Moral Faithfulness is a valuable resource for any Christian who seeks ethical integrity and wholeness."

Steve Wilkens, professor of philosophy, Azusa Pacific University, author of *Beyond Bumper Sticker Ethics*

"This is not a book about general ethical theory and practice but about the ethics of discipleship which is ultimately a responsive and responsible relationship with the trinitarian God. Tyra thus shows that Christian ethics and spirituality are two sides of the same coin. Perhaps its most important contribution is to challenge the reader to take seriously the work of the Holy Spirit which makes the pursuit of a distinctively Christian life possible."

Simon Chan, Earnest Lau Professor of Systematic Theology, Trinity Theological College

"In a world awash with moral compromise, Gary Tyra provides an outstanding resource for Christian educators, students and ministry leaders alike, calling for God-honoring decision making in everyday life. By highlighting Micah 6:8, as well as spiritual practices that position followers of Jesus to hear the voice of the Holy Spirit, he aligns ethical formation and discipleship, a much-needed reaffirmation. Finally, I have found a book that addresses moral discernment, responsibility and choice that is biblically rich, theologically balanced and overtly practical!"

Diane J. Chandler, Regent University School of Divinity

"From his rich experiences as both pastor and professor, Gary Tyra has put his finger on the relatively overall poor condition of Christians' moral discipleship to Jesus, especially due to a pervasive relativism, postmodernism and moralistic therapeutic deism. But he is not just offering here a textbook on moral theories and the identification of what has gone wrong. Nor is he simply trying to develop a decision-making procedure we can methodically apply when facing ethical dilemmas. Much more importantly, he presents a deeply needed corrective to this discipleship deficit. He helps us see the need for balance in our lives between embodying biblical moral principles and virtues, and the need to consider carefully the results of our actions and be responsible for them. Most importantly, he shows us how we can draw upon and listen to the heart of God for guidance in a deeply intimate, personal relationship with him. I highly recommend it."

R. Scott Smith, professor of ethics and Christian apologetics, Biola University

"Gary Tyra tackles a demanding task with courage and conviction, namely, to describe how Christians are to *think* about how to *live*. Tyra not only takes readers through the maze of ethical systems, but nobly constructs a Christ-centered, biblically informed and Spirit-led approach to making moral decisions. It is a great primer on the theory and practice of Christian ethics, but more than that, Tyra proves that if Christians are to make a difference then they have to be different!"

Michael F. Bird, lecturer in theology, Ridley College, Melbourne, Australia

"With keen attention to impulses shaping the moral sensibilities of today's Christians, Gary Tyra carefully guides readers on a serious journey, enabling them to assess their current ethical decision-making practices before helping them better pursue more faithful conduct and character in our ever-changing society. In doing this, he draws from his seasoned experience of teaching a range of students in the globally diverse cultural context of Southern California. *Pursuing Moral Faithfulness*, then, provides a rich and timely resource that will serve numerous generations of believers right down to today's millennials, encouraging us all to be more responsible, Spirit-empowered followers of Christ."

Jason S. Sexton, lecturer, honors department, California State University, Fullerton

Ethics and Christian Discipleship

PURSUING
MORAL
FAITHFULNESS

GARY TYRA

ivp
Academic
An imprint of InterVarsity Press
Downers Grove, Illinois

InterVarsity Press
P.O. Box 1400, Downers Grove, IL 60515-1426
ivpress.com
email@ivpress.com

InterVarsity Press® is the book-publishing division of InterVarsity Christian Fellowship/USA®, a movement of students and faculty active on campus at hundreds of universities, colleges and schools of nursing in the United States of America, and a member movement of the International Fellowship of Evangelical Students. For information about local and regional activities, visit intervarsity.org.

While any stories in this book are true, some names and identifying information may have been changed to protect the privacy of individuals.

Cover design: Cindy Kiple
Interior design: Beth McGill
Images: double fork road sign: © zager/iStockphoto
       forked road sign: © sigurcamp/iStockphoto
       U-turn sign: © P_Wei/iStockphoto

ISBN 978-1-5140-1362-5 (print)
ISBN 978-0-8308-9776-6 (digital)

Library of Congress Cataloging-in-Publication Data
Tyra, Gary, 1955-
   Pursuing moral faithfulness : ethics and Christian discipleship /
Gary Tyra.
      pages cm
   Includes bibliographical references and index.
   ISBN 978-0-8308-2465-6 (pbk. : alk. paper)
1. Christian ethics. I. Title.
   BJ1251.T97 2015
   241—dc23
                                                                           2015010655

P 23 22 21 20 19 18 17 16 15 14 13 12 11 10 9 8 7 6 5 4 3 2 1

Y 43 42 41 40 39 38 37 36 35 34 33 32 31 30 29 28 27 26 25 24

This book is dedicated to the memory of Dr. Lewis Smedes,
a consummately compassionate Christian theologian and ethicist
whose rigorous but gracious tutelage served to transform my life as
a scholar, Christian disciple and human being.

Contents

Acknowledgments   9

Introduction   13

**PART ONE: GETTING STARTED: ASSESSING OUR CURRENT
MORAL FAITHFULNESS QUOTIENT**

  1 Morality Matters: A User-Friendly Introduction to
    Christian Ethics   33

  2 Some Popular Ethical Options (1): Results-Oriented Approaches   57

  3 Some Popular Ethical Options (2): Rules-Oriented Approaches   89

  4 The Religio-Cultural Soup We're All In: Assessing Its Impact
    on Our Moral IQ   127

**PART TWO: TOWARD A MORAL FAITHFULNESS: INTEGRATING
BALANCE AND RESPONSIBILITY INTO OUR ETHICAL LIVES**

  5 More on a Moral Realism (1): The Moral *Guidelines*
    the Scriptures Provide   161

  6 More on a Moral Realism (2): The Moral *Guidance*
    the Scriptures Promise   181

  7 So, What *Would* Jesus Do?   205

  8 Responsible and Responsive Decision Making: A Closer Look
    at "Drawing in the Dirt"   229

  9 The Ethic of Responsible Christian Discipleship: Reasons for
    Its Embrace   255

  10 Actually Becoming an Ethically Responsible Christian
     Disciple: The Process Involved   277

Conclusion   291

Author Index   295

Subject Index   297

Scripture Index   301

Acknowledgments

The publication of a book is usually a team effort. To cite a familiar phrase: "It takes a village!" While this has always been my experience as an author, it was especially so with respect to *Pursuing Moral Faithfulness*. Thus, in the next page or two I want to express my deep gratitude to some folks critical to this work's realization.

To begin, I want to express my heartfelt appreciation to the usual suspects: the library staff at Vanguard University (especially Jack Morgan); the editorial, production and marketing teams at IVP Academic (in particular, the book's editor David Congdon); my former editor, Gary Deddo, who not only secured the project for IVP but also provided some invaluable feedback on an early draft of the work; my son, Brandon, and philosopher friend, R. Scott Smith, both of whom read portions of the book's manuscript and afforded me some helpful counsel; the numerous authors (too many to mention by name, I'm afraid) whose excellent works I interact with in this volume; my friend and Vanguard University colleague, Rich Israel, who functioned as a sounding board and offered many words of encouragement along the way; and finally, my dear wife, Patti, whose patience, love, wisdom and proofreading skills have played such a huge role in all the books I (we) have produced. Though the acknowledgments included in this paragraph might appear to be pro forma, such is not the case. I deeply appreciate the way in which each of these professionals, personal friends and family members contributed to this publishing project.

In addition, I want to express special thanks to those many students who have, over the years, indicated their appreciation for the ethical teaching presented in these pages. It was this enthusiastic response to the moral training I was attempting to provide, along with a growing awareness that too many professing Christians are making important moral choices the way their non-Christian peers do, that eventually convinced me I should pen this work. While I've been careful in all my books to write with my students and not merely other scholars in view, this literary endeavor was special in this regard. With my mind's eye I kept seeing the faces of my students and remembering my interactions with them. These mental images and recollections, pleasant and poignant at the same time, greatly influenced this book in terms of both its message and method. Though any failings inherent in it are my responsibility alone, it's my hope that *Pursuing Moral Faithfulness* does justice to what those who have studied Christian ethics with me say they've taken away from the experience, and that they will appreciate the new material presented here.

Then again, while it's true that the needs of my students (past, present and future) have influenced this work in some significant ways, I obviously didn't produce it only for them. It's also my hope that many students and church members who will never study with me in person will benefit from the book, and that not a few professors, church leaders and student-life professionals will choose to use it as a valued tool in their own disciple-making and moral-formation endeavors.

That said, I suspect it's not uncommon for an author of a newly released book to be a bit anxious about how it will be received, especially if the work breaks new ground or takes a unique approach. In its introduction I make clear how and why *Pursuing Moral Faithfulness* is not your typical Christian ethics text. Thus, I also want to communicate here a word of appreciation to the many university and ministry colleagues who, once they heard about what I was up to in this book, immediately responded with what seemed to be sincere expressions of interest, appreciation and support. While these reactions are certainly no guarantee of success, they did succeed in providing this author with a bit of hope that his newest work might be warmly received by members of its intended audiences—not in spite of its distinctive features, but precisely because of them!

Finally, at the risk of sounding super-spiritual, I want to "acknowledge" our Trinitarian God—Father, Son and Holy Spirit—whose prior faithfulness toward me keeps inspiring a deep desire to render to him a moral (and missional) faithfulness in return. It's my sincere hope that in at least some small manner this book will succeed at encouraging others to want to do the same. While I'd like to think that each of my books is saying something important, it's the thought that *Pursuing Moral Faithfulness* might actually have the effect of enabling Christian disciples to, like Jesus, make moral choices by allowing the Spirit to help them hear and honor the heart of the Father that makes it exceedingly special to me. How could it not be?

In summary, my sincere thanks goes out to everyone who in one way or another helped make this book possible, and to those who have given me reason to believe it can make a difference in the world. I appreciate you all—the members of my village—very much!

Introduction

As a religion professor at a Christian liberal arts university, my responsibilities call for me to participate in the moral as well as spiritual and ministry formation of students. Not long ago an intelligent, culturally savvy student studying Christian ethics with me included in his final paper a telling admission. To be more precise, this young man in his mid- to late twenties prefaced his paper with a twofold confession: First, prior to taking this ethics course, he had neglected to give any serious consideration to the process by which he had been making ethical decisions. Second, as a result of this lack of ethical reflection, he had been guilty of making important moral choices just like many non-Christians do—in an unbalanced and essentially irresponsible manner.

I wish I could say that this twofold confession makes this particular student unique. Actually, my experience has been that just the opposite is true—it makes him iconic instead!

The purpose of this book is to address this situation. Designed to function as a primer on Christian ethics that integrates moral theory with everyday decision-making practice, its grand goal is to enable its readers to come to terms with three things: (1) the notion of a moral faithfulness—the idea that Christians can and should strive to honor the heart of God in their everyday ethical choices; (2) the fact that such a moral faithfulness requires a lifestyle of surrender to the Holy Spirit's endeavors to help Christ's followers discern and do the will of the Father; and (3) the realization that such a moral faithfulness lies at the heart of a genuine Christian discipleship.

Why Such a Book Is Necessary

Having taught Christian ethics for much longer than I'd like to admit, I've witnessed some interesting shifts among students engaged in this particular topic of study. The most significant shift isn't the change that's occurred in how students view social moral issues such as abortion, homosexuality, reproductive and genetic technologies, physician-assisted suicide, euthanasia and so on. Rather, the most dramatic development has to do with an increasing hesitancy among many young adults to engage in the kind of ethical reflection necessary to perform the most basic analysis of moral behavior. Indeed, every year it seems an increasing number of students, like the young man referred to above, show up for the course having given little or no prior thought to the manner in which they've been making ethical decisions. Even more importantly, more and more students are demonstrating a real difficulty coming to terms with the idea that it's not only possible but necessary for Christians to learn to evaluate certain ethical behaviors toward the goal of living their own lives in a morally faithful manner and encouraging others to do likewise.[1]

I will offer here two very basic reasons for the developments I've just described. First, for those still wondering about the effect the advent of postmodernism (or late-modernism)[2] is having on all of us, especially the members of the emerging generations, I can offer this crucial if trite observation: despite any lingering protestations to the contrary, we really are living in an era earmarked by an escalating embrace of a moral relativism.[3] According to the recent research reported on at length in chapter

---

[1]Ethicist William Frankena speaks of the possibility of our being asked by others for help in sorting out moral questions. It's with this thought in mind that he writes: "We are not just agents in morality; we are also spectators, advisors, instructors, judges and critics" (William K. Frankena, *Ethics*, 2nd ed. [Englewood Cliffs, NJ: Prentice-Hall, 1973], p. 12).

[2]As I am using the term, *postmodernism* refers to the view that since everyone's take on reality is culturally and historically determined, no one actually sees reality as it really is. We should therefore be suspicious of any notion of "truth" that purports to be transcendental, applicable to everyone. It's perhaps worth pointing out that the notion of knowledge and reality being culturally and historically determined is actually a distinctively *modern* notion made possible by the philosophical work of David Hume, Immanuel Kant, Friedrich Nietzsche and others. This is why some contemporary philosophers will often refer to postmodernism as hypermodernism, ultramodernism or late-modernism. For more on this, see Dennis P. Hollinger, *Choosing the Good: Christian Ethics in a Complex World* (Grand Rapids: Baker Academic, 2002), p. 107.

[3]While Patrick Nullens and Ronald T. Michener are right to point out that postmodernism is not about the promotion of relativism but about "sensitivity to details, complexities, and close readings

four of this work, pervasive among the members of the emerging generations is the conviction that there are no universally applicable moral standards that might make it possible to evaluate the moral behavior of ourselves and others.[4] The current state of affairs really shouldn't surprise anyone. Years ago, Lewis Smedes, my ethics mentor in seminary, described the contemporary moral climate thusly: "It is a truism today that we are in a crisis of morals. The crisis is not simply that people are doing wrong things; that has been going on since the Fall in Eden. The crisis is the loss of a shared understanding of what is right. Worse, it is a crisis of doubt as to whether there even is a moral right or wrong at all."[5]

Second, I'm tempted to believe that this transition toward a morally relativistic cultural milieu has been aided not only by a neglect on the part of public schools to provide formal ethical instruction for the members of the boomer, Gen X, and emerging generations[6] (not that I'm arguing

---

that have often been ignored or suppressed" (see Nullens and Michener, *The Matrix of Christian Ethics: Integrating Philosophy and Moral Theology in a Postmodern Context* [Downers Grove, IL: IVP Books, 2010], p. 38), it's also true that an epistemological antifoundationalism often associated with postmodernism has had the effect of producing within the younger generations occupying the industrial West a fairly robust embrace of various types of relativism. See Stanley J. Grenz and John R. Franke, *Beyond Foundationalism: Shaping Theology in a Postmodern Context* (Louisville: Westminster John Knox, 2001), p. 19.

[4]See Hollinger, *Choosing the Good*, pp. 19-20, 106-23. Furthermore, referring to postmodernism as the "rise of historical consciousness," Joseph Kotva points out that one of the ways "the growing realization of history's relevance" is altering ethical theory is by "limiting the role and status of rules" (Kotva, *The Christian Case for Virtue Ethics* [Washington, DC: Georgetown University Press, 1996], p. 8). See also Christian Smith, Kari Christoffersen, Hilary Davidson and Patricia Snell Herzog, *Lost in Transition: The Dark Side of Emerging Adulthood* (New York: Oxford University Press, 2011), pp. 15, 55, 60-62, 292-93; Paul G. Hiebert, *Transforming Worldviews: An Anthropological Understanding of How People Change* (Grand Rapids: Baker, 2008), pp. 228-29; Walt Mueller, *Engaging the Soul of Youth Culture: Bridging Teen Worldviews and Christian Truth* (Downers Grove, IL: IVP Books, 2006), pp. 66-67, 89-91; Walt Mueller, *Youth Culture 101* (Grand Rapids: Zondervan, 2007), pp. 51-52, 185-86.

[5]Lewis Smedes, *Mere Morality: What God Expects from Ordinary People* (Grand Rapids: Eerdmans, 1983), pp. 1-2. For a more thorough discussion of the "ethical wilderness" we currently find ourselves in, see David W. Gill, *Becoming Good: Building Moral Character* (Downers Grove, IL: InterVarsity Press, 2000), pp. 11-16. See also the discussion titled "The Ethical Challenge and the Contemporary World," in Stanley J. Grenz, *The Moral Quest: Foundations of Christian Ethics* (Downers Grove, IL: InterVarsity Press, 1997), pp. 14-17.

[6]According to the Center for Generational Studies, the term "Baby Boomers" refers to those Americans born between 1946 through 1964. "Generation X" (also known by the term "Baby Busters") is composed of those born between 1965 and 1980. "Millennials" are those young adults and teens born between 1981 and 1999. Alternate labels for Millennials include: "Generation Y," "Generation Why?" "Nexters" and the "Internet Generation." See "Defining the Generations," Center for Generational Studies (accessed September 7, 2012), www.bobwendover.com/defining-the-generations-how-does-the-center -define-the-current-generations-in-american-society. The term I will often use in this book to refer to

that they should),[7] but also a failure on the part of the home and church to do likewise.[8] Moreover, not a few Christian authors have gone on record lamenting the fact that the dynamic of disciple making as a whole has, in recent years, been neglected within the evangelical Christian community.[9] It only stands to reason that the discipleship deficit currently observable in far too many homes and churches can't be good for the spiritual and moral formation of Christian young people.[10]

Thus it appears that both of these factors—the press of postmodern culture toward a moral relativism and the virtual absence of any sort of existentially impactful ethical training—are at least two principal reasons why an increasing number of students are arriving at college or university having given little or no previous thought to the notion that a moral faithfulness lies at the heart of a genuine Christian discipleship.[11]

Then, to compound the problem, it's my sense that all too often the ethics courses offered at the Christian college, university or seminary are not succeeding at inspiring students toward a morally faithful lifestyle.[12] The result of not being careful to ground the moral life of the believer in the context of Christian discipleship, and of failing to adequately integrate ethical theory with everyday moral decision making, is that far too many students exit these courses with heads full of soon-to-be-forgotten ethical theory but lacking the ability and willingness to spend the rest of their lives striving to "hear" and honor the heart of God in each moral dilemma they encounter.[13]

---

the Millennials or Gen-Y is "emerging generation(s)."

[7]See Smith et al., *Lost in Transition*, pp. 62-63.

[8]See Gill, *Becoming Good*, p. 16. Support for this thesis will be presented in chapter four of this work.

[9]For example, see Kenda Creasy Dean, *Almost Christian: What the Faith of Our Teenagers Is Telling the American Church* (New York: Oxford University Press, 2010), pp. 3-42. See also Gary Tyra, *Defeating Pharisaism: Recovering Jesus' Disciple-Making Method* (Downers Grove, IL: IVP Books, 2009), pp. 194-97.

[10]See Richard R. Dunn and Jana L. Sundene, *Shaping the Journey of Emerging Adults: Life-Giving Rhythms for Spiritual Transformation* (Downers Grove, IL: IVP Books, 2012), pp. 13-21.

[11]This theme, which will be treated not only later in this introduction but in chapter four of this work as well, is explored at length in Patricia Lamoureux and Paul J. Wadell, *The Christian Moral Life: Faithful Discipleship for a Global Society* (Maryknoll, NY: Orbis Books, 2010).

[12]Support for this assertion can be found in Smith et al., *Lost in Transition*, p. 61.

[13]Though Lamoureux and Wadell employ the metaphor of "seeing" rather than "hearing," their approach and mine are in agreement that "the principal business of Christian ethics is learning to see [or hear] truthfully in order to live justly" (Lamoureux and Wadell, *Christian Moral Life*, p. 24). The fact is that despite the laudable emphasis Lamoureux and Wadell place on moral vision, Jesus used the metaphors of both seeing and hearing when speaking of his own interactive relationship with God (see Jn 5:19, 30). With respect to Christian ethics, behind both metaphors is the idea

Though I wish this weren't true, it does no good to keep telling ourselves that it's not.

Thus, awash with the influence of a prevailing moral relativism and bereft of ethical training that inspires toward a moral faithfulness and provides practical counsel on how to make everyday ethical decisions in a morally faithful manner, it's no wonder that the approach of many contemporary Christians, when facing a moral dilemma, is to make the ethical choice the way most non-Christians would: *either by simply going with their gut—relying on their fallen, culturally determined, ultimately untrustworthy ethical instincts*[14] (see Prov 14:12; 16:25; 28:26)—*or based on how they want to be perceived by their peers!*

Furthermore, my experience as both a pastor and professor has been that those in the faith community who do engage in some moral deliberation tend to do so in a *hurried* and often *unbalanced* manner. Any ethical reflection that occurs is focused mainly on the goal of *either* obeying moral rules *or* achieving possible results, with very little attention given to the living out of Christian virtues. The process of ethical reflection often involves *either* the study of Scripture *or* prayer, with both endeavors being performed in a private rather than communal manner. The pace of their ethical reflection, rooted in a desire to get the matter over with as soon as possible, does not allow for any time at all to be spent in an attempt to "hear" or discern where the heart of God is with respect to this particular matter. Even when the Christian moral agent is open to receiving divine moral guidance, the focus is often exclusively on what the Spirit is "saying" to him or her through *either* sacred Scripture, the faith community *or* the individual conscience (rather than all three). For reasons that will be revealed later in this work, such a hurried, unbalanced approach to making moral choices, while well-meaning, will nevertheless often result in moral behaviors that grieve rather than honor the heart of God. As we will see, it's possible to be quite religious, even ethically punctilious, and still not manifest a genuine moral faithfulness.

---

that it's possible and important for Christ's followers to strive to understand where the heart of God is with respect to this or that moral matter.

[14]For a helpful discussion of the relationship between instinct and intuition, see Francis P. Cholle, *The Intuitive Compass: Why the Best Decisions Balance Reason and Instinct* (San Francisco: Jossey-Bass, 2012), p. 28.

I'm convinced that we contemporary Christians can do better. It's with the goal in mind of enabling Christ's followers to do a better job of connecting the dots between ethical theory and practice and, in the process, rendering to God the moral faithfulness he's looking for that I've produced this volume—a primer on Christian ethics that puts forward a balanced, Christ-centered, biblically informed and Spirit-empowered approach to ethical decision making—an approach I refer to as *the ethic of responsible Christian discipleship*.[15]

NOT YOUR TYPICAL CHRISTIAN ETHICS TEXT

The fact that this introduction to Christian ethics has been written by a biblical and practical theologian rather than a classically trained ethicist will, by itself, set it apart from most other volumes belonging to this genre. My particular ethical preparation and professional ministry interests mean that in terms of both *style* and *content*, *Pursuing Moral Faithfulness* will not fall into the category of your typical Christian ethics text.

With respect to the matter of *style*, as I've already stated, my aim in this work is to integrate the theoretical with the practical toward the goal of inspiring and enabling an "everyday" sort of moral faithfulness on the part of contemporary Christians living in an era earmarked by an increasing degree of ethical apathy. Toward this end I've taken pains to

---

[15]Later in the book we will discuss an ethical theory known as "virtue ethics." Those readers who already possess some awareness of ethical theory, especially the character ethics promoted by Stanley Hauerwas, may be aware that virtue theory tends to focus attention away from "exacting procedures for ethical decision making" toward a focus on moral agents and their contexts. See Kotva, *Christian Case for Virtue Ethics*, p. 12. See also Stanley Hauerwas, *Character and the Christian Life: A Study in Theological Ethics* (San Antonio: Trinity University Press, 1975), pp. 7-8; and Nullens and Michener, *Matrix of Christian Ethics*, p. 127. Thus at first glance it might seem that this book's emphasis on making moral decisions that honor the heart of God is at odds with virtue theory. On the contrary, I consider a commitment to *maintaining balance* in one's life (see Eccles 7:18; cf. Prov 4:27) and *acting responsibly* to be two virtues at the heart of a moral faithfulness. In other words, striving to be responsible and balanced rather than irresponsible and unbalanced in the way we make ethical decisions requires virtue and is itself a virtuous action. Surely it's possible and appropriate for a Christian ethic to focus on both the character-building context that forms the moral agent and the decision-making act itself. For a discussion of the reciprocal relationship between actions and character in virtue ethics, see Kotva, *Christian Case for Virtue Ethics*, pp. 30-31. For an even more precise discussion of the relationship between virtue ethics and moral deliberation, see ibid., pp. 31-37. For more on the idea that responsibility is a key virtue with respect to moral decision making, see Vincent E. Rush, *The Responsible Christian: A Popular Guide for Moral Decision Making According to Classical Tradition* (Chicago: Loyola University Press, 1984), pp. 95-99.

make sure that the discussions presented in the main body of *Pursuing Moral Faithfulness* are not overly theoretical in nature. At the same time, the many footnotes also presented in the book provide some very important theoretical and theological foundation for and elaboration of the ideas presented. Throughout the volume my goal is to both inform and inspire—to not only facilitate moral formation but to encourage a lifestyle of moral faithfulness as well. It's up to the reader to decide the degree to which I have accomplished this ambitious objective.

As for the issue of *content*, besides the fact that this work doesn't attempt to accomplish everything a Christian ethics text might,[16] it's also true that I bring to it some theological and ethical presuppositions based on my theological training and three decades of pastoral experience that will also set it apart from others of its ilk. Given the degree to which these premises give shape to what follows, it seems appropriate from the outset to provide the reader with an overview of those theological and ethical emphases that make this book on Christian ethics somewhat unique.

The Distinctive Themes Woven into This Work

Over the years many books have been written that treat the topic of Christian ethics in a helpful manner. I would be foolish in the extreme not to expose my readers to the moral wisdom presented in these texts. At the same time, I've been careful to structure this volume around several distinctive emphases I consider crucial to the task of inspiring and equipping my readers toward a *lifestyle* of *moral faithfulness*.

The possibility of a theological realism. Critical to the ethical theory and

---

[16]For example, the book doesn't provide a detailed exposition of the history of philosophical or theological ethics, or the latest developments in secular ethical theory. Nor does it contain discrete chapters focusing on how Christians in particular might approach specific social moral issues. Some titles I can recommend that possess a singular focus on ethical theory include: R. Scott Smith, *In Search of Moral Knowledge: Overcoming the Fact-Value Dichotomy* (Downers Grove, IL: IVP Academic, 2014); Alexander Miller, *Contemporary Metaethics: An Introduction* (Malden, MA: Polity Press, 2013); Robert Merrihew Adams, *Finite and Infinite Goods: A Framework for Ethics* (New York: Oxford University Press, 2002). Some titles that contain discrete chapters devoted to Christian responses to contemporary social moral issues include: Scott Rae, *Moral Choices: An Introduction to Ethics*, 3rd ed. (Grand Rapids: Zondervan, 2009); David K. Clark and Raymond V. Rakestraw, eds., *Readings in Christian Ethics*, vol. 2, *Issues and Applications* (Grand Rapids: Baker Books, 1996); Robertson McQuilkin and Paul Copan, *An Introduction to Biblical Ethics: Walking in the Way of Wisdom*, 3rd ed. (Downers Grove, IL: IVP Academic, 2014); Patricia Beattie Jung and Shannon Jung, *Moral Issues & Christian Responses*, 8th ed. (Minneapolis: Fortress, 2013).

practice I'm proposing in this work is a particular way of thinking about God and the way we relate to him. A theological realism contends that everything that is owes its existence to God as the ultimate reality. Going further, a theological realism also holds that, because of the birth, vicarious life, death, resurrection and ascension of Jesus the God-man, and the out-pouring of his Spirit on those who belong to him, it's possible for Christ's followers to know and relate to God in a *real* rather than *merely* theoretical, conceptual or ritualistic manner.[17] A hallmark of evangelical Christianity is the belief that the God who is there is a speaking God who has chosen to reveal himself to humanity not only through the inspired writings collectively referred to as the Scriptures (2 Tim 3:14-17) and the written "word of God" (Mk 7:9-13) but also by sending his Son, whom the Bible refers to as the living "Word" (Jn 1:1-2, 14), into the world. As the incarnate Word of God, the Scriptures present Jesus of Nazareth as someone who can and does make the Father known to the faithful in an impeccable manner (Jn 1:18) precisely because he is the "exact representation" of God's being (Heb 1:3). Likewise, according to John 16:13-15, the Holy Spirit (whom Jesus referred to as the "Spirit of truth") has been sent into the world in order to lead Christ's followers into "all truth" by making the revelation that is available in Christ clear to them (cf. Jn 14:26; 1 Cor 2:6-16).[18]

In sum I'm suggesting that the trinitarian understanding of God implicit in Scripture, properly understood, is of great importance because it cannot help but result in a theological realism that impels the believer to take seriously the possibility of an intimate, interactive relationship

---

[17]Please note that my concern here is not that Christians theorize or conceptualize with respect to God. Indeed, in another work I lament the anti-intellectualism (intellectual laziness) manifested by some evangelical Christians (Tyra, *Defeating Pharisaism*, p. 95). Rather the concern here is that it's possible for modern Christians to *overly* conceptualize the Christian faith, allowing this intellectualizing activity to substitute for a real relationship with (lived experience of) God (see Mk 12:18-27). Likewise, my concern is not that Christians engage in rituals but that this can be done in a *mindless, magical* or *myopic* manner. A theologically real understanding of religious rituals sees them as means by which Christian disciples may interact in a meaningful way with a personal God who graciously allows himself to be encountered through certain divinely prescribed ceremonies and behaviors (e.g., baptism, the Eucharist, Bible reading, worship, prayer, confession, giving). In sum, I feel the need to emphasize in this work the important difference between a pneumatologically real, encounter-seeking engagement in religious ritual and a rank *religious ritualism* that divinizes the ritual itself, depersonalizing God in the process.

[18]For more on this see the section titled "Revelation as God's Self-Disclosure," in Michael F. Bird, *Evangelical Theology: A Biblical and Systematic Introduction* (Grand Rapids: Zondervan, 2013), pp. 167-70.

with God the Father that is Christ-centered and Spirit-mediated in nature. As the ensuing discussion will indicate, I'm also suggesting that such a theological perspective will tremendously affect the way we think about and do Christian ethics.

The possibility of a moral realism. Over against the cultural trend toward a moral relativism referred to earlier is the Christian conviction that the God who is there and knowable to us has an opinion about how we human beings are to relate to him, ourselves and one another. This very basic but profound theological observation has huge significance for the ethical endeavor.[19] The Scriptures are rife with passages that assert that because God is a moral being with moral sensitivities, those creatures who bear the *imago Dei* (image of God) should not only, like Jesus, take morality seriously (see Mt 5:17-20) but also, like Jesus, endeavor to hear and honor the heart of God in everything we say and do (see Jn 5:19, 30; 8:28-29; 10:37; 12:49-50; 14:10, 23-24, 30-31).[20] In other words, *an entailment of the theological realism described above is that we Christians have reason to believe that even as God himself is knowable to us by virtue of the revelatory ministries of his Son and Spirit, so is his heart concerning moral matters* (see Eph 5:8-10, 15-17; Phil 1:9-11; Col 1:9-10).[21]

While reserving until later a full discussion of the moral realism I have in mind, I will state here my contention that there are two principal ways the Spirit-inspired Scriptures evidence support for the notion that God is a moral being who desires and makes possible a moral faithfulness on the part of his people. First, there are the transcendent, authoritative *moral guidelines* the Scriptures provide. Second, there is the Christ-centered, Spirit-mediated *moral guidance* the Bible promises. To be more theologically precise, what I'm suggesting is that God has actually provided his people with much more than a set of moral guidelines. What God actually

---

[19]See McQuilkin and Copan, *Introduction to Biblical Ethics*, pp. 182-83.

[20]Robert Adams reminds us: "The transcendence of the Good thus carries over from the divine object of adoration, the Good itself, to ideals of human life, and thus to human ethics" (Adams, *Finite and Infinite Goods*, p. 53). See also McQuilkin and Copan, *Introduction to Biblical Ethics*, p. 13.

[21]As will become apparent in the succeeding discussion, the moral realism presented in this work, influenced by an embrace of the theological realism described above, includes but also goes beyond the philosophical version of this concept that simply holds that "goodness exists independently of the ideas we have about it" (Robin Lovin, *An Introduction to Christian Ethics* [Nashville: Abingdon, 2011], pp. 84-85).

gives is himself in the form of his incarnate Son who embodies both command and promise. On the one hand Jesus serves as an embodied indication of what obedience to God entails (the command). But, going beyond this, Jesus is also the one who provides his followers with the Spirit-enabled freedom to embody this obedience in their own lives (promise). And yet, for Christ's followers to experience through him the command and promise of God in any given ethical situation, much more is required than the reminder to "do what Jesus would do." Instead an engagement in *ethical contextualization* is called for. Put differently, *in order for a moral faithfulness to occur Christian disciples must engage in a theologically real process of moral deliberation that results in the Christ-centered, Spirit-enabled ability to discern and do God's will in this or that ethical situation.*[22]

Again, I'll have much more to say about the scriptural support for a moral realism in a later section of the book.[23] For now, the important point to be made is that it's on the basis of a *moral realism* made possible by the *moral principles* the Scriptures provide, and the *moral guidance* those same Scriptures promise, that we can speak in terms of a *moral faithfulness*. It's possible to *honor* the heart of God only because it's possible, through the Scriptures and the Spirit, to *"hear"* the heart of God. *Pursuing Moral Faithfulness* is intended to inform and inspire its readers with respect to both of these ethically significant discipleship dynamics.

This leads me to comment on yet another distinctive theme of this work.

The possibility of a Spirit-enabled moral guidance. Pressing a bit further, the moral realism I espouse in this book also addresses in some detail the manner in which, according to the biblical revelation, the Holy Spirit enables a moral faithfulness within the lives of Christ's followers (that is, the way he makes real to and within them the moral faithfulness Christ has rendered to the Father on their behalf).[24] In his book *Choosing*

---

[22]See Grenz, *Moral Quest*, pp. 18-20. See also Donald Bloesch, *Freedom for Obedience: Evangelical Ethics for Contemporary Times* (San Francisco: Harper & Row, 1987), pp. 189-91; Nullens and Michener, *Matrix of Christian Ethics*, pp. 109-15.

[23]For an accessible book-length presentation of some philosophical support for a moral realism, see Smith, *In Search of Moral Knowledge*.

[24]Donald Bloesch writes: "Our salvation has already been enacted and fulfilled in Jesus Christ. But the fruits of our salvation need to be appropriated and manifested in a life of discipleship" (*Freedom for Obedience*, p. 12). For an insightful and important discussion of the relationship between Christ and the Holy Spirit—how "since the resurrection of Jesus, life in Christ Jesus is effectively life in the

the Good, ethicist Dennis Hollinger frankly admits that the "Holy Spirit receives scant attention in most ethics texts."[25] *Pursuing Moral Faithfulness* will seek to redress this oversight as I bring to bear on the ethical endeavor a commitment to what I refer to as a *pneumatological realism*— the idea that Christ's followers should expect to interact with the Holy Spirit in ways that are real and phenomenal (that is, perceptible to our senses) rather than *merely* theoretical, conceptual or ritualistic.[26]

In due time I will elaborate on the two main ways the Holy Spirit goes about enabling a moral faithfulness within the lives of Christ's followers. Here I will simply make two bold assertions: First, as Christian disciples engage in certain *spiritual formation* practices (e.g., worship, study, community, ministry praxis and so on), we put ourselves in a place where God's Spirit is able to produce within us the Christlike desire to *honor* the heart of God with respect to life as a whole and moral matters in particular. Second, as Christian disciples engage in certain *spiritual discernment* practices (e.g., Scripture reading and prayer practiced in a theologically real manner), we put ourselves in a place where God's Spirit is able to help us *hear* or sense the heart of God with respect to this or that moral matter, veritably "speaking" wisdom, understanding and insight to us through the Scriptures, the community of faith or directly to the self by means of his still small voice.[27]

Holy Spirit, who carries on the work of Jesus," see Daniel Harrington and James Keenan, *Jesus and Virtue Ethics: Building Bridges Between New Testament Studies and Moral Theology* (Lanham, MD: Sheed & Ward, 2002), pp. 37-38.

[25]Hollinger, *Choosing the Good*, p. 69.

[26]Appreciative of this notion, my friend and colleague Frank Macchia offers this elaboration: "Pneumatological 'realism' takes for granted a biblically-informed vision of life, and of the Christ life in particular, as substantively and necessarily pneumatological. . . . We are made for the Spirit and for the Christ life that the Spirit inspires. . . . There is no life without the Spirit, and . . . there is no salvific or missonal promise or challenge that does not have the presence of God through the Spirit at its very core. . . . A pneumatological realism entails the idea that the New Testament descriptions of life in the Spirit are not merely symbolic portrayals of life that can be translated into modern psychological, moral, or sociological categories. Though such categories can help us better understand how the life of the Spirit impacts us throughout various contexts of human experience, the presence and work of the Holy Spirit as described in the New Testament are to be taken at face value at the root of it all as realities that can be known and felt in analogous ways today" (Frank Macchia, email message to author, August 10, 2014). For more on this, see James D. G. Dunn, *Baptism in the Holy Spirit: A Re-examination of the New Testament on the Gift of the Spirit* (Philadelphia: Westminster John Knox, 1977), pp. 225-26.

[27]I realize that the idea that the Holy Spirit can and will impart moral guidance through *all three* of these means (Bible, community, word of wisdom) has not often been treated in traditional approaches to Christian ethics. For example, in James Gustafson's *Theology and Christian Ethics*, a work in which one might expect a discussion of how a biblically informed pneumatology will affect

It's my sincere hope that the discussion of the possibility of a Spirit-enabled moral guidance presented in this work will prove to be not only provocative but motivational as well.

The crucial need for balance in the believer's moral life. This too is a theme that will show up more than once in this book. As already indicated, at the heart of *Pursuing Moral Faithfulness* are two basic concerns. The first is that too many contemporary Christians are making huge moral choices each day just like their non-Christian peers do: either "from the gut" based on fallen, ultimately untrustworthy ethical instincts (see Prov 14:12; 16:25; 28:26) or on the basis of how the moral agent wants to be perceived by his or her peers. The second big concern is that, because many followers of Christ have not experienced an adequate degree of moral formation—one that is both biblically informed and careful to integrate the theoretical with the practical—it's not at all uncommon for Christians who do engage in some serious ethical reflection to do so in an essentially unbalanced manner. A premise of this book is that an unbalanced decision-making process, well-meaning or not, will nearly always lead to moral behavior that grieves rather than honors the heart of God.

The areas of the moral life in which balance is needed are many: doing justice to *both* the love of God *and* the neighbor; an emphasis in moral deliberation on rules, results *and* virtues;[28] the need to engage in *both*

---

the moral lives of Christians, there are scant references to the Holy Spirit. One of the few has to do with the Spirit's ability to work through the moral discourse that occurs within Christian communities to enable Christians to "become better discerners of God's will" (James M. Gustafson, *Theology and Christian Ethics* [Philadelphia: United Church Press, 1974], p. 117). A similar theme shows up in Paul Lehmann, *Ethics in a Christian Context* (New York: Harper & Row, 1963), p. 47, and the entirety of Bruce C. Birch and Larry L. Rasmussen, *Bible and Ethics in the Christian Life* (Minneapolis: Augsburg, 1976). In a similarly reductionistic manner, Norman Geisler, while maintaining a theoretical or conceptual role for the Holy Spirit in Christian ethics, essentially conflates the Spirit with the Scriptures (Norman L. Geisler, *The Christian Ethic of Love* [Grand Rapids: Zondervan, 1973], pp. 96-97). While I'm in agreement with the notion of the Spirit working through the community of faith and the Scriptures, one of the goals of this work is to advocate for a more robust pneumatology with respect to ethics in general and the dynamic of moral deliberation in particular.

[28]Support for a balanced emphasis on rules, results and virtues can be found in Robin Lovin, *Christian Ethics: An Essential Guide* (Nashville: Abingdon, 2000), pp. 61-63; Rae, *Moral Choices*, pp. 42-44; Nullens and Michener, *Matrix of Christian Ethics*, p. 158; Kotva, *Christian Case for Virtue Ethics*, pp. 170-72; N. T. Wright, *After You Believe: Why Christian Character Matters* (New York: HarperOne, 2010), p. 26; Stanley Hauerwas, *A Community of Character: Toward a Constructive Christian Social Ethic* (Notre Dame: University of Notre Dame Press, 1981), p. 114; Hauerwas, *The Peaceable Kingdom: A Primer on Christian Ethics* (Notre Dame: University of Notre Dame Press, 1983), p. 23;

spiritual formation empowerment disciplines *and* moral formation discernment practices; the need to remain open to *all* the avenues by which
the Spirit might speak to us (that is, the Scriptures, the community of
faith *and* his still small voice speaking directly to the conscience);[29] and
the need to engage in theologically real versions of *both* Scripture study
and prayer at the same time.[30]

Over against an unbalanced exercise in moral deliberation, Jesus
seems to have prescribed an approach to making ethical decisions that
calls for his followers to focus attention on respecting rules, considering
consequences *and* cultivating character. In other words, the ambition of
Jesus is to produce disciples who, like him, are eager and able to discern
the heart of God and act in a manner faithful to it. While asking the
question "What would Jesus do?" is not completely without benefit, the
better question is: "What is the Spirit of Jesus up to in this or that situation and how can/should I cooperate with him in it?"

Yes, this approach to moral deliberation does seem to call for a tremendous degree of intellectual and existential poise (or balance). It also
presumes the possibility of a Spirit-enabled experience of divine moral
guidance and the need for an openness to it. These realities prompt the
question: Where does the inspiration come from to even want to live
one's life in a morally faithful manner?

***The crucial need for the moral life of believers to be grounded in their
understanding of Christian discipleship.*** A final theme distinctive of this
work possesses both a theoretical and practical significance. On the theoretical side of things, Christian ethicist Stanley Hauerwas has been careful
to note the problems that accrue when philosophers, eager to secure
peace between people of diverse beliefs and histories, attempt to forge an

Louis P. Pojman, *How Should We Live? An Introduction to Ethics* (Belmont, CA: Wadsworth, 2004),
p. 188; and Frankena, *Ethics*, p. 65.

[29]See Paul Lewis, "A Pneumatological Approach to Virtue Ethics," *Asian Journal of Pentecostal Studies*
1, no. 1 (1998): 42-61. Online version: www.apts.edu/aeimages/File/AJPS_PDF/98-1-lewis.pdf.

[30]In addition to all of these more practical concerns, there's the more theoretical but still important
need to make sure that our approach to Christian ethics remains balanced theologically so that
our moral lives are influenced in unique ways by God the Father as creator/lawgiver/assessor,
Christ the Son as reconciler/exemplar/intercessor and the Holy Spirit as sanctifier/illuminator/
facilitator. For a helpful discussion of the importance of a Christian ethic that maintains a proper
trinitarian balance, see Nullens and Michener, *Matrix of Christian Ethics*, pp. 158-72.

approach to ethics that's "unqualified"—that is, universal in its application and utility.[31] Hauerwas astutely observes that such an "unqualified" ethic would "make irrelevant for morality the essential Christian convictions about the nature of God and God's care of us through his calling of Israel and the life of Jesus."[32] He goes on to assert that for Christian ethics to possess integrity, rather than being relegated to "some separate 'religious aspects' of our lives, where they make little difference to our moral existence," they must remain distinctively Christian.[33] Indeed, says Hauerwas, "the primary task of Christian ethics is to understand the basis and nature of the Christian life."[34] Among other things, this means that there is, or at least should be, an integral connection between the study of Christian ethics and the life of Christian discipleship.

On the practical side of things, the study of Christian ethics often occurs in a course housed in the "core curriculum" of Christian universities—a noble attempt to integrate faith and learning in the lives of all students (their respective majors notwithstanding). While I appreciate the way this curricular arrangement indicates the special importance of this course, my experience has been that if care is not taken, such a move can not only fail to achieve the kind of cross-disciplinary integration the curriculum designers were hoping for, but it can also serve to bracket off the study of Christian ethics from other courses offered in the religion curriculum. Thus it's not uncommon for some non–religion majors to approach this mandatory course with an apathetic or even antagonistic attitude in place, and for a few religion majors to do likewise!

In my estimation, the solution to the attitudinal problem just referred to is not to excise the study of Christian ethics from the core curriculum but to do all we can to make sure that the bracketing dynamic described above doesn't occur. Christian ethics is something that faculty members across the disciplines need to be discussing among themselves and with their students. Special care needs to be taken within the religion department in

---

[31]See Hauerwas, *Peaceable Kingdom*, p. 17.

[32]Ibid., p. 22.

[33]Ibid., pp. 22-34. (Quote cited is from p. 22.) For a more nuanced discussion of this topic, see the book-length treatment of it provided in James M. Gustafson, *Can Ethics Be Christian?* (Chicago: University of Chicago Press, 1975).

[34]Hauerwas, *Peaceable Kingdom*, p. 50.

particular to make sure that religion majors understand that the study of Christian ethics housed in the core curriculum is an integral part of their theological and ministry training. Finally, those of us who teach Christian ethics, regardless of curricular logistics, need to do our best to do so in a way that's interesting (rather than boring) and that demonstrates the vital importance of the topic to the Christian life as a whole.

What I'm suggesting, ultimately, is that the problem of contemporary Christians making ethical decisions in an irresponsible and unbalanced manner calls for the moral life of believers to be grounded in their understanding of Christian discipleship. Christians of all ages must come to understand that a moral faithfulness, contributing as it does to a missional faithfulness (and fruitfulness), lies at the very heart of what it means to be fully a devoted follower of Christ.

Such an assessment of the importance of a moral faithfulness will affect the way disciple making is practiced, whether at home, church or the Christian university. Put simply, our understanding of Christian maturity needs to take very seriously the commitment and ability of the disciple to make moral choices that seek to honor the heart of God. *We haven't succeeded at making a Christian disciple if he or she ends up making ethical decisions in precisely the same way that his or her non-Christian peers do!*

I'm convinced that, despite the press of the current culture, we don't have to continue living our lives the way most everyone around us does—in an ethically irresponsible and/or unbalanced manner. Furthermore, as Christian disciples we can do more than develop the habit of asking the question "What would Jesus do?" as helpful as that can be. No, the hope I'm holding out is this: with the Holy Spirit's help we can learn to live our lives the way Jesus did—in a morally faithful manner.

How This Text Is Put Together

Having provided a fairly thorough overview of the main themes that are emphasized in *Pursuing Moral Faithfulness*, my discussion of how the book is structured will be comparatively brief. The ten chapters that make up the work are divided into two major sections. Rather than exhaust the reader with a detailed description of all ten chapters, I will simply summarize here the major thrust of each main section.

Part one is titled "Getting Started: Assessing Our Current Moral Faithfulness Quotient" and strives to introduce readers to the discipline of Christian ethics in a way that emphasizes the need for a practical, integration-oriented approach to the study of it. In addition to providing what's designed to be a reader-friendly overview of some very basic ethical theory, the chapters that make up this section of the book also challenge readers to ponder some very important preliminary questions: How do most of our contemporaries tend to approach moral matters? Why is the moral faithfulness the Bible seems to prescribe so very rare among our peers, even those who profess to be Christians? What has been the impact, in terms of our own moral thinking and practice, of the religio-cultural soup most of us are swimming in?[35] How far away are we at present from a lifestyle of moral faithfulness?

Part two of the work bears the title "Toward a Moral Faithfulness: Integrating Balance and Responsibility into Our Ethical Lives." It's here that I present the case for a Christ-centered, biblically informed and Spirit-empowered approach to making moral decisions, which I refer to as *the ethic of responsible Christian discipleship*. It's my contention that a theologically real, contextualizing ethical approach to making moral decisions—one that does justice to rules, results *and* virtues—is the way forward for those followers of Christ who are eager, in a postmodern world, to emulate the responsible and balanced moral decision-making manner practiced and promoted by Jesus himself.[36]

To be more specific, the chapters presented in this second section of the

---

[35] As I'm using the term, *religio-cultural* refers to the way nominal Christian and secular cultural influences combine to create an ecclesial environment that actually works against Christian spiritual health and a moral faithfulness. I will have more to say about this discipleship-defeating dynamic in chapter four.

[36] That is, I'm suggesting that this ethic is the means by which Christians can to do justice to the anthropological imperative (Eph 4:1; 1 Thess 4:1-8) that follows the prior theological indicative—a moral faithfulness before God the Father, vicariously accomplished by Christ the Son, for those who through faith and the sanctifying work of the Spirit are included "in him" (see Eph 1:3-4; cf. Acts 26:18; Rom 15:14-16; 1 Cor 1:2; 6:9-11). See Joseph Kotva's helpful discussion of the relationship between the indicative and imperative in Paul, and how this aligns with a virtue theory of ethics (*Christian Case for Virtue Ethics*, pp. 126-29). A similar discussion can be found in Daniel Harrington and James Keenan, *Paul and Virtue Ethics: Building Bridges Between New Testament Studies and Moral Theology* (Lanham, MD: Rowman & Littlefield, 2010), pp. 52-54. See also the comprehensive treatment of the "Indicative and Imperative" as one of several bases for Pauline ethics in Wolfgang Schrage, *The Ethics of the New Testament* (Philadelphia: Fortress, 1988), pp. 167-72. See the also concise treatment of this theme presented in McQuilkin and Copan, *Introduction to Biblical Ethics*, pp. 84-86.

book make the case for the ethic of responsible Christian discipleship by elaborating on: the nature of the moral and pneumatological realism that are at the heart of this ethical approach, how Jesus himself seemed to model this ethical approach, some important reasons why such an ethic should be embraced and, finally, the process by which a rank-and-file church member actually becomes an ethically responsible Christian disciple.

Make no mistake, as indicated already, *Pursuing Moral Faithfulness* is not intended to function as a comprehensive introduction to ethics in general. Instead, as its subtitle indicates, it's a book about ethics and Christian discipleship—a primer on Christian ethics that focuses on one very serious matter in particular: too many Christians making ethical decisions in essentially the same way as their non- and post-Christian peers.

With that thought in mind, I'm happy to report that the young adult student whose final paper began with an honest admission regarding his prior failure to make moral decisions in a responsible and balanced manner concluded that assignment on a completely different note. He finished the reflection section of the paper with words of appreciation for the way the course had challenged and equipped him to be more mindful concerning the process by which he made moral decisions as a follower of Christ. Though he did not use the phrase "a moral faithfulness" in these concluding paragraphs, I could tell that he "got" it, had become committed to it and would, as an emerging Christian leader, commend it to others.

Honestly, I can't think of a better outcome than what occurred in this young man's life. It's my hope that this book contributes in some small way to the ability of others to have the same experience. I'm convinced that many Christian students and church members, especially those from among the emerging generations, are actually eager to be discipled in a way that enables them to make moral decisions in a distinctively Christian manner. This is what *Pursuing Moral Faithfulness* is all about. Turn the page, and we'll get this very important pursuit started.

Part One

GETTING
STARTED

Assessing Our Current
Moral Faithfulness Quotient

Morality Matters

A User-Friendly Introduction to Christian Ethics

The Bible portrays God as an intrinsically moral being who cares greatly about how human beings created in his image relate to him, one another, themselves and the rest of creation. It's for this reason that, for most Christians, morality matters!

And yet, the manner in which Christian scholars understand and explain this conviction can take different forms. For example, addressing a Christian audience on the topic of "the ethical challenge and the Christian," theologian Stanley Grenz writes:

> We are all ethicists. We all face ethical questions, and these questions are of grave importance. As Christians, we know why this is so: We live out our days in the presence of God. And this God has preferences. God desires that we live a certain way, while disapproving of other ways in which we might choose to live.
>
> Although everyone lives "before God," many people are either ignorant of or choose to ignore this situation. As Christians, in contrast, we readily acknowledge our standing before God. We know that we are responsible to a God who is holy. Not only can God have no part in sin, the God of the Bible must banish sinful creatures from his presence. Knowing this, we approach life as the serious matter that it is. How we live *is* important. Our choices and actions make a difference; they count for eternity! Therefore, we realize that seeking to live as ethical Christians is no small task.[1]

---

[1]Stanley J. Grenz, *The Moral Quest: Foundations of Christian Ethics* (Downers Grove, IL: InterVarsity Press, 1997), pp. 17-18, emphasis original.

This is one way of understanding the significance of ethics for Christians.

However, the famous British literary critic, author and Christian apologist C. S. Lewis also spoke to the importance of the moral choices all of us make but took a slightly different tack in doing so. Addressing himself to a secular rather than Christian audience, the renowned Oxford don wrote:

> People often think of Christian morality as a kind of bargain in which God says, "If you keep a lot of rules I'll reward you, and if you don't I'll do the other thing." I do not think that is the best way of looking at it. I would rather say that every time you make a choice you are turning the central part of you, the part of you that chooses, into something a little different from what it was before. And taking your life as a whole, with all your innumerable choices, all your life long you are slowly turning this central thing either into a heavenly creature or into a hellish creature: either into a creature that is in harmony with God, and with other creatures, and with itself, or else into one that is in a state of war and hatred with God, and with its fellow-creatures, and with itself. To be the one kind of creature is heaven: that is, it is joy and peace and knowledge and power. To be the other means madness, horror, idiocy, rage, impotence, and eternal loneliness. Each of us at each moment is progressing to one state or the other.[2]

According to Lewis, the powerful notion at the heart of Christian morality is that a person's ethical decisions not only reflect his or her character but contribute to it as well. Our everyday moral choices relate to our character in both a correlative and causal manner. With every choice made we become creatures who are either more at peace with God, others and ourselves or less so.[3] Further, though in a manner less explicit than Grenz, Lewis too hints at the idea that our moral choices possess an eschatological as well as existential significance. Our everyday ethical decisions matter greatly because, cumulatively, they determine not only the quality of our existence here and now but also where we will be most comfortable spending eternity![4]

---

[2]C. S. Lewis, *Mere Christianity* (San Francisco: HarperSanFrancisco, 2001), p. 92.

[3]Christian ethicist Lewis Smedes seems to be echoing this assertion when he writes: "Morality is a basic component of any human sort of life, a reality we feel surely even if we cannot define it clearly. We do have choices, and they are sometimes between real moral options. The choice we make can put us in the wrong with God and our ideal selves—or leave us in the right. And being in the right means being in harmony with God's design for our humanity" (*Mere Morality: What God Expects from Ordinary People* [Grand Rapids: Eerdmans, 1983], p. vii).

[4]For more on Lewis's notion that both heaven and hell are choices people make, see C. S. Lewis, *The Great Divorce* (New York: HarperOne, 2009), p. 75.

Ultimately both Grenz and Lewis provide support for the well-known aphorism: "Sow a thought and you reap an action; sow an action and you reap a habit; sow a habit and you reap a character; sow a character and you reap a destiny." Whichever approach you prefer—that of Grenz or Lewis—the bottom line is that for most Christians, morality matters (or at least it should).

Why this discussion of the importance of Christian ethics? The bulk of this chapter has to do with ethical theory. As indicated in the book's introduction, the aim throughout *Pursuing Moral Faithfulness* is to inspire as well as inform. This requires that I do my best to present ethical theory in a way that doesn't seem overly complicated on the one hand or inconsequential on the other. My goal in this first chapter is to introduce Christian ethics to my readers in such a way as to leave them enlightened yet eager for more. Having begun by presenting what was intended as a brief, motivational reflection on the importance of Christian morality, I want to continue by providing some simple yet hopefully interesting answers to several basic questions related to the study of it.

What Is Ethics?

Ethics, along with metaphysics (the study of the nature of reality), epistemology (the study of how we come by our knowledge of reality), logic (the study of correct or proper reasoning) and aesthetics (the study of the phenomenon of beauty), is a subdiscipline included in the larger intellectual discipline known as philosophy (the intellectual pursuit of wisdom or truth in its largest sense).[5] This explains why ethics is sometimes referred to as "moral philosophy."[6]

Speaking broadly, and from a philosophical rather than theological perspective at this point,[7] *ethics is essentially the study of the good life: how*

---

[5]Robertson McQuilkin and Paul Copan, *An Introduction to Biblical Ethics: Walking in the Way of Wisdom*, 3rd ed. (Downers Grove, IL: IVP Academic, 2014), p. 15.

[6]Grenz, *Moral Quest*, p. 23. See also William K. Frankena, *Ethics*, 2nd ed. (Englewood Cliffs, NJ: Prentice-Hall, 1973), p. 4.

[7]According to Dennis Hollinger, philosophical ethics "studies the moral life from within the framework of philosophy and utilizes a rational approach apart from any religious or professional commitments" (*Choosing the Good: Christian Ethics in a Complex World* [Grand Rapids: Baker Academic, 2002], p. 15). Patrick Nullens and Ronald T. Michener go further and articulate the distinction between moral philosophy and moral theology (Nullens and Michener, *The Matrix of Christian Ethics: Integrating Philosophy and Moral Theology in a Postmodern Context* [Downers Grove, IL: IVP Books, 2010], p. 63).

it's conceived of and achieved.[8] The most basic assumption behind this philosophical approach to the study of ethics is that the good life has a moral quality about it; it is achieved by becoming a good person.[9] Indeed, going all the way back to the times of Plato and Aristotle (fifth and fourth centuries B.C., respectively), one way of thinking about ethics has been to ponder the crucial questions: What does it mean to be a good person? What virtues are required?[10]

And yet the study of ethics has come to involve more than simply the study of virtues or ways of *being*. The very idea that there's such a thing as a *good* life lived by a *good* person implies that a distinction can be made between *good* and *bad* ways of *behaving* as well. Thus ethics is also thought of as "the science of determining right and wrong conduct for human beings."[11] This more behavior-oriented understanding of the study of ethics is discernible in the expanded description of this philosophical subdiscipline provided by ethicist Philip Hughes:

> Ethics has to do with the way people behave. The term *ethics* is derived from a Greek word (*ethos*) meaning "custom"; its equivalent, *morals,* comes from a corresponding Latin word (*mos*) with the same meaning. The concern of ethics or morals, however, is not merely the behavior that is customary in society but rather the behavior that *ought* to be customary in society. Ethics is prescriptive, not simply descriptive. Its domain is that of duty and obligation, and it seeks to define the distinction between right and wrong, between justice and injustice, and between responsibility and irresponsibility. Because human conduct is all too seldom what it *ought* to be (as the annals of mankind amply attest), the study of ethics is a discipline of perennial importance.[12]

---

[8]See Robin Lovin, *An Introduction to Christian Ethics* (Nashville: Abingdon, 2011), pp. 10-14; Lovin, *Christian Ethics: An Essential Guide* (Nashville: Abingdon, 2000), pp. 9-16; Grenz, *Moral Quest,* pp. 43-44, 56-57; Henlee H. Barnette, *Introducing Christian Ethics* (Nashville: Broadman and Holman, 1961), pp. 3-4; Scott Rae, *Moral Choices: An Introduction to Ethics,* 3rd ed. (Grand Rapids: Zondervan, 2009), pp. 11-12; McQuilkin and Copan, *Introduction to Biblical Ethics,* p. 13.

[9]See Lovin, *Introduction,* p. 4; Grenz, *Moral Quest,* pp. 23-24; Rae, *Moral Choices,* pp. 11-12.

[10]See David W. Gill, *Becoming Good: Building Moral Character* (Downers Grove, IL: InterVarsity Press, 2000), pp. 64-66, 95-97; Grenz, *Moral Quest,* pp. 23-24, 37, 60-77, 218; Hollinger, *Choosing the Good,* pp. 46-49; Rae, *Moral Choices,* pp. 91-95.

[11]I am indebted to my ethics mentor, Lewis Smedes (now deceased), for this very basic definition of ethics that, according to my notes, I first heard him present in a lecture given on January 9, 1982, as part of a course on Christian ethics offered at Fuller Theological Seminary.

[12]Philip E. Hughes, *Christian Ethics in Secular Society* (Grand Rapids: Baker, 1983), p. 11, emphasis added.

This expanded description is a helpful starting point for understanding the essence of ethics for several reasons. First, it indicates that the study of ethics is about human behavior (doing) as well as being. Second, it explains why the terms *ethics* and *morals* are used by most ethicists in an interchangeable, nearly synonymous manner.[13] Third, it suggests that, while there's such a discipline as descriptive ethics, there's need for an approach to ethics that's prescriptive or normative as well.[14] Fourth, in support of a prescriptive approach to the study of ethics, this definition of the discipline makes the crucial point that at the heart of ethics is the assumption that there exists a moral "ought" that makes it possible to speak in terms of right and wrong, justice and injustice, responsibility and irresponsibility.[15] Finally, it asserts that the study of ethics is an important endeavor precisely because of the negative personal and social consequences that accrue when the ideas of moral duty and obligation are ignored or neglected.

Pressing further, I want to underscore the importance of the idea that at the heart of ethics is a *sense of ought* having to do with both character and conduct. It seems that the deeply rooted sense that there are some ways of being and behaving that simply ought and ought not to occur is a phenomenon *most* people are familiar with.[16] Here's a reflective exercise that was used by Lewis Smedes to help his seminary students get in touch with their sense of moral ought:

---

[13]For example, see Frankena, *Ethics*, pp. 5-6; Grenz, *Moral Quest*, p. 23; Rae, *Moral Choices*, p. 15; Lovin, *Introduction*, p. 9. For their part, Nullens and Michener attempt to distinguish between the terms, suggesting that we think of ethics as the "methodological thinking of morality rather than morality itself" (Nullens and Michener, *Matrix of Christian Ethics*, p. 9).

[14]Actually, most ethicists draw a distinction between at least three types of ethics. For example, apparently following the lead of William Frankena (*Ethics*, pp. 4-5), Stanley Grenz uses the terms *empirical* (descriptive), *normative* and *analytical* when identifying the three major dimensions in which general ethics are often divided (see Grenz, *Moral Quest*, pp. 24-25). Scott Rae goes further, drawing a distinction between four broad categories of ethics: descriptive, normative, metaethics (analytical) and aretaic (see Rae, *Moral Choices*, pp. 15-16). In a nutshell, the discipline of descriptive or empirical ethics merely describes the moral behaviors of a people group. Prescriptive or normative ethics actually develops and commends standards of moral conduct. Analytical or metaethics strives to clarify ethical language and explores philosophical and theological justifications for moral judgments. Aretaic ethics focuses on moral virtues rather than behaviors.

[15]See also Frankena, *Ethics*, p. 9; Grenz, *Moral Quest*, p. 25; Hollinger, *Choosing the Good*, p. 13.

[16]C. S. Lewis referred to the "odd individual here and there" who does not seem to possess an innate sense of moral ought, comparing such a person to someone who is colorblind or tone-deaf. See Lewis, *Mere Christianity*, p. 5. See also Christian Smith, *Moral, Believing Animals: Human Personhood and Culture* (New York: Oxford University Press, 2003), pp. 13-14.

Imagine that you're riding a bus in the downtown region of a city. All the seats on the bus are filled when two young men in their late teens get on board. Looking around for two empty spaces, these late arrivers discover there aren't any. But instead of standing and holding on to the handrails that are there for that purpose, they grab an elderly couple, yank them out of their seats, throw them to the floor and then plop into those spaces themselves, grinning at one another and smirking at the elderly couple afterward. What goes on in your mind as you watch this situation unfold?

Having employed this exercise myself over the years, I can attest to the fact that most persons engaging in it will acknowledge that just imagining such a scenario causes them to experience some rather strong visceral feelings of discomfort, indignation, perhaps even anger. The question is: Why? Why is nearly everyone's reaction to this story negative in nature? Why does nearly everyone seem to possess the same conviction that under these circumstances the behavior of these two young men was simply wrong?

While the scenario depicted in this reflection exercise was concocted, my files are filled with real-life stories of humans behaving badly toward one another. For example, there's the troubling story of a hit-and-run driver who covertly parked her car in her garage and waited patiently for two hours for the injured pedestrian still stuck in her windshield to die so she could then dispose of the body.[17] More disturbing still is the horrible story of the gang rape of a West Palm Beach woman by ten local youths. In addition to physically and sexually brutalizing this Haitian immigrant, the gang felt it necessary to force this mother to perform oral sex on her own twelve-year-old son.[18] As I write this, the distressing story du jour is about a frustrated father who, unable to get his six-week-old daughter to stop crying, put her in the freezer and then fell asleep. He awakened only when his wife returned home some time later. Clothed only in a diaper, the baby's body temperature dropped to 84 degrees before she was finally retrieved from the freezer. She's expected to survive, but the initial medical examination indicates that she also suffers from a broken arm and leg, as well as injury to the head.[19]

---

[17]See "Woman Is Sentenced to 50 Years in Case of Man in Windshield," *New York Times,* June 28, 2003, www .nytimes.com/2003/06/28/us/woman-is-sentenced-to-50-years-in-case-of-man-in-windshield.html.

[18]See "Teen Gets 20 Years for Gang Rape of Woman, Son," *NBCNEWS.com,* November 26, 2007, www .nbcnews.com/id/21982312/ns/us_news-crime_and_courts/t/teen-gets-years-gang-rape-woman-son.

[19]See "Man Accused of Putting 6-week-old Baby Daughter in Freezer," *NBCNEWS.com,* May 28, 2013,

Stories like these are distressing not only because they depict disturbing conduct but also because they indicate a disconcerting lack of character as well. We just don't want to believe that human beings are capable of such perverse, inhumane, bad ways of being and behaving.

At the same time, it's also true that we occasionally hear reports of just the opposite: human heroism. These are the human interest stories we relish—depictions of courageous, altruistic behavior that make our hearts swell, bring tears to our eyes and make us proud of our species.

Again, the question is: Why? Why is it so common for people, when reflecting on either type of story, to experience some pretty strong feelings of either inspiration or disgust? It's my contention that this visceral dynamic is illustrative of the fact that most of us possess a vigorous sense of *moral ought*—a deeply rooted sense that there are such things as appropriate and inappropriate ways of being and behaving. It makes us really sad (and/or angry) when we see or hear of human beings simply following their fallen instincts. We are rendered glad (and/or pleased) whenever we read or hear about someone doing just the opposite. This explains the perennial popularity of the novel or film where the story line portrays a protagonist acting heroically in the end or at the very least experiencing some sort of personal transformation toward becoming a "good" person.

All of this is important to the question: What is ethics? The most basic answer I've come across is this: *Ultimately, ethics is about the innate sense of moral ought most human beings seem to possess.*[20] How do we come by this deeply rooted sense of moral ought? What do we do with it?[21] These are the essential issues the study of ethics endeavors to address.[22]

---

http://usnews.nbcnews.com/_news/2013/05/28/18567782-man-accused-of-putting-6-week-old -baby-daughter-in-freezer?lite.

[20]See Lewis Smedes, "Christian Faith and Moral Obligation" (course handout, Fuller Theological Seminary, Pasadena, CA, 1982), pp. 8-12.

[21]I wish to make clear that I am not suggesting that the experience of a sense of moral ought (to be distinguished from a predictive or prudential ought) equates with an intuitive, prescriptive knowledge of the correct moral action in this or that situation; only that deep down inside, most human beings possess a *haunting* sense that there are ways of being and behaving in which human beings ought and ought not engage. Indeed, I argue throughout the work against any sort of a reliance on a fallen, ultimately untrustworthy moral intuition.

[22]See Lewis Smedes, *Choices: Making Right Decisions in a Complex World* (New York: HarperCollins, 1986), p. 17. See also Rae, *Moral Choices*, p. 12; Frankena, *Ethics*, p. 12.

WHERE DOES THIS SENSE OF MORAL OUGHT COME FROM?

Now that we have a better idea of what ethics is about, let's go on to discuss the origin of the sense of ought that is at the heart of it. Such an endeavor will enable us to make a crucial distinction between philosophical and theological ethics.

Consider once again the way those teenagers behaved on the bus toward the elderly couple. To reiterate, my sense is that most of us feel very strongly that what these two teens did, given the circumstances, was not just unfortunate but actually wrong. But how do we come by this particular conviction?

Some would argue that such a perspective is the result of an instinctive response produced by evolutionary biology. It has become ingrained in our human nature over the course of several thousands of years that, for our species to survive, sometimes the strong have to look after the weak.[23]

Others would counter that this ethical opinion is merely the result of cultural, societal influence. We hold this behavior to be wrong simply because we've been trained to do so by the society in which we've been raised.[24] The implication is that there might be a culture somewhere in which this type of behavior, even in similar circumstances, is considered to be perfectly acceptable, perhaps even laudable.

Still others might insist that the sense of discomfort we're feeling is the result of philosophical reflection. According to this ethical theory, we actually come by our moral convictions by means of moral logic and reasoning. For example, we might have quickly asked ourselves such crucial questions as: What would our society be like if everyone behaved this way? Could we wish that everyone in a similar situation might treat the elderly in such a manner? Then, concluding that it wouldn't be good if everybody mistreated elderly folk, we made the determination that no one should.[25]

Finally, without denying the role that instinct, culture and reasoning play in the ethical decision-making process, there are those who maintain

---

[23]See McQuilkin and Copan, *Introduction to Biblical Ethics*, p. 180. See also Peter Singer, ed., *Ethics* (New York: Oxford University Press, 1994), pp. 5-6.

[24]See Trudy Grovier, "What Is Conscience?" *Humanist Perspectives* 151 (Winter 2004), www.humanist perspectives.org/issue151/whatis_conscience.html.

[25]For more on the ethical rationalism of Immanuel Kant, see chapter three of this book. See also Rae, *Moral Choices*, pp. 77-81; Nullens and Michener, *Matrix of Christian Ethics*, pp. 103-9.

that moral convictions such as this derive from the fact that human beings bear the image of a personal God who has an opinion about how we should treat one another. The view here is that it's because God himself is a moral being with moral sensitivities that humans created in his image possess an innate, foundational, haunting sense of right and wrong.[26] In other words the reason why most people living anywhere would instinctively sense that what the two youths did to the elderly couple was wrong is that God has put within each human heart a fundamental moral sensibility—one that tells us *we should not do to others what we would not want them to do to us (or someone dear to us).* A Bible passage that seems to support this last perspective reads:

> Indeed, when Gentiles, who do not have the law, do by nature things required by the law, they are a law for themselves, even though they do not have the law. They show that the requirements of the law are *written on their hearts,* their consciences also bearing witness, and their thoughts sometimes accusing them and at other times even defending them. (Rom 2:14-15)

According to this passage, one doesn't have to have read the law of Moses to know that behaviors such as lying, stealing, murder, adultery and so on are wrong.[27] The reasoning is thus: the fact that we wouldn't want anyone to do these things to us is an instinctual indication that we shouldn't do them to others. Per the apostle Paul, God's law—and the fundamental sense of moral ought it produces—is inscribed on the human heart!

Obviously, it's this fourth possible explanation of where the sense of moral ought comes from that forms the foundation for an ethic that seeks to incorporate the theological and moral realism referred to in this book's introduction. This is a main point of distinction between a philosophical and a theological approach to ethics. In a theological ethic the source of the sense of moral ought that humans are endowed with comes not from nature, or society or pure rationality but from God. We are moral beings

---

[26]This argument was popularized in the modern era by C. S. Lewis in book one of *Mere Christianity,* a section titled "Right and Wrong as a Clue to the Meaning of the Universe," pp. 3-32. See also Smedes, *Mere Morality,* pp. 10-12, and McQuilkin and Copan, *Introduction to Biblical Ethics,* p. 13. However, Nullens and Michener make the point that some religious philosophers are critical of Lewis's argument, insisting: "The ability to make moral judgments does not lead us to the origin of that moral capacity" (*Matrix of Christian Ethics,* p. 17).

[27]See McQuilkin and Copan, *Introduction to Biblical Ethics,* pp. 18, 66.

precisely because we've been created in the image of a divine moral being. It's because God has an opinion about how creatures made in his image ought to behave toward him, one another, themselves and the rest of creation that he has placed within them a deeply rooted, haunting sense of moral ought. According to the Bible passage cited above, this sense of moral ought can be thought of as residing in the human conscience, which, when functioning according to its divine design, serves to either assure or accuse us with respect to our ethical choices.[28]

Please note that I'm not suggesting that Christian ethics can be grounded in natural revelation (what we can know about God by looking at creation);[29] I'm simply indicating that the notion of ethics in general can be thought of as being about a haunting sense of moral ought—a phenomenon that, according to not only C. S. Lewis but the apostle Paul as well, seems to earmark the human experience.[30] Indeed, rather than trying to ground Christian ethics in natural revelation, I'll go on to make the observation that this conviction that the sense of moral ought operative in the human heart is of theological rather than biological, sociological or philosophical origin actually raises another basic but vitally important question.

WHY IS IT OFTEN STILL VERY DIFFICULT TO KNOW WHAT WE OUGHT TO DO?

One might think that if God is concerned enough about morality to provide human beings with a *conscience* designed to help us know after the fact whether we've succeeded or failed in the ethical endeavor, he might also have provided us with an innate *prescience* (that is, foresight) that allows us to know before the fact, and with absolute certainty, what specific course of action the moral ought is calling for in each life situation we face. However, as indicated above, a biblically informed approach to ethics un-

---

[28]For a much more thorough discussion (from a sociological perspective) of the source of the moral ought within human hearts, see the section titled "Addendum: Why Are Humans Moral Animals?" in Smith, *Moral, Believing Animals*, pp. 33-43.

[29]Hollinger, *Choosing the Good*, p. 12. For a helpful discussion of "natural theology"—that is, "what can be understood about God through human constitution, history, and nature independently of special revelation"—see Michael F. Bird, *Evangelical Theology: A Biblical and Systematic Introduction* (Grand Rapids: Zondervan, 2013), pp. 178-92.

[30]See R. Scott Smith, *In Search of Moral Knowledge: Overcoming the Fact-Value Dichotomy* (Downers Grove, IL: IVP Academic, 2014), p. 36.

derstands that if such a moral prescience was ever active in the human species, it was so damaged in humanity's fall as to be rendered unreliable without the ethical guidance and moral empowerment provided by the Scriptures and the Holy Spirit. Indeed, according to the biblical revelation, one of the results of the fall recounted in Genesis 3 is a profound *inability* on the part of human beings to trust their raw ethical instincts (see Prov 14:12; 16:25; 28:26). This explains why, when faced with some ethical choices, it's not uncommon for even devout, Bible-believing theists to find themselves not at all certain as to what the moral ought requires.

But there's another, even more basic reason why we human beings often find it difficult to know what the "right" thing to do is when faced with the need to make an ethical decision. Allow me to explain what I have in mind here by referring to a real-life incident that occurred in one of my ethics courses.

It's my custom to begin all class sessions with prayer. On one occasion, while teaching a course that focused on ethics in the marketplace, a young adult student felt comfortable enough in the environment to request prayer for some divine direction. He had been offered the job of his dreams—managing a website. On the one hand this computer-savvy student was genuinely excited; the job offer would not only allow him to make a living doing what he loved to do but would also make it possible for him to provide for his family in a more-than-adequate manner. As he put it: "This job is going to pay me a boatload of money to do something I'd gladly do for free!" On the other hand the student was also uneasy. The website he was being recruited to manage provided its subscribers with pornographic images and videos! This was not exactly the kind of website he, as a Christian, envisioned himself overseeing. Thus, his excitement notwithstanding, he was also perplexed, enough so to request prayer.

This student's unpleasant experience of bewilderment was due to the fact that he found himself facing what is known as a *moral dilemma*. On the one hand he felt an obligation to provide for his family in the best possible manner. On the other hand something didn't seem right about doing so in a way that might contribute to problems typically associated with pornography. Though it may do so imperfectly, this story illustrates the reality that in this fallen world it's possible to find ourselves in situations where *we feel tugged at by more than one sense of moral ought at the same time*. More than anything else, it's the phenomenon of the moral dilemma—the uncomfortable experience of feeling tugged at by more than one sense of moral obligation at the same time—that explains why the enterprise of ethics came into existence in the first place.

So, What Do We Do with Moral Dilemmas?

Since the time of Socrates, philosophers and theologians have put forward various approaches to making ethical decisions. By and large these approaches to resolving moral dilemmas have fallen into three distinct categories:

- the ethics of duty (or rules)
- the ethics of consequences (or results)
- the ethics of being (or virtues)

What distinguishes each of these approaches is its primary focus when making an ethical decision. The goal of all three decision-making methodologies is to enable the moral agent to do the "right" thing, whether this is conceived of as achieving the good life or honoring the heart of God.[31] As the next couple of chapters will indicate, there are both theological and philosophical versions of each approach. At this point in our discussion, my goal is simply to provide a brief, no-nonsense description of these three traditional approaches to the ethical endeavor.

Deontology. The ethics of duty is also known as *deontological* ethics.[32] This name is derived from the Greek word *deon*, meaning "what is due."[33] The root idea behind deontologism is the fundamental conviction that morality is objective; a moral action is intrinsically right or wrong irrespective of the moral agent's motive or intention, or the action's outcome.[34] Thus ethics is simply about determining and doing what is the inherently right course of action when faced with a moral dilemma.[35] While there is

---

[31]Actually, Robin Lovin makes the argument that pursuing the good life and honoring God are not necessarily mutually exclusive goals. See Lovin, *Christian Ethics*, pp. 11-15.

[32]Nullens and Michener, *Matrix of Christian Ethics*, p. 52.

[33]See Grenz, *Moral Quest*, p. 29; McQuilkin and Copan, *Introduction to Biblical Ethics*, p. 179.

[34]Nullens and Michener, *Matrix of Christian Ethics*, p. 52.

[35]Grenz, *Moral Quest*, p. 29.

a form of deontologism (act-deontologism) that holds that the intrinsically correct moral action in any given situation can and should be intuited by the moral agent without any resort to moral rules or principles, the most popular version of deontologism (rule-deontologism) asserts just the opposite—that it is "certain rules or principles" that "determine the rightness and wrongness of moral acts," and that consequently, "the ethical life consists of obedience to these rules, whereas unethical conduct is whatever violates them."[36] Therefore, according to this rule-deontological approach, the correct course of action when facing a moral dilemma is to *identify the appropriate moral rule and then do one's duty with respect to it*. Obviously, the emphasis in this ethical approach is on obeying the *rules*.[37]

Teleology. The ethics of consequences is also known as *teleological* ethics.[38] This name is derived from the Greek word *telos,* which means "goal" or "end."[39] The idea here is that when we find ourselves facing a moral dilemma, we are morally obligated to *determine which course of action will result in the greatest balance of good over evil*.[40] As we will discover later on, there may be differing convictions as to how the "greatest balance of good over evil" is conceived.[41] At this point it's sufficient for us to take note of the fact that the emphasis in this ethical approach is on achieving desirable *results*.[42]

Areteology.[43] The ethics of being (or virtue) is also known as *aretaic* ethics.[44] The name derives from the Greek word *aretē,* which means

---

[36]Ibid., p. 30.

[37]See Lovin, *Christian Ethics*, p. 20. As to the question of where the moral rules come from, ethicists such as Scott Rae identify "three primary deontological systems: (1) *divine command theory*, (2) *natural law*, and (3) *ethical rationalism*" (see Rae, *Moral Choices*, p. 17, emphasis original). In other words, the moral rules may come from God, from nature or from moral reasoning. A more thorough discussion of deontology will be presented in chapter three of this work.

[38]Nullens and Michener, *Matrix of Christian Ethics*, p. 50.

[39]See Grenz, *Moral Quest*, p. 33.

[40]Ibid.

[41]See ibid., p. 34. See also Lovin, *Christian Ethics*, pp. 23-26; Lovin, *Introduction*, pp. 10-20.

[42]It should be noted that ethicists can differ slightly in the terminology they use with respect to the focal point of teleology. For example, Robin Lovin prefers to speak of "goals" rather than "results" (*Christian Ethics*, p. 20), whereas Scott Rae uses the term "consequences" (see Rae, *Moral Choices*, p. 17). Regardless of the term used to characterize the focal point of teleology, Stanley Grenz is correct to clarify that the root idea behind the teleological approach is that the rightness or wrongness of a moral action is determined by its outcome (see Grenz, *Moral Quest*, p. 33).

[43]Another common spelling for this term is *aretology*.

[44]See Rae, *Moral Choices*, p. 91. See also Lovin, *Introduction*, p. 74.

"virtue."[45] The idea here is that the motive of the moral agent matters, and the focus in ethics should be on "who a person should become more than what a person should do."[46] Thus the focus in areteology is not on rules or results but character.[47] Whenever we're faced with the question "What should I do?" we should ask ourselves such character-related questions as: What kind of person should I be in this situation? What virtues should I strive to exhibit? Is there a particular virtue or set of virtues I believe should earmark all of my ethical actions (e.g., humility, generosity, honesty, courage)? What virtuous person should I strive to emulate? What would that person of virtue do if he or she were in my place?[48]

The simplicity of the survey presented above notwithstanding, it should be apparent that there's a big difference between these three traditional approaches to ethical decision making. In order to make this more apparent, let's revisit the moral dilemma I referred to earlier that had to do with the student and the tempting job offer that came his way.

Let's imagine that you're in the classroom when this request for prayer is made. This fellow student is a friend of yours. At the break he connects with you and asks for your input. Assuming that you care enough about your friend's well-being to venture to speak into his life (see Col 3:16), how would you counsel him? Which of the three approaches surveyed above would most inform the way you'd try to help him make this ethical decision?[49]

On the one hand it may be that the first thing that occurs to us is the need to remind our friend of the biblical verse that warns: "Anyone who does not provide for their relatives, and especially for their own household, he has denied the faith and is worse than an unbeliever" (1 Tim 5:8). Or on the other hand we might encourage him to ponder those New Testament passages that in one way or another translate the Greek word *porneia*—passages that provide strident warnings against all forms of sexual immorality and lust (e.g., Mt 15:18-19; 2 Cor 12:21; Gal 5:19; Eph 5:3; Col 3:5; 1 Thess

---

[45]See Lovin, *Introduction*, p. 74; Rae, *Moral Choices*, p. 91.

[46]Rae, *Moral Choices*, p. 93. According to Rae, the "foundational moral claims made by the virtue theorist concern the moral agent (the person doing the action), not the act that the agent performs" (p. 91).

[47]Ibid., pp. 91, 93; thus an alternate name for virtue ethics is "character ethics." See Nullens and Michener, *Matrix of Christian Ethics*, p. 53.

[48]See Rae, *Moral Choices*, p. 93.

[49]It's worth noting that in part two of this book I will argue that making a responsible moral choice in a situation such as this actually requires a moral agent to engage in this kind of ethical advice seeking.

4:3-5). In either case, if the expectation is that our friend, once reminded of some pertinent biblical commands, should simply do his duty with respect to them, then this would constitute an essentially deontological (that is, rule-oriented) approach to moral decision making.

Or we might choose instead to launch into a fervent discussion of the consequences pro and con of his taking or not taking this job. On the one hand we could exhort him to contemplate all the psychological, social, marital and spiritual ills caused by online porn. Perhaps we might put to him the question: "Would you really want to contribute to the overall misery and unhappiness in society that such websites are known to produce?" On the other hand (I'm playing devil's advocate here), we might decide to ply our friend with some mission-oriented questions that focus on achieving some desirable ministry outcomes: "Isn't a Christian presence needed near the gates of hell?" "Since it's true that people who want to look at online porn are going to do so somewhere, couldn't it be God's will for you to represent Christ in the lives of those who are involved in the production of this website?" "How will the major players in the porn industry—those who facilitate its dissemination—ever be challenged to change without a witness nearby?" "How can this potentially high-leverage witness occur if someone like you doesn't take this job and enter into this hellish ministry context in Christ's name?"

Whichever tack we take, if the expectation is that our friend should make his decision based on a desire to achieve the greatest balance of good over evil in people's lives, then this would constitute an essentially teleological (that is, results-oriented) approach to moral decision making.

Yet another possibility is to prompt our friend to consider some character-related issues such as: what it would look like for him to exhibit the theological virtues of faith, hope and love in this situation; the need for Christian disciples to maintain an existentially impactful trust in God's ability to provide for them and their families; his responsibility to function as a virtuous role model in the midst of an overly sexualized culture; and so on. Or we might simply choose to encourage our friend to ponder the following: "What would Jesus do if he were offered such a job?" "While it's true that Jesus would not hesitate to associate with sinners (see Mt 9:10-13; 11:16-19), would he actually facilitate their sinful activities (Mt 5:17-19; 13:41; 18:6-9; see Lk 5:32; Jn 8:11)?" The bottom line is that if the expectation is that our friend's greatest responsibility is to maintain his Christian integrity, manifest a trust in God's ability to provide for his family, or emulate the moral and missional faithfulness of Jesus, then this would constitute an essentially areteological (that is, virtues-oriented) approach to moral decision making.

I can report that the student at the center of this real-life case study came to class the next week indicating that he had turned the job offer down. His reasons for doing so are, for our purposes, beside the point. The question that should concern us at present is this: With which of these three traditional approaches to making ethical choices do we most resonate at this point in our journey toward a moral faithfulness?

Some care needs to be taken here for a couple of reasons. First, in part two of this book I will advocate for an ethical approach that strives to do justice to all three approaches (deontology, teleology and areteology) and their respective foci (rules, results and virtues). Though I'm convinced that such a holistic approach is possible, I want to humbly suggest that it would probably be naive for most readers to assume that they're already there—that is, already engaging in the balanced and responsible kind of ethical decision making that a moral faithfulness requires.

Furthermore, I want to be careful not to give the impression that resolving moral dilemmas is easy, even when a balanced and responsible approach is employed. The fact is that the case study cited above may have been a bit too easily resolved for many readers. Perhaps it doesn't adequately connote the degree of intellectual, emotional and spiritual *dis-ease* that occurs when we find ourselves facing an indisputable moral dilemma—a life situation in which the moral rules aren't perfectly clear, desirable outcomes might ensue from various courses of action, and what Jesus would do in the situation is not readily apparent. It's for this reason that I will, toward the goal of helping us all think a bit more deeply about our current inclination as it relates to making ethical decisions, proceed to make use of another case study that shows up in not a few ethics textbooks. This classic case study concerns the hiding of Jews from the Nazis during World War II.

Let's set up the scenario this way:

You belong to a devout Christian family living in Nazi-occupied Amsterdam during the Second World War.

As an evangelical Christian, you take God's Word seriously; you believe it's important to obey the moral commands presented in the Bible. For example, you are very well aware of the fact that the Bible teaches that it's a serious sin to lie, to bear false witness, to intentionally deceive other people (see Ex 20:16; Lev 19:11; Ps 5:5-6; Prov 12:22; Col 3:9-10; Rev 21:8).

The problem is that you and your family are aware that the Nazis are rounding up Jewish men, women, boys and girls and sending them in cattle cars to various extermination camps located in eastern Europe. You and your family pray about this situation and make the decision to hide some Jews in your home. There is a crawlspace under the floor in the dining room, enough room for a family of four to six people to hide should the Nazis ever conduct a search of the premises.

Everything's fine for a while, but eventually the inevitable happens; the Nazis show up at your door. The Gestapo officer asks you point-blank: "Are there any Jews in this home?"

You're enough of a realist to recognize that merely remaining silent is not an option; one way or another the Gestapo is going to beat an answer out of you. It's also readily apparent that trying to run away isn't an option either.

So what would you do? Would you lie to save the lives of the Jews? Would you tell the truth and leave the consequences in God's hands? Or would you try to engage in some form of slippery speech that, while not quite a lie, is also not quite the truth?

Equally important is the reason why. Why would you pursue this course of action in the face of this moral dilemma? How would you justify your moral choice to a fellow Christian struggling with the same dilemma? Honestly, as best as you can tell, what would your motive be for lying, telling the truth or trying to finagle your way out the situation by means of some slippery speech?

Made famous by the inspiring story told in Corrie Ten Boom's *The Hiding Place* and the opening scene of Quentin Tarantino's disturbing film *Inglourious Basterds*, it's probably because this moral scenario is fairly familiar to many of my university students that they are eager to participate in a classroom discussion regarding it.[50] That said, I'll go on to make the observation that, whereas a couple of decades ago I had to work very hard

---

[50]Corrie Ten Boom, *The Hiding Place* (New York: Bantam Books, 1974).

in my role as devil's advocate to get some of my students to consider the possibility that telling a lie in order to save a life might constitute a morally faithful response to this dilemma, nowadays I find myself having to work even harder at getting *any* of my students to consider the possibility that perhaps telling the truth and trusting the outcome to a sovereign God might be the right thing to do in such a situation.

Moreover, when I press my students to explain why they would be so quick to tell a lie despite the many Bible verses that proscribe such behavior, only a few will justify this action on deontological grounds. In other words, only a few of my students are aware that of the fact that the same Bible that forbids lying also directs the people of God to do nothing that would endanger a neighbor's life (Lev 19:16) and contains other passages that seem to legitimize the practice of lying in order to save a life: for example, the story of Rahab related in Joshua 2 (cf. Heb 11:31) and the account of the Hebrew midwives presented in Exodus 1:15-21. As well, very rarely will a student attempt to justify the lie by explicitly referring to his or her desire to exhibit a certain virtue, such as compassion or justice. Instead, the vast majority of my students tend to address this moral dilemma on the basis of teleological (results-oriented) moral reasoning. While I believe that a consideration of the consequences should play a role in a morally faithful lifestyle, the ease with which many members of the emerging generations would tell a lie, and do so apparently without the slightest twinge of conscience, suggests to me that the current widespread popularity of the teleological approach to ethical decision making, even among professing Christians, is to some degree a result of the increasing influence of postmodern thought upon our culture. I (and others) will have more to say about this possibility in chapter four.

In any case, discussions such as these are what the science or study of ethics is about. Ethics is concerned with how people behave when confronted with moral dilemmas and the process by which they make moral decisions. Some of us lean toward a *deontological* approach to moral decision making: we tend to focus first on the rules. Some of us lean toward a *teleological* approach to moral decision making: we tend to focus more on results. Some of us may lean toward an *aretaic* approach to moral decision making: we tend to focus on exhibiting certain virtues and imitating certain role models. A few of us recognize the possibility and propriety of endeavoring to focus on all three—rules, results and virtues—as we strive to emulate the moral decision making we see at work in the life of Jesus.

This leads us to the final question this chapter will attempt to answer.

WHAT DOES IT MEAN TO DO CHRISTIAN ETHICS?

In their book *The Matrix of Christian Ethics,* Patrick Nullens and Ronald Michener explain that "Christian ethics is so much more than simply following a list of rules that you can check off from day to day. It is careful, hard thinking about what it means to be a follower of Jesus in daily decisions, with ultimate respect for God and others."[51]

I appreciate the way this succinct definition of Christian ethics focuses on the issue of following Christ. Throughout this book I continually make the assertion that for an ethical approach to be "Christian," it must be Christ-centered. It's my contention that Jesus not only possessed a certain type of moral character that those committed to imitating him should seek to cultivate, but he also made moral decisions in a certain manner that those professing to be his followers should seek to emulate. Nullens and Michener go on to provide us with this expanded description of the moral faithfulness modeled for us by Jesus:

> Christ demonstrated how we should live by both his words and his deeds. God's character was revealed in his Son. He demonstrated for us what it means to be completely subjected to the will of the Father. He is the Righteous One (1 John 2:1) whose life displayed God's original intention for human beings. Jesus gave us examples of the meaning of service and self-sacrificial love toward others. Both Paul and Peter appealed to Jesus as our moral example (Ephesians 5:1-2; 1 Peter 2:21).[52]

In a similar vein, Scott Rae reminds us that the New Testament makes clear that "the moral obligations for the follower of Jesus are subsumed under the notion of 'becoming like Christ.'"[53]

But how do we engage in this cultivation of Christ's moral character and emulation of his ethical conduct? Given the historical and cultural

---

[51]Nullens and Michener, *Matrix of Christian Ethics,* p. 20.
[52]Ibid., p. 150.
[53]For more on this see Rae, *Moral Choices,* p. 41.

gaps that exist between Jesus' life setting and ours, the question in a Christ-centered approach to the moral life will not be so much *What would Jesus do in this situation?* but instead *How would a person who, like Jesus, is committed to honoring the heart of the Father respond to this particular moral dilemma?* Such a conception of Christian ethics presumes that God has an opinion about how we behave in this life, and that it's possible for us, like Jesus, to possess a pretty good sense of where his heart is with regard to this or that moral issue.

This is where some secondary criteria that spell out what's necessary for an ethic to be Christ-centered prove crucial. In part two of *Pursuing Moral Faithfulness* I elaborate on the moral and pneumatological realism I consider essential to the dynamic of a moral faithfulness, and I present an extended discussion of the balanced and responsible (and responsive) ethical decision making Jesus himself modeled. For now, it must suffice for me to indicate that in order to do Christian ethics we need to be able, like Jesus, to discern where the heart of God is with respect to various life situations and then, with the help of the Holy Spirit, do our best to behave in such a way as to stay in harmony with his heart and mind. Another way to put this is to say that a moral faithfulness involves a commitment and acquired ability to contextualize God's concerns for love, justice and humility (see Mic 6:8) in the face of each moral dilemma we face. One of the main themes of this book is that the only way for Christ's followers to be able to cultivate and emulate Jesus' moral character and conduct (that is, embody in themselves the moral faithfulness the incarnate Son makes possible for those who are in him) is to adopt an ethical approach that is both *biblically informed and Spirit-empowered.*

A Christ-centered ethic is biblically informed. Given the fact that nearly everything we know about Jesus' moral life comes to us through the sacred Scriptures, it only makes sense that a Christ-centered ethic will need to be biblically informed. What this means in practical terms is that in order to do Christian ethics, we will need to spend the rest of our lives paying careful, prayerful attention to:

- the same Old Testament biblical documents that Jesus paid attention to (see Mt 5:17-20);

- the New Testament Gospels that provide a glimpse into the moral life and message of Jesus (e.g., Jn 8:1-11; cf. Jn 5:30);

- the rest of the New Testament, which provides an apostolic commentary on and real-life examples of successful ministry contextualizations of Jesus' ethical genius (e.g., Acts 20:34; Phil 2:3-8; 1 Pet 2:13-23); and

- the biblically faithful insights into the Christian ethical challenge provided by theologians both ancient and contemporary.

A Christ-centered ethic is Spirit-empowered. And yet, as important as a prayerful study of the Scriptures is to Christian ethics, this is not the only means by which Christ's followers are to attempt to discern the heart of God. According to those same Scriptures, we must also spend the rest of our lives paying careful attention to:

- the leading of the Holy Spirit, whom the Bible refers to as Christ's Spirit (e.g., Rom 8:9; 1 Pet 1:11) and whose purpose is to lead and guide us into *all* truth (Jn 16:5-13).

Indeed, according to the Bible, the Holy Spirit not only seeks to enable God's people to "hear" his heart in this or that life situation but to honor it as well (see Rom 8:4; cf. Ps 51:10-12; Gal 5:16-26). This reality lies at the heart of my insistence that it's a pneumatological realism that makes a moral realism possible.

It should be noted that some tacit support for the notion of a Spirit-empowered approach to Christian ethics can be found in the writings of other Christian ethicists. For example, in his book *Choosing the Good: Christian Ethics in a Complex World,* Dennis Hollinger writes:

> Some Christians have argued that morality is fundamentally about a natural law that all human beings can exhibit by nature apart from direct divine initiative or guidance. While people clearly have some sense of the good God desires and can exhibit some actions that reflect that good, Christian ethics is far more than a natural enterprise. It is not only rooted in a particular Christian understanding of reality but is also nourished and sustained by spiritual and divine resources beyond our natural proclivities.[54]

Also indicating the need for Christian ethics to be Spirit empowered is

---

[54]See Hollinger, *Choosing the Good,* p. 12.

Scott Rae who, in his book *Moral Choices: An Introduction to Ethics*, asserts that the New Testament speaks of "an internal source that assists in decision making and enables one to mature spiritually."[55] According to Rae:

> This theme is introduced in the Gospels (John 13–17) and developed in the Epistles, particularly those of Paul. For example, Romans 8 discusses the role of the Holy Spirit in producing sanctification in the individual believer. The person without the Spirit is not able to welcome spiritual things into his or her life (1 Cor 2:14). The process of being transformed from one stage of glory to the next comes ultimately from the Spirit (2 Cor 3:18). Believers who "live by the Spirit" will produce the fruit of the Spirit (Gal 5:16, 22-23), and will not satisfy their innate inclination to sin. *Clearly, the New Testament envisions moral and spiritual maturity only in connection with the internal ministry of the Spirit who transforms a person from the inside out.*[56]

The bottom line is that simply doing our best in our own strength to imitate the character and conduct of Jesus is not an ethical approach that's supported by the Scriptures. Instead the New Testament teaches that there are *spiritual and divine resources* that can and must be relied on for our ethical lives to be considered "Christian" in the fullest sense of that word. It's the Holy Spirit's great desire to empower the followers of Christ to render to God a faithfulness that is both missional and moral in nature. If we let him, the Holy Spirit will enable us to, like Jesus, hear and honor the heart of God.[57]

My goal in this initial chapter is to provide a no-nonsense, user-friendly introduction to Christian ethics that leaves the reader wanting more. The truth is that morality matters, and moral dilemmas happen! In little and big ways we will find ourselves facing tricky, complicated, confusing life situations that represent more than simple temptations to sin. Probably

---

[55]See Rae, *Moral Choices*, p. 47.

[56]Ibid., emphasis added.

[57]It should be noted here that in part two of this work I will provide a description of what a Spirit-enabled moral guidance and empowerment does and doesn't involve. This section of the book will include an important discussion of some things we can do to make sure that we're genuinely interacting with the Holy Spirit rather than simply speaking to ourselves in his name. In anticipation of that discussion, I'll indicate here my conviction that one of the safeguards against too much subjectivity (or psychological projection) in the moral discernment process is the practice of making sure that any promptings provided by the Spirit of God are validated by both the Word of God and the people of God (see 1 Thess 5:19-22).

more than once in this lifetime each of us will face an especially serious moral conundrum in which we will find ourselves being tugged at by more than one sense of ethical obligation at the same time. Sooner or later, all of us will ask or be asked that difficult question: *What should I do?* How to answer that question in a way that strives to hear and honor the heart of God is what Christian ethics and the rest of this book is about.

The next two chapters will collectively present the reader with an overview of the contemporary ethical landscape—a survey of the ethical approaches most commonly utilized by our peers day to day. To what degree do any of these approaches have what it takes to serve as the foundation for a fully Christian ethic? Do any of these ethical options produce the kind of moral faithfulness we believe God is calling for from people made in his image? Let's find out.

Some Popular
Ethical Options (1)

Results-Oriented Approaches

I recently asked my twenty-something daughter to describe for me what's going on in the hearts and minds of her peers, to explain to me the ethos of her circle of friends. She understood that the intent of my query was not to be critical of the emerging generation she's part of but to better understand it. One of the main things I remember her saying that day was that she and her contemporaries really relish options—that is, the freedom to select from a variety of possibilities, take advantage of various opportunities, make choices from a plethora of prospects. In other words, not being tied down to only one way of being or doing just about anything is important to her and the folks she runs with.

Later, when reading a book about emerging adulthood, my eyes widened when I came across a passage that asserts that many members of this generation possess "a general psychological orientation toward maximizing options and postponing commitments."[1] The book's credibility rose in my estimation at that moment. The authors seemed to be in touch with a dynamic at work in my own daughter's life.

Something else that fell into place for me at that time was a better understanding of why my young-adult university students tend to appreciate a certain teaching method. In addition to preferring a dialogical rather than monological approach to the presentation of course material,

[1]Christian Smith, Kari Christoffersen, Hilary Davidson and Patricia Snell Herzog, *Lost in Transition: The Dark Side of Emerging Adulthood* (New York: Oxford University Press, 2011), p. 14.

most of them express real appreciation for the opportunity to survey the various options with respect to any given topic rather than having only one position put before them.

Hence, here in part one of *Pursuing Moral Faithfulness* I include a two-chapter survey of various approaches to making ethical decisions that are currently being utilized by ordinary people in their everyday lives. To what degree are these popular ethical options Christ-centered, biblically informed and Spirit-empowered? Are any of these approaches to making moral decisions a sufficient foundation for a Christian ethic that produces a moral faithfulness before God? These are the crucial questions that will guide the discussion presented in this chapter and the one that follows.

SOME SURVEY SPECIFICS

The fact is that most ethics textbooks provide their readers with the type of overview presented here. Moreover, I've found that most surveys of moral models cover essentially the same ground, with the biggest difference being the order in which the various options are presented, or perhaps the organizing framework used in their classification.

My own approach to such a survey will be distinctive in several significant ways, however. First, given my commitment to produce a Christian ethics text that's both user-friendly and careful to keep integrating the theoretical with the practical, my tack will be to offer brief but pungent examinations of those ethical decision-making options that are, consciously or not, actually being employed every day by ordinary folks, rather than those that are the special projects of moral philosophers and only discussed in academic settings. In other words, the reader should expect this survey to refer to a limited number of truly popular ethical decision-making approaches, and to do so in a fairly concise rather than exhaustive manner.[2]

---

[2]This first survey distinctive raises an important question: *How has the popularity of the various ethical approaches been determined?* Chapter four of this book will report on some statistical research that indicates the kind of ethical decision making currently in vogue in our contemporary, increasingly postmodern, post-Christian culture. To some degree, the statistical research analyzed in chapter four explains the selection of the ethical options treated in this survey, especially the teleological approaches treated in this chapter.

Second, though it's not uncommon for surveys of ethical models to make use of the traditional categories—deontological, teleological and aretaic—there are a couple of issues that need to be addressed. In addition to the reality that some ethical models resist a supercrisp, either-or classification,[3] the truth is that an examination of any slate of ethical *decision-making approaches* can't help but tend toward an emphasis on the *action* of the moral agent rather than his or her *character*. Therefore most popular decision-making models will necessarily qualify as normative ethics of *doing* rather than *being*.[4] In other words, it's an unfortunate fact that the ethics of being (virtue ethics) tends to be something that's more talked about by academics than practiced in everyday life by ordinary people.

The good news is that the ethic of responsible Christian discipleship is an attempt to rectify this lamentable reality! However, since my presentation of this ethical option is reserved for part two of the book, the survey presented in this chapter and the next will necessarily focus on the most popular results-oriented (teleological) and rules-oriented (deontological) *decision-making approaches*. (See figure 2.1.)

THE MOST POPULAR ETHICAL DECISION-MAKING APPROACHES	
Results-Oriented Approaches *(Teleological)*	*Rules-Oriented Approaches* *(Deontological)*

Figure 2.1

A third distinctive feature of this survey derives from the fact that I've also found it helpful when teaching Christian ethics to help students discern the degree to which each of the decision-making approaches surveyed takes seriously the notion of moral absolutes. Again, we must allow for some real-life overlap that makes supercrisp classifications impossible to achieve. This is due to the fact that the issue of moral absolutes is a *meta-*

---

[3]See David K. Clark and Raymond V. Rakestraw, eds., *Readings in Christian Ethics*, vol. 1, *Theology and Method* (Grand Rapids: Baker Books, 1994), p. 144.

[4]One should keep in mind how some ethicists, such as Scott Rae, make a formal distinction between normative and aretaic ethics precisely because the latter focuses on moral virtues rather than behaviors. See Scott Rae, *Moral Choices: An Introduction to Ethics*, 3rd ed. (Grand Rapids: Zondervan, 2009), pp. 15-16.

ethical concern while the manner in which discrete moral choices are made is a *normative* matter. What this means is that a person might choose to make ethical decisions in a teleological manner for deontological reasons. For example, a person might consider it his or her moral duty (an earmark of deontologism) to always act in his or her own best interest (ethical egoism), or to endeavor to bring about the greatest good for the greatest number of people over the long run (utilitarianism). The irony is that ethical egoism and utilitarianism are both considered teleological rather than deontological moral models because the actual choices made end up being relative to the thinking of each moral agent.

It's for this reason that I encourage Christians studying ethics to think in terms of how each decision-making method tends to function in terms of something I refer to as its *metaethical ethos.* That is, does the approach tend to *play out* in an absolutist or relativistic manner? (See figure 2.2.)

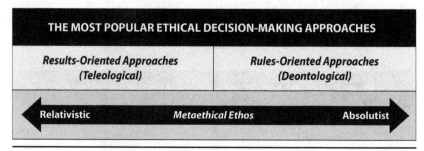

Figure 2.2

As figure 2.2 indicates, I'm suggesting that the rules-oriented approaches to making moral choices tend to be absolutist in terms of their metaethical ethos, while the results-oriented approaches tend to play out in a more relativistic manner. The significance of this distinction will become evident as the survey progresses.

Finally, perhaps another unique aspect of this survey is that none of the various moral models presented strike me as a credible candidate for an adequate foundation for a Christ-centered, biblically informed, Spirit-empowered Christian ethic. Now, in light of the honest admission that I don't personally encourage the employment of any of the decision-making approaches included in this survey, it might be appropriate to ask: What's the point, then? My response would be that I'm not sure it's possible to really comprehend and appreciate what a moral faithfulness involves without viewing it over against approaches to the moral life that, in various ways, fall short of it. Furthermore, if we as Christ's followers are to emulate the manner in which Jesus not only modeled a morally faithful lifestyle but also commended it to others, we need to be able to speak intelligently to our peers about the ethical approaches they're currently employing (whether by design or default) and to comment on how capable each approach seems to be at helping the moral agent hear and honor the heart of God.

Figure 2.3 provides an overview of the ethical decision-making approaches included in this survey.

THE MOST POPULAR ETHICAL DECISION-MAKING APPROACHES	
Results-Oriented Approaches *(Teleological)*	***Rules-Oriented Approaches*** *(Deontological)*
Egoistic	***Reason-Based***
❏ "Promoting My Interests" (egoism)	❏ "Obeying the Dictates of Reason" (moral universalism)
❏ "Following My Heart" (subjectivism/emotivism)	***Bible-Based***
❏ "Trusting My Intuition" (naive intuitionism)	❏ "Following the Letter of the Law" (nonconflicting absolutism)
❏ "Guarding My Reputation" (narcissistic conventionalism)	❏ "Doing the Lesser Evil" (conflicting absolutism)
Altruistic	❏ "Yielding to the Higher Law" (graded absolutism)
❏ "Seeking the Greatest Good" (utilitarianism)	
❏ "Serving the Other in Love" (situationism)	
◀ Relativistic *Metaethical Ethos* Absolutist ▶	

Figure 2.3

It's my suggestion that, more than likely, most of my readers and their peers are utilizing one or more of the ethical decision-making approaches represented in this survey. According to the research that will be reported on in chapter four, most members of our increasingly postmodern culture are making moral choices in a teleological—results-oriented—manner that's either egoistic or altruistic in orientation. What does this mean? To what degree do any of the teleological moral models provide a solid foundation for a Christian ethic? Exploring the answers to these two important questions is what the rest of this chapter is all about. With that thought in mind, figure 2.4 indicates the popular ethical decision-making approaches that are our immediate concern.

THE MOST POPULAR ETHICAL DECISION-MAKING APPROACHES
Chapter 2
Results-Oriented Approaches *(Teleological)*
Egoistic ❑ "Promoting My Interests" (egoism) ❑ "Following My Heart" (subjectivism/emotivism) ❑ "Trusting My Intuition" (naive intuitionism) ❑ "Guarding My Reputation" (narcissistic conventionalism) *Altruistic* ❑ "Seeking the Greatest Good" (utilitarianism) ❑ "Serving the Other in Love" (situationism)
◀ Relativistic   *Metaethical Ethos*   Absolutist ▶

Figure 2.4

EGOISTIC APPROACHES TO ETHICAL DECISION MAKING

Patrick Nullens and Ronald Michener point out that "consequentialist ethics may be divided into at least two major tendencies: *hedonism* and *utilitarianism*."[5] I believe it to be a bit more helpful (accurate) to view the

---

[5]Patrick Nullens and Ronald T. Michener, *The Matrix of Christian Ethics: Integrating Philosophy and Moral Theology in a Postmodern Context* (Downers Grove, IL: IVP Books, 2010), p. 51.

several teleological (results-oriented) moral options as falling under two categories of ethical decision-making approaches: *egoistic* and *altruistic*. The first set of moral models treated in this chapter will be of the egoistic variety.

The "Promoting My Interests" approach (ethical egoism). This very popular decision-making approach is based on the conviction that the morality of an act is determined by one's self-interest.[6] According to this ethical option "we should not fear selfishness but rather embrace it as the highest principle of morality."[7] So, when faced with a moral dilemma, the moral agent should pursue the course of action that will serve to promote his or her own highest good.

The philosophy behind ethical egoism. At this point in the discussion two crucial questions arise: (1) Why this emphasis on one's own highest good? and (2) Precisely how is one's highest good to be conceived?

The emphasis in ethical egoism on one's own highest good (or best interest or long-term advantage) is owing to the fact that, having rejected any sort of divine revelation on which to ground ethics, this ethical option focuses on what's believed to be true in nature. The theory of *psychological egoism*, to which ethical egoism is related, argues that it is *natural* for sentient creatures to look out for their own self-interest—that is, "each of us is always seeking his own greatest good."[8] This observation of what seems to be true in nature is thought to legitimize the notion that it's the pursuit of our own highest good that should guide us as we make ethical decisions. Furthermore, ethical egoism also holds that the key to building a truly healthy society is, ironically, to encourage everyone within that society to make ethical decisions by the "standard of his [or her] own long run advantage in terms of good and evil."[9] A crucial assumption at the heart of ethical egoism seems to be that there exists some sort of "pre-established harmony within the world" that ensures that the pursuit of "self-interest results in the best for all."[10]

---

[6]Rae, *Moral Choices*, p. 67.

[7]Steve Wilkens, *Beyond Bumper Sticker Ethics: An Introduction to Theories of Right and Wrong* (Downers Grove, IL: InterVarsity Press, 1995), p. 46.

[8]See William K. Frankena, *Ethics*, 2nd ed. (Englewood Cliffs, NJ: Prentice-Hall, 1973), p. 21. For a brief but helpful critique of psychological egoism, see pp. 20-23. See also Rae, *Moral Choices*, pp. 71-72.

[9]Frankena, *Ethics*, p. 19.

[10]Ibid. See also Dennis Hollinger, *Choosing the Good: Christian Ethics in a Complex World* (Grand Rapids: Baker Academic, 2002), p. 31.

Leaving aside for the moment the question of whether the aforementioned assumption should be considered valid, let's press on to consider what ethical egoism has in mind when it speaks of the individual's best interest. How is one's highest good to be conceived according to this moral model?

We need to be careful not to oversimplify the answer to this important query. While it's not uncommon for those practicing ethical egoism at a popular level to conceive of their highest good in terms of the experience of personal pleasure or happiness,[11] the fact is that not everyone who employs this ethical option is necessarily a shortsighted, narcissistic hedonist.[12] Scott Rae reminds us that it's possible that "helping others may be a means to the end of a person's own self-interest" and that "one may forgo an immediate advantage to insure long-term interests."[13]

In other words, there is such a thing as an "enlightened" self-interest that acknowledges that living in a way that is moderate in the pursuit of sensual pleasure and that is considerate rather than inconsiderate of others might in the long run be the best way to achieve one's own highest good.

Some famous names associated with ethical egoism are Thomas Hobbes (1588–1679)[14] and Adam Smith (1723–1790), neither of whom encouraged a starkly sensual or narcissistic lifestyle. Even the Greek philosopher Epicurus (341–270 B.C.), one of the first proponents of this moral model, encouraged a pursuit of pleasure that was earmarked by self-restraint, moderation and detachment.[15] Says Dennis Hollinger: "the ethical egoism of Epicurus was thus 'an austere hedonism' and clearly different from the kind of hedonism often associated with the name Epicurean, usually referring to a sensual pursuit of pleasure."[16]

Perhaps the most potent modern advocate for an ethical egoism was Ayn Rand (1905–1982), a novelist and philosopher who fiercely championed an ethic of *rational self-interest*. Rand's atheistic philosophy, known

---

[11]Hollinger, *Choosing the Good*, p. 28.
[12]See Rae, *Moral Choices*, pp. 67-68; Frankena, *Ethics*, p. 18; Stanley J. Grenz, *The Moral Quest: Foundations of Christian Ethics* (Downers Grove, IL: InterVarsity Press, 1997), p. 34; Wilkens, *Beyond Bumper Sticker Ethics*, pp. 46-47.
[13]Rae, *Moral Choices*, p. 69.
[14]For an extended discussion of the moral philosophy of Thomas Hobbes, see Nullens and Michener, *Matrix of Christian Ethics*, pp. 75-81.
[15]Hollinger, *Choosing the Good*, p. 29.
[16]Ibid.

as objectivism, rejected any transcendent (that is, divine) source for ethics and knowledge.[17] With respect to ethics Rand was convinced that both nature and reason supported her scorn for altruism (the practice of putting the welfare of others over one's own).[18] Instead she insisted that "when each person seeks to preserve his or her own self, the world is a more orderly place. Freedom, justice, and self-esteem can come to fruition only when we follow the path of rational self-interest."[19]

A less enlightened version of ethical egoism. However, the fact that various philosophers have contended for the possibility of an enlightened or rational self-interest doesn't mean that this is how ethical egoism usually plays out on the street. Indeed, some polling indicates that "many people operate from a kind of individualism in which personal happiness is the overriding criterion" when it comes to making moral choices.[20]

On December 31, 2001, local newspapers all over North America ran an obituary article announcing the tragic death of the Brazilian rock star Cassia Eller. The article read:

> Cassia Eller, one of the most irreverent singers in Brazilian rock music, has died. She was 39.
>
> Eller was hospitalized Saturday at the Santa Maria hospital in Rio de Janeiro in an "agitated and disoriented" state and died late Saturday, probably after an "external intoxification," hospital spokesman Gedalias Heringer Filho said.
>
> He did not elaborate on what kind of intoxication was suspected, and the results of her autopsy were pending. Eller had admitted to using cocaine in the past.
>
> Eller's fame peaked this year with the sale of about 250,000 copies of her "MTV Unplugged" album and a performance in January's Rock in Rio festival in front of hundreds of thousands of fans, singing along with one of her hits, "I Just Ask God for a Little Indecency."
>
> Shunning middle-class Brazilian morals, Eller was open about her 13-year relationship with another woman and loved to provoke with unconventional punk haircuts or by showing her breasts in televised shows.

---

[17]Ibid., p. 30.
[18]Ibid. See also Wilkens, *Beyond Bumper Sticker Ethics*, pp. 46-49.
[19]Hollinger, *Choosing the Good*, p. 30. See also Wilkens, *Beyond Bumper Sticker Ethics*, pp. 49-50.
[20]Hollinger, *Choosing the Good*, p. 28. See also the discussion of the National Study of Youth and Religion (NSYR) presented in chapter four of this work.

"There is no such thing as right or wrong. You choose what's good for you and it ends up working out well," she said in a recent interview.

Eller was to be buried Sunday evening. She is survived by her 8-year-old-son.[21]

I trust the reader is able to recognize in this sad story the ethical egoism that was at work in Cassia Eller's short life. Frankly, it's hard not to presume that her worldview had been influenced by something akin to Rand's objectivist philosophy. Regardless, my larger point is that, while it may be true that there is such a thing as an enlightened self-interest, the evidence seems to suggest that the popular version of ethical egoism too often tends toward a pursuit of pleasure and happiness that is sensual and shortsighted in nature.

Excursus: A Critique of Ethical Antinomianism in General

The word *antinomianism* literally means "against or instead of law."[22] Ethical approaches of the antinomian variety hold that there are no binding moral laws—nothing outside ourselves that authoritatively indicates good as opposed to bad moral action. And yet, while the appeal here is for a moral autonomy (i.e., self-governance or independence), it's also true that "most antinomians do not deny that persons can choose to live by some moral standards. They simply refuse to accept that these are more than subjective choices of the individual. Whatever moral laws there may be are relative to individuals who choose to live by them. There are no objective moral laws binding on all human beings."[23]

Now, there are several ways in which to critique ethical antinomianism from a Christian perspective. For the sake of expediency, I've presented below a bulleted and therefore extremely spartan list of concerns that apply not only to ethical egoism but to the other egoistic, essentially antinomian moral models included in this survey.

- Antinomian approaches to making ethical decisions don't do justice to the Bible's call for humans to live in the "fear of the Lord."[24]

- Ethical antinomianism patently ignores what the Bible has to say about an eschatological reckoning (future day of divine judgment).[25]

---

[21]"Obituaries in the News: Cassia Eller," *AP News Archive,* December 31, 2001, www.apnewsarchive .com/2001/Obituaries-in-the-News/id-96332b26089d0f18b7f436c95467350c, emphasis added.
[22]See Norman L. Geisler, *Christian Ethics: Options and Issues* (Grand Rapids: Baker, 1989), p. 29.
[23]Ibid., p. 33.
[24]See Ps 111:10; Prov 3:7; 16:6; Eccles 12:13-14; 2 Cor 5:9-11; Rev 14:6-7.
[25]See Mt 12:36; Acts 10:39-43; 17:29-31; Rom 2:5-16; 14:10; 1 Cor 4:4-5; 2 Tim 4:1, 8; Jas 2:12-13; 3:1;

- According to passages such as Matthew 5:17-20, Jesus obviously intended for his followers to take the moral laws found in the Bible seriously.[26]

- Jesus' apostles warned in their day against church members who had adopted an antinomian (lawless, libertine) lifestyle (Jude 4) and made it very clear that genuine Christ followers should avoid this practice like the plague (see 2 Pet 3:17)!

Once again, it's my suggestion that we keep these general, biblically informed critiques of ethical antinomianism in mind as we evaluate all the decision-making approaches included in this survey that are egoistic in nature.

An evaluation of ethical egoism. So, does the "Promoting My Interests" approach to making ethical decisions seem like a solid foundation for a Christ-centered ethic? For several reasons many Christian ethicists would say no.

For one thing, since ethical egoism is an antinomian moral model, the several criticisms of antinomian ethics listed above certainly apply. This by itself should make us wary of the idea that ethical egoism might serve as the foundation for a genuinely Christian ethic.

Second, ethical egoism in particular doesn't do justice to the Bible's call for people bearing the image of God to refrain from living as brute beasts (e.g., Ps 32:8-9; 73:21-24; Jude 17-19; 2 Pet 2:12). For sure, human beings share with animals a creaturely status. This is not to say, however, that humans are mere animals. Bearing the image of God (*imago Dei*) sets us apart from other creatures in a way that is morally significant. Sure, we can live our lives on the basis of mere animal instincts, but God's Word explicitly calls for us not to! We can do better than that; we can learn to hear and honor the heart of God instead.

Moreover, according to passages such as Proverbs 14:12; 16:25, the notion that we can and should make important choices on the basis of what seems good for us in the moment is ultimately self-destructive. Both Proverbs 14:12 and 16:25 provides the warning: "There is a way that ap-

---

5:9; 1 Pet 1:17; 4:5; 2 Pet 3:7; 1 Jn 4:15-17; Jude 14-15; Rev 6:10; 20:12-13.
[26]I'll have more to say about this important passage in chapters three and seven.

pears to be right, but in the end it leads to death." Sadly, Cassia Eller's story serves us as a cautionary tale.

Finally, over against the presumption that "when each person seeks to preserve his or her own self, the world is a more orderly place," we have the Bible indicating just the opposite. According to the book of Judges, a state of moral anarchy resulted when the people of Israel began to do as each one saw fit (Judg 17:6; 21:25) and ended up engaging in evil as a result (Judg 2:11; 3:7, 12; 4:1; 6:1; 10:6; 13:1). The bottom line is that it would seem that ethical egoism is about as antithetical to a moral faithfulness as a decision-making approach can be!

Because ethical egoism is a classic example of this subcategory of te-leological models, my treatment of it has been a bit more thorough than what will be afforded the other versions of egoistic decision-making approaches included in this survey. Still, it's important for us to acknowledge that there are several other egoistic approaches to making moral choices that are very popular in our contemporary culture.

The "Following My Heart" approach (moral subjectivism/emotivism). According to Scott Rae, *moral* (or *ethical*) *subjectivism* is a theory that holds that morality is "determined by the individual's own tastes and preferences."[27] Rae continues: "Expressed in its popular form, ethical subjectivism says, 'What's right for me is right, and what's right for you is right,' even if the person is referring to two diametrically opposed actions."[28] In other words, when applied to ethics, subjectivism teaches that any behavior is morally right as long as the moral agent approves of it. It's the moral agent's approval that makes an action right rather than any extrinsic standard.

Related to moral subjectivism is a theory known as moral emotivism. This rather arcane metaethical theory asserts that because "all moral judgments are nothing but expressions of preference, expressions of attitude or feeling,"[29] they don't actually possess any truth value.[30] The latter theory

---

[27]Rae, *Moral Choices*, p. 85.
[28]Ibid.
[29]See Alasdair MacIntyre, *After Virtue: A Study in Moral Theory* (Notre Dame: University of Notre Dame Press, 1984), pp. 11-12.
[30]Ibid., p. 12. See also Alexander Miller, *Contemporary Metaethics: An Introduction* (Malden, MA: Polity Press, 2013), p. 24; Smith, *In Search of Moral Knowledge*, p. 89; Arthur Holmes, *Ethics:*

(emotivism) arose as a way of defending the former theory (subjectivism) against the criticism that if subjectivism is true, then every moral agent is infallible and no moral behavior can ever be considered wrong.[31] In other words, one way to get around the complaint that moral subjectivism leads to an absurd conclusion is to argue that all we're doing when talking about moral right and wrong is expressing our subjective feelings about them. It's not like anything we say about morality one way or the other corresponds with any sort of objective reality (how the world really is).[32]

The bottom line is that any decision-making approach prompted by an embrace of moral subjectivism/emotivism is going to play out in a radically relativistic manner. According to the research reported on in chapter four, something akin to the "Following My Heart" approach is much employed in our increasingly postmodern, post-Christian society. Apparently, the way many teens and young adults in particular approach making moral choices is simply to do what "feels" right to them—that is, they follow their hearts.

An evaluation of moral subjectivism/emotivism. The fact is that the "Following My Heart" approach to making ethical decisions is very similar to ethical egoism because they are both antinomian in nature. The only difference is that the ultimate criterion for the ethical choice in this case is not necessarily the self-interest of the moral agent but his or her subjective feelings about the moral matter at hand. Though this approach might actually result in an altruistic behavior, it's still egoistic in the sense that it fiercely maintains a sense of moral autonomy—everyone is free to *feel* their way to their own ethical decisions. As an essentially egoistic, antinomian decision-making approach, it's liable to the same criticisms of ethical egoism and antinomianism presented above.

The "Trusting My Intuition" approach (naive moral intuitionism). The basic premise of an ethical theory known as *moral intuitionism* is that morality is "directly intuited by the person making the moral decision."[33] I'm suggesting that yet another popular, very individualistic

---

Approaching Moral Decisions (Downers Grove, IL: InterVarsity Press, 1984), p. 26.

[31]See the online summary of the chapter titled "Subjectivism, Relativism, and Emotivism," in Lewis Vaughn, *Doing Ethics: Moral Reasoning and Contemporary Issues* (New York: W. W. Norton, 2013) (accessed June 13, 2014), www.wwnorton.com/college/phil/ethics3/ch/02/summary.aspx.

[32]Miller, *Contemporary Metaethics*, p. 26.

[33]Rae, *Moral Choices*, p. 82.

method of making ethical decisions that ends up being very relativistic in the way it plays out in everyday life is related to this moral theory. The irony is that the dynamic of intuiting one's way to a correct moral action is a crucial component of an ethical approach known as *act-deontology*.[34] As a deontological moral model, moral intuitionism holds that morality is objective rather than subjective in essence. Put differently, one might say that act-deontology entails the conviction that there is always a patently "correct" way to respond to any given moral dilemma. The ethical challenge, according to this version of deontology, is to discern this correct moral *action* and then do one's *duty* with respect to it.

However, and this is key, moral intuitionism maintains that, rather than rely on a direct appeal to absolute moral rules in order to discern this abjectly "right" course of action (the premise of rule-deontology or legalism),[35] the moral agent must simply *intuit* the obliged course of action through a careful pondering of all the pertinent facts at work in this particular ethical dilemma.[36] According to this ethical option, "goodness" and "rightness" are indefinable qualities that are "knowable only through direct apprehension."[37] In the same way, ethical truth itself is held to be self-evident; one doesn't deduce ethical truth; you simply know it when you see it.[38] What all of this means is that discerning the right thing to do in any particular life situation isn't a matter of taking into account any applicable moral rules but of engaging in an intuitive (though rational rather than merely emotional) deliberation process.[39] *We intuit our way to correct moral action through a careful process of pondering all the facts pertinent to the situation at hand.* It's through an employment of *rational intuition* that we arrive at the correct moral action a particular life situation is calling for.

The research that will be reported on in chapter four of this work indicates that a somewhat vulgar version of moral intuitionism—something that amounts to an ultranaive rendering of this ethical option—is another decision-making approach at work in our culture today. As my

---

[34]Frankena, *Ethics*, p. 23.
[35]Grenz, *Moral Quest*, p. 30.
[36]See Frankena, *Ethics*, p. 23.
[37]Grenz, *Moral Quest*, p. 50.
[38]Ibid., p. 49.
[39]Ibid.

name for this popular decision-making approach implies, when faced with a moral dilemma, many members of our increasingly postmodern, post-Christian society are simply trusting their intuition, relying on what their gut tells them is the right thing to do, *assuming* that their ethical instincts are reliable guides to the moral action that is appropriate for any given situation. Missing from this naive version of moral intuitionism, however, is that careful, thoughtful deliberation process that classical moral intuitionism requires.

An evaluation of naive moral intuitionism. Is the "Trusting My Intuition" approach the touchstone for a Christian ethic that we're looking for? It's for several reasons we might choose not to think so.

First I must point out that, as an antinomian, egoistic moral model, naive moral intuitionism is liable to the same criticisms leveled at ethical antinomianism and egoism listed above.

Second, another huge problem with moral intuitionism as an ethical theory is that its primary premise is flawed. After underscoring the fact that act-deontologism provides us with no criteria or guiding principles to help us in our moral deliberations, William Frankena states the problem with moral intuitionism thusly:

> If we had a distinct intuitive faculty which perceives what is right or wrong, and speaks with a clear voice, matters might still be tolerable. But anthropological and psychological evidence seems to be against the existence of such a faculty, as does the everyday experience of disagreement about what is right in particular situations.[40]

Implied in this critique is the idea that because act-deontologism provides us with no guiding principles for the discernment of correct ethical action, our moral intuition can be skewed as it were by all sorts of subconscious subjective dynamics. This explains why different people intuiting their way to ethical truth end up with widely diverging understandings of it![41] It also explains why I'm suggesting that, even though a classical moral intuitionism speaks of morality being objective in essence, the "Trusting My Intuition" decision-making approach actually plays out in a very relativistic manner

---

[40]Frankena, *Ethics*, p. 23.
[41]See Holmes, *Ethics*, p. 62.

with each individual moral agent "intuiting" his or her way to their own moral choices irrespective of any and all overriding considerations.

Finally, I simply can't move on to my treatment of the next approach without underscoring the fact that, because of what theologians refer to as the *noetic* effect of the fall (the impact of sin on human thinking), the Scriptures speak of the danger of human beings presuming they can think or intuit their way to ethical truth apart from any appeal to or reliance on divine moral guidance (e.g., Prov 14:12; 16:25; cf. Prov 3:5-6).[42]

The "Guarding My Reputation" approach (narcissistic moral conventionalism). Another ethical decision-making approach that's very prevalent in our increasingly postmodern culture derives from a moral theory known as *moral conventionalism* (or *normative relativism*).[43] While moral subjectivism understands the notion of "right and wrong" to be the creation of each individual person (and naive moral intuitionism might as well do likewise), moral conventionalism embraces the basic tenet of cultural relativism, which holds that all values, including moral values, are actually culturally created.[44] Since, according to cultural relativism there are no universal moral principles that are applicable to all cultures and time periods,[45] conventionalism argues that "cultural acceptance determines the validity of moral norms."[46] In other words, since morality is relative to each human culture, the right thing to do in any given situation will be determined by the dynamic of cultural acceptance.[47] Each moral agent ought to always act in keeping with his or her society's moral code.[48] *When facing a moral dilemma, the way to proceed is to give some careful consideration to prevailing cultural norms.* However, for most people, this course of action is conceived of as a *prudential* rather than *moral* ought. Paying attention to prevailing cultural

---

[42]For more on the noetic effect of sin in general, see Michael F. Bird, *Evangelical Theology: A Biblical and Systematic Introduction* (Grand Rapids: Zondervan, 2013), pp. 175-76. For more on the noetic effect of the fall on the ethical endeavor, see the discussion "What Is Wisdom?" in Peter W. Gosnell, *The Ethical Vision of the Bible: Learning Good from Knowing God* (Downers Grove, IL: IVP Academic, 2014), pp. 127-29.

[43]Clark and Rakestraw, *Theology and Method*, p. 26. See also Rae, *Moral Choices*, p. 85.

[44]Rae, *Moral Choices*, p. 85.

[45]Ibid.

[46]Ibid.

[47]Ibid.

[48]Clark and Rakestraw, *Theology and Method*, p. 25.

norms (or convention) is not so much the morally "right" thing to do as it is the "prudent" (or wise or smart) thing to do.

The discussion in chapter four of the moral lives of America's emerging adults (as well as the culture at large) will reveal just how impactful has been postmodernity's embrace of cultural relativism. We will also discover that at work in significant numbers of American adults is a simplistic, less thoughtful, somewhat narcissistic version of conventionalism that has them making important ethical decisions based on *how they want to be perceived by their peers.* The chief concern in this decision-making approach seems to be the moral agent's ethical reputation. While a commitment to guard one's reputation can be considered prudent, the research reported on in chapter four suggests that it can also be prompted by a particular psychological (narcissistic) need. The bottom line is that, since the moral agent has embraced the notion that right and wrong are culturally created categories anyway, a concern to do the right thing before God or in harmony with some objective moral reality is not the primary consideration; doing one's best to engage in some impression management is!

An evaluation of moral conventionalism. Though reluctant to present here a thorough critique of the moral and cultural relativism on which the "Guarding My Reputation" approach ultimately depends,[49] I will encourage my readers to take note of some biblical passages that seem to reflect the idea that honoring the heart of God requires that we exercise care *not* to make spiritual, ethical or lifestyle decisions on the basis of how we will be perceived by those around us. For example, Exodus 23:2 begins with the exhortation: "Do not follow the crowd in doing wrong," and Proverbs 29:25 reads: "Fear of man will prove to be a snare, but whoever trusts in the LORD is kept safe" (cf. Prov 25:26). Furthermore, some New Testament passages that have the effect of cautioning Christ's followers against being overly concerned about how they are viewed by others include: Matthew 6:1; John 12:42-43; Galatians 1:10; and 2 Corinthians 6:14-18.

To summarize what we've observed so far, the four approaches to making ethical decisions previously surveyed have been essentially ego-

---

[49]For such a discussion, see Rae, *Moral Choices*, pp. 84-91; Robertson McQuilkin and Paul Copan, *An Introduction to Biblical Ethics: Walking in the Way of Wisdom*, 3rd ed. (Downers Grove, IL: IVP Academic, 2014), pp. 171-73.

istical (although not necessarily egotistical) in orientation. In other words, the *ultimate* focus in these teleological options has been on the autonomy and/or subjectivity of the person making the moral choices. (This is true even of the "Guarding My Reputation" decision-making approach since, even though there's a focus on community standards, the real concern is how the moral agent is perceived by his or her peers.) It's because all of these egoistical decision-making approaches are essentially antinomian in nature that none of them seem qualified to serve as the starting point for a Christ-centered, biblically informed, Spirit-empowered approach to the moral life. Thus our search for such a starting point continues.

Altruistic Approaches to Ethical Decision Making

Having acknowledged the insufficiency of all the essentially egoistical moral models presented above, it would be understandable to assume that the key to a decision-making approach more consistent with Christian sensitivities is one that calls for us to move in a more altruistic direction. For example, we might endeavor to always act in such a way as to bring about the greatest balance of good over evil in the world as a whole.[50] Or we might choose to focus more attention on what the Bible has to say about always acting toward others with a loving motive in place. Is either of these two altruistic moral moves the key to a Christian ethic capable of producing the moral faithfulness we've come to believe God both desires and deserves? The remainder of this chapter will be devoted to this important question.

The "Seeking the Greatest Good" approach (utilitarianism). There's a category of ethical options that, while denying the existence of authoritative, universally applicable, exceptionless moral absolutes, nevertheless acknowledges the usefulness of certain moral norms and principles acquired through eons of human experience. Utilitarianism is such a moral model.

As its name indicates, this decision-making approach focuses on the notion of utility or usefulness. "An act is right or wrong depending on

---

[50]See Grenz, *Moral Quest*, p. 35; Wilkens, *Beyond Bumper Sticker Ethics*, p. 83.

the degree to which it is useful or harmful."[51] To be more specific, some ethicists articulate the principle of utility thusly: "the moral end to be sought in all we do is *the greatest possible balance of good over evil* (or the least possible balance of evil over good) in the world as a whole."[52] Other ethicists suggest, a bit more simply, that according to this moral model the right thing to do in any given situation is that which will bring about the greatest good for the greatest number of people.[53]

Thus, once again, we find ourselves facing the crucial question: How is the greatest good to be conceived?

Quantitative utilitarianism. One of the founders of classic utilitarianism was Jeremy Bentham (1748–1832).[54] Bentham's form of utilitarianism, often referred to as *quantitative utilitarianism* and sometimes as *hedonistic utilitarianism*, focused on the experience of pleasure as the greatest good.[55] According to Bentham, "Nature has placed mankind under the governance of two sovereign masters, pain and pleasure. It is for them alone to point out what we ought to do, as well as to determine what we shall do."[56] Having thus embraced the notion that nature teaches us that the most basic instinct of human beings is to pursue pleasure and avoid pain,[57] Bentham's principle of utility, which he considered to be self-evident,[58] states that the end of all human action should be the promotion of the greatest happiness for all those involved in any given situation.[59] To be more specific, Bentham insisted that the principle of utility meant that "one should always seek to determine morals on the basis of

---

[51]Grenz, *Moral Quest*, p. 35.

[52]Frankena, *Ethics*, p. 34, emphasis original.

[53]Rae, *Moral Choices*, p. 72; Geisler, *Christian Ethics*, p. 63; Clark and Rakestraw, *Theology and Method*, pp. 20, 64, 161; Hollinger, *Choosing the Good*, pp. 31, 224; Robin Lovin, *An Introduction to Christian Ethics* (Nashville: Abingdon, 2011), pp. 95-96; Wilkens, *Beyond Bumper Sticker Ethics*, p. 83; McQuilkin and Copan, *Introduction to Biblical Ethics*, p. 175.

[54]Rae, *Moral Choices*, p. 73; Hollinger, *Choosing the Good*, p. 32; Nullens and Michener, *Matrix of Christian Ethics*, pp. 81-82.

[55]Rae, *Moral Choices*, pp. 73, 75; Wilkens, *Beyond Bumper Sticker Ethics*, p. 83; Geisler, *Christian Ethics*, pp. 64-67; Hollinger, *Choosing the Good*, pp. 31-33; Robin Lovin, *An Introduction to Christian Ethics*, p. 96.

[56]Jeremy Bentham, *The Principles of Morals and Legislation* (Darien, CT: Hafner, 1949), p. 1, as cited in Hollinger, *Choosing the Good*, p. 32.

[57]Geisler, *Christian Ethics*, p. 64; Lovin, *Introduction*, p. 96; Hollinger, *Choosing the Good*, p. 32.

[58]Geisler, *Christian Ethics*, pp. 64-65.

[59]Ibid.; Grenz, *Moral Quest*, p. 35.

maximizing pleasure and minimizing pain."[60] Thus, when confronted with a moral dilemma, quantitative or hedonistic utilitarianism holds that the right thing to do is to take the course of action that promotes the greatest experience of pleasure for the greatest number of people.

Living and working as he did in the eighteenth and nineteenth centuries "when science was becoming queen of the academic disciplines," and it was believed that nearly everything, including the results of human action, could and should be quantified, Bentham created what is known as the *pleasure* (or *hedonistic*) *calculus*.[61] By this method of calculation one could "determine the amount of pleasure over pain for given situations."[62] While Bentham didn't ignore the distinction between different types of pleasures, such as those of the mind and those of the body, his main focus was on the *quantity* of pleasure over pain.

Toward this end Bentham offered two evaluative processes, one for the individual and one for groups.[63] According to Bentham, the morality of any proposed action can be determined by evaluating (giving a numerical score for) how much pleasure and pain it's likely to produce, using the following seven evaluative criteria:

- intensity (How intense will be the pleasure/pain?);
- duration (How long will the pleasure/pain last?);
- certainty (How certain can we be of the pleasure/pain?);
- propinquity (How soon will the pleasure/pain occur?);
- fecundity (Will this pleasure/pain lead to still others?);
- purity (How much pain accompanies the pleasure and vice versa?)
- extent (How many others will be affected by the pleasure/pain?)[64]

After totaling the "scores" for both pleasure and pain with respect to these criteria, the moral agent was to take note of which total score was highest. In Bentham's own words: "Sum up all the values of all the plea-

---

[60]Hollinger, *Choosing the Good*, p. 32; Lovin, *Introduction*, p. 97.
[61]See Geisler, *Christian Ethics*, p. 64; Hollinger, *Choosing the Good*, p. 32; Frankena, *Ethics*, p. 35; Wilkens, *Beyond Bumper Sticker Ethics*, p. 87.
[62]Hollinger, *Choosing the Good*, p. 32.
[63]Geisler, *Christian Ethics*, p. 65.
[64]Ibid. See also Hollinger, *Choosing the Good*, p. 32; Wilkens, *Beyond Bumper Sticker Ethics*, p. 87.

sures on the one side, and all the pains on the other. The balance, if it be on the side of pleasure, will give the good tendency of the act upon the whole, with respect to the individual."[65]

When it came to decisions affecting a group of people, another step was added. After determining the pleasure and pain scores for each individual, all of these should be added together in order to determine the morality of the act for the group as a whole. Once again the total scores for pleasure or pain are determinative. If a course of action produces more pleasure than pain for the group as a whole, it should be considered a moral act. If not, it should be considered immoral. As Dennis Hollinger has observed, "For Bentham, ethics had become mathematics."[66]

At the same time, Bentham acknowledged that it was not feasible to employ the pleasure calculus before each and every moral decision. In addition to being time consuming, he also understood that because most moral decisions affect more than one person, this process of moral deliberation is "too psychologically and mathematically complex to be practical."[67] But if it's not really possible for one to make ethical decisions by simply calculating the balance of pleasure over pain for everyone involved, and if the notion of authoritative moral rules has been rejected, then how are moral choices to be made?

Qualitative utilitarianism. John Stuart Mill (1806–1873), whose father was a pupil of Jeremy Bentham, is also considered to be one of the ideological founders of utilitarianism.[68] Along with Bentham, Mill's desire was to ground ethics in something other than religious belief.[69] But Mill's version of utilitarianism differed from Bentham's in a couple of important ways.

First, Mill made more of a distinction than did Bentham between the experiences of pleasure and happiness.[70] Mill's version of the principle of

---

[65]Jeremy Bentham, *Principles*, p. 1, as cited in Hollinger, *Choosing the Good*, p. 32. It should be noted that this process aimed at determining the relative morality of individual acts. To resolve a moral dilemma, presumably, the process would need to be completed for each possible solution. The act with the highest ratio of pleasure over pain would be the best moral choice in that particular situation.
[66]Hollinger, *Choosing the Good*, p. 32.
[67]Geisler, *Christian Ethics*, p. 65. See also Frankena, *Ethics*, p. 36.
[68]Rae, *Moral Choices*, p. 75.
[69]Hollinger, *Choosing the Good*, p. 33. See also Rae, *Moral Choices*, p. 75; Lovin, *Christian Ethics: An Essential Guide* (Nashville, Abingdon, 2000), p. 23; Lovin, *Introduction*, pp. 96, 103; Wilkens, *Beyond Bumper Sticker Ethics*, p. 86.
[70]Rae, *Moral Choices*, p. 75.

utility stated that, "Actions are right in proportion as they tend to promote happiness, wrong as they tend to produce the reverse of happiness."[71] Though Bentham himself attempted in later life to soften the hedonistic aspect of his ethic, going so far as to suggest that "happiness" or "felicity" might be better terms by which to understand what he meant by "pleasure," Mill not only made this distinction in a more pronounced way than did Bentham but also went on to differentiate between various types of pleasure.[72] Mill believed that a distinction between pleasures was made necessary by the advanced faculties of human beings. Because of these advanced faculties, human beings not only *can* distinguish between higher and lower pleasures—that is, between cultured/intellectual pleasures and those that are uncultured/physical/sensual in nature—but should do so.[73] Thus, convinced that some pleasures were worth pursuing more so than others, Mill was famous for insisting that "It is better to be a human being dissatisfied than a pig satisfied; better to be Socrates satisfied than a fool dissatisfied. And if the fool or the pig are of a different opinion, it is because they only know their side of the question."[74] The bottom line is that, for Mill, "the primary calculation was not the *quantity* of happiness, but the *quality* of happiness or pleasure."[75]

But, in point of fact, Mill's emphasis on happiness, and his nuanced perspective on the pleasures that contribute to it, do not make it any easier to calculate the consequences of one's actions.[76] It was this recognition that led Mill to differ from Bentham also in the degree to which he emphasized the need for moral norms to guide the ethical decision-making process without determining it altogether.[77]

[71]John Stuart Mill, *Utilitarianism, Liberty and Representative Government* (London: J. M. Dent and Sons, 1910), p. 6, as cited in Grenz, *Moral Quest*, p. 35.

[72]Rae, *Moral Choices*, p. 75; Lovin, *Introduction*, p. 97.

[73]Wilkens, *Beyond Bumper Sticker Ethics*, pp. 88-89. Mill's focus on higher pleasures is reminiscent of Aristotle's notion of *eudaimonia*—true happiness or complete fulfillment, which he considered to be "an activity of our highest faculty, the intellect, and is to be found in the contemplative life of searching for unchangeable truths" and "the pursuit of the social ideal." See Nullens and Michener, *Matrix of Christian Ethics*, pp. 119-20.

[74]John Stuart Mill, *Utilitarianism* (Indianapolis: Hackett, 1979), p. 10, as cited in Hollinger, *Choosing the Good*, p. 33; Wilkens, *Beyond Bumper Sticker Ethics*, p. 89.

[75]Hollinger, *Choosing the Good*, p. 33, emphasis added.

[76]See Frankena, *Ethics*, p. 35.

[77]Geisler, *Christian Ethics*, p. 67.

It was Mill's contention that throughout human history, human beings have been "learning by experience the tendency of actions" and have acquired some beliefs "as to the effects of some actions on their happiness."[78] In other words, Mill was convinced that "there are valid moral rules, beliefs, and codes to guide human decisions toward maximizing the good in society." At the same time Mill insisted that "none of these are exceptionless; all of them can and should be broken for the principle of utility when the greater good is in jeopardy."[79] While no set of moral norms should ever be considered sacred and inviolable, that doesn't mean they should be completely ignored. It only makes sense to routinely follow these time-tested moral norms, only violating them when it becomes apparent that doing so is required in order to achieve the greatest good (happiness) for the greatest number of people.

So distinctive was Mill's approach to making ethical decisions that most ethicists acknowledge at least two versions of the utilitarian moral model.[80] *Act-utilitarianism* (such as the type promoted by Bentham) essentially calls for a strict focus on the principle of utility alone when facing each moral dilemma.[81] In other words, every time I find myself wondering what I should do, I should strive to do what produces the greatest good for the greatest number of people. *Rule-utilitarianism*, on the other hand, places more emphasis on the need for moral norms that can help us make wise ethical choices. The notion here is that normally, generally, we should follow the moral norms at our disposal, only breaking from those norms when it becomes apparent that doing so *in this case* is required in order to achieve the greatest good for the greatest number of people.[82]

An evaluation of utilitarianism. I'll begin by expressing some genuine appreciation for what this moral model brings to the table. It's actually quite appropriate, I believe, for Christians to consider the utilitarian principle—that is, the goal of seeking the greatest good for the greatest number of

---

[78]John Stuart Mill, "Utilitarianism," in *The Utilitarians* (Garden City, NY: Doubleday, 1961), p. 409, as cited in Geisler, *Christian Ethics*, p. 67.

[79]Geisler, *Christian Ethics*, p. 67.

[80]Rae, *Moral Choices*, p. 74. Nullens and Michener, *Matrix of Christian Ethics*, p. 52.

[81]See Rae, *Moral Choices*, p. 74; Frankena, *Ethics*, p. 35.

[82]See Rae, *Moral Choices*, p. 74; Frankena, *Ethics*, p. 39.

people—to be a valid consideration when making ethical decisions.[83] Indeed, not a few Christian ethicists have pointed out the affinity that exists between the utilitarian impulse and what we find God doing in sending his Son to die on behalf of the sins of the world (see Jn 3:16)![84]

Then again, for our purposes, the appropriate question is not: Does the principle of utility possess any ethical value? Rather, the correct questions are:

- Is this a decision-making approach that's really practicable in the rough-and-tumble of everyday life?

- Shouldn't the Bible's emphasis on justice cause us to pause before assuming that the ends always justify the means?[85]

- Aren't there some specific Bible stories that seem to indicate that in God's eyes the end does not always justify the means (for example, Abraham's compromise with respect to Hagar [Gen 16:1-12]; David's compromise with respect to Uriah the Hittite [2 Sam 11:1-26]; Joseph's refusal to compromise with respect to Potiphar's wife [Gen 39:1-23]; the refusal of Daniel and his friends to compromise with respect to King Nebuchadnezzar's command and King Darius's decree [Dan 3:1-30; 6:1-28] respectively)?

- Doesn't the utilitarian approach put us, with our limited understanding, in the precarious position of having to predict what the consequences of this or that action will be (Prov 14:12; 16:25)?

- Does the principle of utility by itself have what it takes to serve as the foundation for a Christian ethic that does justice to the entirety of Jesus' moral teachings (for example, see Mt 5:21-48)?

- Don't we Christians have the hope for a bit more moral guidance from God to help us make our way through this life (for example, see Prov 2:1-9; Ps 32:8-9)?[86]

The "Serving the Other in Love" approach (situationism). Yet another version of an altruistic ethical model asserts that *there actually is at least one*

---

[83]Rae, *Moral Choices*, p. 77; Wilkens, *Beyond Bumper Sticker Ethics*, pp. 91-92.
[84]See Lovin, *Introduction*, pp. 96-97. See also Grenz, *Moral Quest*, p. 35.
[85]See Rae, *Moral Choices*, pp. 86-87.
[86]For more on the problems attached to utilitarianism, see McQuilkin and Copan, *Introduction to Biblical Ethics*, pp. 176-78.

absolute moral law that must be contextualized in each moral situation.[87] What this means is that, unlike any of the ethical models surveyed so far, a contextualizing approach to making ethical decisions insists that the concept of universal, binding, exceptionless moral rules or principles be taken seriously. However, also to be taken very seriously is the specific life situation (or context) that has given rise to the moral dilemma. Referring to a category of ethical models known as "contextualism," Dennis Hollinger explains that "according to this perspective, there are transcendent realities, known through divine revelation, in which we ground our ethics and moral universals. The context, however, determines how we appeal to these trans-cultural norms and virtues and how we seek to apply them within the world."[88] Thus technically speaking contextualism is a category of ethical decision-making approaches earmarked by a commitment to give careful consideration to rules *and* results rather than just one or the other.

However, contextualism as an ethical category encompasses several moral models, at least one of which ends up playing out (in terms of its metaethical ethos) in a very relativistic manner.[89] Indeed, the term *relativistic contextualism* has become nearly synonymous with one option in particular—a model known as *situationism* or "situation ethics."[90]

Though some ethicists distinguish between two versions of situationism (pure and principled), the most popular version of situationism is the one promoted by Joseph Fletcher (1905–1991), primarily by means of his book *Situation Ethics: The New Morality.*[91] Fletcher's desire was to

---

[87]It should be noted that there are various versions of contextualism that differ, among other things, in the degree to which they acknowledge the existence and authority of exceptionless moral rules. See Clark and Rakestraw, *Theology and Method*, p. 144.

[88]Hollinger, *Choosing the Good*, p. 87.

[89]In part two of this book I will argue for another contextualizing approach to making ethical decisions that plays out in a much less relativistic manner.

[90]See Clark and Rakestraw, *Theology and Method*, pp. 116, 143, 175.

[91]*Pure situationism* can be thought of as an abjectly normless approach to making ethical decisions which relies on some form of moral intuition, divinely provided or not, to guide the moral agent in each and every moral situation. (The reader might take note of how reminiscent of the naive moral intuitionism referred to above is this form of situationism.) *Principled situationism*, on the other hand, offers the moral agent at least one moral norm to guide him or her in the moral decision-making moment. See J. I. Packer, "Situations and Principles," in Clark and Rakestraw, *Theology and Method*, pp. 150-53. In addition to Fletcher, one should note also the work of Paul Ramsey, another ethicist who emphasized the "normative value of love" (see Grenz, *Moral Quest*, p. 176) but whose ethical writings did not achieve the level of popularity of Fletcher's (see Grenz, *Moral Quest*, p. 177). For a thorough understanding of Ramsey's ethic of "in-principled love" or what some refer to as

provide an ethical decision-making approach (rather than an ethical system per se) that avoided the abject lawlessness of antinomianism on the one hand, and a slavish and ultimately irresponsible legalism (obsessive focus on rules) on the other.[92] According to Fletcher's version of situationism, the biblical command to love our neighbors as ourselves is *the* universally binding moral absolute.[93] Since love is the only moral absolute, all other laws are breakable if this is done with a loving motive.[94] In Fletcher's own words:

> *Christian* situation ethics has only one norm or principle or law (call it what you will) that is binding and unexceptionable, always good and right regardless of circumstances. That is "love"—the *agapē* of the summary commandment to love God and the neighbor. Everything else without exception, all laws and rules and principles and ideals and norms, are only *contingent*, only valid *if they happen* to serve love in any situation.[95]

On the one hand, this certainly seems to be a *principled* approach that calls for obedience to a transcendent moral rule—love your neighbor.[96] On the other hand, though Fletcher can describe love in ways that are reminiscent of traditional Christian depictions, he goes on to define love essentially as "whatever brings good results."[97] Because of this, some critics have accused Fletcher's understanding of Christian love of being

---

"rule agapism," see Paul Ramsey, *Basic Christian Ethics* (Chicago: University of Chicago Press, 1950). For a brief but helpful overview of Ramsey's approach, see Grenz, *Moral Quest*, pp. 174-77.

[92]James Childress, "Introduction," in Joseph Fletcher, *Situation Ethics: The New Morality* (Louisville: Westminster John Knox, 1966), pp. 2, 4, 17-39. See also Geisler, *Christian Ethics*, pp. 43-45; Hollinger, *Choosing the Good*, p. 34; Lovin, *Introduction*, pp. 105-7; Grenz, *Moral Quest*, pp. 177-78, 250; Wilkens, *Beyond Bumper Sticker Ethics*, pp. 136-38.

[93]Fletcher, *Situation Ethics*, pp. 30, 69-86. See also Geisler, *Christian Ethics*, pp. 43-44, 48; Hollinger, *Choosing the Good*, p. 34; Grenz, *Moral Quest*, p. 177; Lovin, *Christian Ethics*, p. 24; Wilkens, *Beyond Bumper Sticker Ethics*, pp. 134, 138. Scott Rae points out Fletcher's use of Romans 13:8 as support for his focus on love as the supreme moral norm (Rae, *Moral Choices*, p. 86).

[94]Fletcher, *Situation Ethics*, pp. 30-31. See also Geisler, *Christian Ethics*, pp. 44-45, 48, 54; Wilkens, *Beyond Bumper Sticker Ethics*, pp. 134, 136, 138.

[95]Fletcher, *Situation Ethics*, p. 30, emphasis original.

[96]Hence several ethicists refer to situationism as "agapism." See Frankena, *Ethics*, p. 57; Grenz, *Moral Quest*, p. 177; Lovin, *Christian Ethics*, p. 24.

[97]On how Fletcher can describe love in ways reminiscent of traditional Christian depictions, see Grenz, *Moral Quest*, p. 178. On Fletcher's definition of love, see Clark and Rakestraw, *Theology and Method*, p. 144. While Scott Rae acknowledges situationism's references to love as a moral absolute, his brief treatment of this moral model is located in a section titled "Different Forms of Relativism" (see Rae, *Moral Choices*, pp. 84-87).

much too imprecise, even referring to it as a "sloppy agape."[98] Fletcher himself referred to his ethical approach as pragmatic and relativist in orientation.[99] This has caused many ethicists to classify Fletcher's version of situationism as an ultimately teleological or consequentialist moral model.[100] Indeed, it would appear that, in the end, Fletcher's situationism is actually a Christian version of utilitarianism.[101]

I'm going to suggest that it's primarily this association with utilitarianism that makes Fletcher's situationism, despite its theological underpinnings and Christian rhetoric, ultimately problematic for many Christian ethicists.[102] As soon as *Situation Ethics* was published, it proved to be quite controversial.[103] What made Fletcher's book so provocative, especially among Christian readers, were the illustrations he used to explain how an allegiance to a single norm of love would play out in differing life situations. On the one hand it's these case studies that make *Situation Ethics* so readable. On the other hand the pragmatism and relativism reflected in these illustrations were and are disconcerting to those who are even a bit more absolutist than Fletcher in their ethical thinking. For the sake of space I'll have to summarize. In the process of explaining his love ethic, Fletcher ends up promoting such actions as:

- *Altruistic adultery.* According to Fletcher, it would be morally acceptable for a woman in prison to have sex with a guard if her becoming pregnant would get her released so she could be reunited with her family.[104] He also suggests that sexual intercourse outside marriage might be engaged in for therapeutic purposes: for example, to enable a young man "who is afraid he cannot function sexually as an adult and virile man" to overcome his "corrosive self-doubt" and sense of "non-identity."[105]

---

[98]Childress, "Introduction," p. 3.

[99]Fletcher, *Situation Ethics*, p. 43.

[100]Lovin, *Introduction*, pp. 106-7; Wilkens, *Beyond Bumper Sticker Ethics*, p. 138.

[101]Lovin, *Introduction*, pp. 106-7. See also Hollinger, *Choosing the Good*, p. 34; Frankena, *Ethics*, pp. 56-57; Lovin, *Christian Ethics*, pp. 23-24. Grenz refers to Fletcher's "radically contextual" ethic as an "act agapism" (Grenz, *Moral Quest*, p. 177), hinting at its similarity to act-utilitarianism.

[102]See Lovin, *Introduction*, p. 106; Wilkens, *Beyond Bumper Sticker Ethics*, pp. 134, 140.

[103]See Hollinger, *Choosing the Good*, pp. 33-34; Grenz, *Moral Quest*, p. 177.

[104]Fletcher, *Situation Ethics*, pp. 164-65. See also Geisler, *Christian Ethics*, pp. 51-52; Rae, *Moral Choices*, p. 86.

[105]Fletcher, *Situation Ethics*, pp. 126-27.

- *Patriotic prostitution.* Fletcher reflects on a conversation he once had with a young Christian woman who had been approached by a US intelligence agency to function as a "kind of counterespionage agent." She had been encouraged to, using sexual seduction, "lure an enemy spy into blackmail." The way Fletcher relates this account suggests that he encouraged the young woman to consider such an assignment morally acceptable.[106]

- *Sacrificial suicide.* Another suggestion made by Fletcher is that it might be morally acceptable for a terminally ill man to refuse to take medicine that would prolong his life out of concern for the financial expense his family would incur.[107]

- *Acceptable abortion.* Fletcher is fairly passionate in his insistence that it would be morally acceptable for a father of an unmarried schizophrenic patient, pregnant because of rape, to arrange for her to have an abortion.[108]

- *Merciful murder.* According to Fletcher, it would be morally acceptable for: a Christian civilian to have murdered Hitler; a mother to smother her crying baby in order to save her party from being detected and killed by hostile Indians; and a select group of people to be forced out of an overloaded life boat in order to save everyone else from sinking.[109]

An evaluation of situationism. Straightaway I must indicate that a potential problem with the "Serving the Other in Love" approach as put forward by Fletcher centers in his proposal's apparent lack of integrity. We've seen that *Situation Ethics* made prolific use of theological concepts and Christian rhetoric. However, it appears that in another work, Fletcher (himself a philosophical pragmatist)[110] was honest about his using Christian rhetoric in *Situation Ethics* for merely practical reasons.[111] James Childress, an ethics scholar very familiar with Fletcher's work, writes: "Even though Fletcher used 'Christian rhetoric' in *Situation Ethics*, he primarily appealed to readers' reason and experiences in an effort to persuade them that cal-

---

[106]Ibid., pp. 163-64. See also Geisler, *Christian Ethics*, p. 52.

[107]Fletcher, *Situation Ethics*, pp. 165-66. See also Geisler, *Christian Ethics*, p. 52.

[108]Fletcher, *Situation Ethics*, pp. 37-39. See also Geisler, *Christian Ethics*, pp. 52-53.

[109]Fletcher, *Situation Ethics*, pp. 74-75, 113, 125. See also Geisler, *Christian Ethics*, p. 53.

[110]See Childress, "Introduction," p. 2.

[111]Joseph Fletcher, "Memoir of an Ex-Radical," in *Joseph Fletcher: Memoir of an Ex-Radical*, ed. Kenneth Vaux (Louisville: Westminster John Knox, 1993), p. 82, as cited in Childress, "Introduction," p. 9.

culating love (utility) in the situation is the best way to make moral decisions." Moreover, in later life, says Childress, Fletcher essentially denounced the Christian faith as something that did not work. All of this
causes Childress to say of *Situation Ethics*: "The book has a role for religion
and theology, but religion played no role in Fletcher's thought and practice
in later life, not even at the level of motivation—even though he still recognized that religion could provide *others* with motivation."[112]

Now, these revelations regarding Fletcher's rather pragmatic use of
theological concepts and Christian rhetoric don't, by themselves, invalidate his proposal. They do, however, lend support for the notion that his
version of situationism is at the end of the day a version of utilitarianism
adorned in a Christian dress.

This issue of integrity aside, there are several other reasons why many
Christian ethicists are not convinced that situationism is the moral
model on which to base a Christian ethic.

First, the observation has been made that one moral norm does not
an ethic make; a one-norm ethic, especially one as broad and general as
Fletcher's love norm, is in most cases little better than having no norm
at all. Since it's not always easy to know what the "loving" action is, to
encourage someone to resolve a moral dilemma by doing the *loving*
thing is not much more specific than telling him or her to do the *good*
thing or the *right* thing. The bottom line is that one moral law by itself is
too general to be helpful.

Second, if it's true that situationism really is just a Christianized version
of utilitarianism, then the same questions posed above concerning utilitarianism's practicality and sufficiency apply to situationism as well.

Third, some other questions that need to be asked derive from the possibility that in God's eyes some acts are intrinsically evil regardless of the
situation: behaviors as rape, abject cruelty, child abuse, blaspheming the
Holy Spirit, defection from the faith and so on. Can it ever be considered
morally acceptable in God's eyes to engage in such intrinsically evil acts,
even to bring about the greatest good for the greatest number of people?
Should we necessarily assume that God considers these kinds of acts jus-

---

[112]See Childress, "Introduction," pp. 9-10, emphasis original.

tifiable in certain situations? Is it *ever* right to simply honor God's moral principles as articulated in Scripture, trusting him with the results?

Fourth, some ethicists have made the observation that situationism asks more of the Christian moral agent than he or she is able to deliver. Some questions related to this concern include:

- Are we really capable of loving the way God loves without other ethical norms to guide and inform our choices?

- Isn't it true that we possess an innate tendency to rationalize away decisions that bring personal pain and inconvenience?

- Can we truly be objective about what the most loving action is and who the recipient of it should be in this or that situation (Prov 3:5-6; 14:12; 16:25; 28:26)?

Fifth, yet another trenchant observation put forward is that situationism is guilty of collapsing the first commandment to love God supremely into the second commandment to love the neighbor as ourselves (Mt 22:34-40). In other words, for Fletcher, the way we love God is by loving our neighbor. But this conflation of the two commandments has the effect of negating Jesus' use of the qualifiers "first" and "second" with respect to them. Thus yet another crucial question arises: Is it really true that anything goes as long as we can convince ourselves that we are doing the "loving" thing, or should our love for God inform the ways we show love for our neighbors? I will offer that a careful look at the Scriptures as a whole, and Jesus' ethical behavior and teaching in particular, seems to warn against our assuming that, as long as we can convince ourselves that our motive is a loving one, anything goes in terms of our own behavior, or that which we encourage in others.

A final concern relates to Fletcher's valiant attempt to provide an alternative to both antinomianism and legalism. While this was (and is) a noble, necessary goal, we must ask the question: Is Fletcher's version of contextualism the best way to do this? Many Christian ethicists have answered this question in the negative. For example, Stanley Grenz made the observation that Fletcher was much more concerned about refuting legalism than he was resisting antinomianism.[113] Robin Lovin argues that Fletcher's middle way founders on the shoals of imprecision.[114] Even James Childress, in his introduction to *Situation Ethics,* feels the need to ask the question: "Is it a genuine third way between legalism and antinomianism? Or is situation ethics on the slippery slope to antinomianism?"[115] Childress answers his own question when he states: "It is relatively easy to provide sound reasons for rejecting both legalism and antinomianism, but it is not so easy to construct an alternative position that avoids all their problems. Even though Fletcher rejects both, he appears to fear the tyranny of legalism more than the anarchy of antinomianism."[116]

The ultimate conclusion drawn by many Christian ethicists is that, while Fletcher's attempt to steer a middle course between antinomianism and legalism was laudable, the one-norm ethic he proposed falls short of producing the type of moral faithfulness God desires and deserves. So close and yet so far away!

Now, in part two of this work, I will put forward a version of moral contextualism I believe does a much better job than situationism of avoiding the extremes of antinomianism and legalism while doing justice to the notion of moral absolutes. But at this point I must beg the reader's patience. In the next chapter we will conclude this survey of popular ethical options with a careful examination of some rules-oriented decision-making approaches, both reason- and Bible-based. Then the final chapter of part one (chapter four) is designed to help us all better understand the impact an increasingly postmodern culture is having on us and our current capacity for a moral faithfulness. It's only after having wrestled with all these issues that we will be sufficiently prepared to explore the ethic of responsible Christian discipleship.

---

[113]Grenz, *Moral Quest,* p. 178.
[114]Lovin, *Introduction,* p. 107.
[115]Childress, "Introduction," pp. 5-6.
[116]Ibid., p. 4.

Some Popular Ethical Options (2)

Rules-Oriented Approaches

The image of a stern, judgmental person, rigorously applying the law to everyone around him or her in a hardhearted manner, is fairly common in literature and film. Consider, for example, the austere village mayor Comte (Count) Paul de Reynaud, portrayed by Alfred Molina in the movie *Chocolat*. What a vivid example of how one self-righteous, super-scrupulous, inherently unhappy legalist can succeed at making life miserable for an entire community!

But perhaps the most notable legalist in all of literature is the pathetic character Javert in Victor Hugo's masterpiece *Les Misérables*. The famous protagonist of this story is of course Jean Valjean, the backslidden parolee whose life is radically changed for the good when despite his thievery he's shown mercy and grace by a kind and godly church bishop. But the story also has an almost equally famous antagonist, the policeman Javert, who is so compulsive about seeing the law kept that he makes it his great mission in life to see Jean Valjean, despite his transformation, rearrested and re-incarcerated for the rest of his natural life. The tragic irony is that near the end of the story Jean Valjean shows his mortal enemy the same type of mercy and grace that had been extended to him. But Javert will have none of it. So committed is he to the law that he simply cannot receive mercy and grace. Rather than live with any sense of indebtedness to anyone, least of all Jean Valjean, Javert decides to commit suicide instead. What a powerfully sad example of the soul-killing effect of legalism on a human life!

While most legalists are not as extreme in their devotion to the law as Javert, some come pretty close. I've made the case elsewhere that a big reason why so many Americans are post-Christian in their orientation (that is, over Christianity and done with the church) is that a religious and moralistic legalism (and the self-righteous judgmentalism that follows in legalism's wake) are all too rife within conservative Christian churches.[1]

So it's with a definite sense of carefulness that I approach this chapter. On the one hand I'm convinced that all of the ethical options surveyed thus far can be critiqued for their failure to come to terms with the fact that, according to the Scriptures, moral absolutes do exist, and there is more than just one of them. On the other hand my absolutist understanding of Christian ethics is extremely concerned that too many Christians have overcorrected to the relativism that earmarks the ethical thinking at work in the modern and postmodern eras toward a soul-killing, ministry-hampering legalism instead. What all of this means is that *I believe it's important to make a distinction between an acceptance of moral absolutism and an embrace of ethical legalism.* Ironically, in order to nuance this distinction in part two of this work, we need to spend some time in this chapter improving our understanding of how the former can and sometimes does lead to the latter.

Legalism as an Ethical Category

In a religious context, legalism is typically understood as that approach requiring "obedience to divine law as the way of salvation or the means by which we can gain God's favor."[2] But this is not the only way to conceive of legalism.[3] It can also be viewed as an ethical category. Thus Dennis Hollinger refers to a legalism "in which the rules and the principles become ends in themselves—rules for rules' sake."[4] Providing a

---

[1]See Gary Tyra, *Defeating Pharisaism: Recovering Jesus' Disciple-Making Method* (Downers Grove, IL: IVP Books, 2009), pp. 58-68.

[2]Stanley J. Grenz, *The Moral Quest: Foundations of Christian Ethics* (Downers Grove, IL: InterVarsity Press, 1997), p. 243.

[3]For a thorough discussion of the various forms of legalism, see Robertson McQuilkin and Paul Copan, *An Introduction to Biblical Ethics: Walking in the Way of Wisdom*, 3rd ed. (Downers Grove, IL: IVP Academic, 2014), pp. 87-89.

[4]Dennis Hollinger, *Choosing the Good: Christian Ethics in a Complex World* (Grand Rapids: Baker

bit more depth and correctly contrasting legalism with antinomianism, David Clark and Robert Rakestraw speak of ethical systems that "over-emphasize law and develop detailed rules for many specific matters without regard for justice and mercy."[5] Based on a definition such as this, it's possible to conceive of an ethical legalism that's not religious in orientation. I will argue below that the bare-knuckled deontology promoted by the German philosopher Immanuel Kant (1724–1804) qualifies as a legalism even though it sought to be reason- rather than religion-based.

I will, however, go on to suggest that a rather important earmark of an ethical legalism that *is* religion-based is a tendency to view each and every moral command presented in the Bible as a universally binding, authoritative moral absolute. The result of such a tendency is to reduce the Bible to a moral rule book that contains "laws for everything."[6]

It's with this nuanced understanding of an *ethical legalism* in mind that I'm suggesting that the three versions of Christian moral absolutism also treated in this chapter can be viewed as ethical decision-making approaches that tend toward a moral legalism (perhaps moral biblicism is an equally appropriate term). While none of them denies that salvation is by God's grace through faith in the atoning work of Jesus Christ (see Eph 2:8-9), the fact that they tend to treat the Bible as an ethical encyclopedia or rulebook with a law or command for just about everything can suggest that making moral choices that honor the heart of God requires nothing more than a scan of the Scriptures in order to find an applicable moral rule, and then a willingness to do one's duty with respect to it. The question is whether such a perfunctory, principle-obsessed approach to the ethical endeavor, absent an attendant concern for how our moral choices affect other people, is actually reflective of the kind of moral faithfulness we see at work in the life of Christ.

Figure 3.1 reminds us of the popular ethical decision-making approaches that are treated in this chapter.

Academic, 2002), pp. 140, 146, 163.
[5]David K. Clark and Raymond V. Rakestraw, eds., *Readings in Christian Ethics*, vol. 1, *Theology and Method* (Grand Rapids: Baker Books, 1994), p. 175.
[6]Norman L. Geisler, *Christian Ethics: Options and Issues* (Grand Rapids: Baker 1989), p. 43.

THE MOST POPULAR ETHICAL DECISION-MAKING APPROACHES
Chapter 3
Rules-Oriented Approaches *(Deontological)*
Reason-Based ❏ "Obeying the Dictates of Reason" (moral universalism) *Bible-Based* ❏ "Following the Letter of the Law" (nonconflicting absolutism) ❏ "Doing the Lesser Evil" (conflicting absolutism) ❏ "Yielding to the Higher Law" (graded absolutism)
◀ Relativistic   *Metaethical Ethos*   Absolutist ▶

Figure 3.1

A REASON-BASED (ABSOLUTIST) APPROACH TO ETHICAL DECISION MAKING

Ethicists Patrick Nullens and Ronald Michener are careful to distinguish between two versions of absolutist or principle-based ethics. *Theonomous* principle ethics "takes God to be the source of all moral laws," whereas *autonomous* principle ethics "is based on the concept that moral laws are not derived from God but humanity itself."[7] It's the latter type of absolutist ethics that will immediately concern us as we focus our attention on the ethical rationalism promoted by Immanuel Kant.[8]

The "Obeying the Dictates of Reason" approach (moral universalism). Immanuel Kant was one of the most influential thinkers of modern times whose ethical project is widely regarded as supremely representative of de-

---

[7]Patrick Nullens and Ronald T. Michener, *The Matrix of Christian Ethics: Integrating Philosophy and Moral Theology in a Postmodern Context* (Downers Grove, IL: IVP Books, 2010), p. 52.
[8]Scott Rae, *Moral Choices: An Introduction to Ethics*, 3rd ed. (Grand Rapids: Zondervan, 2009), p. 77.

ontological approaches based on reason rather than the Bible.[9] Though Kant's ethic can be regarded as a "purely philosophical system" that's significantly different from theocentric command ethics (such as the ones discussed below), it was unique in the way it accorded a role for a belief in the existence of God.[10] Whether God actually exists was immaterial for Kant. His ethic didn't see moral absolutes originating with God but in human reason.[11] But while Kant didn't believe it was possible to know God in a personal way, he wanted to develop an ethic that could keep civilized, educated people from living like mere animals—that is, hedonists! Kant's reasoning was thus: "Society cannot function without law, and law must be universal in order to be law. If it does not apply to everyone, then it is not a law. Hence, universal moral law, not what is simply socially or personally desirable, is rationally necessary to posit for life."[12] And yet Kant recognized that in order for the members of a society to take these universal laws seriously, they needed some extrinsic motivation to do so.[13] So Kant's ethic "presupposes immortality."[14] Nullens and Michener explain why:

> Ultimately, humans cannot be judged within the boundaries of time and space. While the call to ethical behavior comes from within humankind, final judgment is the task of an entity outside of humankind. It follows that humanity's existence must extend beyond this life. Here lies the necessity for the existence of God for Kant. Morality presupposes a God who acts as judge. Kant did not suggest that we can prove the existence of God; that would go beyond our mental capacity. All he claimed was that ethics required us to believe that God exists. More precisely, ethics did not presuppose the existence of God, but it did presuppose *belief* in God.[15]

And yet we should not make the mistake of thinking that this is a revelation- or Bible-based ethic. Kant's goal was to develop an ethic that was grounded not in religion per se but in rationality, human reason.[16]

---

[9]Ibid., pp. 77-78. See also Robin Lovin, *An Introduction to Christian Ethics* (Nashville: Abingdon, 2011), p. 149; McQuilkin and Copan, *Introduction to Biblical Ethics*, p. 179.
[10]Nullens and Michener, *Matrix of Christian Ethics*, pp. 103, 107.
[11]Ibid., p. 105.
[12]Geisler, *Christian Ethics*, p. 83. See also Nullens and Michener, *Matrix of Christian Ethics*, p. 105.
[13]Rae, *Moral Choices*, p. 77.
[14]Nullens and Michener, *Matrix of Christian Ethics*, p. 107.
[15]Ibid.
[16]Rae, *Moral Choices*, p. 77.

A very basic description of Kant's ethic. It's probably not going too far to say that Kant is another philosopher who wanted to make morality as rational as mathematics. He believed that good acts should not be established by nature on the one hand (the pursuit of pleasure) or special revelation on the other (the Bible) but by a rational standard (logic). He further believed, however, that the goodness of various acts would need to be judged apart from future consequences, apart from situational factors and apart from people's subjective feelings about them. In other words, according to Kant, when a person was approaching a moral choice, his or her focus should not be on special circumstances, strong feelings or possible outcomes. Instead, having identified the patently correct thing to do on the basis of reason, the person should do his or her duty, period.

Of course, this raises the question: How does reason by itself tell us what our duty is in this or that situation?

At the risk of greatly oversimplifying things, I'll reiterate here how important to Kant's ethic was the concept of universalizability. Remember, for Kant one of the main attributes of a moral absolute was its being transcendent or universally applicable regardless of historical location, geographical location, particular personalities involved, specific circumstances at work and so on.

With this thought in mind, Kant distinguished between two types of rules or commands: hypothetical imperatives and categorical imperatives. We obey hypothetical imperatives because doing so is "a means to achieving something else" that we desire.[17] The categorical imperative, on the other hand, is one we obey not as the means to some other end but because the action is "objectively necessary"—an end itself.[18] Dennis Hollinger explains:

> In other words, in regard to the hypothetical imperative, we take a course of
> action because we might regret the consequences if we do not pursue it or
> because the reward for the action is worthy of pursuit. A business person
> might, for example, treat a customer with fairness to keep that person's
> business. Kant saw this as a kind of prudential consideration that always em-

---

[17]Hollinger, *Choosing the Good*, p. 39.
[18]Ibid.

bodied a sense of selfishness; thus it was always less pure in motive and not really the essence of true, rational morality.

The categorical imperative, on the other hand, is an action or principle we choose without recourse to its benefit or results; it is in and of itself good.[19]

This is where the attribute of universalizability becomes crucial. Again, Hollinger is helpful. He writes: "For something to be a categorical imperative, it must be universal, and thus Kant set forth the major principle of the categorical imperative: 'Act only according to that maxim by which you can at the same time will that it should become a universal law.'"[20]

A crude paraphrase of Kant's most basic ethical rule might go like this: Before engaging in any action, ask yourself whether you could wish that everyone would do the same. If universalizing the proposed behavior would constitute a logical impossibility, then back away.[21] If it's not feasible for everyone to do what you're thinking of doing, it's not a permissible behavior.

While Kant insisted that the categorical imperative is a general axiom that is rationally self-evident, and that all other imperatives (duties) and moral principles are derived from it, he did allow for another formulation of it. He referred to this second version as the "practical imperative." It stated: "Act so that you treat humanity, whether in your own person or in that of another, always as an end and never as a means only."[22] Apparently, Kant thought he was able to, on the basis of practical reason (that which is necessary for human societies to flourish), ground a very basic commitment to human dignity.[23] Thus yet another way to conceive of the categorical imperative takes this form: Before engaging in any action, ask yourself whether you could wish that everyone would do the same. If universalizing the proposed behavior would constitute a social impropriety—

---

[19]Ibid.

[20]Ibid. Quotation is from Immanuel Kant, *Foundations of the Metaphysics of Morals*, trans. Lewis White Beck (Indianapolis: Bobbs-Merrill, 1959), p. 39.

[21]For Kant, "the only ethical rules that should be adopted are those which show themselves to be logically consistent and which do not result in self-contradiction." See Steve Wilkens, *Beyond Bumper Sticker Ethics: An Introduction to Theories of Right and Wrong* (Downers Grove, IL: InterVarsity Press, 1995), p. 101.

[22]Hollinger, *Choosing the Good*, p. 39. Quotation is from Kant, *Foundations*, p. 47. See also Nullens and Michener, *Matrix of Christian Ethics*, p. 106.

[23]A critique of this arbitrary ascription of dignity to human beings can be found in McQuilkin and Copan, *Introduction to Biblical Ethics*, pp. 179-80.

that is, would serve to destroy rather than contribute to a civil society—then back away. If it's not desirable for everyone to do what you're thinking of doing, it's not a permissible behavior.

From these two overarching moral principles Kant was able to spin off a multitude of moral maxims or rules, all based in reason rather than religion. For example, Kant's insistence that one should never tell a lie, no matter what the consequences, is paradigmatic.[24] In a tractate titled "On a Supposed Right to Tell Lies from Benevolent Motives," Kant argued against such a supposition, boldly insisting that "to be truthful (honest) in all declarations is therefore a sacred unconditional command of reason, and not to be limited by any expediency."[25] Robin Lovin explains that, according to Kant, it should be apparent that the rule "always tell the truth" is a requirement of reason "because no matter how much we struggle to convince ourselves that there are 'noble' lies and 'white' lies that contribute to the greater good, we cannot conceive a world in which rational people all follow a rule that says, 'Lie when it seems good to you to do so.'"[26]

This is indeed a bare-knuckled, no-holds-barred deontology that brooks no exceptions. An unadulterated absolutist approach to making ethical decisions such as this stands in stark contrast to the relativistic approaches treated in chapter two. Kant would have a huge problem with all of those teleological approaches, not because they lack biblical support but because making ethical choices on the basis of one's self-interest, or the pursuit of the greatest good, or because it feels right, or seems right or possesses a loving motive, is simply not grounded in reason. This is unacceptable to Kant because he held reason to be the ultimate arbiter of all things—the moral as well as the intellectual.

An evaluation of Kant's moral universalism. Several critiques of Kant's ethical proposal have been put forward over the years. What follows is just a few that seem especially pertinent given the nature of this survey.

First, one of the main critiques from a Christian perspective of Kant's ethical project relates to the supreme role that reason and logic play in it.

---

[24]See Nullens and Michener, *Matrix of Christian Ethics*, p. 106.
[25]Immanuel Kant, "On a Supposed Right to Tell Lies from Benevolent Motives," in *The Critique of Practical Reason*, trans. Thomas Kinsmill Abbot, 6th ed. (London: Longmans Green, 1963), p. 363, as cited in Geisler, *Christian Ethics*, p. 363.
[26]Lovin, *Introduction*, p. 149.

Kant's extreme emphasis on rationality has had the effect of suggesting that not just religious behavior but religious belief as well must be justified at the bar of reason. Though over the years some Christians have acquiesced to this Enlightenment-produced mandate, the larger part of the Christian community has not. Moreover, while many Christians will eagerly contend that a commitment to the risen Christ involves a rational, reasonable (rather than irrational) step of faith, most evangelical believers are wary of the notion that human reason by itself is to function as the superlative (if not singular) test of religious belief. Thus the eccentric emphasis Kant placed on human rationality is by itself enough to prohibit an exclusive embrace of the "Obeying the Dictates of Reason" approach to making ethical decisions on the part of most Christian ethicists.

Another concern is that this approach doesn't allow for hard cases that defy a simple solution. According to Kant, the moral life is fairly black and white, cut and dried. This moral model's severely myopic focus on rules/duty/principle over results/consequences/people certainly seems to promote an unbalanced deliberative process. Its abject refusal to allow for any ambiguity in moral matters means that this decision-making approach has a reputation for producing moral choices that strike many people as heartless and cruel (the most notable being Kant's insistence on truth-telling even at the cost of someone's life).[27]

Third, I'll offer the observation that, because this approach doesn't encourage any serious consideration of the consequences of our moral actions—that is, how they affect people involved in the situation at hand—Kant's principle-*obsessed* approach to the moral life seems to be much more reminiscent of the Pharisees (many of whom were actual opponents of Jesus) rather than Jesus himself. As we will see in part two, any decision-making approach that tends toward a hardhearted legalism that prioritizes principles over people in an eccentric, entirely nonnuanced manner is going to be at odds with Jesus' moral behaviors and teachings.

To summarize, just because Kant embraced the notion of moral absolutes and held that a belief in God (and some type of postmortem judgment) is necessary for a society to remain civil doesn't mean that his

---

[27]Geisler, *Christian Ethics*, p. 84.

moral universalism is an adequate foundation for a Christian ethic productive of the type of moral faithfulness this book is about. Thus our search for such a foundation continues.

Three Bible-Based (Absolutist) Approaches to Ethical Decision Making

As indicated above, none of the Christian forms of moral absolutism treated below denies the biblical doctrine of salvation by grace through faith (Eph 2:8-9). They can, however, be thought of as examples of ethical legalism because of a tendency common among them to treat the Bible as an ethical encyclopedia or moral rulebook with a law or command for just about everything. As we will soon see, while this understanding of Christian ethics certainly can't be faulted for not taking the Scriptures seriously, such an approach can lead to some knotty moral dilemmas.[28] Indeed, the main difference between the various versions of ethical legalism surveyed below lies in how each decision-making approach endeavors to answer the question: If in God's economy there exists more than one moral absolute, what does the Christian disciple do when the demands these various moral commands place on him or her seem to conflict?

The "Following the Letter of the Law" approach (nonconflicting absolutism). In a nutshell, nonconflicting absolutism (sometimes referred to as "unqualified absolutism") believes that there are many absolute moral laws and that none of them should ever be broken.[29] In a manner strikingly similar to the moral universalism of Kant, there's a biblically based version of moral absolutism that holds that, since telling the truth is an absolute moral obligation, we must always tell the truth, even if someone dies as a result.[30] Results are *never* to be used as a rationale to break moral rules, even if the results are desirable.

What we're talking about here is yet another hardcore, extreme, deontological emphasis on rules rather than results. But, as indicated above, this approach requires us to ask: What does the Christian moral agent

---

[28]See Grenz, *Moral Quest*, p. 244.
[29]See Robert V. Rakestraw, "Ethical Choices: A Case for Non-conflicting Absolutism," in Clark and Rakestraw, *Theology and Method*, pp. 118-19.
[30]Ibid., p. 119.

do when two or more of these many moral absolutes conflict?

One of the main tenets of a Christian nonconflicting absolutism is that God would not allow a genuine conflict between competing moral commands to occur. Instead there will always be a third alternative, a course of action that will not involve breaking a divinely prescribed moral rule.

Since it's true that many Christians have approached ethical decision making in this way, we need to do our best to understand the reasoning behind it.

The basic premises of nonconflicting absolutism. There are several major premises that make up the nonconflicting absolutism held by many Christians. Briefly stated, they are:

- God's unchanging character is the basis of moral absolutes.[31]

With the assumption in place that moral absolutes have to come from some absolute source—that is, an "absolute moral Prescriber"—this biblically based version of nonconflicting absolutism holds that God's holy character is that source.[32] Furthermore the emphasis in this premise on the "unchanging" character of God (see Mal 3:6) argues for the idea that just as God's holy character is immutable (unchanging), so are the absolutes that derive from it.

- God has expressed his unchanging moral character in his law.[33]

The idea here is that the moral laws presented in Scripture are an accurate reflection of God's moral character. Such certitude tends to result in the classifying of *many* of the moral imperatives clearly prescribed in the Bible as moral absolutes. Thus, contrary to all the ethical options surveyed so far, this moral model insists that the Christian moral agent has a plethora of moral laws to guide him or her in the task of ethical decision making.

But what of the summary of the law provided by Jesus in passages such as Matthew 22:34-40? Most Christian moral absolutists would probably agree with the following statement: "All moral absolutes are extensions of

---

[31]See Geisler, *Christian Ethics*, p. 86; Rakestraw, "Ethical Choices," pp. 123-24.

[32]Geisler, *Christian Ethics*, p. 87. For a book-length defense of the position that moral knowledge can be grounded in the character of the Christian God, see R. Scott Smith, *In Search of Moral Knowledge: Overcoming the Fact-Value Dichotomy* (Downers Grove, IL: IVP Academic, 2014).

[33]Geisler, *Christian Ethics*, p. 86; Rakestraw, "Ethical Choices," pp. 123-24; Rae, *Moral Choices*, pp. 24-25; McQuilkin and Copan, *Introduction to Biblical Ethics*, p. 64.

the one all-encompassing absolute: love for God with all one's being and love for the neighbor as oneself." At the same time, most would likely also concur with Robert Rakestraw's contention that "neighbor-love is best defined as that virtue of mind, emotions, and will which seeks another person's highest good, *according to scriptural standards.*"[34] In other words, most Christian moral absolutists would insist, contra Joseph Fletcher, that we need the other moral laws presented in God's word to help us know what loving someone with God's love does and doesn't look like.

- Since God cannot contradict himself, no two absolute moral laws can really conflict.[35]

The argument being made here is that, given who he is, it would be impossible for God to issue moral commands that could ever really conflict with each other in a given moral dilemma. This is an attempt to ground an important tenet of Christian nonconflicting absolutism in the nature of God.

Obviously, the premise that no two absolute moral laws can really conflict is crucial to a nonconflicting (unqualified) absolutism.[36] It in turn leads to a couple of additional presuppositions that also set this version of absolutism apart from the others introduced later in this chapter.

- God can be counted on to always provide his people with "a way out" from apparent moral dilemmas.[37]

Another important hallmark of this ethical option is that there's always a way out of a moral dilemma if we'll look for it—a "third alternative" we can pursue to avoid having to violate any of God's moral laws. Proponents of nonconflicting absolutism believe they're able to find biblical support for this important premise in one passage in particular:

No temptation has overtaken you except what is common to mankind. And God is faithful; he will not let you be tempted beyond what you can bear. But

---

[34]Rakestraw, "Ethical Choices," p. 119, emphasis added.
[35]Geisler, *Christian Ethics*, pp. 86-87; Rakestraw, "Ethical Choices," pp. 119, 123-24.
[36]Geisler, *Christian Ethics*, p. 79.
[37]Ibid., pp. 86, 88. While Rakestraw doesn't refer to them as "third alternatives" per se, he does emphasize the responsibility of the moral agent to do whatever he or she can, short of literally breaking a biblical command, to resolve a moral conflict (see Rakestraw, "Ethical Choices," pp. 119-20). For instance, in certain situations, says Rakestraw, this might mean "speaking half-truths or unrelated truths if this might help" (p. 120).

when you are tempted, he will also provide *a way out* so that you can endure it. (1 Cor 10:13)[38]

Christians who hold to a nonconflicting absolutism will also point to various Bible stories that seem to portray biblical characters avoiding moral dilemmas by finding clever "ways of escape" (for example, Abraham referring to Sarah as his sister in Genesis 12:10-17 and 20:1-17 in order to escape being killed because of her).[39]

- Furthermore, those Bible stories that are often construed as portraying God blessing those who violate his moral laws are actually being misinterpreted.[40]

An obvious problem for this moral model are those biblical stories that seem to show God blessing people who told lies in order to save lives. For example, Exodus 1:15-21 indicates that God blessed the Hebrew midwives who lied to Pharaoh in order to save the lives of some Jewish baby boys. He also seems to have rewarded the lie told by the harlot Rahab as part of her effort to save the lives of some Jewish spies (Josh 2:1-21; cf. Josh 6:17, 23-24). However, the proponents of the biblically based nonconflicting absolutism being treated here have gone to great pains to explain how God never really blessed anyone in the Bible for breaking one of his laws; it just appears that way. The argument put forward by some of these proponents is that actually God blessed people like Rahab and the Hebrew midwives *despite* their lying, not because of it; the rewards resulted from their *showing mercy*, not their prevarications.[41]

In sum, for all the reasons listed above, a biblically based nonconflicting absolutism insists that the moral agent should think twice before violating any of the moral commandments presented in God's Word.[42] After all, each and every moral commandment is a reflection of the heart of a holy God whose character remains constant and who doesn't con-

---

[38]Geisler, *Christian Ethics*, p. 86.

[39]Ibid., p. 90.

[40]Ibid., pp. 81-82, 85.

[41]Ibid., pp. 81-82.

[42]Most Christian moral absolutists make a distinction between the ceremonial and moral laws presented in the Bible, holding that ceremonial laws such as those having to do with circumcision (see Gen 9:7-14) and clean and unclean food (see Lev 11) were specific to Israelite culture and therefore provisional in nature (see Mk 7:14-19; Gal 5:6; cf. Rom 10:4; Col 2:16-17, 20-23; Heb 8:1-13; 9:1-28).

tradict himself.[43] Indeed, in a fairly striking paragraph, Robert Rakestraw summarizes the nonconflicting absolutist (NCA) position thusly:

> Divinely-given moral absolutes never truly conflict, although there may be occasions when they appear to conflict. NCA holds that there will never be a situation in which obedience to one absolute will entail disobedience to or the setting-aside of another absolute. If a friend's life will almost certainly be taken by a gun-waving maniac unless I lie concerning my friend's whereabouts, whatever else I do I must not lie. The command to speak truthfully (Eph. 4:15) is an absolute that must not be violated. Nothing else I may do or should do to protect my friend is any more clear than my obligation to be truthful. I *am* obligated to protect the friend, because of God's absolute to love my neighbor as myself, but I am to do it without lying. NCA holds that all relevant absolutes can and must be followed in situations of apparent conflict.[44]

Excursus: Some Support for Christian Moral Absolutism in General

Given the stark manner in which the examination of the premises of a biblically based nonconflicting absolutism just concluded, I want to insert into the discussion a not-so-brief excursus expressing some support for a Christian moral absolutism in general. We're searching in this survey for an approach to making ethical decisions that can produce a lifestyle of moral faithfulness. Presented below are four big reasons why I believe that some form of a Christian moral absolutism is what we're looking for.

First, because a Christian moral absolutism is committed to grounding morality in God's unchanging character, it acknowledges God's existence and authority in our lives.[45] As we've seen, most of the ethical options surveyed thus far do not take the existence or moral authority of God seriously. While Joseph Fletcher used

[43]One should note, however, the distinction made by Robert Rakestraw between unqualified absolutism and nonconflicting absolutism. He asserts that the latter "does recognize qualifications and exceptions [to some moral absolutes presented in Scripture], but these are always *within the absolute itself.* They are part of the absolute and are therefore *not exceptions to* the absolute (in which case they would be *external to* the absolute)" (Rakestraw, "Ethical Choices," pp. 119-20). In other words, this argument holds that some moral absolutes have some exceptions and qualifications built into them: e.g., children are to obey their parents, but only to the degree that "parental commands are consistent with the teachings of scripture" (p. 120; see Eph 6:1-4).
[44]Rakestraw, "Ethical Choices," p. 119.
[45]Geisler, *Christian Ethics*, p. 87.

Christian rhetoric in his book *Situation Ethics,* he later denounced the faith and insisted that neither theology nor religion is really crucial to morality.[46] Though Immanuel Kant considered it necessary to emphasize belief in God's existence, this didn't translate into an ethic that was genuinely theocentric. In contrast to the strictly secular or nominally religious moral models we've surveyed so far, a genuinely Christian moral absolutism can and will be a much more theologically astute ethical approach. For those of us concerned to pursue a moral faithfulness before God, such a theocentric starting point for ethics is simply a nonnegotiable.[47]

Second, pressing the issue of divine authority a bit further, a Christian moral absolutism of some type would seem to be the only category of ethical options that takes seriously Jesus' high view of the moral commands presented in Scripture. Later in this work we will have the opportunity to give Matthew 5:17-20 the careful consideration it deserves. For now I will simply offer that what makes this passage especially provocative is the way Jesus expresses his own fundamental conviction regarding the permanent validity of the law while at the same time indicting the Pharisees and teachers of the law as possessing a subpar righteousness before God. Again, I'll have more to say about Jesus' interaction with the Pharisees over moral matters in part two of this work. At present it's enough to observe that any ethical option that doesn't take seriously Jesus' assessment of the abiding authority of the moral commands presented in the Bible can't be considered fully Christian.[48]

Third, it needs to be pointed out how necessary some type of moral absolutism would seem to be for those moral agents wise enough to possess misgivings about their ability to accurately predict future consequences or make moral choices that aren't in some way ultimately self-serving.[49] Steve Wilkens reminds his readers that the value of a moral absolutism is not only that it "takes us back to the intuition that some things are right no matter what" but that it also "helps anchor morality so that we are not swayed by changing moods and emotions or sidetracked by unpredictable consequences."[50] He seems to be asserting that the anchoring dynamic at work in Christian moral absolutism not only seems right intuitively but is crucial to maintaining one's moral course through life. To the degree this is true it's a powerful, practical argument for the adoption of a Christian moral absolutism.

---

[46]See James Childress, "Introduction," in Joseph Fletcher, *Situation Ethics: The New Morality* (Louisville: Westminster John Knox, 1966).

[47]See Hollinger, *Choosing the Good,* p. 140.

[48]For a helpful discussion of Jesus as fulfiller of the Old Testament, see McQuilkin and Copan, *Introduction to Biblical Ethics,* pp. 76-81.

[49]For more on this see Grenz, *Moral Quest,* p. 36.

[50]Wilkens, *Beyond Bumper Sticker Ethics,* p. 108. See also Nullens and Michener, *Matrix of Christian Ethics,* p. 52.

Finally, I will press on to suggest that the anchoring dynamic a Christian moral absolutism provides is crucial not only to maintaining one's moral stability but one's moral buoyancy as well. In other words, there is something about a Christian moral absolutism that is simply indispensable to keeping the pursuit of a moral faithfulness before God afloat.

The fact is that contemporary Christians in the West must make their moral choices within an incredibly relativistic milieu. Such an environment can "sink" a moral faithfulness in a couple of ways. On the one hand it can engender an attitude of moral carelessness; on the other hand it can produce a state of ethical paralysis.[51] Both of these dynamics are nonstarters with respect to the cultivation of a moral faithfulness before God. It seems to me that the key to avoiding both of these moral dangers is the embrace of a moral model capable of inspiring a moral faithfulness on the one hand and informing it on the other. The only ethical option I know of that's up to the task of both inspiring and informing a moral faithfulness before the God of the Bible, and doing so in a manner that's both theologically astute and biblically based, is some version of a Christian moral absolutism.

An evaluation of nonconflicting absolutism. Turning our attention back again to the one version of Christian moral absolutism we've examined so far, let's begin this assessment by acknowledging a couple of the positive distinctives it brings to the table.

First, this is an ethical option that's unique in the manner in which it shows trust in God's providence.[52] Given what the Bible as a whole has to say about the goodness of God (see Ps 145:1-21), his sovereignty (see Ps 33:10-11; Prov 16:9; 19:21; 20:24) and his ability to cause all things to work together for the good of those who belong to him (Rom 8:28), it would seem appropriate for a Christian ethic to have some room in it for the dynamic of God's providence. While the idea that "God's gonna do what God's gonna do" can be abused (more about this below), at the very

---

[51]I'll have more to say about this first dynamic in the next chapter. For more on this second dynamic, see J. Richard Middleton and Brian J. Walsh, *Truth Is Stranger Than It Used to Be: Biblical Faith in a Postmodern Age* (Downers Grove, IL: InterVarsity Press, 1995), p. 51; Gary Tyra, *A Missional Orthodoxy: Theology and Ministry in a Post-Christian Context* (Downers Grove, IL: IVP Academic, 2013), pp. 244-45.

[52]Geisler, *Christian Ethics*, pp. 87-88.

least a healthy respect for God's involvement in the affairs of everyday life means that after doing our best to discern and do his will, we can trust God to work through our moral choices—especially those that are humbly and responsibly made—in order to bring glory to himself and good to the world. While it's certainly possible to be much too cavalier about the consequences of our ethical actions, it's also possible to wrongly assume that God's ultimate purposes in the world hinge solely on them. Here, as everywhere else in the Christian life, a certain balance is necessary lest we lurch into an eccentric way of being and doing. A biblically based version of nonconflicting absolutism brings attention to the fact that it's not *always* inappropriate to respond to an amazingly complicated moral dilemma by humbly heeding the Spirit's call to obey a particular biblical command and then trusting God with the result.

Second, this moral model is unique in the way it emphasizes the possibility of "third alternatives" and encourages moral agents to be careful to look for them rather than rushing to judgment.[53] The fact is that *sometimes* an apparent moral dilemma can be resolved by a third alternative that doesn't involve the breaking of one of God's commands. Obviously, if such a third alternative is available to us, we should feel a moral obligation to employ it.

The problem is that for a variety of reasons these third alternatives aren't always readily apparent to us. My experience tells me that we have to look for them, cry out to God for the wisdom to discern them, recruit others to help us see them and so on. All of this is hard work and usually time consuming as well. We need to be very careful here because, though some moral dilemmas can be time sensitive, one way to be irresponsible in one's ethical decision making is to rush the process simply because we don't enjoy having something so serious hanging over our heads, or because we simply want to get on with our lives. Proverbs 21:5 reads: "The plans of the diligent lead to profit as surely as haste leads to poverty." Viewed within its immediate context (Prov 21:1-8)—a passage rife with a sensitivity to moral matters—this verse could provide some support for the idea that we rarely end up making moral choices that honor the heart of God when the process is rushed simply because of our anxiety in the

---

[53]Ibid., p. 88.

face of ambiguity or due to an impatient desire to move on. It's for this reason that the focus in Christian nonconflicting absolutism on the possibility of third alternatives should be considered a positive distinctive.

However, there are some negative aspects of Christian nonconflicting absolutism. Even though some aspects of this ethical option enjoy a measure of biblical support, it has its detractors, some of whom belong to the evangelical Christian community. Presented below are a few criticisms that have been leveled at this ethical approach.

First, the truth is that, unfortunately, third alternatives are *not* always available.[54] Though we might like to believe that we will never find ourselves facing a moral dilemma that can only be resolved by our breaking a moral command presented in Scripture, most Christian ethicists insist that in real life this is simply not the case. For example, in his book *Christian Ethics: Options and Issues*, Norman Geisler writes:

> It is both unrealistic and unbiblical to assume that moral obligations never conflict. Real life reveals this kind of conflict daily in hospitals, courtrooms, and battlefields. Sometimes one must kill or be killed. Other times the baby must die, or both the mother and baby will die (as in tubal pregnancies). Likewise, the Bible tells of no third alternative for Abraham in killing Isaac (Gen. 22), or for the Hebrew midwives (Exod. 1), or the three Hebrew children (Dan. 3). It is naive to assume that these kinds of situations never happen. And, if the Christian ethic is adequate for all situations, it must have an answer for these real moral conflicts.[55]

But what of 1 Corinthians 10:13 and its supposed support for the premise that there will always be "a way out" of any moral dilemma we face? Once again, Geisler weighs in, pointing out that this passage "is only a promise for victory in temptation—not a guarantee of intervention to avoid moral conflicts."[56] This interpretation seems correct to me, especially in light of the totality of Scripture, with its several accounts of godly people facing some difficult moral dilemmas without any sort of divine deliverance occurring: for example, Abraham (Gen 22), the Hebrew midwives (Ex 1), Rahab (Josh 2), the three Hebrew children (Dan 3) and the apostles

---

[54]Ibid., p. 94.
[55]Ibid.
[56]Ibid., p. 90.

(Acts 4).[57] Thus it seems that this version of a nonconflicting absolutism can be faulted for overstating the availability of third alternatives.

Second, another criticism leveled at this ethical option is that it can cause people to commit sins of omission.[58] In principle a sin of omission occurs when we fail to do something that we should have done. The apostle James seems to provide some biblical support for such a concept when he warns: "If anyone, then, knows the good they ought to do and doesn't do it, it is sin for them" (Jas 4:17).

The idea behind this criticism of Christian nonconflicting absolutism is that we don't have to be the one actually doing evil to be responsible before God for it. Take, for example, the dilemma that centers in whether the Christian moral agent should lie in order to save the life of an innocent person or tell the truth and "punt to providence." According to this critique, when something bad happens to someone because we didn't do what we could have done to stop the evil from occurring, we're guilty before God for having committed a sin of omission. It's not enough for us to say to ourselves, "Well, I didn't actually do anything evil to anyone." The following verse from the book of Proverbs can be understood as saying that if we are aware of the evil action that's taking place in front of us and do nothing about it even though we could have, we're at least partially responsible before God for it:

> Rescue those being led away to death;
>> hold back those staggering toward slaughter.
> If you say, "But we knew nothing about this,"
>> does not he who weighs the heart perceive it?
> Does not he who guards your life know it?
>> Will he not repay everyone according to what they have done? (Prov 24:11-12)

Moreover, in *The Republic,* Plato has Socrates ask a conversation partner:

> But are we really to say that doing right, consists simply and solely in truthfulness and returning anything we have borrowed? Are not those actions that can be sometimes right and sometimes wrong? For instance, if one borrowed a weapon from a friend who subsequently went out of his mind and then asked

---

[57]Ibid.
[58]Ibid., p. 95.

108

PURSUING MORAL FAITHFULNESS

for it back, surely it would be generally agreed that one ought not to return it, and that it would not be right to do so, nor to tell the strict truth to a madman?[59]

The common-sense wisdom reflected in this set of Socratic queries suggests that sometimes sins of omission might be committed by Christians who insist on scrupulously obeying every moral imperative found in the Bible (e.g., Eph 4:15) without regard for the effects such an unnuanced obedience might have on others.

Third, while there needs to be room in a Christian ethic for trust in God's ability to cause all things to work together for good (Rom 8:28), the practice of consistently "punting to providence" strikes most thoughtful people as an irresponsible moral move.[60]

It should be noted how the proponents of nonconflicting absolutism have argued against the idea that obeying a biblical command could possibly result in a sin of omission. For example, Robert Rakestraw insists that, while a Christian moral agent should of course do everything short of breaking a command (like the command not to lie) in order to save a human life, if telling the truth causes the loss of human life, the truth-teller has "done no wrong."[61] In support of this line of reasoning, Rakestraw cites a section of Erwin Lutzer's *The Morality Gap: An Evangelical Response to Situation Ethics.* This provocative passage reads:

> The Christian believes that his responsibility is obedience and that the consequences of moral action are then in the hands of God. If refusing to commit adultery or even telling the truth (if there are no scriptural alternatives) causes others to die, this also is within the providence of God. Surely the God of the Scriptures is not one whose plans for certain individuals are frustrated because someone told the truth.[62]

In response to these attempts to refute the idea that telling the truth could ever amount to a sin of omission, I would offer that it's one thing to put one's trust in the goodness and sovereignty of God after having made a difficult ethical decision in a *responsible* manner (sensitive to

---

[59]Plato, *The Republic*, trans. Desmond Lee (New York: Penguin Classics, 2007), p. 7.
[60]See Geisler, *Christian Ethics*, p. 93.
[61]See Rakestraw, "Ethical Choices," p. 120.
[62]E. W. Lutzer, *The Morality Gap: An Evangelical Response to Situation Ethics* (Chicago: Moody Press, 1972), p. 110, as cited in Rakestraw, "Ethical Choices," p. 120.

both the biblical text and moral context); it's another to routinely make moral choices in a *blithe* manner, content to make God responsible for the outcome, concerned only with maintaining what is presumed to be a righteous posture before the law. Another way to put this is to say that there's a crucial difference between *trusting* in God's providence in the face of a moral dilemma and naively *presuming* on the providence of God as a way of routinely avoiding moral conflict altogether.[63] This is not to say that when it comes to saving a life, anything goes. But the fact that the Bible contains accounts of people being blessed by God even though their life-saving endeavors involved telling some rather bold lies would seem to suggest that a routine habit of slapping moral principles into play and then "punting to providence" lacks the scriptural support the proponents of nonconflicting absolutism have claimed for it.

Fourth, keeping the criticisms presented above in mind, it becomes apparent that the embrace of a nonconflicting absolutism possesses the potential for turning biblical believers into Christian Pharisees.[64] I'm not alone in contending that the New Testament portrays Jesus as criticizing the Pharisees of his day for neglecting the spirit of the law while focusing on the letter of it.[65] According to Jesus this irresponsible approach to making ethical decisions ends up not only hurting people but failing to honor the heart of God as well (e.g., Mt 5:21-48; Mk 2:23-28; Jn 7:21-24). It's possible for contemporary Christians to do the same thing when they, not heeding the warning of Karl Barth against such a practice, adopt an approach to making ethical decisions that effectively exchanges the divine will for a fixed and unbending set of prescriptions.[66]

I will defer until later a more thorough examination of Jesus' ethical approach versus that of the Pharisees of his day. However, I will state here the opinion that a moral legalism, and the judgmentalism, separatism and hypocrisy that often result from it, are all too prevalent among many conservative Christians (and perhaps the biggest reason why so many members of the emerging generations are leaving evangelical churches).[67]

---

[63]For more on this, see Geisler, *Christian Ethics*, pp. 93-94.
[64]Geisler, *Christian Ethics*, p. 95. See also Hollinger, *Choosing the Good*, p. 140.
[65]See Geisler, *Christian Ethics*, pp. 95, 288; Hollinger, *Choosing the Good*, p. 140.
[66]See Barth, *Church Dogmatics*, 2/2:509-51, 3/4:3-46, as cited in Grenz, *Moral Quest*, p. 170.
[67]For more on this, see Tyra, *Missional Orthodoxy*, pp. 38-40, especially p. 39 n. 38.

Thus it's important for us to be aware of the fact that many Christian ethicists, while remaining committed to the validity and value of a moral absolutism, are convinced that the biblically based version of nonconflicting absolutism presented here is not an adequate foundation for a fully Christian ethic.

The "Doing the Lesser Evil" approach (conflicting absolutism). The central assumption behind conflicting absolutism (also known as ideal absolutism) is that, contra the version of absolutism just treated, we live in an evil world where absolute, morally binding laws sometimes do come into conflict.[68] When this happens, we're responsible to obey both laws because no God-given moral law can be broken without guilt. In such cases, therefore, we must discern and do the lesser evil, confess our sin and then seek God's forgiveness.[69]

The basic premises of conflicting absolutism. There are four basic presuppositions at work in this ethical option.

- Like nonconflicting absolutism, conflicting absolutism holds that God's moral laws, as reflections of his holy, unchanging character, are holy, unchanging and to be obeyed absolutely.

Taking very seriously such passages as Psalm 119:4 and Matthew 5:48, the proponents of this view insist that, according to the Bible, God has not made his law to be broken. Instead he expects it to be kept perfectly. While this is a high standard, what else should we expect of a truly holy God? What this means is that *anytime* we break one of God's moral laws, we have committed a sin, period![70]

- Unlike nonconflicting absolutism, it's the contention of this ethical option that, because in the real world moral conflicts do indeed occur, sin is inevitable.

This moral model takes its name from its insistence that moral conflicts happen. According to a principal proponent of this ethical option, the German theologian Helmut Thielicke (1908–1986), it's because we live in

---

[68]See Clark and Rakestraw, *Theology and Method*, p. 115.

[69]Geisler, *Christian Ethics*, pp. 97-98.

[70]Ibid., p. 101. See also Helmut Thielicke, "The Borderline Situation of Extreme Conflict," in Clark and Rakestraw, *Theology and Method*, p. 129.

a fallen, sin-filled world that moral conflicts occur—that we can sometimes find ourselves under obligation to obey more than one divinely
conveyed moral imperative at the same time.[71] For example, Leviticus
19:11 prohibits lying or even deceiving one another, while Leviticus 19:16
warns against doing anything that endangers a neighbor's life. History has
shown that in real life these two God-given commands can compete with
each other for our obedience.[72]

Furthermore, those who hold to conflicting absolutism are not convinced that the Bible teaches that there will always be a third alternative
or "way out" so that the Christian moral agent will be able to resolve the
moral dilemma without breaking one of these conflicting commands. The
stark distinctive at the heart of conflicting absolutism can be stated thusly:
In this fallen world where moral dilemmas actually occur, sometimes, no
matter what we do, we cannot avoid breaking one of God's laws. Therefore,
in certain real life situations, "sin is inevitable"; we simply have to sin.[73]

- When faced with an actual moral dilemma, it's the duty of the Christian
  moral agent to discern and do the lesser evil.[74]

I've found this particular premise to be somewhat provocative for
many of my conservative evangelical students due to the fact that it's
based on the suggestion that in God's economy perhaps not all sins are
of equal weight.[75] This is not to say that some sins aren't serious, just that
there is such a thing as a greater and lesser evil. Citing the work of
Thielicke, Norman Geisler endeavors to explain this particularly provocative premise thusly:

> When decisions are made in conflict situations, we must choose the lesser evil,
> for "there are heavier and lighter sins." They are both sins, but "they do not
> have the same weight." Thielicke makes it clear that there is no justification of

---

[71]Geisler, *Christian Ethics*, p. 99. Quotations are from Helmut Thielicke, *Theological Ethics*, ed. William
H. Lazareth (Philadelphia: Fortress, 1966), 1:596. See also, Thielicke, "Borderline Situation," pp. 128-29.
[72]Indeed, in his discussion of "borderline situations," it appears that Helmut Thielicke has forged a version of conflicting absolutism around the central issue of how one is to respond to a powerful, unjust
enemy, such as the Nazis during World War II. See Thielicke, "Borderline Situation," pp. 125-30.
[73]Geisler, *Christian Ethics*, pp. 100-101, emphasis added.
[74]Norman Geisler suggests that another name for conflicting absolutism might be the "lesser-evil
view." See ibid., p. 98.
[75]For more on the notion of a hierarchy of sin, see McQuilkin and Copan, *Introduction to Biblical
Ethics*, pp. 110-12.

doing the lesser evil. . . . We must simply recognize that in conflict situations
both commands are our moral duty and that sin is inevitable. Nonetheless,
since there are lesser and greater sins, the Christian should do the lesser sin,
knowing forgiveness is available.[76]

In an attempt to provide some biblical support for the controversial
notion that not all sins are the same in God's eyes, the proponents of this
ethical option refer to the following passages:

> "Do you refuse to speak to me?" Pilate said. "Don't you realize I have power
> either to free you or to crucify you?"
>
> Jesus answered, "You would have no power over me if it were not given to
> you from above. Therefore the one who handed me over to you is guilty of a
> greater sin." (Jn 19:10-11)
>
> Anyone who speaks a word against the Son of Man will be forgiven, but
> anyone who speaks against the Holy Spirit will not be forgiven, either in this
> age or in the age to come. (Mt 12:32)

In the first passage presented above we find Jesus referring to a "greater"
sin. The second passage indicates that one sin—speaking against the Holy
Spirit—is "so bad that it is unpardonable."[77] Though we will return to this
topic when treating the third version of moral absolutism included in this
survey, it's enough for now to indicate that it's on the basis of biblical passages such as these that conflicting absolutism holds that it's both possible
and necessary, when one's moral duties conflict, to do the lesser evil, always
making an effort to "maximize the good, even when it is minimal."[78]

This leads us to a fourth and final premise of conflicting absolutism.

- Once the Christian moral agent has been careful to discern and do the
  lesser evil in the face of a moral dilemma, he or she should be careful
  to seek God's forgiveness.

Conflicting absolutism is adamant in its insistence that, even though sin
is sometimes unavoidable, God's forgiveness is always available because of
the atoning work of Jesus Christ.[79] Accepting the paradoxical notion that we

---

[76]Geisler, *Christian Ethics*, pp. 99-100.
[77]Ibid., p. 101.
[78]Ibid., p. 102.
[79]Ibid.

live in a fallen world where the reality of moral conflicts means that sometimes the responsible moral agent must sin in order to do the right thing,
conflicting absolutists are also quick to assert that the grace of God is nevertheless greater than this bitter irony. Moreover, I have to presume that at least
some of the proponents of this ethical option would also emphasize the
ability of God to cause even our imperfect moral choices to ultimately work
for good (Rom 8:28). So it's with a spirit of sobriety that this ethical option
holds that "all one need do in lesser-evil situations is to do the lesser evil,
confess that he [or she] has broken God's law, and receive forgiveness
through Jesus Christ. Sin is unavoidable, but salvation is still available."[80]

An evaluation of conflicting absolutism. In the Clint Eastwood movie
Heartbreak Ridge there's a scene that shows a GI coming upon the body of
an enemy soldier he's just shot and killed. Because this is the GI's first
firefight, the camera is interested in his reaction as he reflects on what he's
done. Staring at the lifeless body, the GI reaches under his shirt for a religious medal hanging around his neck. After kissing the medal, the soldier
whispers the prayer, "God forgive me." He then returns the medal under
his shirt and moves on, keeping pace with the rest of the men in his squad.

I refer to this movie scene not only to provide an illustration of how
an embrace of this ethical option might play out in real life, but also to
suggest that for all its irony it does seem to be a real-life ethic that's
probably employed more often than we might imagine, especially by
religious folk. Thus we need to engage in a careful evaluation of it.

First of all it needs to be kept in mind that this ethical option possesses at
least a couple of the winsome attributes of a Christian moral absolutism in
general: that is, it grounds morality in the holy character of God and takes
seriously Jesus' high view of the moral commands presented in Scripture.

Second, conflicting absolutism and nonconflicting absolutism have in
common the fact that they're both decision-making approaches that
show a measure of trust in God's providence. That said, I will offer that
between these two approaches, it's conflicting absolutism that does the
best job of getting the dynamic of God's providence right. Even though
it relies heavily on God's ability to cause good to come out of an admit-

---

[80]Ibid.

tedly imperfect moral choice, I believe it's fair to say that its call to discern and do the lesser evil is something other than an irresponsible attempt to avoid a moral conflict by slapping a moral command into play and then "punting to providence." There would seem to be a bit more agonizing involved in this approach's deliberation process.

Third, I will go on to offer the opinion that, while conflicting absolutism's emphasis on seeking the forgiveness of God might be viewed by some as a moral cop-out, I believe it can serve an important purpose as it relates to a person's spiritual formation. I'm convinced that a biblical truth that needs to be recovered in this era of increasing moral relativity is the seriousness of sin. Too many people, even churchgoing Christians, possess a cavalier attitude toward this important issue.[81] While it's true that conflicting absolutism seems to authorize the breaking of moral commands under certain situations (something that an adherent of nonconflicting absolutism could never countenance), it does not do this in a flippant manner. Instead, it grieves over what it considers to be a terrible necessity given the fallen condition of the world we inhabit. More than that, it insists that any time a moral command of God is either ignored or transgressed this action must be named a sin and sincerely repented of. To the degree the Bible emphasizes postconversion repentance and confession of sin as part of the life of Christian discipleship (see 2 Cor 7:8-13; 12:21; Jas 5:16; 1 Jn 1:8-10; 2:1-2; Rev 3:1-3) lest the heart of the Christ follower become hardened due to the deceitfulness of sin (see Heb 3:12-13), the emphasis in conflicting absolutism on these very practices should be considered a plus. Working against the assumption that consistently doing the lesser evil must result in a cavalier attitude toward sin is this ethical option's insistence on the need to seek God's forgiveness every time this terrible necessity occurs. Thus I'm suggesting that, done rightly, this spiritual practice might actually sharpen a disciple's moral sensitivity rather than blunt it.

Despite its attractive features, not all Christian ethicists are inclined to endorse conflicting absolutism as the foundation for a Christ-centered, biblically informed and Spirit-empowered ethic. First, some ethicists have pointed out that the concept of *a moral duty to sin* is absurd (that is,

---

[81]For more on the seriousness of sin, see Tyra, *Missional Orthodoxy*, pp. 270-76; McQuilkin and Copan, *Introduction to Biblical Ethics*, pp. 118-19.

such a notion seems to be logically self-contradicting).[82] Christian philosopher Norman Geisler complains: "According to conflicting absolutism, in real moral conflicts we have a moral duty to do the lesser of the two evils. That is, one is morally obligated to do evil. But how can there ever be a moral obligation to do what is immoral? It seems a morally absurd claim."[83]

A second criticism of this ethical option takes on the idea that a moral agent is morally culpable before God as a sinner when in truth the ethical action earning him or her such a status was ultimately unavoidable. According to conflicting absolutism, the fact that in this fallen world sin is inevitable means that we can do our moral duty before God and yet be considered sinners for having done so. The proponents of conflicting absolutism seem to be suggesting that God is in the habit of holding individual moral agents personally responsible for behaving in ways that were personally unavoidable.[84] But is this true? For example, isn't the law of Moses careful to differentiate between murder and the taking of a human life in self-defense? In Exodus 22:2 we read, "If a thief is caught breaking in at night and is struck a fatal blow, the defender is not guilty of bloodshed." Isn't it possible on the basis of biblical passages such as this to come to the conclusion that God does not hold people accountable for tragic, lamentable behaviors that were for them unavoidable?

I admit this is an arcane question and perhaps a bit academic as well. Still, I'll summarize the concern thusly: according to conflicting absolutism, we're morally obligated to do the lesser evil precisely because it's unavoidable. If, at the same time, God holds us guilty for doing the lesser evil, then this would mean that God has commanded us to engage in a sinful act. According to some Christian ethicists, such a position doesn't make sense from either a philosophical or theological perspective.[85]

A third critique of conflicting absolutism that is particularly christological in nature asks the important question: Doesn't a sufficiently high Christology argue against one of the main premises at work in this moral model? It's normally assumed that a Christian ethic will be one that strives

---

[82]Geisler, *Christian Ethics*, pp. 103-4.

[83]Ibid., p. 103.

[84]Ibid., p. 104.

[85]Ibid., pp. 104-6. See also William K. Frankena, *Ethics*, 2nd ed. (Englewood Cliffs, NJ: Prentice-Hall, 1973), pp. 72-73.

to emulate the decision-making method Jesus himself employed. However, because conflicting absolutism insists that it's impossible to negotiate a genuine moral dilemma without sinning, some ethicists have made the observation that this would appear to rule out the idea that Jesus himself made use of this moral model (or that it applies to him).[86]

According to conflicting absolutism, sin is unavoidable in a real moral dilemma where the moral agent must, in order to resolve the conflict, discern and do what he or she decides is the lesser evil. However, Hebrews 4:15 tells us that Jesus is a faithful and sympathetic high priest who was tempted in every way, just as we are, yet was without sin. Therefore for conflicting absolutism to be true, either Jesus must have never faced a genuine moral dilemma (in which case he really can't sympathize with us as our high priest) or he must have sinned (which the Bible says didn't happen, not only here but also in 2 Cor 5:21).

Both of the scenarios just posited constitute huge problems for a well-balanced, biblically informed Christology and would seem to invalidate Jesus as a moral example all Christians can and should follow. They also belie the notion that conflicting absolutism can function as an adequate foundation for a Christ-centered and biblically informed approach to making ethical decisions.

A fourth criticism of conflicting absolutism expresses the concern that, at the end of the day, the decision-making method utilized by this ethical option amounts to yet another Christian version of utilitarianism. If this is so, conflicting absolutism, like situationism, is vulnerable to some of the same criticisms raised against that relativistic moral model.

According to the proponents of conflicting absolutism, doing the *lesser evil* in the face of a moral dilemma involves the moral choice that *maximizes the good and minimizes the evil*.[87] Moreover, it's assumed that the choice that brings about this desired set of consequences will be the one that is grounded in *agapē* (love).[88] But doesn't this focus on maximizing the good and minimizing the evil sound very similar to the principle of utility? And isn't the notion that it's by *acting in agapē* that the lesser evil is achieved quite remi-

---

[86]For example, see Geisler, *Christian Ethics*, pp. 109-10.
[87]See ibid., pp. 102, 104.
[88]See Thielicke, "Borderline Situation," pp. 129-30.

niscent of situationism? Thus it appears that conflicting absolutism ends up employing the same type of ethical decision making as is found in these other moral models except that, once the course of action that constitutes the lesser evil is engaged in, the moral agent is to confess this transgression of one of God's commands as a sin, seeking his forgiveness in the aftermath. But if it's true that ultimately conflicting absolutism ends up making ethical decisions the same way utilitarianism and situationism do, then the same critiques leveled at those two moral models apply to it as well.

Now, as I've indicated already, I believe there are elements of truth inherent in this ethical option and that the desire to discourage a cavalier attitude toward the breaking of any moral command we find in Scripture is to be applauded. But, while I appreciate conflicting absolutism's embrace of ambiguity and paradox as an attempt to function as a real-life ethic, I'm not convinced that a decision-making approach that centers in discerning and doing the lesser evil is sufficient to produce the kind of moral faithfulness God is looking for. Thus it's my suggestion that our search for a foundation for a Christ-centered ethic must continue.

The "Yielding to the Higher Law" approach (graded absolutism). In a nutshell, the final ethical option treated in this survey holds, along with conflicting absolutism, that there are many moral absolutes, and they do sometimes conflict. However, unlike conflicting absolutism, graded absolutism (also known as *hierarchialism*) contends that in God's economy some laws are *higher* (in terms of their moral significance) than others.[89] So, when there is an unavoidable conflict, it's our duty to yield to the higher moral law.

That's a quick overview of this ethical position. Let's take a closer look.

The basic premises of graded absolutism. Along with both Christian non-conflicting absolutism and conflicting absolutism, this moral model holds that there are many absolutes that are grounded in God's holy, unchanging character. In common with conflicting absolutism in particular is the willingness to acknowledge that in real life moral conflicts do occur. Also in common with conflicting absolutism is the notion that not all moral rules carry the same weight; there are higher and lower moral laws. But fairly distinctive to graded absolutism are the following presuppositions:

---

[89]See Grenz, *Moral Quest*, p. 33.

- The moral rules presented in the Bible can be placed in a hierarchy.

In support of the important premise that not all moral laws and/or sins are of equal weight, a principal proponent of graded absolutism, Norman Geisler, has pointed out how that: (1) Jesus made reference to some "weightier" (more important) matters of the law (Mt 23:23 KJV); (2) Jesus also referred to the "least" of God's commands (Mt 5:19); (3) Jesus spoke of one of the two commandments that summarize the entire law as the "first and greatest" (Mt 22:34-40); and (4) Jesus told Pilate that those who had delivered him into Roman hands were guilty of a "greater" sin (Jn 19:11).[90]

Geisler goes on to argue that the "common myth" that all sins are equal is based primarily on a single biblical passage: "For whoever keeps the whole law and yet stumbles at just one point is guilty of breaking all of it" (Jas 2:10).

Some have interpreted this passage in such a way as to suggest that all sins bring equal guilt and therefore equal judgment before God. But on closer examination, it would appear that what this passage is actually saying is that one doesn't have to break all of God's laws in order to be considered a lawbreaker; only one will do!

It's important to keep in mind that graded absolutists are *not* suggesting that some sins are not serious in God's eyes, only that they don't all carry the same moral weight.[91] Thus, continuing his argument against the common myth referred to above, Geisler writes:

> Others have supposed wrongly that simply because Jesus said that one can lust and even murder "in his heart" (Matt. 5:28) that this means it is equally evil to imagine a sin as it is to do it. In the same sermon, Jesus rejected this view, indicating there are at least three levels of sins with corresponding judgments (5:22). Indeed, the whole concept of degrees of punishments in hell (Matt. 5:22; Rom. 2:6; Rev. 20:12) and graded levels of reward in heaven (1 Cor. 3:11-12) indicates that sins come in degrees. The fact that some sins call for excommunication (1 Cor. 5) and others for death (1 Cor. 11:30) also supports the general biblical pattern that all sins are not equal in weight. In fact, there is one sin so great as to be unforgiveable (Mark 3:29). . . . The popular belief is wrong; all sins are not created equal, for there are clearly higher and lower moral laws.[92]

---

[90]Geisler, *Christian Ethics*, p. 116.
[91]See ibid.
[92]Ibid., pp. 116-17.

- The Bible seems to suggest that in God's economy there are likewise "levels of duty" that can and should be prioritized in order to get morality right.

This too is a premise of great importance to graded absolutism. The argument here is that the Bible is replete with exhortations to (or accounts of people being careful to) prioritize *loyalty to God over others in general*, and/or *obedience to God's commands over those issued by some governing authority.*

For example, with respect to the call to prioritize loyalty to God over others, we find in the Scriptures: (1) divine approval for Abraham's apparent willingness to sacrifice Isaac when bidden by God to do so (Gen 22:1-18; Heb 11:17-19); (2) Jesus' declaration that of the two commandments that summarize God's law, the commandment to love God with all one's being is the "first and greatest" (Mt 22:37-38); and (3) Jesus' teaching that loyalty to him must take precedence over one's devotion to everyone and everything else in this life (Lk 14:25-33).

Furthermore, notwithstanding the clear biblical call for believers to "submit to" and "obey" those in authority (Rom 13:1-2; Tit 3:1; 1 Pet 2:13-15), we find in the Scriptures accounts of civil disobedience toward governing authorities meeting with divine approval—for example, the Hebrew midwives lying to Pharaoh (Ex 1); Rahab's lying to the king of Jericho (Josh 6:1-7); Shadrach, Meshach and Abednego bravely choosing to obey God rather than King Nebuchadnezzar (Dan 3); Daniel's boldly choosing to do likewise with respect to King Darius (Dan 6); and the apostles courageously disobeying the clear command of the Sanhedrin (Acts 4:1-31; 5:17-41).[93]

Once again, the proponents of graded absolutism believe they find in biblical passages such as these all the support they need for the premise that the moral commands presented in the Bible form a hierarchy and that the graded nature of God's commands must be taken seriously if we Christians are to get morality right. Says Geisler:

> God does not hold a person guilty for not keeping a lower moral law so long as he keeps the higher. God exempts one from his duty to keep the lower law since he could not keep it without breaking a higher law. This exemption functions something like an ethical "right of way" law. In many states the law declares that

---

[93]Ibid., pp. 121-22.

when two cars simultaneously reach an intersection without signals or signs, the car on the right has the right of way. Common sense dictates that they both cannot go through the intersection at the same time; one car must yield. Similarly, when a person enters an ethical intersection where two laws come into unavoidable conflict, it is evident that one law must yield to the other.[94]

Of course, it's one thing to prioritize God's commands over human commands. But according to the quote presented above graded absolutism goes on to suggest that the many moral imperatives we find in Scripture can be graded in terms of their moral weight relative to one another. This begs the crucial question: How are we to know which of God's laws are higher and lower? The answer to this important query forms another premise:

- The narratives we find in the Bible, along with pertinent expositional passages, are sufficient to help us discern which of God's laws should take precedence over others.

Geisler is adamant in his insistence that graded absolutism is a biblically grounded approach to making ethical decisions.[95] This conviction is clearly evident when he writes: "It is the Christian's obligation in every morally conflicting situation to *search Scripture for an answer*. If one does not know what to do in certain situations, he should heed Jesus' words, 'You are mistaken, because you know neither the Scriptures nor the power of God' (Matt. 22:29 NEB)."[96]

To his credit Geisler makes an effort to demonstrate what such biblical research might result in. In his book *The Christian Ethic of Love*, Geisler identifies some of the most basic moral principles he finds in the Bible. For example: our love for God is to take precedence over our love for humanity (Gen 22; Acts 5:29; Mt 10:37; Lk 9:59-60; 14:26); we should value life saving over truth telling (Josh 2:1-13; Ex 1:15-21); our love for people should take precedence over our affection for things (Mt 6:24; Mk 2:4); our priority should be to show love to as many people as possible in

---

[94]Ibid., p. 120.
[95]It should be noted that there are secular versions of hierarchialism that do not share in this concern to ground ethics in the Bible. An example would be the moral intuitionism of the Scottish ethicist W. D. Ross (1877-1971). See W. D. Ross, *The Right and the Good* (New York: Oxford University Press, 2002).
[96]Geisler, *Christian Ethics*, p. 122, emphasis added.

any given situation (Judg 16:29-30; Rom 9:3); an actual life is to be given priority over a potential life (Ex 21:22-23); a potential person is to be considered of more worth than any number of actual things (Ps 139:14-16); and, while "both complete and incomplete persons are persons and should be loved . . . when the choice is called for, the complete must be considered of more value than the incomplete (Lev 21:18-20)."[97]

Though a careful scrutiny of some of the biblical passages cited above is liable to raise some exegetical eyebrows, Geisler is convinced that this list of moral principles amply illustrates why it's appropriate to grade the moral imperatives we find in Scripture according to their relative moral weight.

This leads us to a final, summative premise of this position.

- When we find ourselves in a moral dilemma, the Christian's duty isn't to do the "lesser evil" but to do the "greater good" by identifying and obeying the weightiest moral law involved in the equation.

As is evident, there's a strong emphasis here on the need to distinguish between the concepts of the "lesser evil" and the "greater good." Geisler believes he's found a way to avoid saying that God holds people guilty for doing the "right" thing in a moral dilemma. Additionally, he also believes that this is the way the characters in the Bible approached the moral decision-making task.

An evaluation of graded absolutism. To be honest, it's not my impression that a large number of my students come to the course having made previous use of this ethical option in their everyday lives. However, once they are made aware of its main premises, a good number, especially those who possess a conservative Christian background, do express some interest in it. It's my sense that this initial interest is due to several benefits it seems to offer.

First, we find here another ethical option that, because it embraces a moral realism, has appeal for people who intuitively sense that morality isn't completely subjective in nature. Like the other versions of Christian moral absolutism surveyed in this chapter, this decision-making approach

---

[97]Norman L. Geisler, *The Christian Ethic of Love* (Grand Rapids: Zondervan, 1973), pp. 76-86. See also Geisler, *Christian Ethics*, pp. 121-22; McQuilkin and Copan, *Introduction to Biblical Ethics*, p. 52.

avoids an abject moral relativism by contending that there are a number of moral absolutes that derive from the very character of God and that it's the Christian's moral duty to take these many moral absolutes seriously.

Another reason why some of my students seem to gravitate toward graded absolutism is because of the very prominent role that the study of the Bible plays in it. Many of my students possess a fairly conservative evangelical heritage. Because they've embraced the concept of the authority of Scripture, the notion that the Bible can and should be appealed to for guidance when facing a moral dilemma just seems right to them.

Finally, the simple fact is that graded absolutism seems to solve a knotty problem that anyone who embraces the notion of multiple moral absolutes must face: what to do when two or more of these moral absolutes seem to conflict. To conceive of the many divine imperatives presented in Scripture as a hierarchy that allows the careful Christian moral agent to discern and do the greater good rather than the lesser evil seems ingenious. Such a clever yet common-sense solution to the problem of conflicting absolutes strikes many students as an ethical option worthy of some serious consideration.

The truth is, however, that this moral model has met with a number of objections.[98] For the sake of brevity, I will give voice here to only three concerns I personally have with respect to this ethical option.

First, I must confess that I'm always a bit troubled by Christian ethical approaches that tend to treat the Bible as if it were intended to function as a moral rulebook. While I appreciate the commitment of graded absolutism to ground ethics in the divine self-revelation presented in the Scriptures (rather than in nature or human rationality), I'm convinced that we err when we think that even a superscrupulous study of Scripture by itself is sufficient to provide the kind of ethical guidance we fallen human knowers need in order to navigate our way through the moral dilemmas real life throws at us. More than this, for reasons that will be elaborated on in part two, I believe that God has purposefully designed sacred Scripture so as *not* to function as an ethical encyclopedia or moral rulebook! So, while I appreciate this ethical option's commitment to making moral choices that are biblically informed, I believe there's more to resolving

---

[98]For a fairly thorough discussion of these objections, see Geisler, *Christian Ethics*, pp. 122-30.

ethical dilemmas in a morally faithful manner than simply scouring our Bibles for pertinent principles, grading them and then putting them in play.

Second, building on the concern previously articulated, I must confess that I'm not convinced that it's possible to create the kind of hierarchy this ethical option posits. Certainly a distinction can be made between two categories of moral imperatives: those vertical in orientation (having to do with our relationship with God) and those horizontal in orientation (having to do with others and ourselves). I've already indicated my concern over how some theologians/ethicists seem to conflate these two categories with the result that our love for and loyalty to God cease to function as criteria by which we might evaluate morally appropriate and inappropriate acts of love toward our neighbors and/or ourselves. That said, I'm not sure that the proponents of a graded absolutism have succeeded in making the case for the idea that a formal hierarchy can be constructed that does justice to all the moral imperatives presented in the Scriptures. For one thing, the biblical support Geisler provides for some of the "principles" he sees in Scripture seems to me to be tenuous at best. Moreover, for all of Geisler's efforts to clarify its application and soften its impact, such a principle as "the complete must be considered of more value than the incomplete," based as it is on the conviction that "all other things being equal, a person with complete mental and physical abilities is more valuable than one without," seems to be not only jarring but antithetical to the principle of justice, Leviticus 21:18-20 notwithstanding (cf. Job 29:1-17; Prov 31:8-9).[99] Thus I'm thinking that even if it were possible to create the formal hierarchy of moral rules that graded absolutism insists on, the model presented thus far isn't sufficient for the task.

Third, I want to suggest that there's an important difference between an ethic that's biblically *informed* and one that's biblically *constrained*. In other words, I'm led to wonder where the Spirit is in this decision-making approach. Some questions I often put to my students having completed this survey of popular ethical options include:

- Which of the approaches to making ethical decisions included in this survey can you imagine Jesus himself employing?

---

[99]Ibid., p. 86.

- Does Jesus' decision-making method seem to focus exclusively on either results or rules, or can you see a concern for both at work in his moral life?

- Keeping in mind that Jesus apparently took moral absolutes seriously (Mt 5:17-20), what do you think he might encourage us to do when facing a moral dilemma besides endeavoring on our own to discern the lesser evil or scouring our Bibles in order to locate the higher moral law?

The purpose of the last question presented above is designed to get people thinking about the role that prayer and waiting on God for some Spirit-enabled moral guidance might play in an ethic that aims to be Christ-centered, biblically informed and Spirit-empowered.[100] Furthermore, it's also appropriate, I believe, to go on to speak of the need for a communal engagement in some spiritual formation activities that possess the time-tested ability to form in Christian disciples the kind of character that's concerned to live a morally faithful life before God in the first place!

It may very well be true that graded absolutism, with its near-exclusive focus on the Bible as *the* resource (*sine qua non*) for moral guidance, is the Christian's best bet for an ethical option that acknowledges the existence of more than one moral absolute. However, in part two of this book I will attempt to show how very important the Holy Spirit and the Christian community are to the ability of Christian disciples to live in a morally faithfully manner before God. To the degree I succeed in this endeavor, it will validate the conclusion offered here that graded absolutism, like nonconflicting absolutism and conflicting absolutism, is by itself an inadequate foundation for a fully Christian ethic.

Even though I'm obviously eager to begin the process of laying out the argument for what I refer to as the ethic of responsible Christian discipleship, there's one more bit of business that must be attended to first. The goal of the next chapter is to help us evaluate the degree to which we as individual moral agents are capable and ready at present to render to God a moral faithfulness. This is intended to be an informative, sobering and

---

[100]I'm not suggesting that any Christian ethicist has made a conscious decision to ignore the Holy Spirit completely, only that this happens. Sadly, the result of this fundamental faux pas is that many versions of Christian ethics end up *not* dealing sufficiently with the need for a theological and pneumatological realism.

yet motivational read. It's my hope that, building on the results of the two-part survey just concluded, the last chapter of part one will produce in the reader a genuine desire to dive into the second half of the book. So let's turn our attention now to a consideration of the impact an increasingly postmodern culture is having on nearly all of us as moral agents, and a process by which we can assess our current moral faithfulness quotient.

The Religio-Cultural
Soup We're All In

Assessing Its Impact
on Our Moral IQ

In the book's introduction I referred to a young-adult student who confessed in a final paper that, prior to taking a college ethics course, he had not given the moral dimension of his life much thought. What are we to make of this lack of moral thoughtfulness? Was it merely an indication in one person's life of what some would refer to as a low moral IQ (moral intelligence)?[1] Or was the ethical naiveté evidenced by this student actually a sign of the times—a to-be-expected byproduct of the religio-cultural soup nearly all young adults have been swimming around in all their lives?

I'm inclined to believe that the latter explanation definitely possesses merit; the culture in which we're immersed can have a fairly dramatic impact on something I refer to as our *moral faithfulness quotient*—our readiness and capacity to hear and honor the heart of God. I'm also of the opinion that it's important before we go any further to give some thought to this dynamic. I trust that doing so will prove to be an eye-opening experience that will not only increase our ability to comprehend and appreciate the argument for the ethic of responsible Christian discipleship proffered in part two of *Pursuing Moral Faithfulness* but will also encourage us to take a long, hard look at the quality of our current

---

[1]For example, see Doug Lennick and Fred Kiel, *Moral Intelligence: Enhancing Business Performance and Leadership Success* (Upper Saddle River, NJ: Wharton School Publishing, 2008); Arthur Dobrin, *Ethics for Everyone: How to Increase Your Moral Intelligence* (New York: John Wiley & Sons, 2002).

walk with Christ (see 2 Cor 13:5). In other words, the goal of this chapter is to prompt the kind of personal reflection necessary for any of us to *want* to improve our ability to live in a morally faithful manner before God. Given the amount of ethical naiveté that seems to be at work in the world today, it's hard for me to imagine a more important endeavor.

CULTURE, WORLDVIEW AND THE MORAL OUGHT

The famous philosopher of communication Marshall McLuhan (1911–1980) once observed: "We don't know who discovered water, but we know it wasn't the fish." I routinely share this quote with students studying the concept of worldview with me. My goal is to help them get a sense of the degree to which we've all been influenced by the cultural environment in which we've existed since birth. "It's hard, if not impossible," I tell them, "if you've been swimming around in something your entire life, to recognize on your own its distinctive qualities and the impact it's had upon you."[2] My experience has been that if I can get my students to acknowledge this profound reality, we can then begin to have a serious conversation about how contemporary culture (a blend of both modernity and postmodernity) has affected the way *all* of us view the world, and the best way to navigate our way through it.[3]

A focus on worldview is appropriate here because, by the reckoning of not a few philosophers and theologians, the basic existential questions most worldviews address ultimately lead to the question of morality: How then should we live?[4] In other words, it certainly appears that one's worldview and convictions regarding the moral ought are inextricably

---

[2]I am not alone in making use of the fish and water analogy. See Don C. Richter, "Growing Up Postmodern: Theological Uses of Culture," in *Starting Right: Thinking Theologically About Youth Ministry*, ed. Kenda Creasy Dean, Chap Clark and Dave Rahn (Grand Rapids: Zondervan, 2001), p. 64; Walt Mueller, *Engaging the Soul of Youth Culture: Bridging Teen Worldviews and Christian Truth* (Downers Grove, IL: IVP Books, 2006), p. 113; and Mueller, *Youth Culture 101* (Grand Rapids: Zondervan, 2007), p. 35.

[3]Paul Hiebert makes the observation: "Modern and postmodern worldviews have coexisted in the West for the past several decades and are competing for general acceptance." See Paul G. Hiebert, *Transforming Worldviews: An Anthropological Understanding of How People Change* (Grand Rapids: Baker, 2008), p. 212.

[4]See Charles W. Colson, *How Now Shall We Live* (Carol Stream, IL: Tyndale House, 1999), pp. xi, xii, 14, 268, 294. See also Brian J. Walsh and J. Richard Middleton, *The Transforming Vision: Shaping a Christian World View* (Downers Grove, IL: InterVarsity Press, 1984), p. 35, and Michael Wittmer, *Heaven Is a Place on Earth: Why Everything You Do Matters to God* (Grand Rapids: Zondervan, 2004), pp. 24, 33.

linked.[5] However, since there's also a fairly indisputable connection between one's worldview and the impress of the culture in which we've
been nurtured, the really important "fish and water" questions are these:
Doesn't it make sense to suppose that a connection might exist between
the cultural soup all of us are swimming in and the manner in which we
approach the moral dimension of life?[6] If so, wouldn't it be a really good
idea for us to be aware of the possible effect of this cultural conditioning
on our desire and ability to cultivate a moral faithfulness? Important
questions such as these deserve a discussion!

THE DISCUSSION'S FOCAL POINT:
THE NATIONAL STUDY OF YOUTH AND RELIGION

For reasons that will be revealed momentarily, my tack in this attempt to
help us all assess our current moral faithfulness quotient will be to draw
attention to some fairly recent sociological analysis that focuses on the
religious, spiritual and moral condition of one generation in particular:
America's young adults. The National Study of Youth and Religion
(NSYR) is a research project directed by Christian Smith, professor of
sociology at the University of Notre Dame, and Lisa Pearce, assistant
professor of sociology at the University of North Carolina at Chapel
Hill.[7] According to research team member Kenda Creasy Dean (associate professor of youth, church and culture at Princeton University), the
research project constitutes "the most ambitious study of American teen-

---

[5]Emerging adult expert Jeffrey Arnett writes: "Another essential part of a world view is a set of values,
that is, a set of moral principles that guides decisions about the issues that come up in the course of
daily life" (Jeffrey Jensen Arnett, *Emerging Adulthood: The Winding Road from the Late Teens Through
the Twenties* [New York: Oxford University Press, 2004], p. 165). For more on the relationship between
ethics and worldview, see Patrick Nullens and Ronald T. Michener, *The Matrix of Christian Ethics:
Integrating Philosophy and Moral Theology in a Postmodern Context* (Downers Grove, IL: IVP Books,
2010), pp. 56-62.

[6]Sociologist Christian Smith answers this question in an unequivocal manner. Explaining his conviction that "human cultures are moral orders," he states that "the most adequate approach to theoriz-
ing human culture must be a normative one that conceives of humans as moral, believing animals
and human social life as consisting of moral orders that constitute and direct social action. Human
culture is always moral order. Human cultures are everywhere moral orders. Human persons are
nearly inescapably moral agents. Human actions are necessarily morally constituted and propelled
practices. And human institutions are inevitably morally infused configurations of rules and resources" (Christian Smith, *Moral, Believing Animals: Human Personhood and Culture* [New York:
Oxford University Press, 2003], p. 7).

[7]See "National Study of Youth and Religion," University of Notre Dame, http://youthandreligion.nd.edu.

agers and religion to date, involving extensive interviews of more than 3,300 American teenagers between the ages of thirteen and seventeen (including telephone interviews of these teenagers' parents)."[8] Though the first phase of the study was conducted between 2002 and 2005, Dean explains that it "also involves an ongoing longitudinal component that has so far revisited more than 2,500 of these young people to understand how their religious lives are changing as they enter emerging adulthood."[9] Because several books based on the NSYR have been published that provide some helpful insight into the religious, spiritual and moral lives of the emerging generations, it's possible to gain a fairly good understanding of the moral faithfulness quotient of many members of the emerging generations.[10]

AN IMPORTANT METHODOLOGICAL PRESUPPOSITION: THE CONNECTION BETWEEN GENERATIONS

As for why I've chosen to focus attention in this chapter on the spiritual and moral lives of America's emerging adults, a crucial presupposition at work here is that, for all the ways in which the emerging generation differs from those that immediately predate it (that is, the boomers and busters), an important connection exists between them. To a great degree, all three of these generations of Americans have been rather strikingly influenced by both modernity and postmodernity. To be more precise, nearly all contemporary conservative American Christians are swimming around

---

[8]Kenda Creasy Dean, *Almost Christian: What the Faith of Our Teenagers Is Telling the American Church* (New York: Oxford University Press, 2010), p. 16.

[9]Ibid.

[10]Books that bear the research study's imprimatur (so to speak) include: Christian Smith with Melinda Lundquist Denton, *Soul Searching: The Religious and Spiritual Lives of American Teenagers* (New York: Oxford University Press, 2005); Mark D. Regnerus, *Forbidden Fruit: Sex and Religion in the Lives of American Teenagers* (New York: Oxford University Press, 2007); Ken Johnson-Mondragon, ed., *Pathways of Hope and Faith Among Hispanic Teens: Pastoral Reflections and Strategies Inspired by the National Study of Youth and Religion* (Stockton, CA: Instituto Fe y Vida, 2007); Christian Smith with Patricia Snell, *Souls in Transition: The Religious and Spiritual Lives of Emerging Adults* (New York: Oxford University Press, 2009); Richard Flory, Korie Edwards and Brad Christerson, *Growing Up in America: The Power of Race in the Lives of Teens* (Stanford, CA: Stanford University Press, 2010); Dean, *Almost Christian*; Lisa D. Pearce and Melinda Lundquist Denton, *A Faith of Their Own: Stability and Change in the Religiosity of America's Adolescents* (New York: Oxford University Press, 2011); Christian Smith, Kari Christoffersen, Hilary Davidson and Patricia Snell Herzog, *Lost in Transition: The Dark Side of Emerging Adulthood* (New York: Oxford University Press, 2011).

in the same religio-cultural soup, with the result that the same blend of nominally Christian and secular cultural influences at work in the lives of the emerging generations is also exercising an effect on the pre-emerging generations as well. In point of fact, since the religious, spiritual and moral condition of America's teens and young adults can be attributed, at least in part, to the larger adult world in which they've been socialized, an important causal as well as correlative connection can be thought of as existing between them.

This is precisely the conclusion arrived at by those conducting the research (NSYR) just alluded to. For example, with respect to the religious and spiritual lives of American teens, Christian Smith and Melinda Lundquist Denton, coauthors of *Soul Searching: The Religious and Spiritual Lives of American Teenagers*, assert that "most American youth faithfully mirror the aspirations, lifestyles, practices, and problems of the adult world into which they are being socialized. In these ways, adolescents may actually serve as a very accurate barometer of the condition of the culture and institutions of our larger society."[11]

As it relates to the religious and spiritual lives of emerging adults, Christian Smith and Patricia Snell Herzog, authors of the follow-up work *Souls in Transition: The Religious and Spiritual Lives of Emerging Adults*, underscore the crucial importance of understanding the religious and spiritual worlds of emerging adults within the broader context of the cultural worlds in which they live, stating: "Emerging adults' religious and spiritual assumptions, experiences, outlooks, beliefs, and practices do not exist in compartmentalized isolation from their larger cultural worldviews and lived experiences but are often related to and powerfully shaped by them."[12] Indeed, the connection between the generations is strong enough, say Smith and Snell, as to warrant the following contention: "By examining the world of contemporary emerging adults, we think we hold up a mirror that reflects back to adults a telling picture of the larger adult world—their own world—into which emerging adults are moving."[13]

Finally, we can find essentially the same contention being made by

---

[11]Smith, *Soul Searching*, p. 191. See also Dean, *Almost Christian*, p. 9.
[12]Smith, *Souls in Transition*, p. 33.
[13]Ibid., p. 4.

Christian Smith and the coauthors of a third work based on the NSYR—
Lost in Transition: The Dark Side of Emerging Adulthood. The authors of
this work are thoroughly convinced that a relationship exists between
"some of the more unsettling aspects of contemporary emerging adult life"
and the "larger culture and society that has formed them morally."[14]

It's this connection between the generations that explains my approach to this chapter and the call it sounds for *everyone* reading it (generational status notwithstanding) to take a closer look at the religio-
cultural soup *all* of us are swimming in and to consider how it may be
affecting *our* moral faithfulness quotient—*our* desire and ability to hear
and honor the heart of God.

THE RELIGIOUS AND SPIRITUAL LIVES OF AMERICA'S TEENS: MORALISTIC THERAPEUTIC DEISM

Many books, articles and blogs have been written commenting on the
findings of the NSYR. Beyond question, the most authoritative work reporting on the study is *Soul Searching: The Religious and Spiritual Lives of
American Teenagers*, penned by project leader Christian Smith along with
Melinda Lundquist Denton.[15] Perhaps the most notable finding presented
in this work is that "the de facto dominant religion among contemporary
U.S. teenagers is what we might call 'Moralistic Therapeutic Deism.'"[16]
(For the sake of convenience, I will sometimes refer to Moralistic Thera-
peutic Deism simply as MTD.)

MTD's core beliefs. According to Smith, five core beliefs form the
basic creed of this dominant worldview:

1. A god exists who created and ordered the world and watches over
   human life on earth.

1. God wants people to be good, nice and fair to each other, as taught
   in the Bible and by most world religions.

2. The central goal of life is to be happy and to feel good about oneself.

---

[14]Smith et al., *Lost in Transition*, pp. 60-61.
[15]For the sake of convenience, I will sometimes refer to the Smith alone as the primary author of this work.
[16]Smith, *Soul Searching*, p. 162.

3. God does not need to be particularly involved in one's life except when God is needed to resolve a problem.

4. Good people go to heaven when they die.[17]

Why Smith and his team refer to this set of beliefs as Moralistic Therapeutic Deism will be spelled out below. But before we launch into that discussion, allow me to provide a justification for it.

The extent of MTD. Because MTD is not an organized religious denomination with official headquarters and ordained clergy, no American teenager would likely refer to himself or herself as a Moralistic Therapeutic Deist. Still, insists Smith, "such a de facto creed is particularly evident among mainline Protestant and Catholic youth" and "is also visible among black and conservative Protestants, Jewish teens, other religious types of teenagers, and even many non-religious teenagers in the United States."[18] So, according to the NSYR, Moralistic Therapeutic Deism is much more prevalent among America's youth than most churchgoing adults realize.[19]

At the same time we need to be clear about the fact that the NSYR is not indicating that MTD is limited to America's teens. As we've just seen, the startling observation made by the authors of *Soul Searching* is that MTD seems to be a "widespread, popular faith among very many U.S. adults" as well.[20] According to Smith and his research team, "our religiously conventional adolescents seem to be merely absorbing and reflecting religiously what the adult world is routinely modeling for and inculcating in its youth."[21] This observation is crucial lest anyone make

---

[17]Ibid., pp. 162-63.

[18]Ibid., p. 163.

[19]Indeed, as someone who works every day with members of the emerging generations, I can attest to the fact that, unfortunately, MTD is alive and well in many evangelical homes and churches. Every semester in more than one course I teach I introduce my mostly evangelical university students to the findings of the NSYR. I've found that, once they are made aware of the research indicating the nature of MTD and its prevalence within their demographic, the response of many of my students follows a predictable pattern: alarm—admission—appreciation. In other words, eventually acknowledging the presence of at least some aspects of MTD in their own lives and those of their peers, not a few students go on to state that being made aware of the jaw-dropping specifics of MTD offers them some powerful motivation toward personal spiritual renewal and provides them with language they can use when expressing concern for the spiritual welfare of their family members and friends. In addition, it's not uncommon for my older ministry students to concede the presence of MTD within the members of the youth groups they are ministering to.

[20]Smith, *Soul Searching*, p. 166.

[21]Ibid.

the mistake of construing *Soul Searching* as just another rant against the emerging generation offered by some cranky baby boomers. No, it's because of the predominance of this de facto religion/worldview in the spiritual and moral lives of huge numbers of Americans of *all* ages that a closer look at why Smith and his research team have chosen to refer to it as Moralistic Therapeutic Deism is warranted.

How MTD is "moralistic." According to the authors of *Soul Searching*, this worldview is moralistic because it "is about inculcating a moralistic approach to life. It teaches that central to living a good and happy life is being a good, moral person."[22] As for what being a good, moral person involves, Smith explains that it means "being nice, kind, pleasant, respectful, responsible, at work on self-improvement, taking care of one's health, and doing one's best to be successful."[23]

At first glance, this emphasis on morality can seem like a good thing. Indeed, given this apparent ethical concern, it might seem counterintuitive to posit that MTD actually decreases a person's moral faithfulness quotient. However, from a biblically informed perspective, there's a big problem with the moralism at work in MTD. A huge difference exists between a readiness to render to God the moral faithfulness he deserves and the idea that the good life is to be achieved in our own strength as we strive to make ourselves good, moral people, successful according to a standard determined not by God but by the culture in which we're immersed. *At the very heart of a moralistic worldview is the notion of salvation by self-improvement.* This is of course at odds with biblical Christianity's emphasis on the need for grace, new birth and the moral empowerment the Holy Spirit provides as we spend a lifetime following Jesus. Based on passages such as Ephesians 2:8-9, we have good reason to believe that the apostle Paul would be very uneasy with the moralism at work in the lives of many churchgoing American teenagers!

How MTD is "therapeutic." The notion that there's a human-centered rather than God-centered orientation at work in MTD's emphasis on morality finds support with Smith's critical observation that this belief system as a whole is "about providing therapeutic benefits to its

---

[22]Ibid., p. 163.
[23]Ibid.

adherents."[24] Missing from this approach to spirituality is any notion of repentance from sin, of a deliberate engagement in spiritual disciplines, of suffering for the cause of Christ and so on. Instead, says Smith, "what appears to be the actual dominant religion among U.S. teenagers is centrally about feeling good, happy, secure, at peace. It is about attaining subjective well-being, being able to resolve problems, and getting along amiably with other people."[25]

Smith and his team report that comments made during interviews indicate that the main reason why many of these teens engage in any sort of religious practice is because of how it makes them feel: good and/or happy.[26] The primary goal of MTD is not to serve God but oneself. The goal of religion is to make the adherent happy and successful. The sovereignty of God has been replaced by a sovereignty of the self. This is another big distinction between MTD and a more biblically informed understanding of the Christian faith and lifestyle.[27]

How MTD is a form of "deism." "Finally," says Smith, "Moralistic Therapeutic Deism is about belief in a particular kind of God: one who exists, created the world, and defines our general moral order, but not one who is particularly personally involved in one's affairs—especially affairs in which one would prefer not to have God involved. Most of the time, the God of this faith keeps a safe distance."[28]

It's this notion of a deity who most of the time keeps a safe distance that causes Smith to see a similarity between the worldview of contemporary teens (and adults) and the deistic understanding of God that flourished in the eighteenth century. According to classical deism, God created the world but then backed away from it, content to allow it to function on the basis of the natural laws woven into the fabric of the created order. The hallmark depiction of the God of deism is that of a watchmaker. According to a deistic worldview, having been "wound up" by its creator, the cosmos as a closed system is now pretty much

---

[24]Ibid.
[25]Ibid., pp. 163-64.
[26]Ibid., p. 164.
[27]For more on this therapeutic understanding of salvation and how it is generated by both modern and postmodern themes, see Hiebert, *Transforming Worldviews*, pp. 35-36.
[28]Smith, *Soul Searching*, p. 164.

running on its own, void of any supernatural "intervention" or "inter-ference" from above or beyond.

And yet Smith is very careful to point out that there is an important *dis-similarity* between MTD and classical deism. Referring to it as the "thera-peutic qualifier," Smith explains that this convenient dissimilarity is due to the fact that: "For many teens, as with adults, God sometimes does get in-volved in people's lives, but usually only when they call on him, mostly when they have some trouble or problem or bad feeling they want resolved."[29]

Thus the distinction between MTD's conception of God and that of classical deism is ultimately not significant. While it moves in the di-rection toward a theological realism, it is still way too anthropocentric (human-centered) and therapeutic in its orientation to be considered truly biblical and Christian. All liturgical confessions aside, the God of MTD is not trinitarian, did not actually speak to Moses on the mount, didn't inspire the sacred Scriptures and was not incarnate in Christ. Moreover, missing from MTD is any serious notion of Christian disci-pleship. Indeed, Smith explains: "This God is not demanding. He ac-tually can't be, because his job is to solve our problems and make people feel good. In short, God is something like a combination Divine Butler and Cosmic Therapist: he is always on call, takes care of any problems that arise, professionally helps his people to feel better about themselves, and does not become too personally involved in the process."[30]

Once again, we see indications that within MTD the sovereignty of God has been replaced with a sovereignty of the self. Though MTD's God can, on occasion, be a bit more involved in people's lives than was the deity in classical deism, he still maintains a safe distance, only becoming involved when the metaphorical lamp he resides in is given a desperate rub by someone who needs his help with a crisis of one type or another.

The effects of MTD. If it seems inconceivable that anyone could ar-ticulate such a view of God with a straight face, we need to keep in mind several additional findings of the NSYR. These additional findings—dis-concerting to Smith and his team—provide insight into the nature of the religio-cultural soup nearly *all* of us are swimming in, and why this

---

[29]Ibid., p. 165.
[30]Ibid.

ethos is antagonistic to the theological and moral realism at the heart of a moral faithfulness.

American teens tend to lack theological fluency. The first of these troubling findings is that the vast majority of the teens interviewed for the study seem to be "*incredibly inarticulate* about their faith, their religious beliefs and practices, and its meaning or place in their lives."[31] The irony is that, as Smith points out, many of the youth interviewed in the NSYR "were quite conversant when it came to their views on salient issues in their lives about which they had been educated and had practice discussing, such as the dangers of drug abuse and STDs."[32] So this lack of theological fluency does not seem to stem from a lack of intelligence or communicative capacity per se. Smith reports instead that "this pervasive teen inarticulacy contributes to our larger impression that religion is either de facto not that important for most teens or that teens are getting very little help from their religious communities in knowing how to express the faith that may be important to them."[33]

Unfortunately, the bad news about MTD's impact on the theological acumen of America's teens doesn't stop there.

American teens tend to lack theological understanding. It's not simply that the teens participating in the NSYR demonstrated a lack of theological fluency; the bigger problem is that they also manifested a troubling degree of theological ignorance. Speaking of the teens interviewed by his team, Smith refers to "their accompanying meager, nebulous, and often fallacious knowledge of the belief content of their own religious traditions which they claim to embrace."[34] Here we find that it's not only a moral thoughtlessness that's at work in the emerging generations but a theological thoughtlessness (indifference) as well. Smith clarifies this distressing observation, saying:

> To the extent that the teens we interviewed did manage to articulate what they understood and believed religiously, it became clear that most religious teenagers either do not really comprehend what their own religious traditions say they are

---

[31]Ibid., p. 131, emphasis original.
[32]Ibid., p. 133.
[33]Ibid., p. 131.
[34]Ibid.

supposed to believe, or they do understand it and simply do not care to believe it. Either way, it is apparent that most religiously affiliated U.S. teens are not particularly invested in espousing and upholding the beliefs of their faith traditions, or that their communities of faith are failing in attempts to educate their youth, or both. The net result, in any case, is that most religious teenagers' opinions and views—one can hardly call them worldviews—are vague, limited, and often quite at variance with the actual teachings of their own religion.[35]

American teens tend to lack a teachable spirit. A third distressing finding of the NSYR worth noting is that the teens surveyed don't seem to be all that teachable regarding theological or moral matters. Smith states that "American youth, like American adults, are nearly without exception profoundly individualistic, instinctively presuming autonomous, individual self-direction to be a universal human norm and life goal." "Consequently," says Smith, it's not only the case that "certain traditional religious languages and vocabularies of commitment, duty, faithfulness, obedience, calling, accountability, and ties to the past are nearly completely absent from the discourse of U.S. teenagers," but also that this profound individualism causes the members of the emerging generations to be "at least somewhat allergic to anything they view as trying to influence them."[36]

American teens seem unable or unwilling to conceive of objective truth. And where did these strong convictions regarding the autonomy and freedom of the individual come from? Ironically, both modernism and postmodernism seem to come into play.

On the one hand, Smith asserts: "From the wells of radical American religious individualism, contemporary U.S. teenagers have drunk deeply, no doubt following the example of their parents and other adults. For most, religious individualism appears to be all U.S. teens can actually conceive of."[37] On the other hand, the resistance to being "taught" manifested by many teens and young adults is also fueled by a conviction

---

[35]Ibid., pp. 133-34.

[36]Ibid., pp. 143-44, emphasis original.

[37]Ibid., p. 147. The radical individualism that seems to be at work in the emerging generations is often viewed as a product of the Enlightenment and therefore an aspect of modernity. For example, see Stanley J. Grenz and John R. Franke, *Beyond Foundationalism: Shaping Theology in a Postmodern Context* (Louisville: Westminster John Knox, 2001), p. 195. See also Hiebert, *Transforming Worldviews*, p. 199.

regarding the relativity of knowledge (that is, epistemological relativism).[38] According to Smith, many if not most members of the emerging generations are genuinely convinced that there are no "right" answers when it comes to religious matters (theology and morality). Combined with their radical individualism, this relativization of knowledge results in the view that everyone is entitled to believe and behave however they want.[39]

American teens are profoundly reluctant to judge. The view just referred to obviously possesses ethical significance. It also explains another salient feature of emerging culture, says Smith—one that will show up later as an important ethical earmark: "a very strong ethos that forswears judging any ideas or people that may be different."[40] As will be pointed out below, there's an important difference between judging and assessing, condemning and critiquing. While the emerging generation's reticence to pass judgment on others is to be applauded, the fact that this cultural ethos is generated by a deeply rooted inability to reckon with the possibility of objective moral truth is fatally antagonistic to the type of theological and moral realism the pursuit of moral faithfulness depends on.

American teens are not contending for the historic Christian faith. Finally, perhaps the most shocking conclusion reported on by Smith and his team has to do with the long-term impact of MTD on the American religious landscape. Indeed, one of the main themes of *Soul Searching* is that only a minority of U.S. teenagers have actually embraced and are faithfully practicing the historic tenets and practices of the religious tradition to which they claim to belong, Instead, "another popular religious faith, Moralistic Therapeutic Deism, is colonizing many historical religious traditions and, almost without anyone noticing, converting believers in the

---

[38]Epistemological relativism is often associated with a deconstructive version of postmodernity. See Grenz and Franke, *Beyond Foundationalism*, p. 19.

[39]Some will argue against the notion that both modernism and postmodernism are to blame for the radical moral individualism that seems to be at work in the emerging generations. It's often contended that American individualism is solely a product of the Enlightenment's (i.e., modernity's) focus on the rational, autonomous self, while the product of postmodernism is an emphasis on plurality (e.g., see Nullens and Michener, *Matrix of Christian Ethics*, pp. 40-41). However, if it's true that postmodernity is actually late modernity (or even a hypermodernity or ultramodernity), then it shouldn't surprise us to find that beneath all the talk of communalism that's supposed to be an indelible earmark of the emerging generations, there's actually a radical moral individualism at work. At least, this is something I've observed in the lives of many of my young adult students.

[40]Smith, *Soul Searching*, p. 144.

old faiths to its alternative religious vision of divinely underwritten personal happiness and interpersonal niceness."[41] Commenting on the impact of MTD on Christianity in particular, Smith and his team offer the dire assessment:

> We can say here that we have come with some confidence to believe that a significant part of Christianity in the United States is actually only tenuously Christian in any sense that is seriously connected to the actual historical Christian tradition, but has rather substantially morphed into Christianity's misbegotten stepcousin, Christian Moralistic Therapeutic Deism. . . . The language, and therefore experience of Trinity, holiness, sin, grace, justification, sanctification, church, Eucharist, and heaven and hell appear, among most Christian teenagers in the United States at the very least, to be supplanted by the language of happiness, niceness, and an earned heavenly reward. It is not so much that U.S. Christianity is being secularized. Rather more subtly, Christianity is either degenerating into a pathetic version of itself or, more significantly, Christianity is actively being colonized and displaced by a quite different religious faith.[42]

I trust it's obvious from what I've presented here that the point of *Soul Searching* is not to rail against what the emerging generations are doing to the Christian faith. This is evident from the fact that throughout the book Smith is careful to indicate his sense that the embrace of Moralistic Therapeutic Deism by so many of America's teens has been enabled by a failure on the part of their adult mentors to: (1) contend for the faith once for all entrusted to the saints (see Jude 3) and (2) adequately model what a biblically informed Christian discipleship actually looks like.[43] Another way to say this is that the religio-cultural soup all of us are swimming in has negatively affected churchgoers of all ages, generational status notwithstanding!

What to do with this information? Obviously, the findings of the NSYR indicate that Christian churches of all stripes (Protestant and Catholic, liberal and conservative) have a big problem on their hands.

I'm happy to report that several books have been published that do an admirable job of providing some wise counsel regarding the remedial action churches and youth ministries need to take posthaste in order to mitigate

---

[41]Ibid., p. 171.
[42]Ibid.
[43]See also Dean, *Almost Christian*, pp. 12, 15-16, 18.

the discipleship-defeating impact of contemporary culture in general and Moralistic Therapeutic Deism in particular.[44] However, the purpose of the rest of this chapter is not to elaborate on these needed ministry correctives. Instead my goal is to explore even more deeply how the religio-cultural context that has facilitated the emergence of an "almost Christianity" in the spiritual lives of so many American teens has exercised a deleterious effect on the moral faithfulness quotient of Americans of all ages. Therefore, keeping in mind the key presupposition that all American Christians are swimming around in essentially the same cultural soup, the next step in this learning process is to explore the impact contemporary church and secular culture have had on the moral lives of America's emerging adults.

MTD and the Moral Lives of America's Emerging Adults

As indicated above, the NSYR is longitudinal in nature, meaning that in 2005 a second telephone interview of most of the subjects making up the original study sample was conducted, along with a personal re-interview of 122 of the same respondents.[45] Then in 2007 and 2008 a third wave of surveys and interviews was conducted, focusing particularly on those eighteen to twenty-three years of age. Recognizing that many transitions were occurring in the lives of these emerging adults, the goal of this component of the NSYR was to discover what was happening in the midst of those transitions to "their religious faith, practices, beliefs, associations, and commitments."[46]

The authoritative resource for the findings of this third wave of the NSYR is the book *Souls in Transition: The Religious and Spiritual Lives of Emerging Adults.* This well-written book is filled with fascinating insights regarding the various "cultural themes" or generational realities that seem to earmark the lives of America's emerging adults (especially those eighteen to twenty-three years old at the time). Sadly, it appears that the same negative effects Moralistic Therapeutic Deism has had on the religious and spiritual lives of America's teens are present in the lives of

---

[44]For example, see Dean, *Almost Christian*; and Richard R. Dunn and Jana L. Sundene, *Shaping the Journey of Emerging Adults: Life-Giving Rhythms for Spiritual Transformation* (Downers Grove, IL: IVP Books, 2012).

[45]Smith, *Souls in Transition*, p. 3.

[46]Ibid., p. 4.

emerging adults as well. At the risk of some redundancy, I feel the need to underscore here those MTD outcomes that appear to be affecting in particular the readiness and capacity of many emerging adults to render to God the type of moral faithfulness this book is promoting.

Emerging adults have a hard time reckoning with an objective reality beyond the self. Reiterated in *Souls in Transition* is the fact that a foundational earmark of the emerging mentality is an inability to even consider the possibility that some things might be real and true apart from how individual persons think and feel about them. Early on in *Souls in Transition* the authors refer to the majority of the emerging adults they interviewed as "soft ontological antirealists and epistemological skeptics and perspectivalists" even though few if any would know what these terms mean.[47] In simpler language, this means that, without doing so in a conscious manner, a significant number of emerging adults "seem to presuppose that they are simply imprisoned in their own subjective selves, limited to their biased interpretations of their own sense perceptions, unable to know the real truth of anything beyond themselves."[48]

As to how this antirealism relates to their moral lives, Smith indicates that because many emerging adults seem to have difficulty even conceiving of objective moral truth that exists apart from human invention, "most simply choose to believe and live by whatever subjectively feels 'right' to them."[49] At this point, the "Following My Heart" decision-making approach I associated with moral subjectivism/emotivism in chapter two comes immediately to mind.[50] It should be apparent that this rather strong commitment to a postmodern, perspectivalist view of truth, arbitrarily ruling out as it does any sort of transcendent moral reality that applies equally to everyone, obviously constitutes a huge impediment for the moral faithfulness endeavor. How or why should someone strive to be faithful to something that doesn't exist?

And yet, despite the absence of a transcendent standard, many emerging adults claim that knowing right and wrong is amazingly easy.

---

[47]Ibid., p. 45.
[48]Ibid.
[49]Ibid., p. 293.
[50]Ibid., p. 46.

The irony, says Smith, is that when asked how difficult or easy it is to make moral choices, many of the study's participants "hardly had to think about it"; "nearly everyone said it is easy." The reason for this, according to Smith, is that, of those emerging adults surveyed, "the vast majority are moral intuitionists—that is, they believe that they know what is right and wrong by attending to the subjective feelings or intuitions that they sense within themselves when they find themselves in various situations or facing ethical questions." This egoistic, intuitional approach to making moral decisions (reminiscent of the ethical option referred to in chapter two as the "Trusting My Intuition" approach) is unquestionably trustworthy, say these respondents, because their subjective moral intuitions are "the product of *right moral principles* implanted deeply within their consciences when they were children by their parents, teachers, pastors, and other adult authorities."[51] Thus, "all one has to do is pay some attention to what one feels or intuits in any situation and one will definitely know what is the *morally right thing* to do."[52] So easy is making moral decisions, said many of those interviewed, that Smith could report that a majority of them "had difficulty thinking of even one example of a situation recently when they had some trouble deciding what was the morally right or wrong thing to do."[53] One of the main messages of the previous chapters is that moral dilemmas happen. Apparently, in the world of emerging adults, not so much! For a huge number of emerging adults, "thinking and living morally is quite ef-

---

[51]Ibid., emphasis added. See also Nullens and Michener, *Matrix of Christian Ethics*, p. 5.

[52]Smith, *Souls in Transition*, p. 46 (emphasis added). As we move forward it will become apparent that there are actually several decision-making approaches at work among the emerging generations, each generated by a different metaethical theory. This observation is prompted by the fact that, even though Smith labels the "vast majority" of NSYR interviewees as "moral intuitionists" who can speak of doing the "morally right thing" because of their impeccable trust in the "right principles" internalized during their youth (suggesting the "Trusting My Intuition" approach), other statements made by interviewees seem to reflect either a conscious or subconscious embrace of a radical moral anti-realism—the metaethical doctrine that there are no objective moral values. (See "Moral Anti-Realism," *The Basics of Philosophy* [website] [accessed June 13, 2014], www.philosophybasics.com/branch_moral_anti-realism.html.) This abject disavowal of any sort of objective moral reality is obviously suggestive of the moral subjectivism/emotivism metaethical theories and the "Following My Heart" decision-making approach generated by them. What's more, as we will see, still other NSYR participants appear to be making moral choices in a manner suggestive of a narcissistic conventionalism and the "Guarding My Reputation" decision-making approach!

[53]Smith, *Souls in Transition*, p. 46.

fortless—you merely pay attention to your inner self, and it all comes fairly naturally."[54]

The simplistic moral reasoning of emerging adults leads to an unbalanced (eccentric) approach to making ethical decisions. The research indicates that the main if not sole moral principle that emerging adults have internalized, and on which they base most of their ethical choices, is "the imperative not to hurt others." What this means, observes Smith, is that most emerging adults are "ethical consequentialists" and that in an eccentric, unbalanced manner. The moral reasoning of most emerging adults amounts to this: "if something would hurt another person, it is probably bad; if it does not and is not illegal, it's probably fine."[55] While it's possible to see a connection between this moral norm and what has come to be known as the Golden Rule (Mt 6:31; 7:12), it is even more evocative of the principle of utility discussed in chapter two.

It should also be noted that the influence of a couple of MTD's core beliefs is apparent here: God wants people to be good, nice and fair to each other; and good people go to heaven when they die. For sure, we should appreciate the fact that the belief system of many emerging adults serves to discourage the type of bad behavior exhibited by the two youths on the bus referred to in chapter one. And yet Smith goes on to draw attention to a reason for concern. "Curiously," Smith says, "very few emerging adults—probably like many adults as well—are able to explain exactly why they think hurting others is morally wrong." When confronted with the fact that there are cultures in the world for whom hurting other people outside the in-group is not only not wrong but considered a good, many study participants simply shrugged it off in a nonplussed but ultimately unflappable manner.[56]

Once again, what seems to be at work here is a lack of moral sophistication (thoughtfulness). Instead, what we find among many emerging adults is a moral naiveté that, when combined with some other ethical attributes, can work against the very notion of a moral faithfulness.

The confused moral reasoning of emerging adults leads to an irresponsible approach to making ethical decisions. This is a bold accusation,

---

[54]Ibid.
[55]Ibid. p. 47.
[56]Ibid.

and I confess that Smith himself, though he comes close, does not actually use the term *irresponsible*. I'm using this term in order to locate under a broad category a host of ethical realities at work among many emerging adults. This will enable me, for the sake of expediency, to condense into one section a number of study findings presented at several different places in *Souls in Transition*. My readers will have to determine for themselves whether the charge of ethical irresponsibility is warranted by the three findings of the NSYR alluded to below.

First, the research indicates that most emerging adults are extraordinarily invested in the idea that "everybody's different," virtually ruling out any commonalities between individuals that can be considered universal or transcendental.[57] Smith is careful to make the point that the stimulus for this strong conviction "is not merely basic American individualism. It is individualism raised on heavy doses of multiculturalism and pumped up on the steroids of the postmodern insistence on disjuncture, *différance*, and differences 'going all the way down.'"[58]

Second, building on this crucial conviction, a majority of emerging adults are equally convinced that "the absolute authority for every person's beliefs or actions is his or her own sovereign self. Anybody can literally think or do whatever he or she wants."[59] Smith goes on to explain that virtually absent from the vocabulary of many emerging adults are such words as *duty, responsibility* and *obligation*. In fact, says Smith, when applied to morality, these concepts strike most young adults as "vaguely coercive and puritanical." One interview respondent put it this way: "I have no other way of knowing what to do morally but how I internally feel. That's where my decisions come from. From me, from inside me."[60]

It's hard to overstate the importance of how individualistic many young adults consider the ethical endeavor to be. While it's true that a significant number of emerging adults (40 percent) believe that moral

---

[57]Ibid., p. 46.

[58]Ibid., p. 48, emphasis original.

[59]Ibid., p. 49.

[60]Ibid. It should be noted how statements such as this seem redolent of the metaethical theory known as moral emotivism—a perspective that, as Arthur Holmes suggests, arose at least in part out of frustration with the persistence of moral arguments. See Arthur Holmes, *Ethics: Approaching Moral Decisions* (Downers Grove, IL: InterVarsity Press, 1984), p. 28.

right and wrong can be defined "primarily by *what other people would think about someone*" (in other words, how the moral agent would be perceived by his or her peers),[61] this interesting yet equally disturbing discovery does nothing to mitigate the fact that "most emerging adults view morality as ultimately a personal, relative affair: morally right and wrong beliefs depend entirely on the specifics of the case and the 'opinions' of the people involved. Not many grasp a strong sense of a natural or universal moral standard or law that in any way transcends human inventions."[62] So whether the ethical decision-making process employed by emerging adults simply involves going with their gut or taking into consideration how they would be perceived by their peers, in the end, the decision is theirs alone to make.

It's my contention that such a radical privatization and relativization of morality not only rules out any possibility of interpersonal critique, but it also works against a sense of interpersonal responsibility. This is indicated by a third finding of the NSYR, which reveals that yet another conviction held by a majority of young adults is that "nobody has any natural or general responsibility or obligation to help other people." Smith elaborates on this conviction so evocative of ethical egoism, indicating that "most of those interviewed said that it is nice if people help others, but that nobody has to. Taking care of other people in need is an individual's choice. If you want to do it, good. If you don't, that's up to you. You don't have to."[63] Even in cases of natural disasters, political oppression or those who are not in any way responsible for their poverty or disabilities, the young adults surveyed insisted: "If someone wants to help, then good for that person. But nobody has to."[64] According to Smith: "Some simply declared, 'That's not my problem.' Others said, 'I wish people would help others, but they really have no duty to do that at all. It's up to them, their opinion.'"[65]

---

[61]Smith et al., *Lost in Transition*, p. 37, emphasis original. See also Mueller, *Youth Culture 101*, pp. 264-65; Nullens and Michener, *Matrix of Christian Ethics*, p. 18. The reader will recall the discussion in chapter two of an ethical decision-making approach I referred to as "Guarding My Reputation."
[62]Smith, *Souls in Transition*, p. 51.
[63]Ibid, p. 68.
[64]Ibid.
[65]Ibid.

Smith concludes his treatment of this apparent ethical attribute of the emerging generations saying: "Again, any notion of the responsibilities of a common humanity, a transcendent call to protect the life and dignity of one's neighbor, or a moral responsibility to seek the common good was entirely absent among the respondents. In the end, each individual does what he or she wants and nobody has any moral leverage to persuade or compel him or her to do otherwise."[66]

Though the word *irresponsible* is not used by Smith and his team as they report on the highly individualistic and relativistic moral perspective of America's emerging adults, I would contend that the idea is certainly conveyed.

This leads me to offer the observation that one is able to sense in Smith's *summary* of the findings of the NSYR a bit of *commentary* as well. Indeed, the fact that Smith and his team approach the subject of morality from a perspective that is more biblically informed than that held by most members of the emerging generations can't help but bleed through the reporting provided in *Souls in Transition*. What's more, the concerns that are somewhat implicit in this book become much more explicit in the subsequent work, *Lost in Transition: The Dark Side of Emerging Adulthood*, written by Christian Smith along with Kari Christoffersen, Hilary Davidson and Patricia Snell Herzog. The very title attached to this third work based on the NSYR implies that some very real concerns for the spiritual health of the emerging generations lie behind its publication. It's to this even more cautious examination of the "troubling and heartbreaking problems"[67] at work in the lives of America's emerging adults that we turn our attention now.

Emerging Morality and the Criteria for a Healthy Moral Faithfulness Quotient

The first chapter of *Lost in Transition* is titled simply "Morality Adrift." What makes this discussion such a valuable resource for our purposes is the set of questions it examines: "How do emerging adults think about morality? How do they know what is moral? How do they make moral decisions? Where do they think moral rights and wrongs, goods and

---

[66]Ibid.
[67]Smith et al., *Lost in Transition*, p. 3.

bads, even come from? What is the source or basis of morality? And how important is it to emerging adults to choose what is morally good?"[68]

While some of the material presented in this more in-depth discussion of emerging morality repeats some of the observations put forward in *Souls in Transition,* the difference is that the declared goal of *Lost in Transition* is to boldly draw attention to what the authors consider to be the "the dark side of emerging adulthood." In other words, the latter work is an even more rock-ribbed analysis of some of the "troubling," "disturbing" and "depressing" dynamics at work in the lives of the emerging adults they've interviewed three times now.[69] Though Smith does not use the phrase *moral faithfulness* to describe the type of moral attitudes and actions he and his team would clearly like to prescribe, it's apparent that these researchers find disconcerting just how far away from what I'm referring to as a moral faithfulness most emerging adults are.

Thus, keeping in mind the presupposition that both a causal and correlative connection exists between the generations and remaining mindful also of what we've already learned from the analyses presented in *Soul Searching* and *Souls in Transition,* I believe it's possible to extrapolate from "Morality Adrift" a set of *criteria* by which all of us regardless of age might assess our own moral faithfulness quotient. The thesis of the final section of this chapter is that *it's by intentionally cultivating the ethical earmarks presented below that all of us can improve our readiness and capacity to hear and honor the heart of God, and more effectively model a moral faithfulness to those around us.* With this thought in mind, I've taken the liberty to follow up the brief discussion of each criterion with a set of reflection questions designed to enhance the reader's assessment experience.

Based on the NSYR, some important criteria for a healthy moral faithfulness quotient include:

A careful rather than cavalier attitude toward the moral dimension of life. We've already seen that a majority of emerging adults consider moral decision making easy, so easy they had difficulty remembering an occasion when they had to wrestle in a serious manner with anything like a moral dilemma. Thus it should come as no surprise to find that as Christian

---

[68]Ibid., p. 19.
[69]Ibid.

Smith and his coauthors[70] begin the critical analysis presented in *Lost in Transition* they warn their readers straightaway that they should not expect the "emerging adult thinking about morality (as with most of the rest of adult Americans)" to be "particularly consistent, coherent or articulate."[71] Later on in the discussion Smith and his team report that emerging adult thinking about moral matters "is not often rigorous or coherent" and that many of those interviewed "hold views that philosophers would say do not rationally belong together."[72] In other words, the research seems to indicate that, as was true in the case of the ethics student referred to in this book's introduction, not many emerging adults have given adequate thought to what morality is and how they go about making moral decisions.[73]

Once again we find Smith being careful to attribute this moral naiveté at least in part to a failure on the part of the adult world—the larger religio-cultural context in which the emerging generation is being so-cialized. According to Smith those belonging to the pre-emerging generations have failed to provide their sons, daughters, students and youth group members with the instruction and example a more substantial ethical life requires.[74] Indeed it's hard to imagine a more direct, causal connection between the generations than the one Smith and his team posit when they write: "But if these emerging adults are lost, it is because the larger culture and society into which they are being inducted is also lost. The forces of social reproduction here are powerful. That so many emerging adults today are adrift in their moral thinking . . . tells us that the adult world into which they are emerging is also adrift."[75]

Regardless of its source, however, the truth is that a lack of moral thoughtfulness does not bode well for the prospect of a moral faithfulness (whatever the generation). In real life, moral dilemmas happen, and making choices in a balanced and responsible manner in the face of them is always a challenging task. Hearing the heart of God and then honoring

---

[70]For the sake of convenience, when referring to the authors of *Lost in Transition*, I will refer to Christian Smith alone rather than include the names of his coresearchers/coauthors.
[71]Smith et al., *Lost in Transition*, p. 20.
[72]Ibid., p. 27.
[73]Ibid., p. 20.
[74]Ibid., p. 21.
[75]Ibid., p. 61.

it, given our fallen state, requires huge amounts of study, fact gathering, counsel seeking and prayer offered in a theologically (and pneumato-logically) real manner. A moral faithfulness before God requires a careful rather than cavalier attitude toward the moral dimension of life.

Some questions we can ask ourselves in order to gauge the level of our *moral thoughtfulness* are:

- When was the last time I really wrestled with a moral dilemma?

- If pressed, could I provide a coherent, articulate explanation of what a moral dilemma is and why, in a fallen world, moral dilemmas happen?

- Can I explain in a thoughtful manner the decision-making process I normally employ in order to resolve a moral dilemma?

- Honestly, to what degree do I tend to think that resolving a moral dilemma is a relatively easy thing to do?

A moral realism that works against a radical ethical relativism. Later in "Morality Adrift" Smith refers not only to a "less than robust grasp of moral issues" and the "weak moral reasoning" at work in the emerging generations but also to a "shaky commitment to the idea of moral truth."[76] This suggests that another concern of Smith and his team is that accom-panying the emerging generation's lack of moral thoughtfulness is a robust embrace of a fairly radical version of ethical relativism.

To be more precise, says Smith, "about three out of ten (30 percent) of the emerging adults we interviewed professed a belief in a strong moral relativism." Then in a parenthetical aside Smith notes that in the nationally representative survey the percentage was much higher: "47 percent of American emerging adults agreed that 'morals are relative, there are not definite rights and wrongs for everybody.'" Even with respect to moral issues such as slavery, a significant number of emerging adults hold that: "there are no real standards of right and wrong"; "morality changes radi-cally across history"; "morality is therefore nothing more than subjective personal opinion or cultural consensus at any given point in time." (The moral subjectivism and conventionalism described in chapter two seem

---

[76]Ibid., p. 35.

apparent here.) According to Smith, the rather virulent version of ethical relativism embraced by at least a third of America's emerging adults insists that morality has no real objective, natural, or universal basis outside of people's heads. Morality is purely a social construction.[77]

As for the rest of America's emerging adults, the news appears to be mixed (from the perspective of someone promoting the pursuit of a moral faithfulness). The good news to be deduced from the research is that two-thirds of those interviewed appear not to be "strong moral relativists; they stopped short of that radical position." The bad news is that this doesn't mean that these emerging adults who "wish to resist the radical implications of a strong moral relativism" are committed moral realists (or absolutists). Instead, says Smith, they should probably be thought of as "reluctant moral agnostics and skeptics." For, while a majority of the emerging adults don't indicate an embrace of a "total moral relativism," neither can they "clearly explain or defend the moral claims that they wished to make or say why moral relativism is actually wrong."[78]

Another way to express this concern is to say that not only does the moral thinking of many emerging adults lack lucidity, also absent from it is the kind of moral realism that steels against a radical moral relativism. Unfortunately, the type of moral relativism that is either aggressively embraced or reluctantly tolerated by significant numbers of emerging adults is at odds with a moral faithfulness that holds not only that God is the transcendent source of morality but that his heart concerning this or that moral matter can and should be known.

Some questions we can ask ourselves to gauge our commitment to a *moral realism* are:

- Honestly, to what degree am I tempted, deep down inside, to accept my culture's commitment to the idea that morality has no real objective, natural or universal basis outside people's heads?

- In what specific ways does my everyday manner of living reflect a serious commitment to the belief that God is a moral being who cares about how human beings made in his image behave toward him, other

[77]Ibid., p. 27.
[78]Ibid., p. 29.

human beings, themselves and the rest of creation?

- To what degree am I, at this point in my life, able to offer a lucid explanation as to why I believe that God's heart regarding moral matters is knowable by those who bear his image?

A commitment to a moral accountability rather than autonomy. So, if a theologically based moral realism is missing from the thinking of huge numbers of emerging adults, on what basis *are* their ethical decisions being made? The actual phrase utilized in *Lost in Transition* for this crucial characteristic is "moral individualism." According to Smith and his team, some sixty percent of the emerging adults interviewed expressed a highly individualistic approach to morality. According to these young adults, "morality is a personal choice, entirely a matter of individual decision. Moral rights and wrongs are essentially matters of individual opinion."[79]

What we are talking about here is a strong commitment to moral autonomy: the right to decide for oneself what is right or wrong over against any sort of transcendent moral standard to which we might be accountable. Once again, it's apparent that there's little room in the lives of most emerging adults for a moral realism that holds that there are such things as knowable, objective moral realities that are true and authoritative regardless of how we feel about them. Instead, for many young adults right and wrong behaviors are subjectively established by individual moral agents on the basis of what they think (and how they feel) about everyday ethical actions.[80]

As was observed in *Souls in Transition,* ruling out as it does the need to take seriously any notion of moral accountability or responsibility, one of the principal ways such a strong commitment to the notion of individual moral sovereignty manifests itself in the lives of the emerging generations is in an equally strong reticence to judge or even assess the moral actions of others. According to Smith and his team, "a strong theme among these moral individualists . . . is a belief that it is wrong for people

---

[79]Ibid., p. 21.

[80]Smith et al. are careful to indicate that a huge difference exists between "(a) moral claims (that are objectively true) being *embraced* subjectively by individuals through a process in which those individuals come to believe them, versus (b) moral claims taking on quasi-true *status* for certain individuals as a result of those individuals believing them to be true." See *Lost in Transition*, pp. 22-23.

to morally judge other people. Each person has to decide for themselves. Nobody else can tell anyone else what to think or do." Indeed, according to many emerging adults, the real problem in contemporary society is not immoral people but those who dare to voice an opinion about the moral actions of others. Smith explains this ethical earmark this way: "In this world of moral individualism, then, anyone can hold their own convictions about morality, but they also must keep those views private. Giving voice to one's own moral views is itself nearly immoral."[81]

In response to this ethical earmark, the authors of *Lost in Transition* are careful to point out that "to judge" doesn't have to connote the idea of condemnation; it can also mean "to assess, discern, estimate, appraise, weigh, evaluate, and critique." They observe, furthermore, that each of these assessing actions "can be done with great humility, openness, reciprocity, care, and even love for the idea or person being judged," rather than in an arrogant, self-righteous, self-serving manner.[82] Thus it seems to prove disappointing to Smith and his team that the commitment to a moral autonomy on the part of many emerging adults is such that any sort of interpersonal critique is considered by them to be completely unjustified and unacceptable.

I'm able to tease out of this discussion several reasons for this sense of disappointment on the part of the authors of *Lost in Transition*. First, just to be clear, it's not that Smith and his team are eager to encourage a mean-spirited moral judgmentalism. Rather it appears they are concerned about the faulty moral reasoning that stands behind this reticence to assess the ethical actions of others. According to these authors: "To try to avoid being *judgmental* is good, by our judgment. But to try for morally grounded reasons to avoid all assessment, evaluation, and criticism of every moral belief and behavior is not only ironic, it is impossible and self-defeating."[83]

Moreover, Smith and his team also seem to be concerned that the antipathy of many young adults toward any sort of assessment of the moral behaviors of their peers, in addition to being intellectually shallow, is ultimately self-serving. The truth is that the conviction that it's never appro-

---

[81]Ibid. pp. 23-24.
[82]Ibid.
[83]Ibid.

priate for us to judge anyone else's moral actions can actually be rooted in a self-serving desire to avoid accountability ourselves. We must keep in mind that a cardinal core belief of MTD, so influential among this demographic, is that the central goal of life is narcissistic in orientation: to be happy and to feel good about oneself. Indeed, Smith and his team report that in response to the survey (and interview question) "If you were unsure of what was right or wrong in a particular situation, how would you decide what to do?" the most frequently chosen answer was "doing what would make [me] feel happy."[84] (This seems to be reflective of the less-than-enlightened version of ethical egoism described in chapter two.) Given the narcissistic nature of this approach to making ethical decisions, it's not unreasonable to suspect that Smith and his team might be justified in their concern regarding the real motivation behind the reticence of young adults to assess the propriety of their peers' moral behaviors. I would add that regardless of their motivation, such individualistic and relativistic beliefs and attitudes can't help but work against the ideas central to a moral faithfulness: that it's possible to hear and honor the heart of God and important to do so.

And yet there is an even more disturbing reason why Smith and his team appear disappointed at the lack of moral accountability present in the lives of many emerging adults. The research seems to indicate that an extreme commitment to *moral autonomy* among this demographic some-times manifests itself in a *moral apathy* as well. According to Smith, the same beliefs and attitudes that drive the antipathy toward judging the moral behaviors of others can also result in the adoption of a less-than-empathetic attitude toward the suffering of others. There's a fine line be-tween a "live-and-let-live" lifestyle and a "live-and-let-die" approach to one's moral responsibility toward other human beings. Sadly the research reveals that a significant minority of emerging adults have not sufficiently made this distinction in their moral development. Instead, the embrace of a moral individualism has produced the belief that "since each person is responsible to take care of themselves, no person is particularly morally responsible to help other people in need."[85] While the research doesn't necessarily indicate that such a moral apathy is widespread among

---

[84]Ibid., pp. 50-51.
[85]Ibid., p. 25, emphasis original.

emerging adults, the fact that an embrace of a moral autonomy can produce such an attitude at all indicates just how contrary to a moral faithfulness such an ethical earmark is.

So, with all of this in mind, some questions we can ask ourselves to gauge the level of our *moral accountability* are:

- To what degree do I resent the idea that I'm accountable to God for my moral actions?

- To what degree do I resent the idea that I'm responsible to other human beings for how I behave?

- Could it be that driving my indignation at the moral judgmentalism of others is a self-serving desire to safeguard my own moral autonomy?

- How would I explain to someone my belief regarding one's responsibility to care for other human beings in dire need?

A commitment to Christ that enables a moral consistency rather than compromise. By all appearances it would seem that very few of those emerging adults who profess any sort of allegiance to Christianity can accurately be described as Christian "disciples." In a chapter titled "Six Religious Types," the authors of *Souls in Transition* make the observation that only 15 percent of the total emerging population "embrace a strong religious faith, whose beliefs they can reasonably articulate and which they actively practice." These are young adults for whom "personal commitment to faith is a significant part of their identities and moral reasoning," and who are "at least somewhat regularly involved in some religious group."[86] Now if it's true that only 15 percent of emerging adults seem to be genuinely committed to their religious faith, and not everyone within this segment of the emerging population self-identifies as Christian, then the conclusion is inescapable: *very few emerging adults can accurately be described as genuine Christian disciples.*

The fact that, as Kenda Creasy Dean puts it, an "almost Christianity" is so very prevalent among churchgoing teens and young adults, is another reality that doesn't bode well for the prospect of a moral faithfulness. Indeed an important issue that's discussed in "Morality Adrift"

---

[86]Smith, *Souls in Transition*, p. 166.

and that might be seen as a direct result of the discipleship deficit apparently at work in the emerging generations has to do with the phenomenon of *moral compromise.*

Let's be clear about what we are and are not talking about here. What's at issue here is not the occasional need to resolve an ethical dilemma by carefully, agonizingly choosing between competing moral imperatives.[87] When Smith and his team speak of "moral compromise" they're referring to the fact that "one in three (34 percent) of those interviewed said they might do certain things *they* considered morally wrong if they knew they could get away with it." What's at issue here is an *abject* moral compromise (or *intentional immorality*) where the moral agent violates his or her own conscience in a deliberate, opportunistic manner. According to Smith and his team, a disturbing number of emerging adults interviewed acknowledged that they have or might engage in such behaviors as lying, cheating and stealing if they could do so without getting caught. The rationale offered for such behavior included the following arguments: (1) a dog-eat-dog world sometimes requires it; (2) everybody does it; (3) even adults teach and encourage it; (4) it's often the easiest course of action; (5) it sometimes brings better benefits to the moral agent; and (6) the experience of financial hardship justifies it.[88]

What I'm suggesting is that the phenomenon of *abject moral compromise* is thoroughly incompatible with a Christian ethic that takes the notion of following Christ seriously. Such an approach to morality might find backing in a belief system such as Moralistic Therapeutic Deism where the sovereignty of the self, the narcissistic pursuit of personal success and happiness, and the radical relativization of morality are guiding principles. However, there are way too many passages in the New Testament that speak of the importance of Christ's followers guarding the condition of their consciences (for their own sake and that of the mission) for the practice of abject moral compromise to ever be considered an appropriate behavior for a Christian disciple.[89]

---

[87]Smith et al., *Lost in Transition*, p. 56.

[88]Ibid., pp. 47-50, emphasis added. For more on the practice of lying and cheating among what he refers to as midadolescents, see Chap Clark, *Hurt 2.0* (Grand Rapids: Baker, 2011), pp. 145-52.

[89]For example, see Acts 24:16; Rom 13:5; 1 Cor 8:7-13; 1 Tim 1:5, 18-20; 4:1-2; 2 Tim 1:3; Titus 1:15; Heb 9:6-14; 10:19-22; 13:18; 1 Pet 3:13-16.

To be sure, Smith and his team go out of their way to stipulate that it's not a majority of emerging adults who seem to be comfortable with abject moral compromise (intentional immorality).[90] Still, they're obviously troubled by the discovery that a "significant minority" are. It's my contention that such a finding should prove disconcerting to anyone interested in promoting a moral faithfulness.

Therefore, some questions we can ask ourselves to gauge the level of our commitment to a Christian discipleship that engenders a *moral consistency* are:

- Honestly, how committed am I to the lordship of Christ? How do my daily activities reflect this?

- Honestly, how committed am I to growing in my understanding of the moral faithfulness of Jesus and embodying it myself?

- How would I explain to someone what it means to live a life surrendered to both the authority of Scripture and the leadership of the Holy Spirit?

- How would I explain to someone the huge difference between resolving a genuine moral dilemma and engaging in abject moral compromise?

- Honestly, am I as careful as the Bible says I should be about guarding the condition of my conscience?

The aim of this chapter has been to encourage readers to, having taken stock of the cultural soup we're all swimming in, assess their readiness and capacity to hear and honor the heart of God. Toward this end, we've taken a rather careful look at the National Survey of Youth and Religion and three books written by the study's main director, Christian Smith, along with various research team members. The presupposition at work here, which is supported by the NSYR's findings, is that the spiritual and moral condition of America's teens and emerging adults is actually a telling indication of the effect that a certain religio-cultural environment has had on huge numbers of Americans, their generational status notwithstanding.

While the picture the NSYR presents is not entirely bad, it's definitely not good. With respect to the topic at hand—Christian ethics—the survey and interview evidence seem to suggest that most emerging

---

[90]Smith et al., *Lost in Transition*, p. 50.

adults currently possess a very, very low moral faithfulness quotient.

Again, what do we do with this information?

It may have occurred to the astute reader that the criteria for a healthy moral faithfulness quotient presented here align loosely with the book's distinctive themes as indicated in its introduction. By way of review, these themes include: the possibility of a theological (and pneumatological) realism, the possibility of a moral realism, the need for an approach to ethical decision making that's balanced and responsible rather than unbalanced and irresponsible, and the need to ground Christian ethics in the life of Christian discipleship. The point I'm trying to make here is that the findings of the NSYR lend some serious support for the presuppositions at work in this book. Thus, having drawn attention in this chapter to what a moral faithfulness does and doesn't look like, and the need for nearly all of us to cultivate a higher moral faithfulness quotient, the rest of the book comprises an attempt to help its readers actually accomplish this.

I'm convinced that it's possible for everyone reading *Pursuing Moral Faithfulness* to avoid an "almost Christianity" and raise their moral IQ. The religio-cultural soup we're all swimming in doesn't have to define us. That being said, let's turn our attention now to part two of the book and its argument for the ethic of responsible Christian discipleship.

Part Two

TOWARD
A MORAL
FAITHFULNESS

Integrating Balance and
Responsibility into Our Ethical Lives

More on a Moral Realism (1)

The Moral Guidelines *the Scriptures Provide*

Andy Le Peau of InterVarsity Press asserts that one way for authors to keep readers reading is to set up a problem of some sort but then not give the answer right away. Instead, "the solution is revealed step by step throughout the book or article." He goes on to indicate that "in a book, the set-up may even take a chapter or two before the remedy is slowly laid out."

Why this literary tack? Le Peau explains:

> After describing the problem people face, the author might discuss Solution A, but show why that doesn't work. Then Solution B is considered, but that also fails. Likewise Solution C. Now readers are really ready for the answer that solves the problem. They are thinking, "If those three seemingly reasonable solutions don't work, then what does?" They are motivated to know.[1]

The fact that I've taken this technique to heart will be apparent to anyone still reading this book.[2] Having laid out the problem in the introduction and chapter one, having explored some possible but ultimately ineffective solutions to the problem in chapters two and three, and having helped the reader engage in some moral and spiritual self-assessment in chapter four, I'm ready now to begin laying out "the answer that solves the problem" in

---

[1]Andy LePeau, "One Way to Keep Readers Reading," *Andy Unedited* (blog), August 9, 2013, http://andyunedited.ivpress.com/2013/08/one_way_to_keep_readers_re.php.

[2]I'm not suggesting that I've employed this literary technique in a perfect manner, just that there was a method to my madness!

the remaining chapters that make up *Pursuing Moral Faithfulness*. My goal will be to accomplish this literary reveal doing my best to keep integrating the practical with the theoretical every step of the way.

As I've been indicating since the very beginning of this project, the key to a moral faithfulness is something I refer to as the *ethic of responsible Christian discipleship*. Assuming it might be helpful to do so, I've provided below a chart (figure 5.1) that locates this preferred moral model on the landscape of ethical options we've surveyed so far.

LOCATING THE ETHIC OF RESPONSIBLE CHRISTIAN DISCIPLESHIP ON THE ETHICAL LANDSCAPE		
Results-Oriented Approaches (Teleological)	*A Results/Rules/Virtues-Oriented Approach (Prophetic Contextualism)*	*Rules-Oriented Approaches (Deontological)*
• ethical egosim • moral subjectivism • naive moral intuitionism • moral conventionalism • utilitarianism • situationism	• the ethic of responsible Christian discipleship	• moral universalism • nonconflicting absolutism • conflicting absolutism • graded absolutism
◄ Relativistic	*Metaethical Ethos*	Absolutist ►

Figure 5.1

The reader will notice that I've introduced into this graphic portrayal of the ethical landscape a third ethical category that combines a focus on rules, results and virtues in a holistic manner. Under this third category, to which I've assigned the name "prophetic contextualism," I've subsumed the moral model I'm referring to in this work as the ethic of responsible Christian discipleship. The goal here is simply to convey the idea that there exists a version of moral contextualism that really shouldn't be put in the same category as situationism. Though this ethical option doesn't absolutize all the moral imperatives found in the Bible (thus avoiding the designation of legalism), it does recognize that according to the Scriptures there are multiple moral absolutes at work in our world. It goes on to insist that a moral faithfulness occurs when the moral agent, with God's help, contextualizes these transcendent moral principles in this or that life situation.[3]

Though this is an overly simplified introduction to the ethic of responsible Christian discipleship, it's a start. The long-awaited process of fully laying out this solution to the *problem* of a moral faithfulness begins with a couple of short chapters designed to make the case for a moral realism— why we should believe that discerning the heart of God is theoretically doable. The focus of this chapter, in particular, is on the moral guidance the Scriptures provide.

OVERVIEW: THE CONCEPT OF A PROPHETIC CASUISTRY

The notion that the Bible provides us with transcendent moral guidelines that can and should be applied in contemporary ethical situations is much debated. In part one of this work we learned that ethicists traditionally differentiate between a *deontological* approach to ethics that focuses on rules and one's duty to obey them, and a *teleological* approach that emphasizes goals or consequences. It stands to reason that the various teleological (results-oriented) theories would be averse to the idea of biblically prescribed moral rules. Though it's possible to distinguish between a moral principle and a moral rule, it's argued by many ethicists that morality will be *either* people-centered *or* principle-driven. Framing the discussion in such a manner usually has the effect of creating a bias toward the former approach over the latter. Who wants to be guilty of prioritizing principles over people?

---

[3]It should be pointed out that while my use of the concept of ethical responsibility has much in common with H. Richard Niebuhr's famous use of the term, it also differs in an important respect. While I appreciate Niebuhr's insistence that moral responsibility involves answering the question "What shall I do?" by posing the crucial question "What is going on?" toward the end of discerning the "fitting action," Niebuhr tends to argue for the "ethic of responsibility" in a manner that has little or no room in it for deontological and/or teleological interplay (see H. Richard Niebuhr, *The Responsible Self: An Essay in Christian Moral Philosophy* [New York: Harper & Row, 1963], pp. 60-61). I should also point out that a significant difference exists between the ethic of responsible Christian discipleship presented in these pages and the ethic of responsibility promoted by Hans Jonas—an ethic that possesses a special focus on the dangers of technology and concomitant need for human beings to exercise responsibility toward the future of humanity and nature, indeed, all that exists. For an extended discussion of Jonas's ethic of responsibility, see Patrick Nullens and Ronald T. Michener, *The Matrix of Christian Ethics: Integrating Philosophy and Moral Theology in a Postmodern Context* (Downers Grove, IL: IVP Books, 2010), pp. 86-91.

However, in his book *Freedom for Obedience: Evangelical Ethics for Contemporary Times,* evangelical theologian Donald Bloesch suggests that, rather than focus on the distinction between deontological and teleological ethics, it's actually more helpful to differentiate between *philosophical* ethics, where the "focus is on the possibilities resident in humanity," and *theological* ethics, which "appeals to a definitive revelation of God in the sacred history mirrored in the Bible."[4] The former, says Bloesch, is anthropocentric: the "right" or "best" thing to do in any moral dilemma is in one way or another both discerned and achieved by human means. The latter is theocentric and Christocentric in orientation: the "right" thing to do with respect to any moral matter is determined by a divine command provided by "Jesus Christ, the God-man, the Word made flesh" that is situation specific.[5] Framing the discussion in this way serves to elevate the importance of paying attention to moral principles, which are viewed now not as human constructions but as divine commands.

But the question then becomes: How is this situation-specific divine command discerned? Is it the result of our having located in the Bible a moral rule or principle that seems to apply to the matter at hand and then slapping it into play in Jesus' name?[6] Or does it come to us by some other means, perhaps some sort of Christian moral intuition ingrained within us as a result of our spiritual formation?[7] For different reasons, both of these options seem problematic. The first seems too similar to a crass absolutism (that is, legalism); the second too redolent of a sanctified situationism (or naive moral intuitionism).

Having surveyed the difference of opinion that exists among various proponents of a theological ethic with respect to the validity of universal

---

[4]See Donald Bloesch, *Freedom for Obedience: Evangelical Ethics for Contemporary Times* (San Francisco: Harper & Row, 1987), p. 19.

[5]See ibid., pp. 19-20. See also Scott Rae, *Moral Choices: An Introduction to Ethics,* 3rd ed. (Grand Rapids: Zondervan, 2009), p. 47.

[6]See Carl F. Henry, *Christian Personal Ethics* (Grand Rapids: Eerdmans, 1957), p. 301. See also Lewis Smedes, *Mere Morality: What God Expects from Ordinary People* (Grand Rapids: Eerdmans, 1983), p. 6.

[7]See James M. Gustafson, *Ethics from a Theocentric Perspective* (Chicago: University of Chicago Press, 1981), pp. 112-13; Gustafson, *Christ and the Moral Life* (New York: Harper & Row, 1968), p. 268; and Gustafson, *Christian Ethics and the Community* (Philadelphia: United Church Press, 1971), p. 99. See also William C. Spohn, *What Are They Saying About Scripture and Ethics?* (New York: Paulist, 1984), pp. 76-77.

principles, Bloesch proceeds to make his case for what he refers to as a "prophetic casuistry"—the idea that there are moral principles presented in sacred Scripture that, with the help of the Spirit, can and should be applied to contemporary ethical situations on a case-by-case basis.[8] Bloesch describes this mediating position thusly:

> In contradistinction to absolutist ethics on the one hand and existentialist [situational] ethics on the other, I propose the alternative of casuistic ethics. I am advocating, however, not a legalistic casuistry . . . but a prophetic casuistry in which the Word of God takes on concreteness and specificity through *faithful hearing*.
>
> Casuistry can be defined as the attempt to apply absolute norms to concrete cases. It deals with mediating principles that carry the force of divine authority. These principles cannot be universalized, but they also cannot be reduced to maxims or guidelines, which are not really binding.[9]

Becoming even more specific, Bloesch explains:

> Evangelical casuistry is the attempt to discern the will of God for a specific situation. We do not begin with abstract norms but with God's self-revelation in Jesus Christ. We see the norms and principles of both the Old and New Testaments exemplified and embodied in the life, death, and resurrection of Jesus Christ.
>
> Casuistry deals with principles and rules of conduct. Evangelical casuistry focuses on directives given by the Spirit of God to the church that enable us to act both faithfully and intelligently in the situation in which we find ourselves. The commandment of God is applied to the way we live in the world of our time.[10]

Now the Christ-centered and Spirit-enabled or "prophetic" aspect of this moral guidance needs to be noted. Bloesch is not proposing that there are universal moral guidelines that are binding on Christians apart from the authority of Jesus Christ and agency of the Holy Spirit. According to Bloesch, the person of Christ is our source of moral guidance. Any moral principles we discern in Scripture should be viewed as "conditional, not unconditional imperatives." To do otherwise, says Bloesch, is to "tie down the freedom of God to an eternal principle."[11]

---

[8]See Bloesch, *Freedom for Obedience*, pp. 50-55.
[9]Ibid., p. 55, emphasis added.
[10]Ibid., pp. 55-56.
[11]Ibid., p. 57.

While I understand this philosophical/theological concern—that God not be viewed as a prisoner to a principle external to himself—and very much appreciate the mediating approach Bloesch has taken with respect to the usefulness of moral principles, I will argue in the next few pages for yet a different possibility. It's my suggestion that there exist a few transcendent moral principles that, because they're grounded in the character and actions of God the Father and phenomenally embodied in the moral faithfulness of Christ the Son, can be viewed as eternal and absolute without making God a prisoner to a principle extrinsic to himself.[12] At the same time the manner in which these moral principles or guidelines are applied to contemporary situations does require, as Bloesch indicates, a *prophetic* encounter with the risen Christ through the Holy Spirit, who provides us with the guidance (command) and empowerment (promise) we need to be able to hear and honor the heart of our trinitarian God.

Excursus: Two Ways of
Understanding the Prophetic Phenomenon

The reference above to the possibility of a "prophetic" encounter with Christ through the Spirit necessitates a brief sidebar discussion. Throughout the remainder of *Pursuing Moral Faithfulness* I refer to such concepts as "prophetic capacity" and "prophetic moral guidance." I want to explain here how I'm making use of the term *prophetic* and why.

In general the Scriptures seem to describe the prophetic phenomenon as occurring in two stages. The first stage is charismatic in nature and involves *discernment*—the Spirit enabling the prophet to somehow "hear" from God so as to receive a message and/or ministry assignment from him. The second stage is confrontational in nature and involves *deployment*—the Spirit empowering the prophet to speak and/or act into the lives of people on God's behalf. Most often these two aspects of the prophetic phenomenon occur in tandem: the prophet hears from God, then speaks and/or acts on behalf of God.[13] It's

---

[12]For a helpful discussion of this philosophical problem, see Scott Smith's discussion of the Euthyphro dilemma in R. Scott Smith, *In Search of Moral Knowledge: Overcoming the Fact-Value Dichotomy* (Downers Grove, IL: IVP Academic, 2014), pp. 31-35. See also Robertson McQuilkin and Paul Copan, *An Introduction to Biblical Ethics: Walking in the Way of Wisdom*, 3rd ed. (Downers Grove, IL: IVP Academic, 2014), pp. 69-70.

[13]For more on this dual understanding of prophetic activity, including the biblical support for it, see

because the Scriptures refer to the prophetic phenomenon in both a discernment and deployment sense that I feel justified in doing likewise.[14]

In subsequent sections of *Pursuing Moral Faithfulness* I'll provide more thorough discussions of the biblical case for a prophetic moral guidance that's charismatic in nature, and how this does and doesn't occur in the daily lives of Christ's followers. While this will be the primary way I'll use the word *prophetic* in this work, I'll also provide at various points along the way indications of how equally apropos the prophetic dynamic in its deployment or confrontational sense is to the ethic of responsible Christian discipleship.

To clarify, what I'm proposing is a theologically real approach to ethical decision making that takes seriously: (1) the fact that the Bible does seem to provide its readers with some transcendent, authoritative moral guidelines, and (2) the possibility of Christ-centered, Spirit-enabled moral guidance and empowerment. Again, we will address the latter reality in chapter six. But before we discuss the manner in which the Holy Spirit enables us to apply to contemporary ethical situations the authoritative moral guidelines the Bible provides, let's devote a few pages to the critical task of identifying what these abiding, transcendent moral principles are.

THE KEY ROLE MICAH 6:8 PLAYS IN A MORAL FAITHFULNESS

Many Christian ethicists will acknowledge the ethical significance of the Ten Commandments and the Sermon on the Mount.[15] However, in

---

Gary Tyra, *The Holy Spirit in Mission: Prophetic Speech and Action in Christian Witness* (Downers Grove, IL: IVP Academic, 2011).

[14]Those familiar with the work of Old Testament scholar Walter Brueggemann will be aware that the main, if not only, way he refers to the prophetic dynamic is in the second (deployment) sense. Early in his book *The Prophetic Imagination*, Brueggemann states his thesis thusly: *"The task of prophetic ministry is to nurture, nourish, and evoke a consciousness and perception alternative to the consciousness and perception of the dominant culture around us"* (Walter Brueggemann, *The Prophetic Imagination*, 2nd ed. [Minneapolis: Fortress, 2001], p. 3, emphasis original). In other words, Brueggemann's understanding of prophetic seems to center in the dynamic of confrontation: the role of the prophet is to challenge the enculturation of the faith community and steer it toward a greater faithfulness vis-à-vis its tradition. While I'm certainly able to endorse the type of prophetic ministry Brueggemann advocates (i.e., his use of the term *prophetic* in its *deployment* or confrontational sense), I also feel justified, given the two ways the Scriptures speak of the prophetic phenomenon, to refer to "prophetic capacity" and "prophetic moral guidance" in its *discernment* or charismatic sense.

[15]In his survey of the ethical approaches put forward by various Christian theologians, Donald Bloesch cites their respective understandings of the value of these two passages in particular. See Bloesch, *Freedom for Obedience*, pp. 54, 60, 129, 142, 189-91, 217.

Micah 6:8 we find a biblical passage that, in the process of clearly re-
vealing God's concern for moral matters, provides an explicit indication
of three key behaviors/virtues a moral faithfulness will require.[16] Set
within its immediate context this powerful passage reads:

> With what shall I come before the LORD
>   and bow down before the exalted God?
> Shall I come before him with burnt offerings,
>   with calves a year old?
> Will the LORD be pleased with thousands of rams,
>   with ten thousand rivers of olive oil?
> Shall I offer my firstborn for my transgression,
>   the fruit of my body for the sin of my soul?
> *He has shown you, O mortal, what is good.*
> *And what does the LORD require of you?*
> *To act justly and to love mercy*
>   *and to walk humbly with your God.* (Mic 6:6-8)

It should be noted that, understood within its immediate context (the
book of Micah) and its larger context within the Hebrew Scriptures as a
whole, this clarion call for God's people to honor him by *acting justly*
(Hebrew: *ʿăśôt mišpāṭ*—that is, "to make just judgments," "to act fairly"),
loving mercy (Hebrew: *ʾahăbat ḥesed*—that is, "to love [with] kindness,
mercy") and *walking humbly before God* (Hebrew: *haṣĕnēaʿ lēkēt ʿim
ʾĕlōhêkā*—that is, "to humbly go with, walk before, follow after, be faithful
to God") goes beyond the ceremonial laws articulated in the Torah,
achieving something of a transcendent, summative status in the process.[17]

---

[16]The connection between behaviors and virtues suggested here is supported by the fact that virtue
theorists such as Joseph Kotva are prone to speak of virtues as both "means to and constituent elements of the human *telos* [i.e., what it means to be a good, authentic or efficient human being]" (*The
Christian Case for Virtue Ethics* [Washington, DC: Georgetown University Press, 1996], p. 22). See
also William K. Frankena, *Ethics*, 2nd ed. (Englewood Cliffs, NJ: Prentice-Hall, 1973), pp. 65-67,
and Rae, *Moral Choices*, p. 96.

[17]Two extensive discussions of what the Old Testament prophets, such as Micah, had in mind when
they referred to "justice" can be found in Paul Ramsey, *Basic Christian Ethics* (Chicago: University
of Chicago Press, 1980), pp. 2-24; and Smedes, *Mere Morality*, pp. 23-33.

Many Christian scholars have sought to demonstrate how, despite the discontinuities that must be
taken into account, a biblically informed Christian ethic can and should be informed by the Old
Testament Scriptures. For example, see W. H. Bellinger Jr., "The Old Testament: Source Book for
Christian Ethics," in *Understanding Christian Ethics: An Interpretive Approach*, ed. William M. Tillman
Jr. (Nashville: Broadman, 1988), pp. 35-58. While my approach to the use of Old Testament ethical

In other words, these three moral behaviors/virtues (collectively referred to by the prophet as the "good") seem to transcend even the specific moral commands articulated in the Decalogue (Ten Commandments), providing a stunning summary of the kind of moral behavior God is ultimately looking for.[18] Indeed, I will go even further and suggest that the prophet (under the anointing of the Holy Spirit) has provided us a glimpse of some cardinal moral virtues that, because they comprise the "good," can be understood as deriving from the very character of God.[19]

Some anticipated concerns regarding this focus on Micah 6:8. Fully cognizant of how reductionistic this line of thinking might appear to be, I should probably address a couple of anticipated concerns straightaway. First, I'm not intending to suggest that the specific virtues/behaviors specified in Micah 6:8 are the only ones presented in Scripture as indicative of God's moral concerns. It's simply my contention that all the moral behaviors commended in the Scriptures can be accurately subsumed under the three categories of acting justly, loving with mercy and walking humbly/faithfully before God.[20]

Second, while I do believe it's possible to understand these cardinal moral virtues—justice, loving mercy and humility/faithfulness—as de-

---

material when doing Christian ethics differs slightly from the one advocated by Bellinger, we're on the same page with respect to the utility of Old Testament ethical material for Christian ethics.

[18]See Michael F. Bird, *Evangelical Theology: A Biblical and Systematic Introduction* (Grand Rapids: Zondervan, 2013), p. 53.

[19]Nullens and Michener lend support for this argument, stating: "Goodness is a descriptive quality of God's character, and his essence provides the basic structure for his creation. The good [as referred to in Micah 6:8] is not some independently existing thing that God serves. This is a confusion of categories. In this sense something is neither good because God loves it—as if something is arbitrarily good whenever God decides it to be—nor does God love something because there is some prior ontological goodness. Instead, goodness is inherently an aspect of God's character from all eternity, and he is the source of anything ascribed the attribute of goodness" (Nullens and Michener, *Matrix of Christian Ethics*, p. 154). See also Dennis Hollinger, *Choosing the Good: Christian Ethics in a Complex World* (Grand Rapids: Baker Academic, 2002), pp. 64-68.

[20]I'm associating the virtue of faithfulness with humility for a couple of reasons. First, passages such as 1 Kings 2:4 suggest that to walk faithfully before God and to walk humbly before him, both referred to as divine requirements, are essentially synonymous actions (cf. Gen 17:1; 1 Kings 8:25; 9:4; 2 Chron 7:17; Ps 101:6). Second, it's my contention that faithfulness is how the third virtue referred to in Micah 6:8 is manifested by God himself in his relation to the other. Support for this association can be found in theologian Michael Bird's listing of faithfulness as one of the communicable divine attributes—that is, those divine attributes that can be replicated in human beings. Says Bird: "Faithfulness remains a cardinal virtue of the Christian life since it expresses a key trait of God's own character (1 Cor 4:2; Col 1:5; 2 Tim 2:22)" (Bird, *Evangelical Theology*, pp. 134-35).

riving from the character of God himself (all three being understood as crucial aspects of the interpersonal relations eternally existent within the Trinity),[21] my position is neither that Micah 6:8 is the only biblical passage by means of which it's possible to glimpse indications of God's moral character, nor that this single passage should be viewed as presenting us with an exhaustive list of the moral qualities that originate in God. While I do believe that this passage is telling us something important about God in terms of his essential character, theological humility (see 1 Cor 13:12) requires an acknowledgment that it's theoretically possible for God to possess morally significant character traits (generative virtues) in addition to justice, loving mercy and faithfulness.[22]

The positive case for the significance of Micah 6:8. These two caveats notwithstanding, a positive case can be made for the idea that Micah 6:8 can and should play a key role in Christian ethics.

Support for the concept of "cardinal" virtues. To begin, we must acknowledge the fact that the concept of "cardinal" virtues is well known in Christian ethics.[23] For example, ethicist Robin Lovin speaks of cardinal virtues as those that "people need to develop in order to live by whatever other virtues are important for them."[24] Lovin goes on to explain that "the idea of the cardinal virtues rests on the insight that we have to acquire some habits in the way we live out our virtues in order to have any virtue work over the long run. Those habits on which the other virtues turn are them-

---

[21]For more on the topic of intratrinitarian relationships, see Bird, *Evangelical Theology*, pp. 118-24. See also Timothy Keller, *The Reason for God: Belief in an Age of Skepticism* (New York: Dutton, 2008), pp. 217-18; and Gregory A. Boyd, *Repenting of Religion: Turning from Judgment to the Love of God* (Grand Rapids: Baker, 2004), pp. 25-26.

[22]Robert M. Adams states: "The realm of value is organized around a transcendent Good.... The Good is transcendent in the sense that it vastly surpasses all other good things, and all our conceptions of the good. They are profoundly imperfect in comparison with the Good itself. This is an aspect of the opposition of the transcendence thesis to antirealism about value. If the Good so surpasses all we understand, it has properties that go beyond anything that we have any way of conceiving or any basis for believing. There must therefore be a distinction, and not merely in principle, between what is true about it and what we conceive or believe or have reason to believe about it. And that is the sort of distinction that is postulated by metaphysical realism about any subject" (Robert Merrihew Adams, *Finite and Infinite Goods: A Framework for Ethics* [New York: Oxford University Press, 2002], p. 50).

[23]Actually, such a concern shows up in Christian theology as well. For example, see Michael Bird's discussion of the three attributes he believes "captures the essence of God's character and being" in Bird, *Evangelical Theology*, p. 139.

[24]See Robin Lovin, *Christian Ethics: An Essential Guide* (Nashville: Abingdon, 2000), p. 69.

selves virtues."[25] I'm suggesting that Micah 6:8 presents us with three key virtues that are both indicative of God's moral concerns and generative of the kind of ethical behavior a moral faithfulness before God requires.

Old Testament support for the significance of Micah 6:8. Keeping this notion of cardinal virtues in mind, we should note that Micah 6:8 is not alone in ascribing to God the virtues/behaviors prescribed within it. Indeed, the fact that the same set of attributes—justice, loving mercy and humility/faithfulness—are alluded to so very often in the Old Testament Law, Prophets and Writings simply can't be accidental. For example, the two passages presented below are examples of many others that provide descriptions of Yahweh containing references to two or more of the virtues alluded to in Micah 6:8:

> Your *love*, LORD, reaches to the heavens,
>   your *faithfulness* to the skies.
> Your righteousness is like the highest mountains,
>   your *justice* like the great deep.
>   You, LORD, preserve both people and animals. (Psalm 36:5-6)

> Righteousness and *justice* are the foundation of your throne;
>   *love* and *faithfulness* go before you. (Ps 89:14)

Perhaps even more compelling, however, are those biblical passages that present us with depictions of God's character *uttered by God himself in a deliberately self-revelatory manner.* For instance, in response to Moses' request to know God better—that is, to behold his glory (Ex 33:18)—Yahweh indicates that, while actually gazing on his face would be too much for Moses to bear, he will allow his goodness to pass before his servant and proclaim the divine name in his presence (Ex 33:19-20). In Exodus 34 we have a record of this encounter, and a wonderful articulation of the divine name:

> And he passed in front of Moses, proclaiming, "The LORD, the LORD, the *compassionate* and *gracious* God, slow to anger, abounding in *love* and *faithfulness*, maintaining love to thousands, and forgiving wickedness, rebellion and sin. *Yet he does not leave the guilty unpunished*; he punishes the children

---

[25]Ibid., pp. 69-70.

and their children for the sin of the parents to the third and fourth generation."

Moses bowed to the ground at once and worshiped. (Ex 34:6-8)[26]

Once again we should note both the explicit and implicit references in this passage to the same three cardinal virtues alluded to in Micah 6:8—justice, loving mercy and humility/faithfulness.

Another example of a biblical passage containing an autobiographical depiction of the divine character is this poignant passage from the book of Hosea. One more time, note the references to the cardinal virtues that are also announced in Micah 6:8:

> I will betroth you to me forever;
>> I will betroth you in righteousness and *justice*,
>> in *love* and *compassion*.
> I will betroth you in *faithfulness*,
>> and you will acknowledge the LORD. (Hos 2:19-20)

New Testament support for the significance of Micah 6:8. We've already taken note of how frequently the Old Testament portrays Yahweh as possessing the cardinal virtues Micah 6:8 refers to collectively as the "good." But what about the New Testament?

I'm arguing in this book for a moral faithfulness that's grounded in a Trinitarian theology.[27] The New Testament makes clear that one of the primary tasks of the incarnate Christ was (and is) to reveal to the world who Yahweh is and what he's about (see Jn 1:18; Heb 1:1-3). This being the case, if what I'm suggesting about the significance of Micah 6:8 is accurate, we should expect to find these same three virtues/behaviors showing up in Jesus' moral life and ethical teaching. In point of fact, we do. Indeed Jesus not only embodied these three behaviors/

---

[26]It should be noted how in their analysis of Micah 6:8 Nullens and Michener point out that the Hebrew word *ḥesed*, usually translated as "lovingkindness," can also hold the meaning of "grace," "mercy" or "compassion" (Nullens and Michener, *Matrix of Christian Ethics*, p. 150).

[27]Toward this end I've contended that a Christian ethic that's productive of a moral faithfulness will, of necessity, be both Christ-centered and Spirit-empowered. But a fully trinitarian ethic will also require some understanding of the agency of the Father. So here's yet another bold suggestion: the blatant manner in which the prophet Micah articulates the moral sensitivities of Yahweh can be viewed as a crucial contribution toward an understanding of a moral faithfulness that's informed by a trinitarian understanding of God. For an extended discussion of this topic that contains many parallels to the one presented in these pages, see the chapter titled "The Triune God and the Good," in Nullens and Michener, *Matrix of Christian Ethics*, pp. 149-72.

virtues; he prescribed them as well![28]

As a prelude to a later, more thorough discussion (in chapter seven) of how Jesus himself embodied and encouraged a moral faithfulness toward the Father in the power of the Spirit, I'll simply point out here a dominical saying found in Matthew's Gospel that certainly seems to have been inspired by Micah 6:8. This passage shows Jesus upbraiding the Jewish Pharisees and teachers of the law for their hypocrisy and moral myopia. Matthew 23:23 reads:

> Woe to you, teachers of the law and Pharisees, you hypocrites! You give a tenth of your spices—mint, dill and cumin. But you have neglected the more important matters of the law—*justice, mercy* and *faithfulness*. You should have practiced the latter, without neglecting the former. (Mt 23:23)

I trust that the correspondence between Jesus' advocacy of justice, mercy and faithfulness and the prophetic call found in Micah 6:8 can be acknowledged (cf. Lk 11:42).[29]

Going forward, we should also take note of how the rest of the New Testament—especially the apostolic literature—presents us with ethical exhortations evocative of both the moral faithfulness embodied by Jesus and Micah's cardinal virtues. For instance, in Paul's letter to the Colossians we read:

> Therefore, as God's chosen people, holy and dearly loved, clothe yourselves with *compassion, kindness, humility, gentleness* and *patience*. Bear with each other and forgive one another if any of you has a grievance against someone. *Forgive as the Lord forgave you.* And over all these virtues put on *love*, which binds them all together in perfect unity. (Col 3:12-14)

It's possible to see a connection between the cardinal virtues of loving mercy and humility/faithfulness with Paul's references in this passage to "compassion," "kindness," "humility," "gentleness" and "patience."[30] While

---

[28]Actually, I want to suggest that the very act of God the Son becoming incarnate was reflective of the cardinal virtues announced in Micah 6:8.

[29]See Craig L. Blomberg, *Matthew*, New American Commentary (Nashville: Broadman, 1992), pp. 345-46. According to R. T. France, "The 'weightier matters' listed here are strongly reminiscent of the famous summary in Mic 6:8" (R. T. France, *The Gospel of Matthew*, New International Commentary on the New Testament [Grand Rapids: Eerdmans, 2007], p. 873).

[30]See F. F. Bruce, *The Epistles to the Colossians, to Philemon, and to the Ephesians*, New International Commentary on the New Testament (Grand Rapids: Eerdmans, 1984), p. 154.

it's true that any Greek word that might be translated as "justice" (e.g., *dikē, dikaios* or *krisis*) is missing from this passage, I will argue that the concept is not.[31] After all, the just, fair, equitable thing for the followers of Christ to do is to treat others the way the Lord has treated them.[32] Thus Paul's plea for his readers to "forgive as the Lord forgave you" in verse 13 is, ironically, an implicit call for them to act justly as well as to love with mercy. This same type of ethical exhortation, implicit of the dynamic of grace-oriented justice, also occurs in Romans 15:7 and in Ephesians 4:32. Indeed, if this observation holds, then a careful read of Ephesians 5:1-2 with its call to imitate God as dearly loved children and to live a life of love *just as* Christ loved us will likewise prove evocative of the ethical exhortation found in Micah 6:8 to act justly, love with mercy and walk humbly (faithfully) before God (albeit in reverse order).

Some other New Testament passages that seem redolent of Micah 6:8, according to biblical theologian Michael Bird, are James 1:27 and 1 John 3:17. After rehearsing the ethical imperatives presented in these two passages, Bird writes: "In summary, we can say that a messianic community should make every effort 'to act justly and love mercy and to walk humbly with your God' (Mic 6:8). . . . The reign of God is a dynamic reality that can be demonstrated in loving action to those suffering and in justice that is brought on the wicked."[33]

Support for the significance of Micah 6:8 from other ethicists. Perhaps it was a recognition of the prominence of these three cardinal virtues in the Bible as a whole that prompted biblical ethicist T. B. Maston to refer to Micah 6:8 as "the most comprehensive statement of the ethical teaching of the prophets" and "the perfect ideal of religion." Indeed Maston goes on to state: "In this verse is united the strictly religious (vertical) and the ethical (horizontal), which is typical not only of prophetic religion but also of the basic teachings of both the Old Testament and the New Testament."[34]

Of course, an emphasis on Micah 6:8 shows up in the writings of other

---

[31]In other passages Paul refers to the need for Christians to behave in a just (Greek *dikaios*) manner: e.g., Col 4:1; 1 Thess 2:10; Titus 1:8.
[32]See Bruce, *Epistles*, p. 155.
[33]Bird, *Evangelical Theology*, p. 755.
[34]T. B. Maston, *Biblical Ethics: A Guide to the Ethical Message of the Scriptures from Genesis to Revelation* (Macon, GA: Mercer University Press, 1997), p. 58.

Christian ethicists as well. Just a few notable instances include: the assertion of Robin Lovin that Micah 6:8 presents us with a summary of the ethical thrust of the Hebrew prophets, the manner in which Arthur Holmes refers to the moral virtues/behaviors prescribed in Micah 6:8 as "principles of God's kingdom" and "the principles of a Christian ethic, to guide our judgments and conduct," and the way Glen Stassen and David Gushee devote some special attention to this important passage, saying,

> If the church is functioning as it should, it will continually and very earnestly engage in a search for authoritative direction and insight concerning its character and its conduct. It will desire above all else to know and to live out the answer to the prophet's question, "What does the Lord require?" (Mic 6:8), recognizing that the question needs to be asked again and again, rather than once and for all.[35]

In addition, in their book *The Matrix of Christian Ethics*, Patrick Nullens and Ronald Michener assert:

> The prophet Micah gave us biblical morality in a nutshell: "He has showed you, O man, what is good. And what does the LORD require of you? To act justly and to love mercy and to walk humbly with your God" (Micah 6:8). Rather than undertaking deep philosophical speculation, he straightforwardly expressed what God revealed to him as "the good"—precisely what we are looking for in ethics![36]

MICAH 6:8 AND A MORAL REALISM

Keeping the overarching premise of this chapter in view, the upshot of what we've discovered thus far is that the possibility of a moral realism is strengthened by the fact that the Spirit-inspired Scriptures, especially Micah 6:8, provide us with what seem to be some transcendent moral guidelines (moral principles) that are grounded in the very character of God. Going further, I will articulate here a bold, provocative, vitally important assertion: while not every moral command presented in Scripture

---

[35]Respectively, see Robin Lovin, *An Introduction to Christian Ethics* (Nashville: Abingdon, 2011), pp. 5-6; Arthur Holmes, *Ethics: Approaching Moral Decisions* (Downers Grove, IL: InterVarsity Press, 1984), p. 55; Glen H. Stassen and David P. Gushee, *Kingdom Ethics: Following Jesus in Contemporary Context* (Downers Grove, IL: InterVarsity Press, 2003), p. 82.
[36]Nullens and Michener, *Matrix of Christian Ethics*, p. 149.

rises to this level, there are such things as knowable moral absolutes—
ethical standards of behavior that transcend time and cultural location.[37]
In other words, what I'm proposing in this work is that *behind all the
moral commands articulated in the Bible are at least three moral absolutes—
acting justly, loving with mercy and walking humbly (faithfully) before God.*
These three transcendent moral imperatives, grounded as they are in the
character of God, in turn provide the ground not only for the Ten Commandments and ethical content of the Sermon on the Mount (including
the Beatitudes) but for all the moral commands found in the Old and New
Testaments. *These three divinely revealed moral absolutes seem to be presented in Scripture as reflective of the heart of God regarding all matters
moral.* It's *always* God's will for human beings to act justly, love with
mercy and walk humbly before him. It's *never* God's will for us to behave
in a manner that fails to honor these three moral commands.[38]

Micah 6:8 and the New Testament's Emphasis on Love

"But," it may be asked, "what about the teaching of Jesus regarding the
love of God and the neighbor?"[39] "Isn't it common for Christian ethicists,
citing Colossians 3:14 and 1 Corinthians 13:13, to refer to love as *the* tran-

---

[37]For a brief but cogent justification for the notion of moral absolutes, see Smedes, *Mere Morality*, p. 10.

[38]Arthur Holmes essentially makes this same assertion (Holmes, *Ethics*, p. 55). Moreover, in his book
Choices, Lewis Smedes proposes two moral absolutes: love and justice (*Choices: Making Right Decisions in a Complex World* [New York: HarperCollins, 1986], pp. 54-56); see also Smedes, *Mere
Morality*, pp. 4-5. Likewise, William Frankena, though technically he denies the existence of absolute moral rules (see Frankena, *Ethics*, pp. 55-56), insists that two principles—beneficence and
justice—form the foundation of all moral duties (p. 52). Indeed, Frankena boldly asserts: "if we ask
for *guidance* about what to do or not do, then the answer is contained, at least primarily, in two
deontic principles and their corollaries, namely, the principles of beneficence and equal treatment.
Given these two deontic principles, plus the necessary clarity of thought and factual knowledge, we
can know what we morally ought to do or not do, except in cases of conflict between them. We also
know that we should cultivate two virtues, a disposition to be beneficial (i.e., benevolence) and a
disposition to treat people equally (justice as a trait)" (pp. 66-67). As to the existence of moral absolutes, I'm going to side with Smedes over Frankena. However, with respect, I'm also going to go
beyond both Frankena and my mentor (Smedes) and suggest that, according to Micah 6:8, the call
to walk humbly rather than arrogantly—faithfully rather than unfaithfully—before God also qualifies as a moral absolute, one that is often crucial to the manner in which the calls to love and justice
play out in our relations to others and ourselves.

[39]For some exegetical background that includes a helpful comparison of the various ways in which
the synoptic authors (Matthew, Mark and Luke) present the double love commandment of Jesus,
see Daniel Harrington and James Keenan, *Jesus and Virtue Ethics: Building Bridges Between New
Testament Studies and Moral Theology* (Lanham, MD: Sheed & Ward, 2002), pp. 77-80.

scendent virtue that 'embraces and holds together all the virtues'?"[40] These are some legitimate questions that should be addressed.

I will respond by saying that, while an argument can be made against the idea that the law of love exhausts Jesus' ethical teaching,[41] I want to suggest that there is no contradiction between Jesus' summary of the Law and the Prophets presented in the Gospels (Mt 22:34-40; Mk 12:28-34; Lk 10:25-28) and Micah 6:8.[42] Instead, while it's accurate to summarize the Christian ethic as an ethic of love for God and the neighbor, I will point out that: (1) it's possible to argue that the commands to love God and the neighbor can be understood as nearly synonymous with the call to act justly, show mercy and walk humbly/faithfully before God; (2) the fact is that we human beings require more than one moral norm, standard or virtue to help us navigate most moral dilemmas; and (3) it's precisely because the Old Testament Scriptures—the Bible of the apostolic authors—so often combine references to these three foundational moral concepts that the New Testament authors could speak of the primacy of charity, knowing full well that their readers would understand that inherent in the apostolic call to love are the notions of acting justly and walking humbly/faithfully before God![43] Indeed, I could argue that the pastoral instruction presented in 1 Corinthians 13:4-7 (the so-called love chapter) implies an engagement in all three of the transcendent principles/virtues referred to in Micah 6:8!

Allow me to elaborate just a bit on points two and three of the three-pronged argument presented above. The reality is that it's not always easy to know what loving my neighbor looks like in this or that ethical or cultural

---

[40]See ibid, pp. 81-82.
[41]See the discussion titled "Matthew: Love and Law," in Joseph Kotva, *The Christian Case for Virtue Ethics* (Washington, DC: Georgetown University Press, 1996), pp. 113-18. See also the discussion of "Faithful Discipleship," in Patricia Lamoureux and Paul J. Wadell, *The Christian Moral Life: Faithful Discipleship for a Global Society* (Maryknoll, NY: Orbis Books, 2010), pp. 7-9, and the critique of pure agapism in William Frankena, "Love and Principle in Christian Ethics," in *Faith and Philosophy*, ed. Alvin Plantinga (Grand Rapids: Eerdmans, 1964), as cited in Ramsey, *Basic Christian Ethics*, pp. 104-16.
[42]Indeed, in his exhaustive commentary on the Gospel of Matthew, R. T. France references a rabbinic discussion located in the Babylonian Talmud (*Makkot*) that identifies Micah 6:8 as a summary of the law in three principles. See France, *Gospel of Matthew*, p. 844.
[43]On humans requiring more than one moral norm, see the thoughtful discussion in Holmes, *Ethics*, pp. 54-55.

situation.[44] Loving the neighbor is especially difficult when there's more than one neighbor involved and when we're honest enough to admit that in our fallen state it's incredibly difficult to make sure that our neighbor-love isn't actually self-serving. It's also possible to completely collapse the first commandment (to love God) into the second (to love my neighbor) so that my love for God ceases to inform what showing love to my neighbor should and shouldn't involve.[45] Could it be that the three moral behaviors/virtues alluded to in Micah 6:8 are actually crucial to our ability to fulfill Christ's call to love God and the neighbor or, to put it differently, to love the neighbor in a way that truly honors the heart of God?[46] We have to remember that Micah 6:8 was part of the sacred Scriptures from which Jesus, Peter and Paul took their moral cues. This may explain why in Matthew's Gospel we find "an ethic of justice (12:18, 20; 23:23), mercy (9:13; 12:7), and cross bearing [faithfulness] (10:38; 16:24)" as well as the call to love.[47] Here's a bold proposal: Could it be that the key to the New Testament ethic of showing love to our neighbor is to follow the course of action that does the best job of exhibiting, *at the same time*, the ethical virtues of justice, loving mercy and humility/faithfulness before God?[48]

---

[44]See Kotva, *Christian Case for Virtue Ethics*, p. 114, and Gustafson, *Christ and the Moral Life*, pp. 267-68.

[45]See Donald Bloesch on how "the divine commandment does not overthrow law but transforms it" (Bloesch, *Freedom for Obedience*, pp. 2-3). Thus in *Freedom for Obedience* Bloesch devotes several chapters to discussions of how a biblically informed ethic will combine: law and grace (pp. 6-13), love and justice (pp. 88-103), and law and gospel (pp. 126-46). It's my contention that, without saying as much, what Bloesch is advocating is an ethic that allows Micah 6:8, with its emphases on both justice and loving mercy exercised in humility before God, to inform what it means to follow the law of love as practiced and promoted by Jesus.

[46]For more on this possibility see the discussion of various versions of rule-agapsim versus various versions of act-agapism (or pure agapism) in Paul Ramsey, *Deeds and Rules in Christian Ethics* (Lantham, MD: University Press of America, 1983). See also the discussion of the role of rules in the moral life found in Lovin, *Christian Ethics*, pp. 57-60. I should also point out here that in those instances where it appears a moral action affects only ourselves rather than a neighbor, the call in Micah 6:8 to walk humbly/faithfully with God will inform what a legitimate love for ourselves might and might not involve.

[47]See Kotva, *Christian Case for Virtue Ethics*, p. 114.

[48]Ethicist Paul Ramsey writes: "The question is simply whether there are any general rules or principles or virtues or styles of life that embody love for fellowman, and if so what these may be" (Ramsey, *Deeds and Rules*, p. 132). The response from a Judeo-Christian perspective to Ramsey's question is: Yes, there are. This is precisely what we find in Micah 6:8. This may explain why Lewis Smedes could summarize the essence of the moral ought in a manner so reminiscent of Micah 6:8. According to Smedes: "Morality is all about how we treat people, including ourselves. Treating people unfairly and unlovingly—this is what moral wrong is. Treating people fairly and lovingly—this is what moral right is." See Lewis Smedes, *Choices: Making Right Decisions in a Complex World* (New York: HarperCollins, 1986), pp. 17-18.

In summary, the concept of a moral faithfulness implies a moral and theological realism. We simply must possess some divinely conveyed indication of which kinds of behaviors are pleasing to God and which are not. Do we possess such an indication? We do. Yahweh, the Father of Jesus, is a speaking, self-revealing God who has mercifully made his moral sensitivities known to those creatures who bear his image. Both the written word (the Scriptures) and the living Word (Jesus) provide us with some rather explicit clues as to three behaviors/virtues in particular that, because they derive from God's holy, unchanging character, should be considered holy and unchanging (that is, absolute): acting justly, loving with mercy, walking humbly before him. Put simply, a moral faithfulness—hearing and honoring the heart of God—involves the Holy Spirit enabling the moral agent to behave in this or that situation in a way that honors *all three of these moral absolutes at the same time.*

I'm not suggesting by this that a moral faithfulness is easy; far from it. However, the ethical model I'm putting forward goes on to insist that the Scriptures not only provide moral guidelines, they promise moral guidance also. In other words, a moral faithfulness is possible not only because God has *endowed* us with some moral principles but also because he's willing and able to *empower* us to discern and do his will as well. The next chapter focuses the reader's attention on the possibility of a Spirit-enabled moral guidance. Let's move straightaway to that important discussion.

More on a
Moral Realism [2]

The Moral Guidance
the Scriptures Promise

In chapter one of his book *Mere Morality,* Lewis Smedes writes:

> He is a little man in a long green coat and a cocked hat, standing with one leg
> on a steep roof, playing the fiddle. He is all of us, trying to make some mean-
> ingful music out of our lives but lacking a level place to stand on. "We are all
> fiddlers on the roof, trying to scratch out a pleasant little tune without falling
> down and breaking our necks."[1]

Smedes is suggesting that getting morality right involves a delicate,
perhaps even dangerous, balancing act. He goes on to pose some pretty
important questions:

> To know in advance what God expects us to do—before a new wind threatens
> to blow us off the roof, before a new crisis shakes our foundations—would be
> a great gift! *Is it possible? Are there signals from God—directions norms, rules,*
> *commandments?*
>
> To people cut off from any moral or spiritual tradition, perhaps hankering
> for something to help them keep their balance on the slippery shingles of
> freedom, any claim to represent what God expects us to do may evoke recol-
> lections of a childhood faith forever lost. Still, freedom without direction and
> responsibility without rules get to be burdensome after a while, and we may
> be more ready than we have been for a while to ask whether there is a way to

---

[1]Lewis Smedes, *Mere Morality: What God Expects from Ordinary People* (Grand Rapids: Eerdmans,
1983), p. 1.

know the will of God. *Is there any help for us fiddlers as we try to scratch out our individual tunes without falling off the roof?*[2]

In the previous chapter we discovered that the answer to Smedes's rhetorical queries is a resounding "Yes!" God has provided us with some powerful indications of where his heart is. In sum, it's always God's will for his people to choose that course of action that strives to honor three moral imperatives *at the same time*: acting justly, loving with mercy, walking humbly before him (Mic 6:8).

But just because we have some transcendent moral guidelines doesn't mean that it's a simple matter in any given moral dilemma to discern and do the course of action that accomplishes the moral balancing act Micah 6:8 seems to call for. Furthermore, precisely what an attempt to act justly, love with mercy and walk humbly before God *at the same time* might call for may differ somewhat depending on our historical and cultural location.[3] So, while the recognition that being faithful to these three moral behaviors/virtues is precisely what we are called on by God to do in order to honor his heart with respect to this or that moral matter, *we still need help with the contextualization of these commands.* This is why it's important for Christians to recognize that the Scriptures not only *provide* us with moral *guidelines* but *promise* us moral *guidance* (and empowerment) as well.

As we've seen, the evangelical ethic of Donald Bloesch allows for the possibility that the risen Christ can and will make known to his followers

---

[2]Ibid., emphasis added.

[3]Joseph Kotva points out that one of the ways the rise of historical consciousness is altering ethical theory is by stressing the need to give attention to one's historical context. According to Kotva, "The more aware we become of the fluid and changing nature of history, the more our moral judgments must attend to the details of the concrete situation. If nature and society are basically unchanging, then general principles are fine and we simply do whatever those before us did. But if nature and society change and develop, then we must attend to contextual variety and situational specificity. In other words, an awareness of history forces attention on the details and specific features of the situations in which moral decisions are made. The continuities of human life are no doubt important but historical consciousness pushes ethical theory to acknowledge the potential uniqueness of each moment" (Joseph Kotva, *The Christian Case for Virtue Ethics* [Washington, DC: Georgetown University Press, 1996], pp. 8-9). See also the book-length treatment of this theme in Patrick Nullens and Ronald T. Michener, *The Matrix of Christian Ethics: Integrating Philosophy and Moral Theology in a Postmodern Context* (Downers Grove, IL: IVP Books, 2010). Because I see Jesus himself engaging in this type of ethical contextualization, albeit striving to hear the heart of God in each specific situation, the ethical approach I'm promoting can be viewed as striving to be sensitive to the postmodern perspective without capitulating to deconstructive versions of it.

the command (and promise) of God in this or that contemporary ethical situation. This is a theologically real approach to Christian ethics. Does such an ethical option enjoy biblical support? In the next few pages I'll attempt to provide a biblical theology of Spirit-enabled moral guidance that both supports and extends Bloesch's basic proposal.

SOME OLD TESTAMENT SUPPORT FOR
THE CONCEPT OF DIVINE MORAL GUIDANCE

Beginning again with the Old Testament, I want to focus our attention on a portion of Scripture in which we find a discussion of morality that, because of its ground in a theology of creation and the apparent influence of some wisdom literature from other ancient cultures seems to transcend the historically and culturally conditioned ceremonial and covenant laws provided by Moses to the nation of Israel.[4] I'm referring to the book of Proverbs—chapters 1–9 in particular. Ostensibly presenting to the reader the counsel of a concerned father to his young adult sons, the first nine chapters of Proverbs keep pronouncing the message: the God who created the world to operate in a morally sensitive manner is eager to enable his people to render to him a moral faithfulness. To be more specific, I want to suggest that a close look at Proverbs 2, in particular, will reveal three vitally important themes.

First, in the universe we inhabit, it's possible for people and things to be either good or evil. Proverbs 2:7-15 makes several references to people, paths and perspectives in an evaluative, morally significant manner:

> He holds success in store for the *upright*,
>   he is a shield to those whose walk is *blameless*,
> for he guards the course of the *just*
>   and protects the way of his *faithful* ones.

---

[4]On a theology of creation see R. N. Whybray, *The Book of Proverbs*, Cambridge Bible Commentary (London: Cambridge University Press, 1972), p. 85. See also John Paterson, *The Wisdom of Israel: Job and Proverbs* (New York: Abingdon, 1962), p. 86. On wisdom literature from other ancient cultures see Roland E. Murphy, *Wisdom Literature: Job, Proverbs, Ruth, Canticles, Ecclesiastes and Esther* (Grand Rapids: Eerdmans, 1981), pp. 9-12. Referring to the presence of a utilitarian emphasis on consequences in many of the Proverbs, Scott Rae writes: "The intended readership of the Wisdom Literature extended outside the community of Old Testament Israel. As a result, the authors could not rely on the same style of reasoning that other authors used with Israel. In fact, conspicuous by its absence in the Wisdom books are many themes that characterize the Law, such as the Promised Land, the sacrifices, the religious festivals, and the fine points of the Law, all of which were compelling only to the nation of Israel" (Scott Rae, *Moral Choices: An Introduction to Ethics*, 3rd ed. [Grand Rapids: Zondervan, 2009], p. 26).

Then you will understand what is *right* and *just*
    and *fair*—every *good* path.
For wisdom will enter your heart,
    and knowledge will be pleasant to your soul.
Discretion will protect you,
    and understanding will guard you.
Wisdom will save you from the ways of *wicked* men,
    from men whose words are *perverse*,
who have left the *straight* paths
    to walk in *dark* ways,
who delight in doing *wrong*
    and rejoice in the *perverseness* of *evil*,
whose paths are *crooked*
    and who are *devious* in their ways. (Prov 2:7-15)

Apparently there is a universal standard by which people, paths and perspectives can be evaluated: the God who created the world is a moral being with a point of view. In sum, to be "upright" and "blameless" before God is to be "just" and "faithful"; to follow the "good path" rather than "doing wrong."

Second, within God's economy, the consequences for doing right and wrong are highly significant. Proverbs 2:16-22 goes on to compare the consequences that accrue to good and evil behavior respectively. The contrast between these differing consequences is meant to be striking:

Wisdom will save you also from the adulterous woman,
    from the wayward woman with her seductive words,
who has left the partner of her youth
    and ignored the covenant she made before God.
Surely her house leads down to *death*
    and her paths to the spirits of the *dead*.
None who go to her return
    or attain the paths of *life*.
Thus you will walk in the ways of the good
    and keep to the paths of the righteous.
For the upright will *live* in the land,
    and the blameless will *remain* in it;
but the wicked will be *cut off* from the land,

and the unfaithful will be *torn* from it. (Prov 2:16-22)

The warning provided by this father to his young adult sons needs to be underscored: the difference between righteous and wicked behavior is literally a matter of life and death![5]

Third, the God who has an opinion about how his image bearers behave in the world he created is able and willing to provide human beings with a wisdom that often takes the form of moral guidance. We should take note of how Proverbs 2:1-6 refers to the possibility of God giving "wisdom" and speaking "knowledge" and "understanding" into people's lives:

My son, if you accept my words
    and store up my commands within you,
turning your ear to *wisdom*
    and applying your heart to *understanding*—
indeed, if you call out for *insight*
    and cry aloud for *understanding*,
and if you look for it as for silver
    and search for it as for hidden treasure,
then you will understand the fear of the LORD
    and find the *knowledge* of God.
For the LORD gives *wisdom*;
    from his mouth come *knowledge* and *understanding*. (Prov 2:1-6)

Here's one way to think about the wisdom God is eager to provide his people: it's an understanding of the way the world we inhabit works and how best to navigate our way through it. The fact that the *wisdom* referred to in Proverbs 2:1-6 often takes the form of *moral guidance* is indicated not only by the rest of Proverbs 2 but also by several other passages found in Proverbs 1–9 as well.[6]

---

[5]It should also be noted how the particular moral faux pas referred to in this passage (verse 16) has to do with something other than a behavior proscribed by Israel's historically and culturally conditioned ceremonial law. The act of marital adultery not only violates the eighth commandment presented in the Decalogue; it is contrary to all three of the prescribed behaviors listed in Micah 6:8 as well! It's no wonder, then, that the New Testament echoes so vibrantly the Old Testament's warnings regarding this particularly tempting but ultimately self-sabotaging moral misstep (e.g., see Mt 5:27-32; 15:10-20; 19:16-19).

[6]See Prov 1:20-33; 3:1-7; 4:10-19; 5:1-23; 6:20-35; 7:1-27; 8:12-16; 9:1-6.

SOME NEW TESTAMENT SUPPORT FOR
THE CONCEPT OF DIVINE MORAL GUIDANCE

Moreover, support for the notion of divine moral guidance is not limited to the Old Testament. We find allusions to this dynamic in the New Testament as well.

For one thing, the fact is that, as in the book of Proverbs, the New Testament contains many passages that portray God as an eager, gracious giver of wisdom (e.g., see Acts 6:3; 1 Cor 12:8; 2 Cor 1:12; Eph 1:17; Jas 1:5; 3:13-17). Given the manner in which divine wisdom is associated with moral discernment in Proverbs 2, this fact is not without significance.

In addition, the New Testament contains many passages that seem to link moral guidance with the ministry of God's Spirit in the lives of Christ's followers. For instance, consider the following passage from John's Gospel:

> But very truly I tell you, it is for your good that I am going away. Unless I go away, the Advocate will not come to you; but if I go, I will send him to you. When he comes, he will prove the world to be in the wrong about sin and righteousness and judgment: about sin, because people do not believe in me; about righteousness, because I am going to the Father, where you can see me no longer; and about judgment, because the prince of this world now stands condemned.
>
> I have much more to say to you, more than you can now bear. But when he, the Spirit of truth, comes, he will guide you into *all the truth*. He will not speak on his own; he will speak only what he hears, and he will tell you what is yet to come. He will glorify me because it is from me that he will receive what he will make known to you. (Jn 16:7-14)

For sure, this passage does more than promise divine moral guidance; the idea of Christian mission is obviously in view. We should note, however, that it's immediately after announcing that the role of the Spirit will be to "prove the world to be in the wrong about *sin, righteousness* and *judgment*" (obviously ethical categories), that Jesus refers to the Holy Spirit as the "Spirit of truth" who will "guide you into all the truth." The idea being communicated in this passage and its complement in John 14:15-26 is that the Holy Spirit is to function as "another counselor"—a theologically real re-presentation of Jesus in the lives of his disciples, enabling them to among other things bring to mind *everything* that Jesus had taught them (Jn 14:26) and wishes (in an ongoing way) to teach them (Jn 16:14). Given the enduring and ethical aspects of Jesus' teaching ministry, is there any reason to assume that the spiritual guidance into "all the truth" provided by this vicarious "counselor" *wouldn't* and *won't* include matters moral as well as missional?[7] Besides, is it not the case that a missional faithfulness both requires and reflects a moral faithfulness?[8]

Furthermore, support for the idea of divine moral guidance can be found in the letters of Paul as well. Christian ethicist Joseph Kotva has pointed out that "Paul continually exhibits and calls for a kind of discriminating wisdom or skillful judgment that seeks in the particular situation to 'discern the will of God—what is good and acceptable and perfect' (Rom 12:2)."[9] A couple of other Pauline passages that seem to convey a similar call include Philippians 1:9-11 and Colossians 1:9-10. In both of these passages Paul indicates to his readers how he's praying for them. Apparently the apostle was in the habit of praying that the members of churches he felt responsible for would be the beneficiaries of some divine moral guidance:

> And this is my prayer: that your love may abound more and more in knowledge and depth of insight, *so that you may be able to discern what is best* and may be pure and blameless for the day of Christ, filled with the fruit of righteousness that comes through Jesus Christ—to the glory and praise of God. (Phil 1:9-11)[10]
>
> For this reason, since the day we heard about you, we have not stopped praying for you. *We continually ask God to fill you with the knowledge of his will through all the wisdom and understanding that the Spirit gives*, so that you may live a life worthy of the Lord and please him in every way. (Col 1:9-10)

In the section that follows I'll have more to say about the manner in which the Holy Spirit can and will help Christ's followers discern the will

---

[7]Support for the idea of a Spirit-enabled moral guidance on the basis of these passages can be found in Henlee H. Barnette, *Introducing Christian Ethics* (Nashville: Broadman and Holman, 1961), pp. 90, 94, and Paul Lewis, "A Pneumatological Approach to Virtue Ethics" (March 30, 2013), www .apts.edu/aeimages/File/AJPS_PDF/98-1-lewis.pdf. See also Rae, *Moral Choices*, p. 47.

[8]See Nullens and Michener, *Matrix of Christian Ethics*, pp. 21-22.

[9]See Kotva, *Christian Case for Virtue Ethics*, p. 123.

[10]Certainly this passage refers to the dynamic of moral discernment on the part of Christ's followers and suggests that it's made possible by a growth in "knowledge" and "depth of insight." That Paul had in mind a divine source and object of the "knowledge" and "insight" that produces moral discernment is made evident in the parallel passage: Eph 1:15-19 (cf. Eph 3:14-19). See F. F. Bruce, *The Epistles to the Colossians, to Philemon, and to the Ephesians*, New International Commentary on the New Testament (Grand Rapids: Eerdmans, 1984), pp. 268-70. I'll have more to say about this passage in the book's conclusion.

of God. This moral discernment possesses utility for life in general and
those discrete situations in which we find ourselves confronted with an
especially difficult moral conundrum. At this point in the discussion it's
enough to reiterate that, based on what we read in the Bible as a whole
and Proverbs 1–9 in particular, an embrace of a theological realism seems
to justify an attendant allegiance to a moral realism that asserts that there
are indeed knowable, universally applicable moral standards that make
it possible (and necessary) for us human beings to evaluate the moral
behavior of ourselves and others. What's more, the moral realism pictured here entails the notion that God is eager to enable his people to
render to him a lifestyle of moral faithfulness. It's my contention that a
commitment to such a moral realism is a game-changer for the doing of
ethics in an increasingly postmodern, post-Christian world. It's a moral
realism that makes a moral faithfulness possible![11]

THE POSSIBILITY OF A SPIRIT-ENABLED MORAL GUIDANCE

Pressing a bit further, the moral realism I espouse in this work holds that
there are two main ways that the Holy Spirit goes about enabling a moral
faithfulness within the lives of Christ's followers (that is, there are two
ways he enables us as disciples to embody the moral faithfulness Jesus
rendered to the Father on our behalf).[12]

First, as we engage in certain *spiritual formation* practices—worship,
nurture, community and mission—we put ourselves in a place where God's

---

[11]Though I've already introduced the reader to the concept of a moral faithfulness, I feel the need to
offer here an important clarification, if only by way of a footnote. To maintain that a moral faithfulness is possible is not the same as saying that it's automatic. The promise of wisdom (i.e., moral
guidance) presented in the early chapters of Proverbs takes the form of an *invitation* that can either
be accepted (see Prov 1:8; 2:1-4; 3:1; 4:1, 5; 5:1-2; 6:20-21; 7:1-4; 8:1-6, 10, 17, 32-34) or ignored
(see Prov 1:20-33; 4:5-6, 13; 5:7; 6:20; 8:33, 36). The language of contingency present in these passages should not be overlooked. Because God is faithful, moral guidance is available. Still, we must
open our lives to it; God does not force his moral guidance on us. A moral faithfulness occurs when
his people, inspired by his prior faithfulness to us, choose to *respond* to him (rather than merely
react to the situation at hand) by doing what is necessary to make moral choices that honor his heart.
[12]Donald Bloesch writes: "Our salvation has already been enacted and fulfilled in Jesus Christ. But the
fruits of our salvation need to be appropriated and manifested in a life of discipleship" (Bloesch, *Freedom
for Obedience: Evangelical Ethics for Contemporary Times* [San Francisco: Harper & Row, 1987], p. 12).
For an insightful and important discussion of the relationship between Christ and the Holy Spirit, and
how "since the resurrection of Jesus, life in Christ Jesus is effectively life in the Holy Spirit, who carries
on the work of Jesus," see Daniel Harrington and James Keenan, *Jesus and Virtue Ethics: Building Bridges
Between New Testament Studies and Moral Theology* (Lanham, MD: Sheed & Ward, 2002), pp. 37-38.

Spirit is able to produce within us the Christlike desire to *honor* the heart of God with respect to life as a whole and moral matters in particular.[13] It's when the character of Christ is formed within that it occurs to us to rather routinely pose to ourselves the two questions that are crucial to both a missional and moral faithfulness: Where is the heart of God with respect to this situation? How can I (we) act in cooperation with what the Spirit of Jesus is up to in it?[14] The *desire* to respond to various life situations in ways that are faithful to Micah 6:8 is produced over time as we engage in the character-forming practices alluded to above in the power of the Spirit.[15]

Second, as we engage in certain *spiritual discernment* practices—Scripture study and prayer practiced in a theologically real manner—we put ourselves in a place where God's Spirit is able to help us *hear* or sense the heart of God with respect to this or that moral matter, virtually "speaking" wisdom, understanding and insight to us through the Scriptures, the community of faith or directly to the self by means of his still small voice.

It's one thing to desire to behave in ways faithful to Micah 6:8; it's another to know how to do so in a contextually sensitive manner—that is, in a way that's in step with what God is up to in the situation for his glory and the good of the world. It's my conviction that the spiritual discernment practices referred to above are very important to the process of forming the Christlike ability to *hear* (that is, sense or discern) where the heart of God is with respect to life as a whole and moral matters in particular. The kind of moral realism I see presented in Scripture and have experienced

---

[13] According to Joseph Kotva, our desires are important because "they help determine what actions we pursue and which we avoid. Put most simply, since we often pursue what we desire, the content of our desires is terribly important" (Kotva, *Christian Case for Virtue Ethics*, p. 12).

[14] Though for a variety of reasons some Christian ethicists don't consider the Jesus of the Gospels to be relevant to Christian ethics (ibid., p. 87), Joseph Kotva argues to the contrary, and not simply because Jesus championed the law of love. No, according to Kotva, the significance of Jesus for Christian ethics goes beyond his advocacy of the law of love to the manner in which he lived that law out during the entirety of his life. Jesus' life story becomes the guide for Christian disciples toward the normative way of being human as God intends. See ibid., pp. 88-90.

[15] Kotva reminds his readers that there are some ethicists who flatly reject the idea that virtue theory is compatible with the Christian faith, with its emphasis on divine commands (i.e., rules), a concern for others (rather than self-realization) and the need for grace (rather than self-actualization) (ibid., pp. 48-49). However, I would argue that viewing the ethical exhortations presented in Micah 6:8 as both behaviors to be engaged in and virtues to be cultivated so that we might become the kind of persons who, when facing a perplexing moral dilemma, ask the right contextualization questions as fully devoted followers of Jesus, is a way of building a case for the compatibility of virtue theory with Christian discipleship.

in my own life is open to the possibility that when followers of Jesus find themselves needing to make a specific ethical decision while also surrounded by a cloud of moral ambiguity, the Spirit of God is often willing to provide us with some fairly specific, situation-sensitive moral guidance. (At the very least, he can be counted on to provide a gentle "nudge" toward one course of action or another.) Once again the crucial prompt for this experience occurs as we pose to ourselves the ethical contextualization questions: Where is the heart of God with respect to this situation? How can I (we) act in cooperation with what the Spirit of Jesus is up to in it? Given the third takeaway from Proverbs 2 cited above—the idea that our God is willing and eager to provide his people with moral guidance as well as moral guidelines—I'm absolutely convinced that routinely pondering such questions is anything but a fool's errand.

THE NATURE OF SPIRIT-ENABLED MORAL GUIDANCE

Let's be clear: an individual Christ follower or community of Christians can benefit from the ethic of responsible Christian discipleship without embracing the notion of specific, situation-sensitive, Spirit-enabled moral guidance. That said, I want to go on to clarify in the next few pages what my thesis is and isn't.

Beyond the general, overall moral wisdom presented to us in the Spirit-inspired Scriptures (especially Micah 6:8), and in addition to the way the Holy Spirit works through the spiritual formation practices of the church to form within us the kind of character that desires to *honor* the heart of God, is the way that same Holy Spirit can enable Christ's followers to *hear* (that is, sense or discern) the heart of God. In other words, traveling in a trajectory very similar to the one described in Bloesch's prophetic casuistry, my thesis is that it's possible for the Holy Spirit to provide Christian disciples with some specific, situation-sensitive (that is, "prophetic") guidance as to how to contextualize what it means to act justly, love with mercy and walk humbly before God with respect to this or that moral dilemma.[16]

---

[16]Indeed, it's possible to argue for the concept of personal, Spirit-enabled moral guidance on the basis of Micah 6:8 itself. The Hebrew phrase translated "walk humbly with your God" in the NIV rendering of this passage (*haṣĕnēaʿ lĕkēt ʿim ʾĕlōhêkā*) also contains the idea of a humble following after God. This might suggest that built into the passage is a recognition of the need for the moral agent to receive ongoing guidance from God as to how to balance the demands of justice and loving mercy. This

How does this "prophetic" moral guidance occur? I also want to make clear that the kind of Spirit-enabled moral guidance I have in mind can come about in more than one way. On the one hand, it might involve the Holy Spirit's bringing to the mind of the disciple a certain moral action or virtue that is modeled and/or commended somewhere in God's word. Within the context of a prayerful indwelling of the Scriptures, the Holy Spirit is able to impress on the follower of Christ the significance of an aspect of the biblical story that is especially apropos to the ethical dilemma confronting him or her. This is not a matter of simply finding a moral rule and putting it in play. No, there's a sense of call involved: Jesus is calling the disciple through his or her prayerful indwelling of the Spirit-inspired Scriptures to embody a moral behavior or virtue modeled by him or some other character within the biblical story—a moral action that seems faithful to all three of the behaviors/virtues commended in Micah 6:8.

On the other hand, the phenomenon of "prophetic" moral guidance might also involve the dynamic of Christ "speaking" to the disciple through his Spirit, prescribing a specific course of action to be taken in the midst of an especially tricky, confusing ethical situation. In this case the follower of Christ experiences an extraordinarily strong impression, deep within, that he or she is being led by the Lord to speak or act into the situation in such a way as to do justice to Micah 6:8, honoring the heart of the Father in the process. It's not that the disciple has heard an audible voice (though a *realistic* read of Scripture should cause us to be open to even this possibility[17]). Rather he or she simply feels a prompting (whether strong or gentle) to take a particular course of action. This prompting can derive from something that is said by a member of our faith community, from a passage of Scripture that seems significant to the current situation (see Ps 119:18) or from the still small voice of the Spirit speaking directly to one's conscience (see Jn 14:26; Acts 10:19; 13:2).[18] At the same time such a prompting, especially if it derives from a sense of God's Spirit speaking directly to our hearts, must be vali-

---

interpretation may enjoy some implicit support from the NIV rendering of Hosea 12:6, a parallel passage of sorts, which reads: "But you must return to your God; maintain love and justice, and wait for your God always."

[17]See Dallas Willard, *Hearing God: Developing a Conversational Relationship with God* (Downers Grove, IL: InterVarsity Press, 1999), p. 10.

[18]See Nullens and Michener, *Matrix of Christian Ethics*, p. 159.

dated against the Scriptures as a whole and the community of faith (including the church's rich history of biblical interpretation). These are some important ways we guard against the dynamic of psychological projection— our projecting onto the Holy Spirit promptings that actually originate within our subconscious selves.[19] In chapter eight I will have much more to say about how to mitigate the possibility of our speaking to ourselves in the name of the Spirit. At this point I will simply make the very important point that, while my experience has been that a strong (or gentle) inner prompting, when it's from the Spirit of God, is always accompanied by an equally strong (or gentle) sense of inner peace, a *balanced* and *responsible* experience of specific, Spirit-enabled moral guidance will *never involve a moral action that violates the clear teaching of Scripture or that we're unwilling to put before our brothers and sisters in Christ.*[20]

I trust it's apparent that I'm *not* suggesting that in every moral dilemma a Christ follower faces he or she should expect to hear a voice behind him or her saying, "This is the way; walk in it" (see Is 30:21). My intention is simply to point out *all* the possible ways that, according to the Scriptures, the Holy Spirit can guide us in our ethical endeavors. The larger point this book is striving to make is that *instead of relying on our own understanding when it comes to making ethical decisions* (see Prov 3:5-6), *we can and should count on the Holy Spirit's help at gaining a vitally important sense of where God's heart is with respect to this or that ethical option.* Some might suggest

---

[19]See Michael F. Bird, *Evangelical Theology: A Biblical and Systematic Introduction* (Grand Rapids: Zondervan, 2013), p. 73.

[20]For those readers who are worried that the kind of Spirit-enabled moral guidance described here is much too subjective to be reliable, I wish to express my agreement with Pentecostal ethicist Paul Lewis who, while rightly emphasizing the role of the Spirit in a theologically savvy Christian ethic, is also careful to issue an important caveat: "One aspect of a Pentecostal ethic is the awareness of the immediacy of the Trinity's role within the ethical behavior of the believer. Although orthodoxy is aware of the three persons of the Trinity's joint rule within a person, in theological discourse it is the Holy Spirit who mediates the virtues from God to humankind. This mediatory work of the Spirit works through three avenues: the Bible, the community and the self. None of these three are final authorities within themselves, and each by the Spirit's authentication certifies the others to the believer. The interrelationship of these three provides the checks and balances needed within the life of a Christian. In fact, these three are inseparable, and necessary to a believer's ethical walk, otherwise a believer who overemphasizes one avenue above the others will fall into solipsism, collectivism, or biblicism, each of which will ultimately be detrimental to Christian faith and practice. It is through the Spirit's work immediately in the self, through the community and by the Bible that the believer is led into a greater ethical life" (Paul Lewis, "A Pneumatological Approach to Virtue Ethics" [March 30, 2013], www.apts.edu/aeimages/File/AJPS_PDF/98-1-lewis.pdf).

that maintaining an openness to the type of Spirit-enabled moral guidance I've just described is an incredibly irresponsible action. I would aver that, given the tendency of contemporary churchgoers to make moral decisions the very same way their non-Christian peers do, it's irresponsible *not* to maintain such an openness. I'm convinced that the Spirit of God wants to enable Christian disciples on a day-to-day basis to adequately contextualize a love for God and neighbor—a love that is informed by Micah 6:8. A willingness to be a part of this contextualization process, as messy as it can be, is a big part of what it means to live a morally faithful life.[21]

SOME BIBLICAL SUPPORT FOR THE DYNAMIC OF SPIRIT-ENABLED MORAL GUIDANCE

All of this prompts the question: But is there really biblical support for the experience of a moral guidance from God that is specific and situation-sensitive (that is, "prophetic") in nature?

I'll begin my response to this important query by reiterating that my study of Scripture as a whole has led me to the conclusion that the coming of the Spirit into the lives of Christ's followers provides them with what I refer to as a *prophetic capacity*. As it relates to the *missional* dimension of Christian discipleship, this phenomenon imparts to us the ability to hear God's voice, receive ministry assignments from him, and speak and act into people's lives on God's behalf, making a difference in the world for God in the process.[22] As it relates to the *moral* dimension of Christian discipleship, I'm suggesting that the Bible as a whole appears

---

[21]I am not alone in suggesting that striving toward a moral faithfulness will necessarily be a somewhat messy endeavor. Joseph Kotva makes the same argument based on an acknowledgment of "Christianity's many moral concerns and modes of reasoning" (Kotva, *Christian Case for Virtue Ethics*, p. 157). In addition, Daniel Castelo, citing the works of N. T. Wright (biblical studies) and Kevin Vanhoozer (theological studies), refers to the Scriptures as providing a "script for the holy life that has to be enacted" by Christian disciples in something of an improvisational manner (Daniel Castelo, *Revisioning Pentecostal Ethics: The Epicletic Community* [Cleveland, TN: CPT Press, 2012], pp. 94-97). One should take special note of how the notion of Christian ethics as moral improvisation is elaborated on in Samuel Wells, *Improvisation: The Drama of Christian Ethics* (Grand Rapids: Brazos, 2004). Finally, Stanley Hauerwas has similarly observed that Christian ethics is about learning to "live truthfully in a world without certainty" and that "[t]he task of Christian ethics is not to relieve us of the ambiguity but to help us understand rightly what it means to live in the world we do" (Stanley Hauerwas, *The Peaceable Kingdom: A Primer on Christian Ethics* [Notre Dame: University of Notre Dame Press, 1983], p. 16).
[22]For more on this, see Gary Tyra, *The Holy Spirit in Mission: Prophetic Speech and Action in Christian Witness* (Downers Grove, IL: IVP Academic, 2011), pp. 68, 98, 120, 129, 161, 189.

to teach that it's possible for God to provide his people with some in-the-moment, Spirit-imparted wisdom as to how to contextualize Micah 6:8 and the love of God and the neighbor for everyday life situations.

Old Testament support for "prophetic" moral guidance. We've already taken note of how Proverbs 2:6 refers to wisdom, knowledge and understanding coming from the "mouth" of God. We've also taken note of those passages in Proverbs 8–9 that portray a personified wisdom "calling out," providing wisdom to those who will "listen" (Prov 8:1-6, 32-34; 9:1-6). Biblical scholar Roland Murphy has offered that, since it appears that the Spirit of God is sometimes personified in the Hebrew Scriptures as Lady Wisdom, what is said about Wisdom in the book of Proverbs can be said about the Holy Spirit as well.[23] This association of the Holy Spirit with the personified Wisdom of Proverbs 1–9 obviously provides some tacit biblical/theological support for the notion of a Spirit-enabled moral guidance.

Along with this I'm intrigued by the way several passages in the Psalms, with their emphasis on the dynamic of an intimate, interactive relationship with God, seem to suggest the possibility of a personal, "prophetic" type of moral guidance. Psalm 32:8-9 is a particularly intriguing passage, which reads:

> I will instruct you and teach you in the way you should go;
> > I will counsel you with my loving eye on you.
> Do not be like the horse or the mule,
> > which have no understanding
> but must be controlled by bit and bridle
> > or they will not come to you. (Ps 32:8-9)[24]

Implied in this passage is a call for its readers to make the decision to willingly yield themselves (unlike the horse or mule) in an ongoing way to the life counsel a loving God desires to provide.

But how does this ongoing life counsel come to us?

---

[23]Roland Murphy, *The Tree of Life: An Exploration of Biblical Wisdom Literature*, 3rd ed. (Grand Rapids: Eerdmans, 1990), pp. 118-20, 144, as cited in Patricia Lamoureux and Paul J. Wadell, *The Christian Moral Life: Faithful Discipleship for a Global Society* (Maryknoll, NY: Orbis Books, 2010), p. 228. See also Whybray, *Book of Proverbs*, p. 51, and Craig S. Keener, *The IVP Bible Background Commentary: New Testament* (Downers Grove, IL: InterVarsity Press, 1993), p. 301.

[24]Support for the idea that the promise of life counsel made in this passage is of divine origin is provided by Ps 25:12.

Passages such as Psalm 143:10 provide support for the supposition that such moral guidance is not only personal but Spirit-enabled as well: "Teach me to do your will, for you are my God; *may your good Spirit lead me* on level ground" (Ps 143:10). I'm going to suggest that we need to keep in mind the way this verse unmistakably connects the Holy Spirit with divine moral guidance as we peruse some other passages from the Old Testament that seem to refer to the same phenomenon—a Spirit-enabled moral guidance that comes to God's people in some manner other than the letter of the law.

For example, in the ode to the law that is Psalm 119 we find a collection of verses that seem to suggest an ability to receive moral instruction from God that, while going beyond a verbatim rehearsal of the commands and statutes of the written law, are faithful to them. Indeed the moral instruction alluded to in these verses can be thought of as Spirit-enabled guidance as to how to obey God's written word in this or that specific situation.[25] I have in mind passages such as:

Teach me, LORD, the way of your decrees,
    that I may follow it to the end.
Give me understanding, so that I may keep your law
    and obey it with all my heart.
Direct me in the path of your commands,
    for there I find delight. (Ps 119:33-35)

Teach me knowledge and *good judgment,*
    for I trust your commands. (Ps 119:66)

I am your servant; *give me discernment*
    that I may understand your statutes. (Ps 119:125)

Direct my footsteps according to your word;
    let no sin rule over me. (Ps 119:133)

Of course, Psalm 119 is not alone in its apparent support for the notion of a moral instruction that is personal; perhaps even "prophetic" (Spirit-

---

[25]Commenting on Psalm 119, Walter Brueggemann underscores its emphasis on a personal interaction between the psalmist and God—an interaction that's grounded in grace and effected through the Spirit. See Walter Brueggemann, *The Message of the Psalms: A Theological Commentary* (Minneapolis: Augsburg, 1984), p. 41.

enabled) in nature. Other passages from Israel's psalter that also appear to refer to the possibility of God providing personal, ongoing guidance as to how to apply his law to everyday life include:

> I will praise the LORD, who *counsels* me;
>   even at night my heart instructs me. (Ps 16:7)

> He *guides* me along the right paths
>   for his name's sake. (Ps 23:3)

> *Show me* your ways, LORD,
>   *teach me* your paths.
> *Guide me* in your truth and teach me,
>   for you are God my Savior,
>   and my hope is in you all day long. (Ps 25:4-5)

> Who, then, are those who fear the LORD?
>   He will *instruct* them in the ways they should choose. (Ps 25:12)

These are just a few passages from just one section of the Old Testament Scriptures that present us with the possibility of personal, ongoing moral guidance from God that, while faithful to the Torah, seems to come to the moral agent in some sort of immediate, interactive manner. The best supposition, I'm suggesting, is that this personal, ongoing moral instruction is provided by God's Spirit.

Such a supposition is strengthened by the promise we find in the prophetic book of Ezekiel. Speaking through the prophet at the end of the old covenant era, God refers to a new era in Israel's history—an era earmarked by a Spirit-enabled ability to render to God the moral faithfulness he desires and deserves. This poignant passage reads:

> For I will take you out of the nations; I will gather you from all the countries and bring you back into your own land. I will sprinkle clean water on you, and you will be clean; I will cleanse you from all your impurities and from all your idols. I will give you a new heart and put a new spirit in you; I will remove from you your heart of stone and give you a heart of flesh. *And I will put my Spirit in you and move you to follow my decrees and be careful to keep my laws.* (Ezek 36:24-27)

New Testament support for "prophetic" moral guidance. I'll introduce this discussion noting how ethicist Scott Rae insists that the New Testament

> provides an internal source that assists in decision making and enables one to mature spiritually. This theme is introduced in the Gospels (John 13–17) and developed in the Epistles, particularly those of Paul. . . . Clearly, the New Testament envisions moral and spiritual maturity only in connection with the internal ministry of the Spirit who transforms a person from the inside out.[26]

That the Holy Spirit plays a role in the spiritual maturation of Christian disciples is a given. The two questions I want us to ponder here are: Precisely how does the Holy Spirit assist the follower of Christ in making ethical decisions? Does the New Testament provide at least some inferential support for the concept of moral guidance that's prophetic in nature? Obviously, I believe that the answer to the latter question is yes. Here's why.

To begin, it's my contention that a careful analysis of the book of Acts will reveal many examples of Christ's first followers engaging in missional activities (evangelism, edification and equipping) that, because they were Spirit-initiated and enabled, can be considered prophetic in nature. Nearly every chapter in Acts reflects someone engaging in missional ministry at the behest of the Spirit.[27] I've referred several times already to the idea that a significant, dynamic relationship exists between a missional and moral faithfulness: a missional faithfulness both requires and reflects a moral faithfulness.[28] Building on this notion, I'll put forward here the argument that *since the book of Acts is replete with accounts of missional guidance that is prophetic in nature, it's not illogical to presume that some prophetic moral guidance was occurring as well.* A passage such as Acts 15:22-29, which portrays the early Christians making an important, morally significant missional decision in a prayerful, communal, charismatic manner, would seem to support such a supposition. While the case

---

[26]Rae, *Moral Choices*, pp. 46-47.

[27]See Tyra, *Holy Spirit in Mission*, pp. 65-67, 80-97.

[28]It seems axiomatic that a fruitfulness in one's attempt to contextualize the gospel for new people groups requires a certain moral faithfulness on the part of the missionary; anything less would undermine the missionary's attempt to provide a compelling presentation of the gospel! This explains why the apostle Paul considered it crucial to behave in a morally faithful manner before God and those to whom he proclaimed the gospel (see 2 Cor 1:12; 1 Thess 2:10-12) and to encourage his ministry protégées and the members of the churches to do likewise (see Tit 1:5-8; 2:7-8).

for a prophetic moral guidance doesn't hinge on this Acts-based argument, the tacit support it provides should not go unnoticed.

That being said, support for the thesis of a Spirit-enabled moral guidance can be found in other New Testament writings as well. For example, in 1 Corinthians 2:6-16 Paul refers to the Spirit's ability to enable Christian disciples to somehow "have the mind of Christ." In both Romans 8:1-14 and Galatians 5:16-25 Paul underscores the importance that being "led" by the Spirit has for the Christian life in general and the moral life in particular. Reading passages such as these in tandem certainly seems to support the notion of a divine moral guidance that is Spirit-enabled.[29]

Also, we should keep in mind the way Paul prayed for the church members in Philippi and Colossae. His petition was that with the help of the Holy Spirit they would be able to know God's will (that is, discern the *best* course of action in this or that situation), and in doing so live morally faithful lives until the return of Christ (Phil 1:9-11; Col 1:9-10). Commenting on Colossians 1:9, H. M. Carson observes:

> It is significant that knowledge of the will of God is looked on as preceding a life that is pleasing to Him. The word *filled, plēroō,* suggests the idea of filling out to completeness. Hence the thought is that the imperfection and inadequacy of our knowledge of God's will must be more and more corrected by our growth in a deeper understanding. . . . Such knowledge is not the product of the fleshly wisdom of the world which puffs up but does not enlighten the inner man (cf. 1 Cor 1:20; 2:5, 6, 13; 3:19). It comes rather from the illumination of the Holy Spirit. He it is who gives that *wisdom* and *understanding* which enables us to know the will of God.[30]

Furthermore, what are we to make of the fact that Ephesians 4:17-19 suggests that the phenomenon of immorality is due to a loss of some type of spiritual sensitivity? And how significant is it that the exhortation in Ephesians 4:30 not to "grieve" or disappoint (Greek *lypeō*) the Holy Spirit is located in a pericope rife with moral (and missional) significance (Eph 4:25-32)?

---

[29]See the interesting and provocative discussion of "The Spirit and Moral Discernment" in Lamoureux and Wadell, *Christian Moral Life*, pp. 229-45. See also the chapter titled "Ethics of the Holy Spirit" in Barnette, *Introducing Christian Ethics*, pp. 87-97.

[30]H. M. Carson, *Colossians and Philemon*, Tyndale New Testament Commentaries (Grand Rapids: Eerdmans, 1984), p. 35, emphasis original. For more on the role of the Spirit in providing the wisdom and revelation required of a moral faithfulness, see Bruce, *Epistles*, pp. 268-70.

Also worth noting is the relationship that possibly existed in Paul's mind between discrete, ethically significant passages in Ephesians 5. In Ephesians 5:8-10 we find Paul encouraging his readers to live morally faithful lives by being careful to "find out what pleases the Lord." Just a few verses later in Ephesians 5:17-18 the apostle explains that the key to understanding "what the Lord's will is" is to continually be being "filled with the Spirit."

Finally, it must not escape our notice how often in Revelation 2–3 we find the mantra: "Whoever has ears, let them hear what the Spirit says to the churches" (Rev 2:7, 11, 17, 29; 3:6, 13, 22). A careful read of these two chapters of the Apocalypse will make clear that the motivation behind the repeated exhortations for the members of the seven churches to "hear" what the Spirit is saying to each of them is a concern for a faithfulness that is moral as well as missional in nature. Furthermore, the ethical instructions provided by the Spirit to these churches are definitely situation-specific.

SUPPORT FOR THE DYNAMIC OF SPIRIT-ENABLED MORAL GUIDANCE FROM THE ETHICAL LITERATURE

Due in no little part, I'm sure, to the biblical witness, many moral theologians have commented on the role of the Holy Spirit in ethical decision making, and that in a rather specific manner. For instance, in their book *The Christian Moral Life: Faithful Discipleship for a Global Society*, Patricia Lamoureux and Paul Wadell offer a thoughtful description of moral discernment that's evocative of the contextualizing dynamic at the heart of the ethic of responsible Christian discipleship.

First, these authors clarify that the moral discernment they have in mind "is concerned with the art of determining what God is asking of us, and what our life of discipleship requires in this particular time and place."[31]

Lamoureux and Wadell go on to assert the importance of the Spirit to the discernment process. In so doing they affirm the pneumatological realism I've been championing in this book. They make the bold assertion that

> for much of the history of moral theology, there has been an overemphasis on the intellectual and rational aspects of moral reasoning, while neglecting the role of the Spirit. Rational discourse has gradually been disassociated from its

---

[31]Lamoureux and Wadell, *Christian Moral Life*, p. 232.

roots in the affective and intuitive dimensions of human nature that have close experiential rapport with the Spirit and the gifts of the Spirit.[32]

Moreover, having acknowledged the importance of the gifts of the Spirit, especially the gift of wisdom, to the discernment dynamic, Lamoureux and Wadell affirm that "it is with the assistance of the Holy Spirit, particularly through the infused virtues and the gifts of the Spirit, that a sound moral choice is made."[33]

Finally, these moral theologians go on to clarify the gifts of the Spirit they have in mind and to explain the role of these spiritual gifts in moral decision making. Though the concept of "prophetic," as I'm using that term, may not have been on their minds, the way these scholars refer to the role the Holy Spirit plays in the moral discernment process accords nicely with the notion of a Spirit-enabled moral guidance presented in this book. Lamoureux and Wadell write: "The gifts of the Holy Spirit . . . *make us more amenable to the interior promptings of the Spirit.* They . . . enable us to operate with a certain inclination toward what is of God. The gifts augment the capacity for leading virtuous lives, *discerning God's call*, and making sound judgments."[34]

It's in thoughtful, eloquent ethical works such as this that we find additional support for the concept of Spirit-enabled moral guidance. Can we afford to ignore a potential resource for ethical discernment and decision making that both the Bible and the literature devoted to the ethical enterprise refer to in such striking ways?

DEVOTIONAL BALANCE: THE KEY TO PUTTING OURSELVES IN A PLACE TO "HEAR" GOD

As I pointed out in the introduction to *Pursuing Moral Faithfulness*, the areas of the moral life in which balance is needed are many. There's a need when engaged in ethical deliberation to balance an emphasis on rules, results and virtues, and to maintain a balanced engagement in both spiritual formation practices and spiritual discernment practices.[35] Furthermore, a moral faith-

---

[32]Ibid., pp. 232-33.
[33]Ibid., p. 233.
[34]Ibid., p. 233, emphasis added.
[35]Support for a balanced emphasis on rules, results and virtues can be found in Robin Lovin, *Christian Ethics: An Essential Guide* (Nashville, Abingdon, 2000), pp. 61-63, and Rae, *Moral Choices*, pp. 42-44. See also Kotva, *Christian Case for Virtue Ethics*, pp. 170-72; N. T. Wright, *After You Believe: Why*

fulness requires that when seeking moral guidance we must remain open to all the avenues by which the Spirit might speak to us: the Scriptures, the community of faith and his still small voice speaking directly to our conscience. Finally, in order to put ourselves in a position to hear God speaking directly to us there's the need to make sure that we engage, *at the same time*, in theologically real versions of both Scripture study and prayer.

The last area of needed balance referred to above probably calls for yet another word of clarification. I occasionally hear fellow Christ followers express concern that they have never experienced the dynamic of having God speak directly to their conscience by means of his still small voice. It's my contention that taking another look at Proverbs 2:1-6 will yield yet another critical observation: *an engagement in not one but two guidance-seeking activities at the same time is crucial to our putting ourselves in a position to receive any specific, situation-sensitive moral guidance God wants to give.* According to this passage, in order to acquire the wisdom, knowledge and understanding that comes from God's mouth (Prov 2:6) we must first, so to speak, put ourselves in a place where we can "hear" it. The note of contingency conveyed by means of the "if . . . then" language Proverbs 2:1-6 employs implies a responsibility on the part of the moral agent. In support of this exegetical take biblical scholar Richard Clifford writes: "These verses hold in perfect balance divine initiative and human activity."[36]

Thus the father speaking to his sons in this passage, having encouraged them to pay attention to his instruction (Prov 2:1), goes on provide them with two exhortations: "turn your ears toward wisdom" and "apply your hearts toward understanding" (Prov 2:2). Then he states in a rather matter-of-fact manner that in order to experience God's wisdom they must do more than simply sit back and wait for it to come to them. Instead they are to "call out for insight and cry aloud for understanding" (Prov 2:3), and to "look for it as for silver and search for it as for hidden treasure" (Prov 2:4).

Christian Character Matters (New York: HarperOne, 2010), p. 26; Hauerwas, *Peaceable Kingdom*, p. 23; Stanley Hauerwas, *A Community of Character: Toward a Constructive Christian Social Ethic* (Notre Dame: University of Notre Dame Press, 1981), p. 118; Louis P. Pojman, *How Should We Live? An Introduction to Ethics* (Belmont, CA: Wadsworth, 2004), p. 188; William K. Frankena, *Ethics*, 2nd ed. (Englewood Cliffs, NJ: Prentice-Hall, 1973), pp. 65-67.

[36]Richard J. Clifford, *Proverbs* (Louisville: Westminster John Knox, 1999), p. 47. For a helpful discussion of how God's grace does not eliminate the need for human effort in the moral life, see Kotva, *Christian Case for Virtue Ethics*, p. 130.

I admit to exercising a bit of creative exegetical license when I suggest that it's possible to find in Proverbs 2:1-6 exhortations to proactively engage in two basic guidance-seeking endeavors: (1) a sincere, interactive *praying* that actually expects a response from the Spirit of God and (2) a careful, diligent *study of God's Word*, ever open to the possibility that the Spirit who inspired the Scriptures might choose to "speak" to us in an existentially meaningful manner through it, enabling us to recognize the relevance of a particular biblical text or story to a moral matter currently confronting us. Psalm 119 is filled with references to both of the guidance-seeking practices I believe Proverbs 2 is promoting. For example, the psalmist intones: "May my cry come before you, LORD; give me understanding according to your word" (Ps 119:169).[37]

Could it be that the reason why some of Christ's followers have never sensed the phenomenon of specific, prophetic moral guidance is that they've not intentionally engaged in both of these guidance-seeking practices *at the same time*? Having interacted with thousands of students and parishioners over the years, it's my impression that many churchgoing Christians tend not to seek guidance from God at all or to do so by *either* studying God's written word *or* by crying out to him in prayer. Furthermore, it's been my experience that unless we're very careful we can be guilty of engaging in both of these devotional activities in a merely *theoretical, conceptual* or *ritualistic* rather than *theologically real* manner. In other words, the God of the Bible is, either consciously or subconsciously, conceived of by us as a mere concept or philosophical principle rather than as a real, personal being with whom human beings can interact in a real, intimate manner. Indeed, even though I am quite keen with respect to this issue, I find that in my own devotional life it's not only possible but easy to slip into the habit of praying to the *idea* of God rather than really conversing with him. This amounts to an exercise of worrying in his presence rather than truly casting my cares upon him. It's also possible to read the Bible with an "I-It" rather than an "I-Thou" mentality in place.[38] The difference is one of

---

[37]For a discussion of how the wisdom referred to Proverbs 2 comes by revelation and discipleship, see Derek Kidner, *The Proverbs: An Introduction and Commentary* (Downers Grove, IL: InterVarsity Press, 1964), pp. 36, 61.

[38]This is a reference to the work of philosopher Martin Buber in his book *I and Thou* (New York: Scribner, 2000). Applied to this discussion, the idea is that we can approach Scripture either as an

expectancy: do we really expect God to "speak" to us through his written word? Are we there to master God's Word, or to be "mastered" by God's Spirit through our prayerful interaction with God's Word?

Influenced by a commitment to a theological realism (the idea that God can and should be related to in an intimate, interactive, *realistic*, rather than merely *theoretical, conceptual* or *ritualistic* manner), my read of Proverbs 2:1-6 leads me to assert that perhaps it's not God's fault that some of us lack the sense of having experienced the kind of personal moral guidance Proverbs 2 promises. Maybe we need to take another look at this biblical passage with its apparent call for us to proactively put ourselves in a position to receive moral guidance from God through a balanced, simultaneous engagement in *prayer and Scripture study conducted in a theologically real manner.*[39]

Even more will be said about the extensive, crucial role the Holy Spirit plays in the life of Christian discipleship in later chapters. I'll conclude this discussion by asserting that the teaching of the Bible as a whole, along with my own experience as a Christian moral agent, has convinced me of the value of engaging in a moral deliberation process that includes an openness to the possibility of some specific, situation-sensitive, Spirit-enabled moral guidance. Indeed it's my contention that to the degree we allow him the Holy Spirit can be counted on to enable the sincere Christ follower to not only discern the will of God in this or that situation but to do it as well (see Rom 8:1-4). Though the moral guidance the Spirit provides in any given ethical situation is not always going to be spectacular in the way it occurs, it will always be sufficient, if only to provide us with an invaluable sense of peace about moving forward in this or that direction, trusting in God's ability to use our moral action to support what he is up to in the lives of everyone involved. Even if the moral guidance provided by the Spirit is often of this subtle variety, the process of endeavoring to "hear" what the Spirit might be saying to us mitigates the tendency of too many church members to make moral choices in

---

"It" to be studied, handled, managed or as a "Thou" to be interacted with in a respectful manner as the medium of God's self-revelation to us.

[39]On the other hand, since the experience of prophetic moral guidance can be quite subtle, I believe it's very likely that many sincere, Spirit-filled Christ followers have experienced this phenomenon without realizing it!

precisely the same the way their non-Christians peers do.[40] A primary goal of *Pursuing Moral Faithfulness* is to spread the message that it's because the Holy Spirit longs to provide Christ's followers with *both* moral *discernment* and *empowerment* that a moral faithfulness is possible.[41]

In the next chapter our focus will shift to Jesus and the way he approached the ethical decision-making task and encouraged his followers to do likewise. Such a discussion is obviously crucial to the task of forging an ethic that's Christ-centered. I'm convinced that Jesus himself made moral choices that were both biblically informed and Spirit-empowered. Keep reading, and I'll show you what I mean.

---

[40]This is an important point that needs to be underscored. As H. Richard Niebuhr maintained, an ethic of responsibility does not guarantee that we will never "miss the mark" in terms of God's perfect will, but it does function as an "aid in accuracy in action" (*The Responsible Self: An Essay in Christian Moral Philosophy* [New York: Harper & Row, 1963], pp. 16-17). In other words, the very process of striving to make a responsible moral choice makes it more likely that the resulting moral action is one that honors the heart of God. Hence the title of a chapter in the book *Choices* by Lewis Smedes: "When You Can't Be Sure, Be Responsible" (*Choices: Making Right Decisions in a Complex World* [New York: HarperCollins, 1986], pp. 91-114).

[41]For more on the Spirit's role in ethical empowerment see Barnette, *Introducing Christian Ethics*, pp. 89-91; Dennis Hollinger, *Choosing the Good: Christian Ethics in a Complex World* (Grand Rapids: Baker Academic, 2002), pp. 68-69.

So, What *Would* Jesus Do?

It was in the 1890s when the phrase "What Would Jesus Do?" was first popularized by Congregational minister Charles Sheldon by means of his bestselling book *In His Steps*. The fictional work told the story of a homeless man whose impassioned complaint about churchgoers who don't look at all like the Christ they claim to follow motivated a minister, the Reverend Henry Maxwell, to invite his congregation to take a pledge with him: For one year, before making any important decision, everyone in the church was to ask themselves the question "What would Jesus do?" Then they would act accordingly, no matter what consequences might result.[1]

Nearly a hundred years later, in the late 1980s, the phrase once again commanded wide attention when bracelets bearing the acronym WWJD became a fashion fad. Since then the phrase "What Would Jesus Do?" has been uttered often but seldom in a serious manner. Having become a mere cliché, some bastardized variations of this query include: "What Would Jesus Drive?" "Who Would Jesus Bomb?" and "What Would Bear (Grylls) Do?"[2]

The truth is, however, that "the *imitatio Christi* ideal—imitating Jesus in his purposes, thoughts, and behavior—is as old as Jesus himself. 'Follow me,' Jesus told his would-be disciples; 'do as I do.' This idea is repeated throughout the New Testament" (Lk 9:23; Jn 13:15; Rom 8:29; Eph 5:1; Phil 2:5; 1 Pet 2:21; 1 Jn 2:6).[3] Thus Scott Rae can make the assertion that "the New Testament is clear that the moral

---

[1] Victoria Emily Jones, "WWJD, Part 1: Origin of the Phrase," *The Jesus Question* (blog), January 6, 2012, http://thejesusquestion.org/2012/01/06/wwjd-part-1-the-origin-of-the-phrase/.
[2] Ibid.
[3] Ibid.

obligations for the follower of Jesus are subsumed under the notion of 'becoming like Christ.'"[4]

Still, it's not uncommon for Christian theologians to point out that the WWJD question by itself doesn't a Christian ethic make. Such an approach runs the risk of not sufficiently taking into account the vicarious manner in which Jesus lived his life on our behalf, not just as a model for us to follow in our own feeble strength but as someone whose moral faithfulness becomes the moral faithfulness of everyone who is "in" him through an act of existential trust (biblical faith) and the regenerating and sanctifying work of the Holy Spirit.[5] While it's true that our embodying the moral faithfulness of Christ doesn't occur automatically but requires a surrender to the leadership of his Spirit in our lives, simply asking the question "What would Jesus do?" and then attempting with our own understanding and strength to respond to it, while well-meaning, is fraught with many of the same difficulties attached to any one-norm ethic. Perhaps this is why every so often this essentially good question arises as an ethical fad and then abates once again into essential nonuse.

I'm of the opinion, therefore, that, while the WWJD question when taken seriously is not altogether without value, it's better to ask: "How would a person who, like Jesus, is committed to honoring the heart of the Father respond to this particular moral dilemma?" or "What is the Spirit of Jesus up to in this situation and how can/should I cooperate with him in it?" or "What is Jesus, through the Holy Spirit, commanding and empowering me to do in this specific missional and moral context?" Such questions take seriously the call to follow the risen Christ but do so in a theologically (and pneumatologically) real manner.

That said, the ability of a Christian disciple to answer any of these questions does require some familiarity with the moral manner of Christ. How did Jesus himself make moral choices? What kind of ethical instruction did he provide his first followers?

The aim of this chapter is to give some consideration to the question: "So, what *would* Jesus do?" My approach to this important discussion will be somewhat unique. Rather than provide a lengthy survey of what

---

[4]Scott Rae, *Moral Choices: An Introduction to Ethics*, 3rd ed. (Grand Rapids: Zondervan, 2009), p. 41.
[5]See this book's introduction, p. 28, n. 36.

various Christian ethicists and biblical scholars have to say about how Jesus conceived of morality, I'm going to let Jesus speak for himself, so to speak, focusing the reader's attention on several key incidents recorded in the Gospels that, I'm convinced, provide ample biblical support for a particular understanding of Jesus' moral manner and message.

SEVEN ESSENTIAL ATTRIBUTES OF
THE ETHICAL APPROACH OF JESUS

I've written elsewhere of the importance of understanding Jesus' teaching on discipleship in light of what the Gospels have to say about the antagonistic relationship that existed between him and the religious leaders of his day, especially the Pharisees and teachers of the law.[6] Because of the relationship between Christian ethics and Christian discipleship I've posited in this work, it should come as no surprise to find me arguing here that to properly understand Jesus' moral manner and message we must take into account his polemical relationship with those same ministry antagonists.

In my defense I'll indicate straightaway that I'm not alone in holding this perspective. It's not uncommon for Christian ethicists to distinguish Jesus' take on ethics from the one the Gospels attribute to the Pharisees. For example, Scott Rae, in his book *Moral Choices: An Introduction to Ethics*, summarizes Jesus' ethical genius over against the Pharisees thusly:

> Jesus himself deepens and reapplies the principles of the Law that were misused by the Jewish religious leaders. For example, in the Sermon on the Mount (Matt. 5–7) he does not nullify the Law (5:17-20; John 10:33-35). Rather, he critiques the Pharisees for their misunderstanding and misapplication of it. He extends the requirements of the Law and promotes to both the religious leaders and general population a deontology that is both action and intent oriented. Jesus teaches in the Sermon on the Mount that the intention is just as important as the action, and that a correct action with the wrong intention is not a correct action at all. The Pharisees exemplify some of the abuses of an unbalanced commitment to principles with their system of rigid rules and insensitivity to both the people involved and the consequences of such strict attention to rules.[7]

---

[6]See Gary Tyra, *Defeating Pharisaism: Recovering Jesus' Disciple-Making Method* (Downers Grove, IL: IVP Books, 2009).

[7]Rae, *Moral Choices*, p. 42. A similar take on Jesus' approach to the ethical endeavor can be found in Patrick Nullens and Ronald T. Michener, *The Matrix of Christian Ethics: Integrating Philosophy*

> In rebuking the Pharisees for their rigid misapplication of the Law, Jesus sought a radical change in the primary perspective of ethics among first-century Jews. He rejected a rigid and callous commitment to principles that were not consistent with the Law. He aimed for a deontology that accurately applied the Law, combining a commitment to principles with the virtue of compassion for people.[8]

I'm going to suggest that embedded in these summarizing statements are several key concepts that are true to the biblical portrayal of Jesus' approach to the ethical endeavor and therefore crucial to a Christ-centered, biblically informed and Spirit-empowered ethic. By my reckoning, these critical concepts—which I refer to as seven essential attributes of the ethical approach of Jesus—are as follows:

1. Jesus' ethic is essentially deontological and absolutist in nature; he possesses a high view of the moral commands presented in the Scriptures.

2. Jesus was critical of many of the Pharisees of his day for their misunderstanding and misapplication of these moral commands (despite their superscrupulous nitpicking with respect to them).

3. Rather than veering toward any sort of antinomianism, however, Jesus' ethic actually has the effect of deepening the impact of the biblical commands in people's lives.

4. Jesus calls for his followers to give careful consideration to the original *intent* of a divine command as well as the *impact* it will have on the lives of people in this or that particular context.

5. According to Jesus motive is important, so important that it's possible to be immoral (miss the heart of God) by doing the right thing for the wrong reason.

6. Jesus' ethic seems to require an attempt to be sensitive to the heart of God in the face of each new ethical dilemma.

7. Jesus' ethical decision-making approach seems to combine an emphasis on rules, results *and* virtues, rather than to focus on just one to the neglect of the others.

---

and Moral Theology in a Postmodern Context (Downers Grove, IL: IVP Books, 2010), pp. 26-27.
[8]Rae, *Moral Choices*, p. 43.

These are seven essential attributes of Jesus' ethical approach that I'm able to exegete from the excerpts from Rae presented above. Now the question is: How accurate is this assessment of Jesus' moral manner and message? Put differently, we might frame the issue thusly: To what degree do the Gospels lend support for the seven essential attributes of Jesus' ethical approach presented above?

SOME NEW TESTAMENT SUPPORT FOR
THE SEVEN ESSENTIAL ATTRIBUTES

For his part Rae cites such passages as Matthew 12:1-14 (the story of Jesus healing a man with a withered hand on the Sabbath) and Mark 7:1-20 (Jesus' response to the accusation that he's not sufficiently loyal to Jewish religious traditions) as he expounds on the two summary statements alluded to earlier. In addition to the biblical support Rae provides for the seven essential attributes, I'd like to offer some more. But rather than treat each of the bulleted concepts presented above seriatim (methodically, one after another), I'm going to invite the reader to explore with me several additional Gospel pericopes (passages from the Gospels) that appear to underwrite what both Rae and I are saying about Jesus' approach to the ethical endeavor.

Like the two passages cited by Rae, each of the Gospel portions examined below portrays Jesus interacting either directly or indirectly in a polemical (antagonistic) manner with the Pharisees.

The reader will recall how in chapter five I cited Matthew 23:23, a passage that shows Jesus upbraiding the Jewish Pharisees and teachers of the law for their hypocrisy and moral myopia. By way of reminder, this passage reads thusly:

> Woe to you, teachers of the law and Pharisees, you hypocrites! You give a tenth of your spices—mint, dill and cumin. But you have neglected the more important matters of the law—justice, mercy and faithfulness. You should have practiced the latter, without neglecting the former. (Mt 23:23)

I'm going to suggest that we would do well to keep this acerbic accusation leveled by Jesus against the Pharisees in mind as we explore how four other Gospel pericopes seem to provide some significant support for the seven essential attributes of Jesus' ethical genius.

We will begin this exploration with a careful look at two passages from Jesus' Sermon on the Mount. It's my contention that what we find in Matthew 5–7 is a disciple-making speech that uses the Pharisees as negative examples of what it means to live one's life under the rule and reign of God.[9] While this is true of the Sermon as a whole, nowhere is this contra-Pharisee motif more apparent than in Matthew 5:3-12 and Matthew 5:17-48. It just so happens that both of these passages are hugely indicative of Jesus' approach to a moral faithfulness before God.

Jesus, the Pharisees and the core values of the kingdom of God— Matthew 5:3-12. The Sermon on the Mount begins with a famous section of Scripture we've come to know as the Beatitudes (Mt 5:3-12). While it's true that the Beatitudes are significant for Christian ethics, it's my contention that a proper understanding of this import requires that we not divorce them from what the Matthean Jesus seems to have been doing in the Sermon (and his ministry) as a whole.[10]

What we find in the Beatitudes is a set of actions and attitudes we might think of as the core values of the kingdom of heaven—the central theme of Jesus' preaching ministry (see Mt 4:17, 23). As a whole, the Beatitudes seems to constitute a description—a declaration even—of the kind of people who are genuinely blessed: the kind of people who according to Jesus are to be envied because they are truly approved of by God.[11] We might even say that the Beatitudes are earmarks of those who've learned to live *the good life* from a kingdom perspective.

The question is: How do we understand the meaning of each beatitude? Over the years many varying interpretations have been offered; so many, in fact, that surveying them can be a confusing rather than clarifying experience!

I believe that an important key to understanding the basic meaning of each of the Beatitudes, in addition to keeping the polemical nature of the Sermon as a whole in view, is to do our best to identify and ponder those Old Testament passages that seem to have informed Jesus' own

---

[9]For more on this, see Tyra, *Defeating Pharisaism*, pp. 101-5.

[10]Some of what follows in this discussion is adapted from my book *Defeating Pharisaism*, pp. 127-30.

[11]See D. A. Carson, *The Sermon on the Mount: An Evangelical Exposition of Matthew 5–7* (Grand Rapids: Baker, 1978), p. 16; David Hill, *The Gospel of Matthew*, New Century Bible Commentary (Grand Rapids: Eerdmans, 1972), p. 110.

understanding of what it means to be blessed before God.[12] This herme-neutical method helps us narrow the range of possible meanings Jesus might have intended when he uttered this list of kingdom core values.[13]

It's also important, I believe, to bear in mind the role the Beatitudes played in Matthew's version of Jesus' most famous sermon. Not enough commentators reckon with the fact that the Beatitudes functioned as the introduction to the Sermon on the Mount—an introduction that, in harmony with the Gospel of Matthew as a whole, appears to portray the Pharisees in a rather negative light as very religiously minded folk whose lives were, ironically, severely lacking with respect to the core values of the kingdom.[14] Any effective preaching pastor will verify how important a good sermon introduction is. One classic way to capture the attention of an audience is to begin a sermon by saying something shocking, un-expected, *ironic*. What I'm suggesting is that, when we keep in mind the anti-Pharisee theme that runs throughout the Gospel of Matthew,[15] it makes perfect sense for the Matthean Jesus to begin his sermon with a list of kingdom core values that would have been extremely shocking to

---

[12]We need to remember that a truly high (orthodox) Christology takes the humanity of Jesus as seri-ously as his divinity. While still retaining his essential deity, a truly human Jesus would have devel-oped his theology the way other Jews of his day would—by studying the Old Testament Scriptures (see Lk 2:52)!

[13]It's worth noting that Carson refers to the Beatitudes as "norms of the kingdom" (Carson, *Sermon on the Mount*, p. 16).

[14]In his commentary on the Sermon, August Tholuck does make reference to the role of the Beatitudes as the introduction of Jesus' sermon (*Commentary on the Sermon on the Mount* [Philadelphia: Smith English, 1860], p. 62). See also Craig L. Blomberg, *Matthew*, New American Commentary (Nashville: Broadman, 1992), p. 95. For more on the Pharisees in Matthew see Tyra, *Defeating Pharisaism*, pp. 87-91. For some support for this interpretive take see Georg Strecker, *The Sermon on the Mount: An Exegetical Commentary* (Nashville: Abingdon, 1988), p. 40, where the author argues that the demand of purity that is present in the "pure in heart" beatitude is "turned indirectly against the attitude of the Pharisees, who are pictured as the antitype in Matthew's Gospel." See also Carl G. Vaught, *The Sermon on the Mount: A Theological Interpretation* (Albany: State University of New York Press, 1986), pp. 15-16, where the author suggests that the key to understanding the "poor in spirit" beati-tude is to reflect on Jesus' parable of the Pharisee and the tax collector praying in the temple (Lk 18:10-14). See also Sinclair Ferguson, *The Sermon on the Mount: Kingdom Life in a Fallen World* (Carlisle, PA: Banner of Trust, 1997), p. 47.

[15]For example, see E. P. Sanders, *Jesus and Judaism* (London: SCM Press, 1985), pp. 260-61. At the same time, most scholars exhibit a marked and valid concern to make it clear that the vitriol present in Matthew's Gospel is not directed toward the Jewish people as a whole but at their religious lead-ers specifically, especially the Pharisees. For example, see Jack Kingsbury, *Matthew as Story* (Phila-delphia: Fortress, 1988), p. 115; R. T. France, *Matthew: Evangelist and Teacher* (Exeter, UK: Pater-noster, 1989), p. 218; Donald Senior, *Matthew* (Nashville: Abingdon, 1998), p. 30; Donald Hagner, *Matthew 1–13*, Word Biblical Commentary, vol. 33A (Dallas: Word, 1993), p. lxxii.

his audience on the mount, not just because they seemed to contradict the prevailing notions of happiness and success in their society but also because they would have immediately recognized the absence of these particular attitudes and actions from the lives of most (not all) of the scribes and Pharisees![16] Keeping in mind how very popular the scribes and Pharisees were in Jesus' day—how they were viewed by the common folk as spiritual heroes—this would have rendered the Beatitudes a supremely effective way for Jesus to have immediately gained the rapt attention of his audience while also forecasting what the dual theme of his sermon would be: (1) an explication of life in God's kingdom and (2) the nature of authentic Christian discipleship over against the hypocritical practices of the Pharisees.[17]

If we take these two exegetical presuppositions seriously—that is, the need to give consideration to those Old Testament passages that seem to inform the Beatitudes, and the role the Beatitudes played as an edgy sermon introduction—we come up with the following list of kingdom virtues and behaviors Jesus encouraged his followers to cultivate.

According to Jesus, those truly blessed of God are:

- the *poor in spirit*—those who recognize their radical need for God rather than assuming that material things can provide soul satisfaction or that they can live truly God-pleasing lives in their own strength and on the basis of their own resources (see Is 57:15; 66:1-2; cf. Mt 6:19-24; Lk 16:13-15);[18]

- those who *mourn*—who, instead of minimizing their sin and continually justifying themselves before God and others, are profoundly aware of and grieved by the presence and effect of sin in their own lives (see Is 61:1-3; cf. Mt 23:13-15; cf. Lk 18:9-14);

- the *meek*—those who keep trusting in God to protect and provide for

---

[16]W. D. Davies, *The Sermon on the Mount* (Nashville: Abingdon, 1966), p. 86.

[17]On the Pharisees as spiritual heroes see Blomberg, *Matthew*, p. 105; John Wick Bowman and Roland W. Tapp, *The Gospel from the Mount* (Philadelphia: Westminster Press, 1957), p. 63; William Coleman, *Those Pharisees* (New York: Hawthorn Books, 1977), p. 27; Marcel Simon, *Jewish Sects at the Time of Jesus* (Philadelphia: Fortress, 1967), p. 10; W. D. Davies, *Introduction to Pharisaism* (Philadelphia: Fortress, 1967), p. 17.

[18]Nullens and Michener see an explicit connection between the blessing Jesus pronounces on the poor in Spirit and the call in Micah 6:8 to walk humbly before God (Nullens and Michener, *Matrix of Christian Ethics*, p. 151).

them rather than feel the need to return tit for tat or engage in conspicuous, shameless self-promotion (see Ps 37:1-11; cf. Mt 23:1-12);

- those who *hunger and thirst for righteousness*—who proactively cultivate an insatiable appetite for an intimate, interactive relationship with God rather than rest content with a religion based on a myopic, obsessive focus on rules and rituals (see Ps 42:1-2; 63:1-5; cf. Mt 23:23-24);[19]

- the *merciful*—those who have cultivated a capacity for compassion rather than harsh judgmentalism in their dealings with others (see Mic 6:8; Zech 7:9-10; cf. Mt 9:10-13);

- the *pure in heart*—those who avoid spiritual hypocrisy by striving to maintain an integrity in their professed devotion to God (see Ps 24:3-6; cf. Mt 23:25-28);

- the *peacemakers*—those who, refusing the temptation to return evil for evil, promote peace rather than strife and conflict in the world around them (see Ps 34:11-21; cf. Mt 23:29-32); and

- those who are *persecuted because of righteousness*—who are willing and able to endure hostility at the hands of others because of their loyalty to God and his kingdom cause (see Ps 22; 69; 119; cf. Mt 23:33-39).

Now, some support for this interpretive take on the Beatitudes lies in the view embraced by some biblical scholars that Matthew deliberately structured his Gospel so that each major section is thematically connected to another major section in a chiastic, concentric or symmetrical manner. It just so happens that many versions of this structural theory connect the Sermon on the Mount with Jesus' strident denunciation of the Pharisees in chapter 23.[20] Such a notion lends support for the idea that as the Matthean Jesus enunciated the blessings contained in the Beatitudes he may very well have had the failings of the Pharisees in mind—failings that would be fully exposed and critiqued later in the Gospel.[21]

---

[19]I'm indebted to Dallas Willard (lecture presented in Fuller Seminary Doctor of Ministry seminar "Spirituality and Ministry," Sierra Madre, CA, June 20, 2002) for the idea that Jesus possessed an "intimate, interactive" relationship with God and desired to teach his disciples how to do likewise.
[20]For example, see Robert H. Gundry, *Matthew: A Commentary on His Literary and Theological Art* (Grand Rapids: Eerdmans, 1994), p. 166; Hagner, *Matthew 1–13*, p. lii; France, *Matthew: Evangelist*, p. 148.
[21]The fact that Luke's iteration of the Sermon (Lk 6:20-26) combines versions of both the blessings presented in Matthew 5 and the woes enunciated in Matthew 23 might be seen as providing some

Perhaps even stronger support for this understanding of what Jesus was doing in the Beatitudes is evident in the remarkable correspondence that exists between these core values of the kingdom and the prophetic call to do justice, love with mercy and walk humbly before God. I'm not alone in sensing this correspondence. In his book *The Christian Case for Virtue Ethics,* Joseph Kotva observes:

> The Beatitudes depict the kinds of people and actions that will receive a full share in God's coming kingdom. In pronouncing blessings on the "poor in spirit" (5:3), on those who "hunger and thirst for righteousness" (5:6), and on those who are "pure in heart" (5:8), Matthew's Jesus promises God's reign to those who are humble before God, who yearn for and desire God's justice, and who live from a position of genuineness and integrity.[22]

Surely the parallel between the virtues Kotva sees Jesus promoting in the Beatitudes and those extolled in Micah 6:8 is easily discerned.[23] That said, the larger point I wish to make is this: we've already seen how that in Matthew 23:23 Jesus seems to be indicting the Pharisees for their failure to take Micah 6:8 seriously. I'm arguing here for the idea that Jesus was doing something similar in Matthew 5:3-12—his introduction to the Sermon on the Mount. Now if this were the case, should we not expect to find in the Beatitudes echoes of the cardinal virtues that this key Old Testament passage prescribes in such a dramatic manner? The fact that this is precisely what we do find is telling. In the Beatitudes Jesus was implicitly calling for his hearers to do better than the Pharisees and teachers of the law at rendering to God a genuine moral faithfulness (see Mt 5:20). In the process he articulates a short list of kingdom core values redolent of the prophetic call to act justly, love with mercy and walk humbly before God.

Jesus, the Pharisees and the real righteousness God is looking for— Matthew 5:17-48. Even more support for the interpretive take regarding the ethical significance of the Beatitudes presented above can be found in the next section of the Sermon, where Jesus pointedly positions his

---

support for this structural theory.

[22]See Kotva, *Christian Case for Virtue Ethics*, p. 104.

[23]See also the succinct but still substantial synopsis of the Beatitudes presented by Patricia Lamoureux and Paul J. Wadell—an overview that is redolent of the behaviors/virtues prescribed in Micah 6:8 (Lamoureux and Wadell, *The Christian Moral Life: Faithful Discipleship for a Global Society* [Maryknoll, NY: Orbis Books, 2010], pp. 62-63).

ethical teaching over against that of the Pharisees and teachers of the law.[24] Because this section is both lengthy and dense, I'm going to bracket off Matthew 5:17-20 and Matthew 5:48 and treat them as separate introductory and concluding texts respectively that, because of their special functions, merit some special attention.

Matthew 5:17-20. Actually these four verses not only introduce a major section of the Sermon on the Mount, but they stand at the very heart of Matthew 5 and perhaps the Sermon as a whole. Jesus makes it very clear in this passage that he has not "come to abolish the Law or the Prophets; I have not come to abolish them but to fulfill them" (Mt 5:17).[25]

He goes on to insist in a somewhat dramatic manner that he has a high rather than low view of the commands contained in the Law:

> For truly I tell you, until heaven and earth disappear, not the smallest letter, not the least stroke of a pen, will by any means disappear from the Law until everything is accomplished. Therefore anyone who sets aside one of the least of these commands and teaches others accordingly will be called least in the kingdom of heaven, but whoever practices and teaches these commands will be called great in the kingdom of heaven. (Mt 5:18-19)

He then concludes this ethically significant warning with a startlingly ironic statement regarding the need for a righteousness that surpasses that of the Pharisees and teachers of the law:[26]

> For I tell you that unless your righteousness surpasses that of the Pharisees and the teachers of the law, you will certainly not enter the kingdom of heaven. (Mt 5:20)

Once again this now-explicit indictment of some of Israel's religious leaders would have struck Jesus' hearers as highly ironic. Keeping in mind the reputation for a superlative righteousness the Pharisees and teachers of the law enjoyed in Jesus' day, it would have been quite unexpected and

---

[24]Some of what follows in this discussion is adapted from my book *Defeating Pharisaism*, pp. 130-44.
[25]R. T. France is careful to point out that when Jesus referred to "the Law or the Prophets" he was actually referring to the Old Testament Scriptures as a whole; the third element in the Hebrew Scriptures, the "Writings," did not need to be specifically included (R. T. France, *The Gospel of Matthew*, New International Commentary on the New Testament [Grand Rapids: Eerdmans, 2007], p. 181).
[26]It should be noted that France refers to the fact that Matthew's references to the Pharisees and teachers of the law seem to overlap (France, *Matthew: Evangelist*, pp. 220-21).

provocative for Jesus' audience on the mount to hear him say that the righteousness exhibited by the hyperscrupulous Pharisees and teachers of the law actually fell short of the mark of what God was looking for in his people.[27] And yet it's hard to imagine a better way for Jesus to have arrested the attention of his hearers, virtually daring them not to attend closely to what he was about to say regarding what's really involved in honoring the heart of God. It's for this reason that some biblical scholars view Matthew 5:20 as the interpretive key to the Sermon as a whole![28]

Matthew 5:21-47. I'm convinced it's possible to view this lengthy portion of the Sermon as possessing a common, unifying theme. Having just made the startling statement that he fully expects his followers, as newly naturalized citizens of God's kingdom, to manifest a righteousness that far surpasses that of the Pharisees and teachers of the law, Jesus goes on to provide his hearers with no less than six examples of how—ironically—the hermeneutical approach of the Pharisees and teachers of the law had caused them to miss the heart of God and to forge a lifestyle that, while adhering to the letter of the law, was nevertheless lacking in true righteousness.

The scholarly consensus is that Jesus' frequent refrain, "You have heard that it was said" (Mt 5:21, 27, 31, 33, 38, 43), refers to the teaching of the scribes and Pharisees—the teachers and leaders of the synagogue.[29] *In each case, Jesus boldly counters the ethical teaching of the Pharisees and teachers of the law with his own announcement of the kind of virtue/ behavior God is really looking for.* Matthew's readers would have understood that in the course of providing his hearers with these six antitheses ("You have heard that it was said . . . But I tell you . . .") Jesus was not just demonstrating that it's possible to focus on the letter of the law and still miss the spirit of it; he was also indicting the Pharisees for several hypocritical actions and attitudes.[30] This is what happens when religious

---

[27]See Blomberg, *Matthew,* p. 105; see also Bowman and Tapp, *Gospel from the Mount,* p. 63, and Hagner, *Matthew 1-13,* p. 110.

[28]Donald Hagner cites Joachim Jeremias's view that Mt 5:20 can be considered the "theme" of the Sermon. See Hagner, *Matthew 1-13,* p. 83.

[29]William B. Tolar, "The Sermon on the Mount from an Exegetical Perspective," *Southwestern Journal of Theology* 35 (1992): 72.

[30]Clarence Bauman, *The Sermon on the Mount: The Modern Quest for Its Meaning* (Macon, GA: Mercer University Press, 1985), p. 156. Bauman cites the view of Karl Bornhäuser that each and every antithesis presented in Mt 5:21-48 constitutes an implicit indictment of a specific Pharisaic teaching

people treat the Bible as a moral rulebook rather than as a means by which the moral agent might grow in his or her desire and ability to contextualize the will of God in this or that ethical situation. The truth

THE SIX ETHICAL ANTITHESES OF MATTHEW 5:21-47			
What Was Being Taught	**The Likely Old Testament Foundation**	**A Hyperliteral, Loophole-Seeking Interpretation**	**Jesus On the Heart of God**
"You shall not murder, and anyone who murders will be subject to judgment" (Mt 5:21).	Ex 20:13; 21:12	*As long as we don't literally kill anyone, it's OK for us to hurl hurtful epithets their way.*	God desires that we avoid murdering people mentally and with our mouths (Mt 5:22)!
"You shall not commit adultery" (Mt 5:27).	Ex 20:14; Lev 20:10	*It's OK to leer at others lustfully as long as we don't go on to act physically on the impulse.*	God desires that we not view people as sexual objects, committing adultery with them in our hearts (Mt 5:28)!
"Anyone who divorces his wife must give her a certificate of divorce" (Mt 5:31).	Deut 24:1-4	*As long as we legally divorce and remarry each time, we're free to experience sexual intimacy with many people over a lifetime.*	God desires that we take marriage seriously, not divorcing and remarrying in order to change sexual partners (Mt 5:32)!
"Do not break your oath, but fulfill to the Lord the vows you have made" (Mt 5:33).	Ex 20:7; Num 30:2; Deut 6:13	*As long as we don't actually use the name of God when swearing an oath we're free not to make good on it.*	God desires that we not use slippery speech but simply say what we mean and mean what we say (Mt 5:34-37)!
"Eye for eye, and tooth for tooth" (Mt 5:38).	Lev 24:19-20	*It's morally justifiable to seek recompense from anyone who injures us.*	God desires that we not only overlook everyday slights but dare to be radically generous toward others also (Mt 5:39-42)!
"Love your neighbor and hate your enemy" (Mt 5:43).	Lev 19:18; Ps 139:21-22	*All God requires is that we love the in-group; no need to concern ourselves over the welfare of outsiders.*	God desires that we learn to care for everyone (even the outsider) the way he does (5:44-47)!

Figure 7.1

or practice. See also Robert Guelich, *The Sermon on the Mount* (Dallas: Word, 1982), p. 17; John R. W. Stott, *Christian Counter-Culture: The Message of the Sermon on the Mount* (Downers Grove, IL: InterVarsity Press, 1978), pp. 78-80; Michael Green, *The Message of Matthew* (Downers Grove, IL: InterVarsity Press, 1988), pp. 92-97; Bowman and Tapp, *Gospel from the Mount*, pp. 64-105.

is that an innate, fallen human tendency to look for loopholes will cause even the most superspiritual church member to minimize in self-serving ways the ethical imperatives found in Scripture. This is what the Pharisees had been doing, and Jesus was about to bring attention to their hypocrisy and faux righteousness in a very public manner.[31]

Since I've elaborated at length elsewhere on what I see Jesus doing in his enunciation of the six antitheses that make up Matthew 5:21-47, I have, at the risk of greatly oversimplifying things, condensed the essence of that discussion and placed it in the table presented above. (See figure 7.1.) Again, the key to understanding this table is to recognize that implicit in each of the six antitheses is an awareness on the part of Jesus and his hearers of some behaviors engaged in by at least some of the Pharisees and teachers of the law—behaviors that, while holding to the letter of the law, failed to honor the heart of God.[32]

Matthew 5:48. I want to suggest that the key to understanding what Jesus was up to in all of the antitheses was articulated in his startling call for his disciples to "Be perfect, therefore, as your heavenly Father is perfect" (Mt 5:48).

In other words, it appears that at the heart of Jesus' teaching regarding the ethics of the kingdom is an emphasis on the possibility of a personal, intimate, interactive relationship with God as our heavenly Abba. The reason why we can learn to engage in all the "radical" behaviors prescribed by Jesus in the foregoing section of the Sermon is that, as members of the new humanity created in Christ, we not only bear the image of the Father but we also, so to speak, now possess the spiritual DNA of his ever-faithful Son! Such a theologically real approach to ethics changes everything![33]

In his book *The Sermon on the Mount: A Theological Interpretation,* Carl Vaught offers a nuanced interpretation of what Jesus had in mind

---

[31]Again, it's possible that Matthew intended his readers to see, on the one hand, a loose but direct relationship between these six indictments and the seven woes pronounced on the Pharisees in chapter 23, and, on the other hand, a loose, inverse (ironic) relationship between this list of indictments and the eight kingdom core values (the Beatitudes) with which Jesus began this sermon (Mt 5:3-12).

[32]For some additional, more specific support for this thesis, see Tyra, *Defeating Pharisaism,* pp. 148-50, nn. 38-46.

[33]For more on the significance of the new humanity formed in Christ, see Gary Tyra, *A Missional Orthodoxy: Theology and Ministry in a Post-Christian Context* (Downers Grove, IL: IVP Academic, 2013), pp. 240-48.

when he used the word "perfect" (Greek: *teleios*) in Matthew 5:48 to describe the goal of his ethic. Vaught writes:

> It is important to focus on the Greek word that is translated "perfection" in this passage. The word *telios* [sic] is the term from which we get the word *telos*, or "end." As a result, the word translated "perfection" means the end toward which a developing being is oriented so that when it reaches that end, it will finally be mature, and by implication, be what it was meant to become. The universe about which Jesus spoke . . . was a world understood in terms of purposes, ends, and goals. As a result, the crucial question to be asked about a person or a thing was not a question about its internal constitution, but a more fundamental question about what that thing or person was meant to be.
>
> In the passage before us, Jesus formulates this fundamental question by using the term *telios,* which can be translated with the English word "perfection" but which can perhaps be rendered more adequately in terms of the concept of maturity. "Be engaged," Jesus says, "in the task of becoming what you were meant to be, reaching the *telos*, the purpose, the goal, and the maturity for which you were intended." In these terms, the Sermon on the Mount intends to bring the followers of Jesus into a kingdom that has both come and is coming and into a way of life that makes it possible for us to live in terms of the end toward which we ought to be directed.[34]

According to this interpretation, Jesus' call for his followers to be perfect even as their heavenly Father is perfect is as much a promise as it is a command. The idea is that we belong to a loving, compassionate God who delights in empowering his children to likewise behave in loving, compassionate ways.[35] In other words, what we have in Matthew 5:48 is a dramatic, no-nonsense call for Jesus' followers to internalize the radical love of their heavenly Abba so that they, like him, might actually manifest a righteous, loving, gracious lifestyle that differed drastically from the faux righteousness of the Pharisees and teachers of the law.[36] Jesus' message to his disciples seems to have been this: "Because of what I have done, am doing and will do on your behalf, you can do this! A moral

---

[34]Vaught, *Sermon on the Mount,* p. 11.

[35]Note that in Luke's version of this exhortation (Lk 6:36) the call is for Jesus' disciples to be merciful as their (heavenly) Father is merciful.

[36]Ferguson, *Sermon on the Mount,* pp. 114, 116. Ferguson insists that the "heart of the problem" with the Pharisees was that they did not know God as their heavenly Father (*Abba*).

faithfulness is possible! Let me, as your savior and sanctifier, help you grow in your capacity to hear and honor the heart of God."[37]

Even though what was provided here was a only a cursory exposition of a major section of Jesus' most famous sermon, I trust that the reader is able to find in it some solid support for most if not all of the seven essential attributes listed earlier in this chapter. In particular I want to underscore how that a careful read of this Gospel pericope provides an indication that for Jesus, honoring the heart of God requires a deliberative approach that emphasizes rules, results and virtues. That this is so will become even clearer in the sections that follow.

Jesus, the Pharisees and the call to make "correct judgments"—John 7:14-24. As additional scriptural support for the seven essential attributes of Jesus' approach to the ethical endeavor, I will offer here the opinion that the stinging rebuke Jesus directed at his antagonists in John 7:24—"Stop judging by mere appearances, but instead judge correctly"—also possesses ethical significance.[38] While it's true that this exchange is presented in John's Gospel as part of a larger discussion of Jesus' true identity as Israel's messiah, the immediate context for the rebuke uttered in John 7:24 is focused on the question of whether it's appropriate for his antagonists to criticize him for healing on the Sabbath. Viewed within its immediate context, Jesus' morally meaningful exhortation reads thusly:

> Jesus said to them, "I did one miracle, and you are all amazed. Yet, because Moses gave you circumcision (though actually it did not come from Moses, but from the patriarchs), you circumcise a boy on the Sabbath. Now if a boy can be circumcised on the Sabbath so that the law of Moses may not be broken, why are you angry with me for healing a man's whole body on the Sabbath? *Stop judging by mere appearances, but instead judge correctly.*" (Jn 7:21-24)

The reference in this passage to Jesus' having healed a man on the Sabbath—a healing that infuriated his legalistic opponents—harks back

---

[37]I have in mind here Jesus' vicarious life, death and resurrection, the future outpouring of his Spirit, and his ensuing high-priestly ministry.

[38]See Frederick Dale Bruner, *The Gospel of John: A Commentary* (Grand Rapids: Eerdmans, 2012), p. 473.

to a contentious exchange we read of in John 5:1-18.[39] John indicates the upshot of that contentious exchange thusly:

> So, because Jesus was doing these things on the Sabbath, the Jewish leaders began to persecute him. In his defense Jesus said to them, "My Father is always at his work to this very day, and I too am working." For this reason they tried all the more to kill him; not only was he breaking the Sabbath, but he was even calling God his own Father, making himself equal with God. (Jn 5:16-18)

This summary of the incident reported on in John 5 makes it clear that the frustration of the Pharisees had to do with two things: (1) the way Jesus behaved on the Sabbath, and (2) the way he was referring to God as his Father. Passages such as John 9:13-16 underscore just how important to the Pharisees was the first concern listed above. Indeed in John 9:16 we read: "Some of the Pharisees said, 'This man is not from God, for he does not keep the Sabbath.'" Thus it's my suggestion that *the warning directed at the Pharisees in John 7:24 actually possessed a dual meaning.* It's true that when Jesus exhorted his interlocutors to "Stop judging by mere appearances, but instead judge correctly," he was ultimately challenging them to think more deeply about his true identity. But, given the focus on the question of the morality of healing on the Sabbath in both the immediate and larger contexts in which this warning was given, I'm suggesting that it's possible to derive from John 7:24 some very basic, if inferential, ethical instruction. *Jesus seemed to be asserting that, instead of rushing to judgment (about such issues as healing on the Sabbath), a morally faithful life before God requires that the moral agent slow down and think deeply and biblically about where the heart of God is with respect to the moral matter at hand.*[40]

It's true that nothing in John 7:14-24 explicitly refers to a desire on the part of Jesus to help his hearers learn this crucial lesson about what's involved in manifesting a moral faithfulness before God. And yet, as we've seen, such a concern *is* evident in a major section of Jesus' Sermon on the Mount (Mt 5:17-48) as well as Matthew 23:23. Furthermore, I will suggest below that it's

---

[39]Bruner, *Gospel of John*, pp. 476-77; D. A. Carson, *The Gospel According to John* (Grand Rapids: Eerdmans, 1991), p. 314; N. T. Wright, *John for Everyone, Part 1* (Louisville: Westminster John Knox, 2004), pp. 97, 101; F. F. Bruce, *The Gospel of John: Introduction, Exposition, Notes* (Grand Rapids: Eerdmans, 1994), pp. 176-77.

[40]See Bruner, *Gospel of John*, pp. 477-78; Carson, *Gospel According to John*, pp. 315-16; Wright, *John*, pp. 100-102; Bruce, *Gospel of John*, p. 177.

also inferred in the way Jesus himself handled ethically tricky situations like the one described in John 8:1-11. Let's turn our attention now to that provocative passage, doing our best to be open to the possibility that it too will provide some support for the seven essential attributes listed above.

Jesus, the Pharisees and the woman caught in the act of adultery—John 8:1-11.[41] Yet another pericope that's at least potentially pregnant with ethical significance is the biblical account of how Jesus responded when his ministry antagonists used an adulterous woman caught *in flagrante delicto* (redhanded or in the very act) in an effort to force him to say or do something that would either get him in trouble with the Sanhedrin or alienate him from the crowd of people who were hanging on his every word.[42] Apparently the case of a woman who was guilty of having committed an act that according to the law of Moses was indeed a grave offense had come to the attention of the teachers of the law and the Pharisees. These religious leaders decided they would attempt to pressure Jesus into weighing in on this matter, and to do so in a public setting. For the reasons stated above, this move was clever; it put Jesus in between a rock and a hard place.[43]

But Jesus went to the Mount of Olives.

At dawn he appeared again in the temple courts, where all the people gathered around him, and he sat down to teach them. The teachers of the law and the Pharisees brought in a woman caught in adultery. They made her stand before the group and said to Jesus, "Teacher, this woman was caught in the act of adultery. In the Law Moses commanded us to stone such women. Now what do you say?" They were using this question as a trap, in order to have a basis for accusing him. (Jn 8:1-6a)

---

[41]Use of this passage to provide biblical support for just about anything having to do with Christ is tricky since the authorship, date and original placement of this pericope are highly disputed. (For example, Bruner, *Gospel of John*, pp. 507-8; Herman Ridderbos, *The Gospel of John: A Theological Commentary* [Grand Rapids: Eerdmans, 1997], pp. 285-87; Carson, *Gospel According to John*, p. 333; Leon Morris, *The Gospel According to John* [Grand Rapids: Eerdmans, 1995], pp. 778-79; Bruce, *Gospel of John*, p. 413.) I make use of it, having embraced the notion put forward by Ridderbos, Carson, Morris and others that even if this passage were not an original part of the Fourth Gospel, it was, nevertheless, an insertion that was reflective of a real incident from Jesus' life. See Ridderbos, *Gospel of John*, p. 287; Carson, *Gospel According to John*, p. 333; Morris, *Gospel According to John*, p. 779.
[42]Ridderbos, *Gospel of John*, p. 288; Carson, *Gospel According to John*, p. 335; Morris, *Gospel According to John*, pp. 782-83; Bruce, *Gospel of John*, p. 415; Wright, *John*, p. 112; William Barclay, *The Gospel of John* (Philadelphia: Westminster Press, 1975), 2:1-2.
[43]F. F. Bruce offers that the question was "calculated to put Jesus on the horns of a dilemma" (Bruce, *Gospel of John*, p. 415). William Barclay uses similar language (Barclay, *Gospel of John*, 2:1-2).

According to the second part of verse 6, Jesus responded to this moral dilemma by kneeling down and drawing in the dirt. "But Jesus bent down and started to write on the ground with his finger" (Jn 8:6b). I'm suggesting that a careful look at this story can provide us with a powerful lesson regarding the Christlike way to respond when facing ethical situations that seem just too knotted to untangle. Jesus' "drawing in the dirt" can serve as an apt metaphor for what's involved in making ethical decisions that strive to honor the heart of God.

Before going any further, it should be noted that what follows is more of a theological reflection than an exercise in biblical exposition. In other words, I'm *not* suggesting that the biblical author (or redactor) had the moral instruction of his readers primarily in mind as he penned (and/or included) this passage. This doesn't mean, however, that the author/redactor couldn't have had more than one purpose or life application in view. Regardless, it's my hope that the reader will find some value in this attempt, by means of a theological reflection that doesn't completely ignore exegetical matters, to let the risen Christ speak to us through this poignant passage with its suggestive depiction of how he once resolved a tricky moral dilemma himself.

What "drawing in the dirt" represents. I'm going to offer immediately that "drawing in the dirt" (as a metaphorical approach to ethical decision making) involves two things. First, we draw in the dirt when we, like Jesus, are careful to *respond* to our circumstances rather than merely *react* to them. If we were honest, many of us would have to admit that, facing a similar conundrum, we would probably offer a rushed reaction to our antagonists rather than a careful response. One of the many things I admire about Jesus is his ability to remain cool, calm and collected even when under immense pressure. His ability to remain unflappable regardless of the circumstances is certainly on display here.[44] To draw in the dirt means, first of all, that when we find ourselves facing an ethical dilemma, we pause long enough to form a thoughtful, prayerful *response* to our circumstances rather than reacting hastily to them.

Something else is involved in learning to draw in the dirt, however. Not only did Jesus endeavor to respond to this situation rather than react, he

---

[44]See Bruner, *Gospel of John,* p. 506.

also sought to offer a *responsible,* virtuous solution to the moral problem that confronted him—an ethical decision that was *responsive* to the heart of God (cf. Jn 14:10, 31; 5:30; 8:28; 12:49; 14:24; 15:15). All too often we tend to seek the easy way out of the ethical dilemmas we periodically encounter. The easy way out is to simply focus our attention on obeying rules *or* producing results *or* exhibiting virtues in any given situation, rather than attempting to do justice to all three at the same time per Micah 6:8 and the command to love God supremely and our neighbors as ourselves. Frankly, it's hard work to balance a focus on rules and results while also striving to manifest the virtues God is looking for his people to possess.

With this thought in mind, I believe it's vitally important for evangelical Christians, given our commitment to the authority of Scripture, to recognize that Jesus didn't *merely* focus his attention on the rules that applied to the moral dilemma he was facing. Had he, the story would have ended much differently. He might have simply agreed with the scribes and Pharisees that the woman should be stoned according to the law of Moses (Lev 20:10; Deut 22:22-24).[45] Thus I'm suggesting that drawing in the dirt involves us in doing more than *merely* respecting the rules.

On the other hand, this approach to ethical decision making also requires that we do more than *simply* consider the consequences. As we've seen, a single-minded focus on the consequences of a moral action constitutes another imbalanced approach to ethical decision making. Due to the influence of both modernism and postmodernism, too many church-going Christians fail to sufficiently respect the rules for moral conduct provided for us in God's Word. Though I've argued in this work that the Bible shouldn't (and really can't) be treated as a comprehensive menu of moral responses that address every conceivable dilemma we might face in this life, I've also contended that it does serve as a crucial resource for making good moral choices. It will very often provide specific ethical instruction that is directly applicable to a given situation.[46]

---

[45]Ibid., p. 505; Ridderbos, *Gospel of John,* p. 287; Morris, *Gospel According to John,* p. 781; Bruce, *Gospel of John,* p. 414; Barclay, *Gospel of John,* 2:2.

[46]Indeed, it probably bears repeating that not all ethical situations constitute a genuine moral dilemma as defined in chapter one of this work. Sometimes we simply find ourselves as Christian disciples facing nothing more than a temptation to sin. When this is the case, and a biblical command is obviously relevant to the matter at hand, there is no dilemma per se; we just obey the divine command, proving

So the ethical manner of Jesus seems to call for us to take the moral teaching found in the Scriptures seriously while also giving careful consideration to the possible consequences of each and every discrete moral choice. To learn how to do both, while also striving to emulate the wisdom, courage and compassion of Jesus, is what it means to "draw in the dirt," metaphorically speaking.[47]

Why did *Jesus draw in the dirt?* It's time now to ask the exegetical question: Is there any support in the text, implicit or explicit, for this theological/ethical understanding of what Jesus was doing when he drew in the dirt? In other words: *How appropriate is it for us to even think that we might find in this Gospel pericope (Jn 8:1-11) a metaphor for an ethical decision-making process that strives to honor the heart of God?* Why *did* Jesus kneel and draw with his finger in the dirt when confronted with this moral dilemma?

Scholars are not at all in agreement as to what Jesus actually wrote in the dirt, many concluding that no one knows for sure.[48] A number of scholars are willing to suggest, however, that whatever the content, his drawing was intended as some sort of "delaying tactic."[49]

But why the need for a delay? While it's possible that Jesus was concerned to draw attention away from the shamed woman standing there on display, it has also been argued that Jesus, in his very real humanity, needed some time in order to quickly and quietly pray, asking God for help and guidance in this new and difficult test.[50] As William Barclay puts it: "He may simply have wished to gain time and not be rushed into a decision. In that brief moment he may have been both thinking the thing out and taking it to God."[51]

---

to be doers of God's word rather than hearers only (see Jas 1:22; cf. Mt 7:21; Lk 6:46-49)! Moreover, even when the Bible does not in an obvious manner present us with us normative ethical instruction, it still serves us in our ethical decision making as something the Holy Spirit uses to form in us the kind of godly character and spiritual sensitivity necessary for making moral choices that reflect the wisdom of God and redound to his glory. It's for all of these reasons our Bibles must not be neglected!

[47]Another way to say this is that "drawing in the dirt" occurs whenever we're careful to give due consideration to the divine *intent* of any moral commands that seem relevant to the situation at hand, doing our best with the help of the Holy Spirit to discern what doing justice, loving with mercy and walking humbly/faithfully before God looks like in this particular ethical context.

[48]For example, see Carson, *Gospel According to John*, p. 336; Ridderbos, *Gospel of John*, p. 289; Morris, *Gospel According to John*, pp. 783-84; Wright, *John*, p. 113; Bruce, *Gospel of John*, p. 415.

[49]For example, Carson, *Gospel According to John*, p. 336. See also Ridderbos, *Gospel of John*, p. 289.

[50]Bruner, *Gospel of John*, pp. 505-6.

[51]Barclay, *Gospel of John*, 2:3.

I want to encourage the reader not to dismiss such a suggestion too hastily. A high Christology is one that takes both the divinity and humanity of Jesus seriously.[52] Based on passages such as Hebrews 2:10-18, we need to be careful not to construct an image of Jesus that totally discounts the possibility that he in his assumed humanity genuinely needed, like the rest of us, to experience the illuminating, empowering work of the Holy Spirit in order to render to God the missional and moral faithfulness he desires and deserves (see Lk 3:21-22; 4:1-2, 14; 5:16).

Could it be that this is why Jesus drew in the dirt? Though the exegetical support for this explanation of Jesus' mysterious behavior is admittedly inferential at best, I believe we would do well to at least consider the possibility that Jesus, by kneeling to draw in the dirt, was actually pausing long enough to thoughtfully and prayerfully forge a response to this ethical dilemma—a virtuous response that sought to do justice to both the rules and the results at the same time.

Such an interpretive take finds some tacit support in our analyses of the Gospel pericopes presented in the three sections previous. Additional support for this idea can be found in F. D. Bruner's commentary on the Gospel of John, in which he opines: "With this response Jesus manages to both recognize (if not to honor) the ancient Bible's capital teaching (*'stone her'*) and at the same time to honor even more his unique compassion for this and for every shamed (even if sinful) human being and so to avert a cruel use of the Bible."[53]

The rest of this tantalizingly suggestive passage from John 8 reads:

> They were using this question as a trap, in order to have a basis for accusing him.
>
> But Jesus bent down and started to write on the ground with his finger. When they kept on questioning him, he straightened up and said to them, "Let any one of you who is without sin be the first to throw a stone at her." Again he stooped down and wrote on the ground.
>
> At this, those who heard began to go away one at a time, the older ones first, until only Jesus was left, with the woman still standing there. Jesus straightened up and asked her, "Woman, where are they? Has no one condemned you?"

[52]Bruner, *Gospel of John*, p. 506.
[53]Ibid., emphasis original.

"No one, sir," she said.

"Then neither do I condemn you," Jesus declared. "Go now and leave your life of sin." (Jn 8:6-11)

I believe Bruner's observation of what was going on in this passage is spot-on. On the one hand, because of those Old Testament passages referred to earlier that speak of stoning people caught in the act of adultery, there is some scholarly support for the idea that Jesus, by calling for someone to hurl the first stone, was acknowledging that in principle the woman was indeed guilty of a capital crime under Jewish law.[54] On the other hand, many scholars are of the opinion that it would have been inherently unjust for this particular woman to be stoned there on the spot. Some argue that the absence of her partner in infidelity suggests that the woman had been in some way "set up" (or that the Pharisees had a special grievance against her).[55] Others wonder whether, under the circumstances, the punishment being promoted by the woman's accusers didn't amount to a form of lynching that lacked true legal authority.[56] Either way it's clear that *the Pharisees and teachers of the law didn't have the original intention for the law prohibiting adultery in mind as they publicly paraded this woman in front of Jesus in order to try to trap him.* Thus it's my suggestion that Jesus' drawing in the dirt was his way of prayerfully discerning how the call in Micah 6:8 to do justice, love with mercy and walk humbly before God might apply in this particular life situation.[57]

So, once again, I'll ask: Could it be that Jesus' drawing in the dirt was driven by a desire to render to God, his Father, a moral faithfulness? Is it possible that he drew in the dirt on this occasion because it took some time, even for him, to engage in the discernment process necessary to arrive at

---

[54]For example, see Morris, *Gospel According to John*, p. 784, where the author proposes that Jesus' call for someone to throw the first stone (Jn 8:7) was a tacit admission of the validity of the law in this case.

[55]See Bruner, *Gospel of John*, pp. 505-6; Morris, *Gospel According to John*, p. 781; Bruce, *Gospel of John*, p. 414; Lewis Smedes, *Choices: Making Right Decisions in a Complex World* (New York: HarperCollins, 1986), p. 35.

[56]See Morris, *Gospel According to John*, p. 782.

[57]It's probably unnecessary for me to alert the reader to the fact that most commentaries are careful to indicate how John 8:11 specifies that while Jesus did not choose to condemn the woman, neither did he condone her behavior. Indeed he labeled it a sin that must be avoided going forward. See, for example, Bruner, *Gospel of John*, p. 510; Ridderbos, *Gospel of John*, pp. 290-91; Carson, *Gospel According to John*, pp. 336-37; Morris, *Gospel According to John*, p. 785; Wright, *John*, p. 113; and Barclay, *Gospel of John*, 2:4, 7-9.

a moral choice that would be both responsible and responsive—a moral choice that would honor the heart of his heavenly Father? Even if the biblical author/redactor didn't have such a message in mind, *doesn't the story provide us with an apt metaphor for an ethical decision-making process that seeks to be both responsible and responsive?* If any of the foregoing is true, then this pericope can be viewed as providing some stunning support for the seven essential attributes of Jesus' ethical genius presented earlier. Furthermore, as disciples of Jesus, we're obliged to follow his example here as elsewhere. In other words, it's my contention that, as difficult as it may be, learning to "draw in the dirt" should be one of our aspirations as sincere Christ followers eager to render to God a moral faithfulness.

Even more will be said about the responsible and responsive nature of this approach to ethical decision making in the next chapter. But before we go there, I'll conclude this chapter with a summary statement of my own. What all of this means ultimately is that a biblically informed answer to the question "So, what *would* Jesus do?" will go something like this: According to Jesus himself, in order to make moral choices that honor the heart of God, we must, like him, become the kind of people who are eager and able to "hear" his heart so that we might live in a manner that's faithful to it (see Jn 5:30). This is a big part of what Christian discipleship is all about. This is how we, in union with Christ, allow the Holy Spirit to make real in our lives the moral faithfulness of Jesus himself.

Can anything besides the desire to also manifest before God a missional faithfulness be considered as important as what we're talking about here? A presumed negative answer to this concluding query will, I hope, prompt the reader to keep reading. It's possible to be even more precise about what's involved in making *responsible* moral judgments that are also *responsive* in nature. The next chapter, very practical in nature, will show us how this can be done.

8

Responsible and Responsive
Decision Making

*A Closer Look at
"Drawing in the Dirt"*

Mark 3:1-6 tells the story of some Pharisees (cf. Mk 2:23-28) watching Jesus closely to see whether he would heal a man with a withered hand even though it was the Sabbath. According to Mark 3:2, they were "looking for a reason to accuse Jesus." In other words, they were apparently hoping to catch him healing someone on the Sabbath so that they might have cause for his condemnation.

We read in verse 3 of this passage that Jesus had the man with the withered hand "stand up in front of everyone." Then verse 5 tells us that just before healing the man, Jesus "looked around at them in anger . . . deeply distressed at their stubborn hearts." It's important, I think, to notice that Jesus wasn't simply frustrated with their conduct; he was distressed at their character. I cite this passage as an indication that Jesus doesn't just care about what we do; he's concerned also about what's going on inside of us, the kind of people we are.

The reader will recall that in the survey of popular ethical options presented in part one of this work, we examined some *teleological* (results-oriented) and *deontological* (rule-oriented) but not any *aretaic* (virtues-oriented) approaches to making ethical decisions. In the previous chapter we took note of the fact that an ethic that's biblically informed can't help but be somewhat deontological. At the same time, we discovered that if we take the ethical style and teaching of Jesus seriously, this essentially deontological approach to Christian ethics will also pay attention to consequences. So we've come to the conclusion that an ethic that's both biblically informed and Christ-centered is going to be *both* deontological *and* teleological in nature.[1] The question is: Where does this leave virtue ethics, or the ethics of being?

Furthermore, we've seen that Proverbs 2 tells us that divine guidance is available for us when facing a moral dilemma, but in order to receive this guidance we must engage in theologically real versions of both Scripture study and prayer, and do so at the same time. Of the six popular approaches to ethical decision making surveyed in chapters two and three, some don't encourage us to do either of these things (the teleological approaches), while the others (the deontological approaches) encourage us to focus mainly, if not exclusively, on rules we find in the Bible. So an additional question we need to ask ourselves is this: Where's the decision-making approach that encourages us to dig deep into God's word and engage in some serious prayer at the same time, actually expecting a response from God?

I'm convinced that engaging in a process of moral deliberation that resembles what Jesus was doing when he drew in the dirt is at the heart of a Christ-centered, biblically informed, Spirit-empowered Christian ethic—a holistic ethic that does justice to the manner in which Jesus himself paid attention to rules, results and virtues. It's time now to get practical. What, specifically, does "drawing in the dirt" as a method of moral deliberation involve?

The idea that Jesus' drawing in the dirt might serve as an apt metaphor for what's involved in making moral decisions that honor the heart of God first occurred to me while studying ethics at Fuller Theological Seminary with the late Lewis Smedes. In his book *Choices: Making Right Decisions in a Complex World*, Smedes focused his attention on helping readers know how to make *responsible* moral decisions.[2] This involves four steps: after having taken care to (1) *face the facts*, (2) *respect the rules*, and (3)

---

[1]For more on how an ethic can and should strive to combine a concern for both character and conduct, see Stanley J. Grenz, *The Moral Quest: Foundations of Christian Ethics* (Downers Grove, IL: InterVarsity Press, 1997), p. 41.
[2]Lewis Smedes, *Choices: Making Right Decisions in a Complex World* (New York: HarperCollins, 1986), pp. 13, 37, 38, 41, 44-45, 90, 91-114, 116.

consider the consequences, Smedes encouraged his readers to (4) *be responsible* (that is, strive to make the moral call as a responsible person).

In addition to these four steps, I want to humbly suggest a fifth. In order to make moral choices that have the very best chance of hearing and honoring the heart of God, we should also (5) *be responsive* (that is, strive to be sensitive to whatever moral guidance the Spirit of God deigns to provide).

There's a sense in which this entire five-step process is what's involved in "drawing in the dirt." In other words, the metaphor represents an ethical decision-making process that seeks to *respond* rather than *react* to the situation at hand by: (1) taking the time necessary to get all the facts about the issue before us; (2) being careful to pay due attention to what, if anything, the Bible has to say about such a situation; (3) giving some serious consideration to what the consequences are liable to be with respect to each possible course of action; and then striving to process all of this in a way that's both (4) responsible (rather than irresponsible) and (5) responsive (sensitive) to whatever moral guidance the Holy Spirit has for us.

Now, because the first three steps have to some degree been touched on already in previous chapters, I'm going to focus some special attention in this chapter on just the latter two. After a brief analysis of what Smedes has to say about what it means to strive to make moral choices as a responsible moral agent, I'll go on to discuss what it means to engage in a deliberation process that seeks to be responsive to whatever moral guidance God deigns to provide.

What It Means to Be a "Responsible" Moral Agent

Writing for a general rather than specifically Christian audience, Smedes sets up his discussion of this topic by way of an analogy nearly everyone can relate to. He reminds his readers of the fact that, since there isn't a traffic rule for every conceivable situation we might encounter on the freeway, the accepted wisdom or "catchall rule for driving on the freeway that covers all situations" is that everyone should strive to *drive responsibly*. He goes on to assert that "the moral side of life is this way too."[3] While it's true that God and nature provide us with rules to live by, "there are not enough of these

---

[3]Ibid., p. 92.

rules to go around. Life's situations are almost infinitely varied and absolute rules are limited."[4] This is why, says Smedes, "Like driving on the freeway, life's broad plains of freedom are covered by one broad law: *live responsibly.*"[5]

Smedes proceeds to make the crucial point that "to live responsibly, we need to *be* responsible."[6] His thinking about what it means to be responsible was greatly influenced by the ethical work of H. Richard Niebuhr (1894–1962). According to Niebuhr, for a person to be considered responsible they must possess three qualities: (1) they are able to initiate action, (2) they are able to make a genuine response to the situation they are in, and (3) they are able to account for their actions.[7]

What follows is a brief interpretive summary of Smede's treatment of these three crucial qualities. I can't help but think of Jesus, kneeling to draw in the dirt, as I contemplate afresh these three earmarks of a responsible person.

First, *responsible people initiate action.*[8] Smedes's focus here is on the idea that responsible people are not only able to take action but willing to. They are not averse to making decisions that have consequences. Rather than waiting for someone else to make a decision, or for life to figure itself out, these are folks who, when required, will boldly step up to the plate and take their turn at bat.

Second, *responsible people's actions are an answer to what is happening around them.* According to Smedes, responsible people don't take action just because they can; these are folks who strive to be sensitive to each new situation so they might initiate an action that's *appropriate* or *fitting* for it. Their perspective is that every new set of circumstances presents the moral agent with the question: "What will you do about me?" Responsible people take this question seriously. As Smedes puts it: "They try to understand what is going on, and then respond in a way that fits the question. Their actions are answers, responses—not reactions."[9]

Third, *responsible people are willing to explain their answers.* This is

---

[4]Ibid., p. 115.
[5]Ibid., pp. 92-93.
[6]Ibid., p. 93.
[7]Ibid.
[8]Ibid.
[9]Ibid.

another way of saying that truly *responsible* people are willing to *take responsibility* for their actions, to be held accountable for them. Moreover, says Smedes, responsible people "do not try to account for their acts by saying, 'Well, I was in the mood,' or 'We have always done it this way.'" Instead, responsible moral agents are those who are willing to "help other people see *why* the thing they did made sense in that situation, and can show why they thought their action was fitting."[10]

I've already suggested that this description of the responsible person is suggestive of the moral agency of Jesus as portrayed in the New Testament. At this point, I want to turn the attention of my readers to the Old Testament, where we find a brief passage that bids us recognize an enormously important life truth. Proverbs 17:3 announces: "The crucible for silver and the furnace for gold, but the LORD tests the heart." According to the biblical author, this is what the Lord does: he tests hearts. Given the vagueness inherent in the verse, the reader is left wondering whether life as a whole is not a huge test. At the very least, we might find some support here for the practice of viewing the occasional moral dilemma we find ourselves facing as some sort of test with respect to our character—a test designed not only to evaluate but to cultivate, to inculcate, to strengthen.

All this to say that it's on the basis of Jesus' example, the writings of Niebuhr and Smedes, and biblical passages such as Proverbs 17:3 that I'm inclined to encourage my students to make the existential choice to become *responsible actors on the stage of human history*. What does this mean? Keeping all of the above in view, it's a call for them to become responsible moral agents—men and women who take action in life, addressing rather than shirking the tough moral questions, who strive to respond rather than merely react to each new set of circumstances they face, and who are willing to be held to account, now and later, for what they've done and left undone in this life.

This is a tall order, for sure. But I'm convinced that with God's help, this type of moral responsibility is possible. After all, the moral faithfulness he's expecting of us depends on it, and Jesus himself seems to have gone out of his way to model it for us.

---

[10]Ibid., p. 94.

I'm pretty sure my former ethics professor would agree with this conviction. And, having done so, he would probably want to add that the key to living a responsible life before God, as daunting as that sounds, is to develop the habit of making responsible moral choices.[11] The journey toward a moral faithfulness begins with a commitment to spend the rest of our lives learning how to make ethical decisions in a responsible rather than irresponsible manner.

Great! Now, how's that done?

WHAT'S REQUIRED FOR MORAL CHOICES TO BE MADE IN A "RESPONSIBLE" MANNER

At the heart of the chapter in *Choices* titled "When You Can't Be Sure, Be Responsible" is a set of questions Smedes says we can use over and over again in order to "test ourselves for responsibility."[12] The idea here is that when we find ourselves facing a moral dilemma for which there doesn't seem to be an *obviously* correct choice, the next best thing we can do is make sure that the process by which we're making the ethical decision is a responsible one.

The eight questions Smedes proposes in this book as tests for responsibility are:

1. Have I used discernment?

2. Have I interpreted the question?

3. Did my action fit the situation?

4. Does it support my commitments?

5. Is it congruent with my roles?

6. Have I used my imagination?

7. Am I willing to go public?

8. Am I willing to accept the consequences?

Because I'm going to offer my own version of this set of self-reflection/responsibility test questions below—a revised iteration that reflects an em-

---

[11]Ibid., pp. 94-95.
[12]Ibid., p. 95.

phasis I believe is somewhat missing from Smedes's approach—I will, at the risk of greatly oversimplifying things, simply offer here the observation that pondering the eight questions Smedes suggests we ask ourselves during a season of moral deliberation will serve to encourage us as moral agents to do our best to: (1) discern what's really going on in the situation at hand; (2) not allow a prewritten script to determine what we do; (3) act in a way that's uniquely appropriate to the particular situation we're currently facing; (4) honor the most important commitments we've made; (5) act in a manner that's congruent with the significant roles we normally play in life; (6) use our imagination before acting, striving to arrive at the very best response; (7) never do anything we wouldn't want the people we care about to hear of; and (8) picture ourselves in advance accepting the consequences for our action, whatever they may be.[13]

Once again, the idea here is that, even when we can't be sure about what the "correct" answer to a moral dilemma is, we can and should strive to be responsible in our ethical deliberation. This encouragement to integrate the virtue of responsibility into ethical decision making is nothing short of profound. It's based on the daring presupposition that, God being who he is—a responsible being in his own right—a moral choice that's made in a responsible manner is more than likely going to be at or very near the heart of God.

Furthermore, says Smedes, even when it becomes apparent that a moral action has missed the mark somewhat, "it's nice to know that bad choices do not have to be fatal."[14]

What does this mean?

The final chapter of *Choices* bears the title "Being Wrong Is Not All Bad." Even though, as I've stipulated, Smedes aimed this work for a wide readership (not necessarily a specifically religious audience), its concluding paragraphs are filled with references to God's willingness to forgive. Consider, for instance, these grace-infused lines: "The last word about choices is this: nothing you do wrong can get God to love you less than he did when you did things right. Nothing need ever separate you from the love of God. After all is said and done, being right is not the

---

[13]Ibid., pp. 95-113.
[14]Ibid., p. 115.

most important thing in the world. Being forgiven is."[15]

Because there's no reference to John 3:16 in this chapter, it might appear that Smedes was encouraging his readers to adopt a nonchalant attitude toward the possibility of getting morality wrong. But a careful consideration of the book as a whole will serve to dispel such a notion. I'll suggest instead that Smedes was deftly encouraging his readers, regardless of their level of religiosity, to take into consideration the grace and greatness of God—his steadfast commitment to forgive and remarkable ability to cause any moral choice *responsibly made* to work ultimately, mysteriously for good. That this was the gospel-suggesting message that Smedes the consummately compassionate Christian theologian had in mind is indicated by the manner in which he pressed into service a quote from the work of Søren Kierkegaard (1813–1855). According to Smedes, "that complicated Danish philosopher . . . once said a prayer that went something like this: 'Lord, I have to make a choice, and I'm afraid that I may make the wrong one. But I have to make it anyway; and I can't put it off. So I will make it, and trust you to forgive me if I do wrong. And, Lord, I will trust you, too, to help make things right afterward. Amen.'"[16]

It should be apparent just how much I deeply appreciate this endeavor to infuse into the ethical decision-making process a concern to be responsible. And yet, with all due respect to my former ethics professor, in the end I'm also led to wonder whether a theologically (and pneumatologically) real approach to the moral life, especially one that strives to be Christ-centered, biblically informed and Spirit-empowered, doesn't promise and require of us a bit more. It's for this reason that I want to press on in this chapter to talk about the possibility of Christian disciples making moral choices that strive to be *responsive* as well as *responsible*.

WHAT'S REQUIRED FOR MORAL CHOICES TO BE "RESPONSIVE" AS WELL AS "RESPONSIBLE"

What I'm suggesting here is that in addition to the three qualities of responsible moral agents originally put forward by Niebuhr and then endorsed by

---

[15]Ibid., p. 121.
[16]Ibid.

Smedes, we can add a fourth: *truly responsible people are humble enough to call on God for guidance before they act as well as for forgiveness afterward.*

I certainly don't want to give the impression that Smedes was categorically opposed to or dismissive of the dynamic of divine moral guidance. In the final chapter of *Choices* he speaks of prayer as a powerful resource and even refers to a kind of "seeing" and "hearing" that is spiritual in nature.[17] With respect to the latter two dynamics, Smedes writes: "Some people have intuition. . . . Some people simply see with the help of spiritual eyes, hear with the aid of spiritual ears, know with the certainty that comes from a resource lying beneath the mind. And if you are lucky enough to have this power, you should respect it. And use it."[18]

Again, we need to keep in mind that Smedes was *not* writing for an exclusively Christian audience. Still, even though Smedes indicates an openness to something akin to divine moral guidance, it's a theoretical openness at best; one that appears in *Choices* as if it were an afterthought, definitely not a cardinal component of his ethical decision-making approach.

Because I'm convinced that a Christ-centered, biblically informed and Spirit-empowered approach to making ethical decisions has room in it for a much more robust appeal to God for moral guidance than we see in Smedes, I've created a set of self-reflection questions that not only encourage the virtue of responsibility but also work toward moral choices that strive to be responsive to whatever spiritual guidance God is willing to provide us in the matter at hand.

As I treat each of the nine questions presented below, I will not only reference what Smedes has to say about the topic but also indicate how we might see a connection between this self-reflection query and the metaphor inherent in Jesus' drawing in the dirt. The reader will also notice that I've attempted to incorporate into this set of questions some mechanism by which we can assure our having done an adequate job of getting the facts, respecting the rules and considering the consequences. Such a move is motivated by my conviction that *all* of these steps in the deliberation process are crucial to its proving ultimately to be responsible and responsive in nature.

---

[17]Ibid., pp. 116-19.
[18]Ibid., p. 116.

Have I done a really good job of gathering all the facts so that I might accurately discern what's going on in front of me? Proverbs 13:16 reads: "All who are prudent act with knowledge, but fools expose their folly." The idea here is that it's a really good idea to fully assess the situation before making judgments about it. This is one of the key differences between *responding* to a moral dilemma and just *reacting* to it.

Smedes has much to say about the need to be *discerning* whenever we're deliberating a moral question—to keep our eyes and ears open to what's going on before us. Commenting on the crucial importance of discernment to the decision-making process, he writes: "Discernment separates the moral artist from the moral bungler. Bunglers know the rules but do not see what is going on in front of their eyes. They do not make good choices because they have not discerned what the situation calls for."[19]

The actual exercise of discernment begins with our being careful to become familiar with the facts: *all the facts* that are at work in a situation. In addition, says Smedes, we must take our time with these facts rather than rush to judgment. We wait, checking the "impulse to shoot from the hip," doing and saying nothing until we have "gotten a good sense of what the situation really calls for." Finally, Smedes clarifies that we must also do our best to keep our subjectivity in check. We do that by continually asking ourselves: "Have I paid unbiased attention to all that is going on; have I resisted the temptation to see only what I want to see?"[20]

I want to suggest that John 8:1-11 shows Jesus exercising discernment. He seems to have been aware of the ignoble motives of those who had paraded the adulterous woman into public view. Could it be that, like any human being, Jesus had to be careful to use some discernment so as to fully appreciate what was happening before him? Is this part of what made Jesus the moral artist he was?

Regardless of how we answer these hermeneutical and theological questions, it should be obvious how important this first self-reflection query can be as a test for responsibility. It's not too much to say that it's a commitment to get all the facts so that we might exercise some discernment that enables us to avoid judging by mere appearances, judging

---

[19]Ibid., p. 96.
[20]Ibid., pp. 96, 99.

correctly instead (see Jn 7:24). Whether Jesus literally asked himself this question as he drew in the dirt is not the point. The really important issue is whether we see him modeling this aspect of responsible moral agency for us. I think the answer to that question is obvious.

Have I identified the most significant moral issue at work in this situation and what all of my options are with respect to it? Smedes insists, correctly I believe, that every moral dilemma presents to us the question: "What will you do about me?"[21] Put in terms more in keeping with this section's emphasis on being *responsive* as well as responsible, we might say that the question we face with each moral dilemma can also be stated thusly: "Where's the heart of God here?" or "How can I cooperate with what God is up to in this situation?"

Regardless of how we frame the question, Smedes is also wise to point out how necessary it is for us to reinterpret this question in a fresh way every time we face a new moral challenge, and to use our imagination in a diligent manner so as to not rule out any God-honoring answers to it. Forcing ourselves to do this is what frees us from habitually *reacting* to moral dilemmas on the basis of prewritten scripts that have in one way or another been delivered to us or that we have created for our own use. It also puts us in a position to experience what the apostle Paul asked God to do in the lives of the members of the Philippian church: enable them to discern, in every life situation, the very *best* course of action (see Phil 1:9-11).

This is all to say that responsible and responsive moral choices aren't pre-scripted! They are freshly contextualized attempts to do justice to Micah 6:8 in each and every individual circumstance. It's extremely important that we properly interpret the moral question being put to us and imaginatively identify *all* the possible answers to it before we offer a response. The very possibility of honoring the heart of God with our moral choices hinges on this.

I've already referred to Jesus' having discerned the real motive of those eager to entrap him at the expense of an adulterous woman's humiliation (and perhaps even her execution). It's equally important to focus on the fact that he was also clear on the original intent of those divine com-

---

[21]Ibid., p. 99.

mands presented as part of the old covenant that have to do with the punishment of adulterers. This clarity allowed Jesus to boil down the matter before him so that the real, most significant moral issue could become evident. In other words, Jesus took the time necessary to put his finger on the weightiest, most fundamental moral question that was being asked of him. This, combined with an imaginative survey of his options, plus perhaps the guidance of the Holy Spirit, allowed him to make a moral choice that honored the heart of God, *to act in a way that facilitated what God was up to in that particular situation.* Jesus was a master at this (see Jn 5:17, 19, 30; 14:10). As Christ's disciples, we can and must, with the empowerment of his Spirit, learn to do the same thing if our ethical decisions are to be responsible and responsive ones.

Have I been careful to engage in a thoughtful examination of what God's Word has to say about this kind of situation—which moral principles presented in Scripture might apply? Like the proponents of the three types of Christian absolutism surveyed in chapter three of this work, Smedes encourages a hearty respect for the moral commands presented in sacred Scripture. In chapter four of *Choices*, Smedes provides his readers with a nuanced, helpful discussion of the various types of moral rules and how they should and shouldn't be employed as part of an ethical decision-making process.[22] What makes this chapter especially helpful is the manner in which Smedes discusses the role of rules in a moral model that insists on combining deontological and teleological impulses. This balanced discussion by itself is worth the price of the book!

Given the nuanced manner in which Smedes discusses the role of rules in responsible decision making, it might seem that he's guilty of downplaying the importance of paying attention to the moral imperatives we find in the Scriptures. Nothing could be further from the truth. An earlier book titled *Mere Morality: What God Expects from Ordinary People* contains an extended exposition of the Ten Commandments and their import for morality. The fact that Smedes had a distinctly religious readership in view as he penned this volume is evident from the outset. Early on he explains the book's focus on the Decalogue, saying:

---

[22]Ibid., pp. 43-66.

I am going to the commandments because, of all the places where God's voice may be heard, they speak it most urgently and clearly. Where else does God confront people as urgently as in his undebatable "Thou shalt?" Where does he preempt people's freedom to do wrong as clearly as when he utters his "Thou shalt not?" Never mind, for the moment, that he spoke his "Thou shalt's" and "Thou shalt not's" long ago. The fact is that he did speak them, and biblical faith holds that in speaking them to others, he somehow spoke them to us. There they are in print, the commandments of God—not the only way, but the one way that no one can ignore.[23]

To be sure, Smedes makes it clear in this passage that he's not contending that the Decalogue is the only way God makes his moral will known. Moreover, in subsequent paragraphs, he also stipulates that he does not mean to say that *all* the commandments presented in the Bible possess the same moral weight, or that "all we need in order to know God's will is a book of commandments, indexed to help us find the one that applies." Still, he goes on to make the tremendously important point that "a morality guided by biblical commandments is not necessarily legalism."[24] Statements such as this indicate that the ethical approach promoted by Smedes has plenty of room in it for a deontology that is biblically informed; it's very important for our moral deliberation to be affected by some serious study of God's word.

As for Jesus' resort to the rules, even a rudimentary understanding of the Gospels will take into account how familiar he was with the Old Testament Scriptures. But just because Jesus possessed an extraordinary understanding of God's Word, and that at a remarkably young age (see Lk 2:41-51), doesn't mean that he was born with that wisdom in place. Instead, Luke 2:52 can be interpreted to mean that Jesus' understanding of God's Word increased over time. If this is true, we really can't rule out the possibility that, in his real humanity, Jesus, like any human, might have needed to give some thought from time to time as to how the Scriptures applied to this or that situation. The fact that we can't say with absolute certainty that Jesus' drawing in the dirt was part of a meditative process

---

[23]Lewis Smedes, *Mere Morality: What God Expects from Ordinary People* (Grand Rapids: Eerdmans, 1983), p. 5.
[24]Ibid., pp. 5-6.

designed to help him sense the heart of God in that situation doesn't mean
that his followers don't need to do this. Responsible and responsive moral
choices are born of this type of prayerful, biblical reflection.

Have I done a really good job of trying to predict what the conse-
quences of each possible response to this situation are likely to be? We're
discovering that in a Christian approach to ethical decision making *both*
principles *and* people matter. Though this crucial truth is evidenced
throughout the Gospels, nowhere is this more apparent than in the story
related in John 8:1-11. We get the feeling that the creative response Jesus
offered in the face of this moral dilemma was motivated more by a desire
to minister God's grace to a sinner than by any need that he in his real
humanity might have possessed to best some pesky ministry antagonists.

What this emphasis on people in Jesus' moral method means is that
Christian moral agents need to be concerned about the consequences of
their actions. But this brings us back again to those several criticisms
often leveled against teleological approaches: (1) can we trust our ability
to accurately predict consequences? (2) how do we ensure that our endeavor to produce a good outcome isn't ultimately self-serving? and (3)
how do we guarantee a just distribution of the good we're trying to
produce through our moral actions?

All I can offer in the face of these concerns is that if Jesus models for us
a concern for the consequences of moral choices, we dare not do otherwise.
Just because it's not easy to do doesn't mean that it shouldn't be done. A
truly responsible and responsive decision-making process mandates that
we rack our brains, doing our very best to list and then prayerfully evaluate
the possible consequences, pro and con, of each viable response to the
moral dilemma at hand. It's simply impossible to hear the heart of God
without engaging in this agonizing process, striving to be sensitive to any
Spirit-imparted wisdom, insight or discernment along the way.

Which of the actions I'm considering allows me to function with the
strongest degree of integrity—to behave in a manner congruent with the
virtues I've always espoused, the various roles I've been called to play in
life, and the most important commitments I've made to the people who
depend on me? If responsibility is a crucial virtue for Christian ethics, so
is *integrity*. According to Proverbs 10:9, "Whoever walks in integrity

walks securely, but whoever takes crooked paths will be found out." Likewise, Proverbs 11:3 reads: "The integrity of the upright guides them, but the unfaithful are destroyed by their duplicity." These are just two of many biblical passages that in one way or another encourage God's people to behave with integrity and to avoid hypocrisy.[25]

One way to think about integrity is in terms of congruency. Is any given action congruent with those virtues we're in the habit of lauding in others and claiming to want to inculcate within ourselves? Does it comport with the way I normally live my life, supporting rather than diminishing my ability to be for others the husband or wife, father or mother, brother or sister, friend, teacher, pastor, moral example they've come to depend on me to be? Would engaging in this behavior constitute a breach of promise I've made to someone important to me, or an act of faithfulness? All of this is involved in the kind of integrity a responsible moral decision calls for.

While Smedes is careful to clarify that we're not the roles we play, he insists that they are still important. He writes: "Roles, freely accepted and faithfully played, are the personal lynchpins of any caring community. . . . So one test of whether we are being responsible is this question: 'Am I being congruent with my significant roles?'"[26]

Another dynamic that's crucial to a healthy experience of community (and thus to human flourishing in this life) is the keeping of commitments. With respect to this dynamic Smedes writes: "Commitments are the backbone of human relationships, so the question of whether the things we do support or violate our commitments makes or breaks our life together."[27]

While Smedes is enough of a realist to know that there are times when it's appropriate to "break a commitment badly made and wrong to keep,"[28] our default should always be to honor rather than dishonor our commitments, especially those we've made to the people and institutions most

---

[25]Of course, it's hard not to also call to mind the many times Jesus warned his followers to avoid the hypocrisy of the Pharisees and teachers of the law (see Mt 6:2, 5, 15; 7:5; cf. Mt 15:1-9; 22:15-18; 23:13, 15, 23, 25, 27, 29). See also 1 Kings 9:4-5; 1 Chron 29:17; Neh 7:1-2; Ps 26:1-4; 51:10; 119:1-5; Prov 4:24-27; Mt 24:45-51; 2 Cor 1:12; 1 Tim 4:1-2; Tit 2:6-8.

[26]Smedes, *Choices*, pp. 107-8.

[27]Ibid., p. 105.

[28]Ibid., p. 104.

important to us. The genius of this self-reflection question lies in its ability to help us bring some deontological objectivity to the subjectivity that plagues a teleological concern to do good in the world. In other words, one way we can know when the end doesn't justify the means is by keeping our primary commitments in view. Thus, Smedes offers that "when responsible people make a decision, they ask themselves, 'How will it impact my significant commitments?'"[29]

And what do we do when find ourselves not knowing for sure whether a given moral action will undermine an important commitment? Interestingly, though Smedes acknowledges that this is a legitimate question, he doesn't really have an answer for it. Instead he simply reasserts how irresponsible it would be for us to not keep an eye on our commitments. It seems this is one of those areas of the moral life where Smedes encourages his readers to use their intuition.[30]

But the wrinkle in this is that, as we've seen, Smedes seems to suggest that not everyone possesses the same intuitive capacity. It's only certain, "lucky" people who possess this gift.[31]

Without wanting to sound as if I'm playing a game of "Gotcha!" with my former professor, I have to ask: Is this not a problem? Moreover, doesn't Proverbs 2 promise more in terms of divine moral guidance? Isn't it possible to engage in an approach to moral deliberation that goes beyond the crucial need to be responsible? Shouldn't we at least entertain the notion of a decision-making method that emphasizes the need to be responsive as well?

Once again, I can't say for sure that Jesus literally had the issue of integrity/congruence in mind as he knelt and drew in the dirt. I can assert that his response to the moral dilemma that prompted such a deliberative technique allowed him to act with integrity and congruence with respect to the virtues he promoted, the roles he played and the commitments (to God *and* to hurting people) he considered inviolable. I can also suggest that if we want, in the rough-and-tumble of everyday life, to do the best job possible of likewise acting with integrity and congruence, we

---

[29]Ibid., p. 105.
[30]Ibid., pp. 105, 117.
[31]Ibid., p. 116.

might consider engaging in a deliberation process that strives to be responsive as well as responsible.

Am I willing to have the people most important to me know about this decision—to accept the consequences for it without trying to shift blame to someone else? While there was no way for Jesus to cloak in secrecy his response to the moral question put to him by the Pharisees as depicted in John 8, we sometimes have this option. Smedes reminds us that "cover ups are always the strategy of the irresponsible" and that responsible decisions are *most often* the ones we don't mind the world knowing about.[32] Just as Jesus boldly stood to his feet and challenged the crowd surrounding him, so we must be willing to have our world know about the choices we make. Special circumstances aside, a good rule of thumb is this: *an ethical decision may be less than wholly responsible if we're abjectly unwilling for the people most important to us to know of it.* Conversely, Smedes insists that while our willingness to own the consequences of our moral actions doesn't guarantee that it's the "right" thing to do, it is a "fine test" of whether we are making the decision in a responsible manner.[33]

John 7:1-52 indicates that the days and hours just prior to the incident reported on in John 8:1-11 were filled with tension. The author of the Fourth Gospel makes very clear how committed Jerusalem's religious leaders—especially the Pharisees—were to seeing Jesus arrested and/or assassinated (see Jn 7:1). It's not going too far to suggest that Jesus, even while kneeling to draw in the dirt, knew very well that the response he was about to provide his antagonists would only serve to fuel their fury. This leads me to assert that "drawing in the dirt"—that is, engaging in a season of moral deliberation that strives to be both responsible and responsive—leads us to make decisions we can live with no matter what the consequences of our actions might be. This is a vital earmark of a

---

[32]Ibid., p. 111.

[33]When I indicated in a class session one evening that I was considering the removal of this particular query from my list of self-reflection questions, a young woman, normally not outspoken in class, spoke up, insisting that I not make that move. Her take was that, for all the talk of how the members of her generation prize community, she was a witness to a tendency in many of her peers toward a moral autonomy and a penchant for privacy. She went on to comment on how important it is that people her age be challenged to make themselves accountable to others for their moral choices. She very nearly pleaded with me to leave the list alone. It is due in large part to her passionate appeal that I have.

responsible ethical decision: it's a moral choice we're willing to accept the consequences for, whether good or bad, convenient or costly.

What does acting justly, loving with mercy and walking humbly before God look like in this particular situation? The genius of Jesus' response to the moral dilemma portrayed in John 8:1-11 is how it did justice to Micah 6:8. When you think about it, isn't it remarkable how Jesus navigated that complicated, precarious life situation in a way that embodied the three behaviors/virtues that the Bible enjoins on all of humankind?

I've argued that what we find in Micah 6:8 is a prophetic (Spirit-inspired) articulation of nothing less than three moral absolutes. A profoundly important moral principle that derives from this argument is that *in any given situation the moral choice that's closest to the heart of God will always be the one that does the best job of acting justly, loving with mercy and walking humbly/faithfully before him.*

In *Choices,* Smedes offers some tacit support for this thesis as he discusses the nature of moral rules. Referring to moral absolutes as "rules of every game" and speaking first with respect to literal games, Smedes explains: "There are a few rules, not many, that we simply have to obey in every game we play. No matter what sort of game it is, no matter who plays it, or where." The kind of transcendent rules Smedes has in mind include: "we ought always to play fair" and "we ought to play the game the best we can."[34]

Then, switching gears, Smedes presses on to inquire rhetorically: "Are there *rules of every game,* absolutes for ordinary people in the serious game of life—the marriage game, the family game, the business game, the political game, and the many other games we play, all of them involving significant relationships with people?" Immediately, Smedes answers his own query, asserting that there are indeed two transcendent rules in the game of life—the two most important rules we could possibly live by: "One of them is a carbon copy of the first rule of every game: be fair. The rule of justice! The other is, care for people who need you. The rule of love!"[35]

It's true that Smedes doesn't refer in this particular excerpt to Micah's call for humility. Indeed the norm for Smedes, in *Choices,* is to talk about

---

[34]Ibid., p. 54.
[35]Ibid.

there being just two moral absolutes or "rules for every game." He explains:

> In every case, there are two moral absolutes, they follow us into every nook
> and cranny of our lives and, whatever the game we are playing, whatever re-
> lationship we are in, they pin us down with the dual demand: help people who
> need your help, but be fair whatever you do. These are absolute, they give us
> no escape hatches: everyone, always, in every human relationship, ought to
> have a heart to be helpful and a mind to be fair.[36]

However, Smedes immediately goes on to make the following assertion, his general readership notwithstanding: "The ancient prophet Micah gave the people rules for every game: 'What does the Lord require of you but to do justice, and to love kindness, and to walk humbly with your God.'"[37] So it seems that my former ethics mentor would concur with this basic premise: there are a few moral absolutes that need to be heeded in absolutely every life situation we find ourselves facing. To be more specific, it's my contention that honoring the heart of God requires that we make moral choices that have us acting justly, loving with mercy and walking humbly before God.[38]

Whether Jesus had Micah 6:8 in mind as he drew in the dirt, I can't say for sure. What I am certain of is that his response to that particular moral dilemma was true to all three behaviors/virtues prescribed in that passage and that any moral deliberation process we engage in, if it's to be both responsible and responsive, will aim to do likewise.

Of course, this is easier said than done, which is why I've included two more self-reflection/responsibility test questions in my revised list.

Have I been careful to bathe this entire moral deliberation process in some serious prayer offered in a theologically real manner? I concluded the two-chapter survey of popular ethical options presented in part one of this book hinting at the need for readers to ask themselves such questions as: What role might prayer and waiting on God for prophetic moral guidance play in a Christ-centered, biblically informed and Spirit-empowered approach to making ethical decisions? and How important is it for church members to engage in certain spiritual formation

---

[36]Smedes, *Choices*, p. 56.
[37]Ibid.
[38]See Smedes, *Mere Morality*, pp. 33, 105, 252, where the need for spiritual humility is stated explicitly.

practices so as to form the kind of character that's concerned to live a morally faithful life before God?

The next two self-reflection questions on my revised list lead us toward more thorough discussions of these two important issues. First, let's talk a bit about the importance of prayer offered in a theologically real manner to making moral choices that are responsive as well as responsible.

Like the proponents of the three Bible-based absolutisms surveyed in chapter three, Smedes encourages the Christian moral agent to engage in a serious study of the Scriptures. However, in a manner much more pronounced than in those other deontological decision-making approaches, Smedes also emphasizes the role prayer can play in moral deliberation, referring to it as "a massively neglected resource for making right choices" and "a way of tapping into wisdom better than our own.[39]

As for the importance of prayer being offered in a *theologically real* manner, to be sure, Smedes was no mystic.[40] Actually, he seems to have been somewhat reluctant to endorse the notion of the Holy Spirit responding to prayers for direction by speaking directly to people. Thus, honesty requires that I acknowledge that my former mentor would likely be a bit nervous about the emphasis I'm placing in this work on the possibility of prophetic moral guidance.

I will have more to say about this apparent reticence on the part of Smedes to encourage his readers to "wait on God" for any moral direction he would deign to provide in the next section. At this point my primary task is to underscore how important it is that we infuse the moral deliberation process with some serious prayer, open to the possibility that God might respond by at the very least nudging us toward or away from a particular moral action.

Did Jesus whisper a prayer for guidance and direction as he knelt to draw in the dirt? While I can't provide exegetical proof that he did, is it not reasonable to think that the one who possessed an intimate, interactive, prayer-based relationship with God—and who taught his dis-

---

[39]Smedes, *Choices*, p. 117.

[40]On the other hand, Smedes once remarked in an interview that after a moment of awe and gratitude prompted him in a rather ecstatic manner to raise his hands in praise, he began to playfully refer to himself as "closet charismatic." See "Lewis Smedes," *Chicago Sunday Evening Club* (accessed September 29, 2013), www.csec.org/index.php/archives/23-member-archives/553-lewis-smedes-program-3805.

ciples to pray persistently and with a pronounced sense of expectancy in place—might have been in the habit of praying thusly himself?[41]

In other words, making moral choices that are responsive in nature requires that, as we face the facts, respect the rules, consider the consequences, and test ourselves for the virtue of responsibility, we pray. And after we pray, we actually listen, open to the possibility that a personal, responsible and responsive God might choose to respond to us per the promises presented in passages such as Proverbs 2.

Let's go on now to consider a final crucial self-reflection/responsibility test question.

Have I consulted with other members of my community of faith, humbly seeking their counsel and prayers regarding this issue? Proverbs 12:15 reminds us that "The way of fools seems right to them, but the wise listen to advice." Jesus taught his disciples that special things happen when they agree together in prayer (Mt 18:19-20). As we've seen, the book of Acts shows Christian disciples making important, morally significant missional decisions in a prayerful, communal, charismatic manner (Acts 15:22-29; cf. Acts 13:1-3). This leads me to suggest that, if the goal is a biblically informed moral deliberation process that's responsive as well as responsible, then it will likely possess a prayerful, communal, charismatic aspect to it.

This brings us back again to the apparent reticence on the part of Smedes to endorse the idea that making excellent moral choices might include an openness to a charismatic dynamic. I use the word "apparent" to describe this reticence because nowhere to my knowledge does Smedes in either *Choices* or *Mere Morality* explicitly denounce the possibility of what I'm referring to as Spirit-enabled moral guidance. Still, I must admit there is a passage in *Mere Morality* that seems to come pretty close. As part of his attempt to justify a book-length exploration of the moral value of the Ten Commandments, Smedes posed the following question, obviously anticipating a negative answer: "Does God speak to each of us privately through the intimations of the spirit, heart to heart,

---

[41]On prayer in the Gospels, see Mt 7:7-11; Mk 1:35; Lk 5:16; 18:1-8; Jn 5:19, 30; 8:28-29; 10:37; 12:49-50; 14:10, 23-24, 30-31. Support for the notion that Jesus prayed thusly himself can be found in the many exhortations found in the rest of the New Testament to take prayer seriously: 1 Thess 5:17; cf. Rom 12:11-12; Eph 6:18; Phil 4:6; Col 4:2; 1 Tim 5:5.

mind to mind, divine Word direct to human soul? Must each of us go it alone while waiting for the voice of the Lord?"[42]

I will humbly suggest that Smedes, while correct to emphasize the importance of God's commands to the moral life, is somewhat guilty here of overstating his concern against a too-private approach to moral deliberation and of not taking into account the role of the Spirit in the conveyance of God's commands.

Since I've made my case for the possibility of prophetic moral guidance in previous chapters, I'll focus here on the question of whether a moral deliberation process that possesses a charismatic component must be private and individualistic in nature. Let me go on the record: I'm certainly not suggesting that *prophetic* moral guidance must equal *private* moral guidance. In point of fact, my contention is just the opposite. Any direction provided immediately to the moral agent by the Spirit needs to be validated by the Scriptures and the community of faith. Furthermore, it's also by means of the Scriptures and the community of faith that the Spirit often speaks to people!

In my book *A Missional Orthodoxy* I relate a story from my ministry files that illustrates both of these contentions. This story is simply too appropriate for this discussion not to rehearse here.[43]

> A young couple came to faith in Christ in one of the churches I pastored. One day the husband (I'll call him Rich) called the church office to let me know that he and his wife (I'll refer to her as Miranda) would not be attending the small group meeting that was scheduled to occur at my home that evening. He went on to indicate the reason why. He and Miranda were in the midst of a significant disagreement over a serious matter and did not think it would be a good idea to be around other couples that evening. They both felt that it would seem hypocritical to come to the meeting, pretending that everything was fine in their lives when the reality was otherwise.
>
> When I asked Rich if he wanted to talk about what was going on, he told me the story. In brief, Miranda had recently received news from her OB/GYN confirming a suspicion that she might be pregnant. Immediately, without dis-

---

[42]Smedes, *Mere Morality*, p. 2, emphasis added.
[43]I'm thankful to the folks at IVP for granting permission to use this copyrighted material. Gary Tyra, *A Missional Orthodoxy: Theology and Ministry in a Post-Christian Context* (Downers Grove, IL: IVP Academic, 2013), pp. 352-54.

cussing the matter with Rich, she had scheduled an appointment to have the pregnancy terminated. My wife Patti recollects that there was some sort of health concern at work in the situation. All I remember is Rich explaining that Miranda did not want to be pregnant again at that point in her life. Their daughter was just emerging from the "terrible twos" and they had both been looking forward to certain changes in their lifestyle which that development would bring. Rich indicated to me that though he was sympathetic to Miranda's desire not to be pregnant again, he felt that such a huge decision merited a discussion between the two of them and some serious consideration of where God's heart was on the matter. Becoming more and more heated, the disagreement had begun to spiral out of control. According to Rich, they had come to the point where they were not communicating at all.

Though I indicated to Rich that it's often during such tough times that a Christian couple most needs the love and support of a caring community, I put no pressure on him with respect to the small group meeting scheduled that evening. I told him I would be praying for him and Miranda and would, of course, keep the matter we had just discussed to myself.

Later that evening, the small group meeting was about to begin when, to my surprise, Rich and Miranda arrived, filling two empty chairs to my immediate left. Pleased that this young couple, new in the faith, had made the decision to attend the meeting after all, I began the meeting in the usual way by asking the members of the group to "check in," sharing what they sensed the Lord was currently "up to" in their lives based on their experiences the previous week, their study of Scripture, or perhaps what the Spirit of the Lord had spoken to them by means of his still small voice. It seemed wise at the time to begin with the person on my right who happened to be Patti, my wife. As Patti explained briefly what she sensed the Lord might be doing in her life at the moment, I took note of the fact that what she shared had an amazing degree of relevance for Rich and Miranda. Apparently Miranda sensed this as well; she began to dab at tears welling up in her eyes.

The really astounding thing is that this dynamic of the Holy Spirit speaking to Rich and Miranda through the "innocent" sharing of the others in the group repeated itself over and over again as everyone else checked in, commenting on what they felt like God was saying to or doing in them. And what was happening was not lost on this couple, especially Miranda. Before long she was a mess, mascara running down both cheeks!

Eventually, it came to be Rich's turn to weigh in. He simply deferred to

Miranda. Everyone in the room sensed that God was, at that moment, effecting some work within her. When she was finally able to speak, she slowly articulated what was going on: that she had discovered that week that she was pregnant; that she had wasted no time in scheduling the procedure that would end the pregnancy. "But," she went on to say, "God has spoken to me through the sharing of each and every one of you tonight. I now know that I can't go through with the procedure. God wants me to have this baby."

Walking around somewhere today is a young woman in her late twenties who owes her very existence, at least in part, to the fact that her mom and dad were once part of a community of Spirit-filled Christ-followers doing its best to obey the exhortation: "And let us consider how we may spur one another on toward love and good deeds, not giving up meeting together, as some are in the habit of doing, but encouraging one another—and all the more as you see the Day approaching" (Heb 10:23-25).

It has been experiences such as this that have encouraged me to believe that if our moral deliberation is going to do the *best* job possible of hearing and honoring the heart of God, it can and perhaps should strive to be responsive as well as responsible—that is, sensitive to any guidance the Spirit deigns to provide. Furthermore, I'm also convinced that a crucial test for both criteria is whether we've been careful to seek the counsel and prayer support of other members of our faith community. I'd like to think that, framed in this manner, Dr. Smedes would smile at such a suggestion.

I'm pretty sure Jesus would too. Although he did have to "go it alone" while enduring the moral dilemma pictured in John 8:1-11, he's also the one who encouraged his disciples with respect to the value of communal prayer. In fact, I'll conclude this discussion by citing one of the most profound promises Jesus made to his disciples—a promise important to the pursuit of both a missional and moral faithfulness: "Again, truly I tell you that if two of you on earth agree about anything they ask for, it will be done for them by my Father in heaven. For where two or three gather in my name, there am I with them" (Mt 18:19-20).

Okay, enough talk about drawing in the dirt! In the next chapter I'll do my best to explain why I believe that the ethic of responsible Christian discipleship is an ethic that should be taken seriously. In the process we'll also give some consideration to what it means to say that a moral faithfulness requires a moral model that's grounded in the context of authentic Christian discipleship. It's one thing to say that real Christian disciples are those who strive to hear and honor the heart of God. It's another to assert that truly hearing and honoring the heart of God requires a biblically informed and Spirit-empowered engagement in Christian discipleship. Is either contention correct? Let's find out.

The Ethic of Responsible Christian Discipleship

Reasons for Its Embrace

Several years ago a young woman—a college student around nineteen years old and new to the faith and the church I was serving at the time—came to my office seeking pastoral counsel. She was pregnant as a result of a one-night stand with someone she barely knew. Though she had already decided to terminate the pregnancy, she wanted to know what I thought about her planned course of action. She had no one else to talk to since her erstwhile lover was unwilling to be involved and she was determined to keep her condition a secret from her family.

In the course of our conversation I inquired as to whether she had considered giving birth and then allowing a couple eager but unable to have children to adopt the baby. Indicating that the possibility had not even crossed her mind, her immediate reaction was to dismiss it out of hand since it would require that her parents be informed of her situation. "Besides," she said, "I don't know if I could live with myself, knowing that I had given a baby away for someone else to raise."

It struck me that this naive, confused and frightened young lady might not be properly interpreting the moral question confronting her. It was also apparent that she was yet to ask herself any of the other responsibility test questions presented in the second half of the previous chapter. My helping her to do so made a huge difference. Months later she brought her newborn baby in for me to see. With her family's help she had decided not only to complete the pregnancy but also to raise the child herself.

This story illustrates the need for a responsible and responsive moral deliberation process. It also indicates how important an engagement in authentic Christian discipleship is to a moral faithfulness. This young woman, so emblematic of others in her demographic, needed more than some assistance in making a single moral choice, as important as that one choice was. Rather, as a new believer in the gospel, she needed to be discipled toward becoming a responsible and responsive Christian moral agent. She needed someone to help her understand the crucial difference between mere churchianity and genuine Christianity, and between making moral choices the way everyone else does and the way a Christian disciple who's striving to embody the moral faithfulness of Jesus will.

In this book's introduction I made the point that a moral faithfulness, contributing as it does to a missional faithfulness and fruitfulness, lies at the very heart of what it means to be fully a devoted follower of Christ. I also suggested that a comprehensive disciple-making process will include an emphasis on becoming a responsible and responsive Christian moral agent. In plain language: we haven't succeeded at making a Christian disciple if he or she ends up making ethical decisions in precisely the same way that his or her non-Christian peers do!

In this chapter my aim is to explore a related but slightly different theme: why a moral faithfulness requires the ethic of responsible Christian discipleship. As we discovered in part one of *Pursuing Moral Faithfulness*, there are many moral models we might choose from. Why should the reader take the one presented in part two of this book seriously? Is it simply because the name I've attached to it refers to responsible Christian discipleship? Or is there more to it than that?

I will argue in this chapter that the ethic of responsible Christian discipleship has much more going for it than its name. In a nutshell, there are three really big reasons why we need to take this moral model seriously: First, it's an ethic appropriate for the real world in which we live. Second, it's an ethic in touch with what authentic Christian discipleship is ultimately about. Third, it's an ethic that takes seriously what the New Testament has to say about being led by the Holy Spirit. Let's take a brief look at each of these reasons one at a time.

AN ETHIC APPROPRIATE FOR THE REAL WORLD

I'll admit it: an obvious criticism of the approach to making ethical decisions that *Pursuing Moral Faithfulness* is promoting centers in how "messy" it is—that it doesn't always provide the moral agent with an absolute sense of certainty that he or she has done the right thing. Actually, I will contend in the face of this criticism that it's precisely because of this approach's messiness and uncertainty that it should be embraced by us!

The fact is that we live in a world that's filled with paradox and therefore ambiguity. Even the Bible contains a measure of ambiguity, especially when it comes to the moral life:

- It doesn't provide us with a specific moral command for every situation we face in life.

- Sometimes the moral commands it does provide seem to conflict with one another.

- Often it's hard to be clear about what the moral commands actually call for!

At some point in a book such as this some hard questions need to be asked: Why all this ambiguity? Why didn't God provide humankind with a moral rulebook? Wouldn't such a move have served to increase the amount of moral faithfulness at work in the world?

I'll contend, in response to these hard questions, that God has allowed a measure of moral ambiguity to exist in our world for a reason: *it's the ambiguities present in our lives that keep forcing us to our knees in prayer, seeking a personal encounter with him.* The moral faithfulness our God is looking for can only occur within the context of a real relationship. The most scrupulous obedience to some moral rules codified in an ethical encyclopedia, no matter how inspired its origin, is simply not what the God of the Bible is after. He's looking for moral choices on our part that are both responsible and responsive with respect to his heart. This is why, I believe, God allows so much ambiguity in our world.

Excursus: Job and the Notion of a Purposeful Ambiguity

As an example of what I'm talking about, consider the biblical story of Job.

It's common for interpreters to suggest that the purpose of the book of Job is to function as a theodicy—"an essay in the justification of the ways of God to man."[1] To be more specific, it's often suggested that the story "seeks to justify the arbitrary dispensation of injustice by God for His private ends."[2] Stated plainly, this proposal holds that, whether we like it or not, the purpose of the book of Job is to function as a bald declaration of God's sovereign right to do whatever he wants with the people he created.

It's also somewhat common for scholars to suggest that the book of Job's single purpose is to function as a sort of catharsis. The message of the book is simply that *ambiguity happens!* According to this view, the question of undeserved suffering that's at the heart of the work is never fully answered. How could it be in an essentially ambiguous world? And yet the reader experiences a strange and ironic comfort as he or she identifies with Job and the bold maintenance of his integrity against all accusers, human and divine. Thus, one proponent of this perspective asserts: "all the hero can do, if he is visited as Job was, is to persevere in the pride of his conviction, to appeal to God against God, and if he is as fortunate as Job, hear his questionings echo into nothingness in the infinite mystery and the glory."[3]

I have another idea in mind.

My suggestion is that, while the story does concern the ambiguities that attend an apparent arbitrariness on the part of God, the purpose of the story is to indicate that this ambiguity is itself purposeful. In other words, I'm suggesting that the sufferings of Job were purposeful in that they effected a divinely intended *development* from one state of being to another. Thus the message of the story of Job is that, while ambiguities happen, we humans can rest assured that any "injustice" that God seems a party to is not for "His private ends" but for the ultimate good of people he dearly loves and with whom he desires a personal, intimate, interactive relationship.

Now I'm not the only person to hold that the sufferings of Job were *developmental* in their nature and purpose. For example, Old Testament scholar Bruce

---

[1]David Wolfers, *Deep Things Out of Darkness: The Book of Job* (Grand Rapids: Eerdmans, 1995), p. 68. See also Robert Davidson, *The Old Testament* (Philadelphia: Lippincott, 1964), pp. 166-68; Bruce Waltke, *An Old Testament Theology* (Grand Rapids: Zondervan, 2007), p. 929.

[2]Wolfers, *Deep Things*, p. 68.

[3]See Richard B. Sewall, "The Book of Job," in *Twentieth Century Interpretations of the Book of Job*, ed. Paul S. Sanders (Englewood Cliffs, NJ: Prentice-Hall, 1968), p. 34.

Waltke suggests that "the book is about the development of Job to become not only the most righteous among mortals, but also the most wise. . . . In other words, the author traces the trajectory of Job's development from a good man to a wise man."[4] According to this view, the development that occurred in Job's life was *sapiential* in nature (that is, it had to do with his acquiring a wisdom he didn't possess before). It's with this thought in mind that Waltke provides his readers with this brief overview of the entire story:

> In the prologue we observe Job as an idealist in elementary school (chaps. 1-2); in the dialogue, Job is a sophomore in college on the way to becoming wise (chaps. 3-31); finally, the *I AM* speeches address him as a student in graduate school, where he is humbled and accepts that there are sufficient reasons to trust *I AM* without demanding of him rational explanations (37:1–42:6).[5]

Thus, according to this interpretation, the story of Job is not meant to be merely cathartic in its effect on the reader but instructive as well. Waltke refers to Job as "a sapiential, literary icon" and asserts that "the narrator teaches sufferers through Job's protestations that God is neither limited nor evil but sovereign and good beyond human understanding."[6] In other words, the reader is encouraged to acquire vicariously the *wisdom* Job had to glean the hard way—by means of the tremendous suffering he experienced in the school of life.

While appreciative of this emphasis on the development that occurred in Job, I want to offer a slightly different take. I'm suggesting that the development that occurred in Job's life as a result of his suffering wasn't merely *sapiential* in nature but was *spiritual* as well. I'm going to argue that the story portrays Job moving from a religious approach that was fear-based to one that's trust-based—from one that focused on a *phobic* obedience to rules and *obsessive-compulsive* observance of sacrificial rituals to one that was about a real relationship.

In the next few pages I'll attempt to make the case for this spiritually impactful take on the book of Job. (While it's true that any interpretation of the story of Job that sees God using ambiguity in Job's life for a benevolent purpose will support the main point this section seeks to make, I believe this particular interpretation has something extra to offer in terms of our development as Christian disciples.)

The significance of the story's prologue (Job 1:1-5). In the beginning of the story we read that Job was a very righteous person. "In the land of Uz there lived a man whose name was Job. This man was blameless and upright; he feared God and shunned evil" (Job 1:1).

---

[4]Waltke, *Old Testament Theology*, p. 929.
[5]Ibid., pp. 929-30.
[6]Ibid., p. 928.

Indeed, Job's piety was beyond dispute. Later in the book, Job describes his own ethical demeanor prior to the onset of his suffering. In that autobiographical passage (Job 31) we find a vivid portrayal of someone in the ancient Near East doing his best to embody the three behaviors/virtues that just so happen to be prescribed in Micah 6:8.

However, here at the very beginning of the book, the reader is immediately made aware that Job's religious life seems to have been extraordinarily legalistic/ritualistic in orientation—and that in a somewhat phobic and obsessive-compulsive manner.[7]

> His sons used to hold feasts in their homes on their birthdays, and they would invite their three sisters to eat and drink with them. When a period of feasting had run its course, Job would make arrangements for them to be purified. Early in the morning he would sacrifice a burnt offering for each of them, thinking, "Perhaps my children have sinned and cursed God in their hearts." This was Job's regular custom. (Job 1:4-5)

Commenting on Job's "regular custom" of offering sacrifices on behalf of his kids, Bruce Waltke, citing yet another Old Testament scholar, writes: "Job would have them purified," showing his "*extraordinary scrupulousness* that must cover even unseen sin, that must bestir itself 'early in the morning,' that must offer not one sacrifice but ten, that must never fail in its responsibility but 'do so continually.'"[8]

Now it could be that this revelation concerning Job's habit of routinely sacrificing numerous burnt offerings on behalf of his adult kids just in case they might have displeased the deity in some way was simply the author's method of portraying the extent of Job's piety or his family values, or both. Such a perspective might explain why many commentators hardly touch on this detail at all. On the other hand, this brief but interesting glimpse into Job's religious routine might actually be critical to a fuller understanding of the mystery-shrouded story that's about to unfold.[9]

Based on what we find in Job 1:9—Satan's accusation against Job—many

---

[7]I want to reiterate here that my concern is not with an encounter-seeking engagement in religious ritual but with a magical approach to the same. It's legitimate, I believe, to at least wonder about the motivation behind Job's extraordinarily scrupulous engagement in religious ritual. Was his regular custom of offering numerous sacrifices in a prophylactic manner on behalf of his kids a way for Job to grow in his (or their) relationship with a personal God, or an attempt to, through a religious ceremony, obtain from the deity a certain outcome?

[8]Waltke, *Old Testament Theology*, p. 930, citing David J. A. Clines, *Job 1-20*, Word Biblical Commentary, vol. 17 (Waco: Word, 1989), p. 17, emphasis added.

[9]I'll point out here that Eleonore Stump likewise views Job's story as "intricately crafted" (see Eleonore Stump, *Wandering in the Darkness: Narrative and the Problem of Suffering* [Oxford: Oxford University Press, 2010], p. 178) and sees significance especially in the way the story begins and ends (pp. 179-80).

commentators will point out that it appears that Job's extraordinary religiosity was motivated by his desire to continue in his prosperity.[10] This, I will suggest, gets it partially right. But along with any desire on Job's part to earn or maintain God's favor (through acts of religious ritual and rule keeping) was also a deep-seated sense of need to mitigate his displeasure. Some support for this latter interpretive take can be found in several passages scattered throughout the book (near the beginning, the middle and the end) that serve to indicate that Job's fear of God was not merely reverential but actually phobic in nature.[11] These telling passages include:

> What I *feared* has come upon me;
>> what I dreaded has happened to me. (Job 3:25)

> That is why I am *terrified* before him;
>> when I think of all this, I *fear* him. (Job 23:15)

> For I *dreaded* destruction from God,
>> and for *fear* of his splendor I could not do such things. (Job 31:23)

The last passage just cited is especially important. Passages such as Isaiah 1:11-17; Hosea 6:1-6; 8:11-14; Amos 5:21-24 and Micah 6:6-8 are representative of a prophetic critique of a participation in religious rituals that is not accompanied by righteous moral behavior (cf. 1 Sam 15:22; Ps 50:7-23; 51:16-17; Prov 21:3).[12] While Job 31 as a whole makes it clear that Job's life was not lacking with respect to righteous behaviors, verse 23 of that autobiographical passage suggests that Job's impeccable piety was not grounded in his love for and trust in the goodness, bigness and dependability of God but a terrible dread of him instead.

All this to say that I'm wondering whether it's not possible to see in the prologue to the story of Job an indication that the main character's extraordinarily righteous lifestyle was rooted in a fear of God that went beyond reverence and manifested itself in a superscrupulous, actually obsessive-compulsive obedience to rules and observance of religious ritual. The problem with Job, however (and any people in ancient Israel the biblical author[s] may have intended him to represent), was not his hyperpiety but an expectation that went along with it:

---

[10]For example, see G. Buchanan Gray, "The Purpose and Method of the Writer," in *Twentieth Century Interpretations of the Book of Job*, ed. Paul S. Sanders (Englewood Cliffs, NJ: Prentice-Hall Inc., 1968), p. 37.

[11]See Wolfers, *Deep Things*, pp. 97-98.

[12]For more on the prophetic critique of the Israelite cultus found in the literature of the psalms and prophetic writings, see James W. Thompson, "Hebrews 9 and Hellenistic Concepts of Sacrifice," *JBL* 98 (1979): 567-78. See also Robert Merrihew Adams, *Finite and Infinite Goods: A Framework for Ethics* (New York: Oxford University Press, 2002), p. 228.

a *quid pro quo* expectation that such a hyperpiety would necessarily guarantee blessing and obviate disaster. Could it be that there were people in ancient Israel who felt that their loyalty to the temple cultus and pious behavior fairly obligated God to function in their lives in a certain manner? Is it possible that even in the ancient era people could engage in a Pharisaic religiosity that, if only at a subconscious level, functioned as an attempt to tame and domesticate God, turning him into a predictable purveyor of blessings? Might it be that the same need the Pharisees of Jesus' day possessed for a sense of certainty and control with respect to their spiritual status was present in the lives of some of the pious living in Old Testament times?[13] Or, considering yet another possibility, had some people in ancient Israel been guilty of perhaps unintentionally demoting God *de facto* to the rank of a guardian angel?[14]

Here's the question I want to ask: What if God wanted to move Job (and those whom Job was designed to represent) away from a fear-based religion of rules and rituals to a more trust-based personal relationship? What if, *even in the Old Testament era*, God was concerned that his people not allow a super-scrupulous focus on rules and rituals to substitute for a theologically real relationship with him?[15] How might God go about accomplishing such a development in the life of Job, sending a message through him to Israel and the entire world in the process?

One way to achieve this aim might be to throw the extraordinarily scrupulous Job some existential curve balls designed to help him see that true spiritual fulfillment requires more than rules and rituals—that a legalistic/ritualistic approach

---

[13]For more on this, see Gary Tyra, *Defeating Pharisaism: Recovering Jesus' Disciple-Making Method* (Downers Grove, IL: IVP Books, 2009), pp. 68-75.

[14]I trust it's unnecessary for me to point out how the heavenly scenes depicted in Job 1:6-12; 2:1-6 emphasize the authority of God over the entire angelic community.

[15]Some support for this possibility is provided by Walter Brueggemann who, when commenting on Psalm 119 and its emphasis on a personal interaction between the psalmist and God that is grounded in grace and effected through the Spirit, observes: "Psalm 119 thus is structured with delicate sophistication about the life of the spirit. On the one hand, the psalm understands that life with Yahweh is a two-way street. Torah keepers have a right to expect something from Yahweh. Obedience gives entry to seek God's attention and God's gift. . . . On the other hand, those legitimate expectations from God are given an evangelical cast. Finally having earned the right to speak, the speaker nevertheless throws himself on the mercy of God and waits for a move from God—a free, unfettered, uncoerced move from God. There is, to be sure, some comfort in recalling the torah (v. 52). But finally the psalm does not overrate torah. It is Yahweh who is the portion of the speaker (v. 57), not the torah nor one's keeping of the torah. Thus the torah becomes a point of entry for exploring the whole range of interactions with Yahweh. Clearly this psalm probes beyond the simplistic formulation of Psalm 1. A life of full obedience is not a conclusion of faith. It is the beginning point and an access to a life filled with many-sided communion with God. It is by mercy and not by obedience that this one lives (v. 77)" (Walter Brueggemann, *The Message of the Psalms: A Theological Commentary* [Minneapolis: Augsburg, 1984], p. 41).

to religion, while sometimes productive of righteous behavior, isn't sufficient to help human beings actually fulfill the holy purpose for which they were created.[16]

The significance of Job's ensuing suffering (Job 1:6–37:24). Perhaps this explains why the rest of the book of Job seems to show God *using* Job's unexplained suffering to bring this very thing to pass. At the risk of greatly over-simplifying a majestically rich literary work, I'll suggest that in order to properly interpret the significance of Job's suffering, it's important for the reader of the book of Job to keep four crucial details in mind.

First, the ensuing series of painful sufferings Job experiences, while directly caused by *Satan* (the accuser), are actually instigated by God (Job 1:6-12; 2:1-6). It's apparent to the careful reader that God is in control of this story from start to finish. According to Old Testament scholar Paul House, Job 1:6–2:6 makes it clear that "Yahweh is King in charge of angels, Satan, human affairs and ultimately the tests people endure."[17]

Second, the sufferings of Job are complicated, ironically, by the attempts of some "friends" to get him to confess the secret sin they believe must be present in his life. As Job maintains his integrity in the face of his friends' encourage-ments for him to "come clean," the tenor of the conversation between them changes, becoming more and more hostile in tone. Before it's over, the real aim of his friends becomes clear: their real goal is Pharisaic in nature—*to defend God's honor* (see Job 13:7-8) and in the process maintain a view of the world that, because it allows for no ambiguity, affords the experience of psychological safety.[18] Such a worldview sees everything, especially morality, in terms of black and white. An entailment of such a perspective interprets all suffering as penal. It simply has to be lest God be guilty of either incompetence or injustice, or both![19]

Third, though Job never actually curses God in his speeches to his "friends," he does come close, essentially accusing God of acting in a capricious manner toward him and by extension the whole world.[20] G. Buchanan Gray explains Job's thought process thusly:

> Because he has no other theory of suffering than that of the friends, he can imagine no other *just* cause for his own sufferings than sin on his part; since, then,

---

[16]See William Sanford LaSor, David Allan Hubbard and Frederic William Bush, *Old Testament Survey: The Message, Form, and Background of the Old Testament* (Grand Rapids: Eerdmans, 1982), p. 565.
[17]Paul R. House, *Old Testament Theology* (Downers Grove, IL: InterVarsity Press, 1998), p. 428.
[18]See Job 4:7-9, 17; 8:3-7; 11:1-6; 15:11-16; 18:5-21; 20:4-29; 22:1-5, 21-30; 25:1-6; 36:1-17.
[19]For more on the belief system and motive of Job's "friends," see Gray, "Purpose and Method," pp. 38-41. See also Robert L. Alden, *Job*, New American Commentary (Nashville: Broadman & Holman, 1993), p. 40.
[20]For example, see Job 7:17-21; 9:16-18, 22-24; 10:1-3; 16:7-17; 19:1-7; 23:11-17; 24:1, 12; 27:2-6; 30:20-26; cf. Job 33:8-11; 34:5-6; 40:8.

as he knows directly and for certain that such just cause does not exist, he *infers* that his suffering has been unjustly inflicted, that God—the God at least of his own old and his friends' still cherished theory—is unjustly causing his suffering, has changed without good cause from being his friend into his enemy.[21]

Moreover, even when Job isn't explicitly expressing misgivings regarding God's faithfulness toward him, he's doing so inferentially by wishing that he had never been born (e.g., Job 3:1-26; 10:18-19). Can one conceive of a more passive-aggressive way of indicting God for having performed his duties poorly?

Fourth, as Job's compounded suffering goes on and on, he becomes more and more desperate for a personal encounter with God.[22] Moreover, as time passes, Job begins to accuse God of being unwilling to meet with him lest he be forced to acknowledge Job's righteousness and his own capriciousness![23] Is it possible that this is precisely where God wanted Job: crazy hungry for a personal encounter with his Creator—literally desperate for an existentially impactful experience of the living God?

The significance of the divine speeches (Job 38–41). My take on the purposeful nature of the terrifying ambiguity experienced by Job hinges on the notion that when God does show up to converse with him, the rhetorical questions that make up his two speeches are doing more than asserting his sovereign right to do whatever he pleases. They are *also* subtle declarations of his goodness, bigness and dependability. It's not simply that only God can create and sustain the universe but that he has and does![24]

In his commentary on Job, Francis Anderson makes an important observation that unfortunately too many commentators overlook. He states:

> There is a kindly playfulness in the Lord's speeches which is quite relaxing. Their aim is not to crush Job with an awareness of his minuteness contrasted with the limitless power of God, not to mock him when he puts his tiny mind beside God's vast intellect. On the contrary, the mere fact that God converses with him gives him a dignity above all the birds and beasts, assuring him that it is a splendid thing

---

[21]Gray, "Purpose and Method," p. 39, emphasis original. See also LaSor, Hubbard and Bush, *Old Testament Survey*, pp. 565-66.

[22]Gray, "Purpose and Method," pp. 40-41. See also Claus Westermann, *The Structure of the Book of Job: A Form-Critical Analysis* (Minneapolis: Fortress, 1981), pp. 68-69. Indeed, according to Westermann, Job's "main wish" is "for a direct encounter with God. This is the real wish toward which Job has been struggling all along." Westermann also observes that "this is the most elaborate wish in the whole Book of Job" (p. 69).

[23]For example, see Job 10:2; 13:3, 15-24; 19:7; 23:3-9; 30:20; 31:35-37; cf. Job 35:12-14.

[24]See Pascal P. Parente, "The Meaning of Job," in *The Voice Out of the Whirlwind: The Book of Job*, ed. Ralph E. Hone (San Francisco: Chandler, 1960), p. 112; Westermann, *Structure of the Book*, pp. 126-27; House, *Old Testament Theology*, p. 437.

to be a man. To look at any bird or flower—and how many of them there are!—is a revelation of God in His constant care for His world.[25]

Likewise, Eleonore Stump contends:

It is a mistake, then, to characterize God's speeches to Job as demonstrating nothing but God's power over creation. The speeches certainly do show God's power; but, equally importantly, they show God in second-personal connection to all his creatures. . . . God deals as a parent with his creatures, from the sea and rain to the raven and the donkey and even the monstrous behemoth and leviathan. He brings them out of the womb, swaddles, feeds, and guides them, and even plays with them. Most importantly, he talks to them; and somehow, in some sense or other, they talk to him in return.[26]

Stump goes on to offer this bold conclusion: "The divine speeches suggest that God's relationship to all his creatures is personal, intimate, and parental."[27]

In other words, what I'm suggesting is that in his two speeches (Job 38:1–40:2; 40:6–41:34), God is engaged in some crucial self-revelation,[28] essentially saying to Job (and the reader): "The world is more complicated than you think; being God is more involved than you could ever imagine. But because I'm the kind of God I am, it's both inappropriate and unnecessary for you to ever assume that I'm acting capriciously toward you. I'm not only great and good; I'm filled with wisdom as well (cf. Job 28). This reality calls for some trust in the face of mystery (cf. Ps 131:1-3). Though it's true that, like the Leviathan and Behemoth, I can't be tamed or domesticated (that is, made your pet), such a notion should never occur to you in the first place. Spiritual certainty is overrated, and a sense of psychological safety doesn't depend upon your being in control. I'm a good, big and dependable God, and I'm here for you!"[29]

Such a take on the significance of God's speaking to Job from the storm seems to be one that Eleonore Stump might agree with, as evidenced by this bold interpretive observation:

Nothing in God's speeches to Job specifically describes God's relations with human beings, of course, but there is certainly a ready reference—both for Job

---

[25]Francis I. Andersen, *Job: An Introduction and Commentary* (Downers Grove, IL: InterVarsity Press, 1976), p. 271.

[26]Stump, *Wandering in the Darkness*, p. 190.

[27]Ibid., p. 191.

[28]Ibid., p. 127.

[29]Support for the idea that this is the message of the story of Job as a whole can be found in Alden, *Job*, p. 41; House, *Old Testament Theology*, p. 437; Stump, *Wandering in the Darkness*, pp. 187-92; and Robert Gordis, *The Book of God and Man: A Study of Job* (Chicago: University of Chicago Press, 1965), pp. 127-34.

and for the audience of the book—from the way God deals with the rest of his creation to the way in which he deals with human persons. If God deals as a good parent with even the inanimate parts of his creation, if he seeks to produce good even for infant ravens, then a fortiori in his dealings with a human person God will operate in the same way, allowing that person's suffering only in the case he can turn it to some outweighing good not otherwise available to the sufferer.[30]

The significance of Job's ultimate response (Job 42:1-6). And yet, the story isn't over. All the interpretive takes put forward so far lead to a final expositional observation: as the book wraps up, the only resolution to the story offered to the reader is that in the face of this powerful, personal, existentially impactful encounter with God, Job essentially says of his sufferings: "It's all good. Once upon a time I knew about you, but now I've seen you up close and personal. I repent of ever having mistrusted you and of wishing myself dead" (see Job 42:1-6).[31]

We will recall that, according to the developmental theory promoted by Bruce Waltke, the point of the story is to portray Job as evolving from being merely a righteous man to one who is wise as well. Francis Andersen seems to have just such a development in mind when, commenting on Job's response to the divine speeches, he observes:

> Job is satisfied. His vision of God has been expanded beyond all previous bounds. He has a new appreciation of the scope and harmony of God's world, of which he is but a small part. But this discovery does not make him feel insignificant. Just by looking at ordinary things, he realizes that he cannot even begin to imagine what it must be like to be God. The world is beautiful and terrifying, and in it all God is everywhere, seen to be powerful and wise, and more mysterious when He is known than when He is but dimly discerned. The Lord has spoken to Job. That fact alone is marvellous [*sic*] beyond all wonder. Job has grown in wisdom. He is at once delighted and ashamed.[32]

---

[30]Stump, *Wandering in the Darkness*, p. 191. It should be noted that Stump, sensitive to the criticism that such an interpretation by itself doesn't adequately account for the suffering of Job's wife and kids, offers the suggestion that the story of Job is best understood as a "complex fractal." Put simply, an example of a fractal would be "a picture within a picture within a picture, and so on, each picture of which is similar to the picture of the whole, only reduced in scale" (p. 220). Thus, says Stump, the way God deals with all his creatures possesses a fractal quality about it. She explains: "Understood as a kind of complex fractal, the book of Job is an illustration of the way in which God's relations with creatures is to be understood. God is able to use those creatures whom he treats as ends in themselves within their own stories *also* as means to ends for others of his creatures, who are ends in themselves within *their* stories. This interpretation thus suggests a way of looking at all the other suffering, apart from Job's mentioned or implied in the book of Job" (p. 221).

[31]See Westermann, *Structure of the Book*, p. 128.

[32]Andersen, *Job*, p. 291. See also Stump, *Wandering in the Darkness*, p. 191.

Absolutely! And yet, it's my sense that Job's admission is reflective not only of a sapiential development in his life but a spiritual one as well. The growth Job has experienced is not just in the area of wisdom but the very nature of his relationship with God!

It's with this very thought in mind that, after discounting the popular notion that the purpose of Job was to serve as a theodicy, Bernhard Anderson, Stephen Bishop and Judith Newman assert: "To be sure, the poet wrestles with an inescapable problem of human life: the suffering of the innocent. But the problem of suffering—and its counterpart, the question of divine justice—provides the occasion for probing a much deeper question: *What is a person's relationship to God?*"[33]

And precisely how does Job's story address this crucial relational question? Essentially echoing my own argument, this trio of authors explain:

> Outside the "I-thou" relationship for which human beings were created, suffering can drive people to despair or to the easy solutions of popular religion. Within the context of *faith*—the relationship that finally defined Job's existence—suffering can be faced in the confidence that the times of a person's life "are in God's hand" (Ps. 31:15) and that God in a surprising manner brings good out of evil (Gen. 50:20; compare Rom. 8:28). Thus the climax of the Job poetry occurs at the very end, when a *false relationship based on a conception of God received from tradition* ("I had heard of you by the hearing of the ear") is converted into a *relationship of personal trust and surrender*—"but now my eye sees you" (Job 42:5).[34]

G. Buchanan Gray provides some additional support for this relational emphasis in Job. Commenting on the effect his encounter with God had on Job, Gray writes:

> But the speech of Yahweh accompanies an appearance or direct manifestation of Yahweh to Job, and in this respect is the direct response of Yahweh to Job's deepest desire: Job has at last found Yahweh; and in spite of the rebuke of his words beyond knowledge, he has found Yahweh on his side, no more estranged from him than in the days of his former prosperity, but *more intimately known*; as compared with his former, his present knowledge is as sight to hearing, as direct, first hand personal to second hand and traditional knowledge.[35]

Going a bit beyond Gray, I'm suggesting the possibility that it's not only true

[33]Bernhard W. Anderson, Stephen Bishop and Judith H. Newman, *Understanding the Old Testament* (Upper Saddle River, NJ: Pearson Prentice-Hall, 2007), p. 545, emphasis original.
[34]Ibid., p. 551, emphasis added.
[35]Gray, "Purpose and Method," p. 43, emphasis added.

that Job's communion with God has been intensified through this experience of suffering and encounter but that he has actually moved from a fear-based, legalistic and obsessively ritualistic religious posture to a personal, interactive, faith-based relationship with God.[36] But whether one accepts Gray's position or mine, the fact is that we both contend that the book of Job is not simply a bald declaration of God's sovereign right as Creator and Lord to do whatever he wants with us. No, it's a bold but gracious acknowledgment that God is not beyond using the experience of suffering to chase people he cares about deeply into an existential space where they become virtually desperate for a personal encounter with him (cf. 2 Cor 12:1-10). *The story of Job in particular, and the Bible as a whole, seems to be telling us that God has allowed a certain amount of ambiguity in the world because that's what it takes to cause merely religious (and irreligious) people to awaken to the reality that they desperately need a real relationship with him.*[37]

It appears that even though God is good, he sometimes plays "rough" with his kids. Walter Brueggemann can be interpreted as affirming precisely this when he observes that what we find in the book of Job is "a pattern of *orientation, disorientation,* and *new orientation*"—that is, an introduction into the messy and sometimes costly life of faith. In his imitable manner, Brueggemann explains: "The dramatic power of the book of Job attests to the reality that faith, beyond easy convictions, is a demanding way to live that thrives on candor and requires immense courage. Faith of this kind that pushes deeply beyond covenantal quid pro quos or sapiential *consequences* that follow from *deeds* is no enterprise for wimps or sissies."[38]

---

[36]LaSor, Hubbard and Bush opine: "The answer comes not so much in the flood of new information as in a *new* relationship with the Lord of the universe: 'but now my eye sees thee' (v. 5)" (LaSor, Hubbard and Bush, *Old Testament Survey*, p. 568, emphasis added).

[37]A possible objection to my treatment of Job might derive from the fact that, after indicting Job's "friends" for not speaking the truth about him as Job had, God instructs them to go to Job, sacrifice a burnt offering and then ask Job to pray for them (Job 42:7-9). Doesn't this apparent sanction of ritual sacrifice at the end of the story invalidate the notion that the purpose of Job's suffering was to move him away from ritual religion toward a real relationship? In response, I'll remind the reader that nowhere in this exposition have I suggested that it was inherently wrong for people in the Old Testament era to engage in ritual sacrifice. That said, I do find it interesting that the text doesn't say that God accepted the sacrifice offered by Job's "friends" per se but that he accepted Job's intercessory prayer on their behalf. Furthermore, Job 42:10 goes on to specify that it was "after Job had prayed for his friends" that "the LORD restored his fortunes and gave him twice as much as he had before." I find it significant that there's quite a bit of emphasis here on Job's prayerful intercession. Perhaps a lesson Job has learned is that the best way to intercede for others is not by means of ritual sacrifice but through a personal, prayerful communion with God. Isn't this precisely what we would expect to find if the point of the story had been what I've proposed: God's concern to bring about a spiritual development in Job's life away from a rank ritualism toward an intimate, interactive relationship?

[38]Walter Brueggemann, *An Introduction to the Old Testament: The Canon and Christian Imagination* (Louisville: Westminster John Knox, 2003), p. 302, emphasis original.

Now, the point of this interpretive summary of the story of Job is this: if it's true that for whatever reason God has allowed a measure of ambiguity to exist in our world, then a real-world ethic simply must take this existential reality into account. Rather than surprise or scandalize us, the suggestion that a moral faithfulness before God requires an ethical decision-making approach that's somewhat messy in nature should be readily embraced. It's the ambiguity at work in the world that forces us to do more than treat the Bible as a moral rule book. It's this ethic's recognition of this ambiguity that encourages us as moral agents to both search the Scriptures and cry out to God, eager if not desperate for a personal encounter and the divine moral guidance Proverbs 2 just happens to promise.

AN ETHIC IN TOUCH WITH WHAT AUTHENTIC CHRISTIAN DISCIPLESHIP IS ULTIMATELY ABOUT

It stands to reason that any moral model claiming to be Christ-centered, especially one claiming to promote a responsible Christian discipleship, must be grounded in a theologically astute understanding of the ultimate purpose of Christ's disciple-making ministry. In Mark 1:14-15 we read:

> After John was put in prison, Jesus went into Galilee, proclaiming the good news of God. "The time has come," he said. "The kingdom of God has come near. Repent and believe the good news!" (Mk 1:14-15)

So what was Jesus was up to as he went about announcing the availability of the kingdom of God and calling people to faith, repentance and a devoted followership? How important to an authentic Christian discipleship is this thing Jesus refers to as the kingdom of God?

I'm going to suggest that in order to properly understand what Christian discipleship is about we need to understand the nature of Jesus' kingdom announcement. Furthermore, to understand what the kingdom of God is about we must seek to understand the nature of our trinitarian God and what he's ultimately after. Presented below is my attempt at a necessarily brief yet theologically sensitive treatment of the ultimate aim of authentic Christian discipleship.

The relational nature of God. According to C. S. Lewis, the God of the Bible is not only superpersonal but ultrarelational as well.[39] The teaching of Scripture seems to be that at the heart of the Godhead is a community of three divine persons—Father, Son and Holy Spirit—eternally engaged in a sort of dance produced by the eternal, loving interaction between them.[40] *In other words, our God is all about the dynamic of interpersonal relationship.*[41] We might even say that he is a hyperpersonal, ultrarelational God who is radically interested in a personal (though not private) relationship with each and every human being created in his image.[42] To paraphrase a bold assertion made by theologian Emil Brunner, when we Christians use personal, relational, communal language in reference to God, we're not projecting onto him our personal attributes and capacity for community. Rather, the reason why we human beings are both community-capable and community-craving creatures is that we bear the *imago Dei!*[43]

The relational nature of God's kingdom. The Bible is replete with passages that support the idea that, precisely because God is concerned for the spiritual well-being of individuals, he desires that individuals enter into and maintain a *personal relationship* with him through Jesus Christ (a personal though not private relationship that most certainly has communal implications).[44] Moreover, the Bible concludes with the prophetic promise that the intimate, interactive intimacy between God and humanity that is now experienced in a provisional, halting, imperfect manner will someday become perfect, and that for all of eternity:

---

[39]C. S. Lewis, *Mere Christianity* (San Francisco: HarperSanFrancisco, 2001), pp. 175-76.

[40]See Timothy Keller, *The Reason for God: Belief in an Age of Skepticism* (New York: Dutton, 2008), p. 215. See also Stanley Grenz, *Theology for the Community of God* (Grand Rapids: Eerdmans, 2000), p. 72.

[41]Michael Bird observes: "That there are personal relationships within the Godhead means that relationality is essential for what it means to be God" (Michael F. Bird, *Evangelical Theology: A Biblical and Systematic Introduction* [Grand Rapids: Zondervan, 2013], p. 134).

[42]Ibid, p. 167.

[43]See Emil Brunner, *Dogmatics*, vol. 1, *The Christian Doctrine of God* (London: Lutterworth, 1949), p. 140.

[44]Some New Testament passages that reflect God's interest in a personal relationship with people created in his image include: Mt 16:24-27; Mk 8:38; Lk 15; Jn 7:17; 10:3; 14:23; Rom 10:11; 1 Cor 3:17; 11:29; 16:22; 2 Cor 5:17; Gal 1:15-16; 2:19-21; Phil 4:13; Heb 3:12; 4:1, 10; Jas 1:23-26; 2:14; 2 Pet 1:8-9; 3:9; 1 Jn 2:4-6; 4:8, 15-16; and Rev 3:20-22; 22:12, 17.

> Then I saw "a new heaven and a new earth," for the first heaven and the first earth
> had passed away, and there was no longer any sea. I saw the Holy City, the new
> Jerusalem, coming down out of heaven from God, prepared as a bride beautifully
> dressed for her husband. And I heard a loud voice from the throne saying, "Look!
> God's dwelling place is now among the people, and he will dwell with them. They
> will be his people, and God himself will be with them and be their God. 'He will
> wipe every tear from their eyes. There will be no more death' or mourning or
> crying or pain, for the old order of things has passed away." (Rev 21:1-4)

The word *kingdom* (Greek *basileia*) does not appear in the passage just cited.
But if we were to allow this vivid portrayal of the eternal state to inform our
understanding of God's supreme intention with respect to his people, we
might very well conclude that it's surely indicative of what the kingdom is
ultimately about—an existence earmarked by an eternal experience of righteousness, peace and joy (Is 32:16-18; cf. Rom 14:17) made possible by an
unmitigated relational intimacy with the God of creation. Talk about psychological safety! All of God's people enjoying a never-ceasing experience
of the kind of community eternally occurring within the Godhead itself:
this, I'm proposing, is the ultimate goal of God's forever kingdom.

The relational nature of Christian discipleship. What all this suggests
is that an intimate, interactive, world-impacting relationship with God
is what Christian discipleship is all about. Such a relationship is what the
first humans enjoyed for a season in the garden and, as we've just seen,
what redeemed humanity will ultimately experience in the eternal
kingdom (cf. Jer 31:33-34; Rev 22:3-5). When the incarnate Christ came
preaching the good news that "the kingdom of God is at hand," he was
announcing the availability of this kind of personal, intimate, interactive
relationship with God as one's "Abba." Such a theologically real relationship with God is a huge part of what Christian discipleship is designed to achieve. Jesus of Nazareth is really good at loving God supremely and loving his neighbor as himself. Jesus of Nazareth is really
good at doing justice, loving mercy and walking humbly before God
(Mic 6:8). *If we let him, the risen Jesus will enable us to do this too!*[45] This

---

[45]Timothy Keller insists that an implication of the fact that ultimate reality is a divine community
of three persons—Father, Son and Holy Spirit—eternally engaged in knowing, loving and joyfully
serving one another is that this life is all about those who bear the *imago Dei* likewise becoming

is another reason why the message of *Pursuing Moral Faithfulness* should be taken seriously: it's about an ethic that's in touch with what Christian discipleship is ultimately about.

AN ETHIC THAT TAKES SERIOUSLY WHAT THE NEW TESTAMENT HAS TO SAY ABOUT BEING LED BY THE SPIRIT

A third positive feature of the ethic of responsible Christian discipleship is the way it pays heed to the New Testament's teaching regarding the importance of a pneumatologically real approach to Christian discipleship. As churchman and biblical scholar John Stott put it: "the Christian life is essentially life in the Spirit, that is to say, a life which is animated, sustained, directed and enriched by the Holy Spirit. Without the Holy Spirit true Christian discipleship would be inconceivable, indeed impossible."[46] Such an observation is validated by the fact that the writings of Jesus' apostles are replete with passages that underscore the prominent role the Holy Spirit is to play in the Christian life and how important it is for Christ's followers to surrender themselves to his leadership.[47]

For our purposes, two of these passages are of particular importance: Romans 8:1-4 and Galatians 5:22-25. Both passages are absolutely pivotal not only to the message Paul is conveying in each letter but also to his theology overall, especially his understanding of Christian ethics.

Romans 8:1-4 (and the verses that follow). In the first of these two pivotal passages, Paul writes:

> Therefore, there is now no condemnation for those who are in Christ Jesus, because through Christ Jesus the law of the Spirit who gives life has set you free from the law of sin and death. For what the law was powerless to do because it was weakened by the flesh, God did by sending his own Son in the likeness of sinful flesh to be a sin offering. And so he condemned sin in the flesh, *in order that the righteous requirement of the law might be fully met in us, who do not live according to the flesh but according to the Spirit.* (Rom 8:1-4)

---

enabled to know, love and joyfully serve God and their neighbors (see Mt 22:34-40). See Keller, *Reason for God*, pp. 216-17.

[46]See John R. W. Stott, *The Message of Romans: God's Good News for the World* (Downers Grove, IL: IVP Academic, 2001), p. 216.

[47]For example, see Jn 3:3-8; 16:7-15; Acts 1:8; 16:6-10; Rom 8:15-16, 26-27; 15:13; 1 Cor 12:4-8; Eph 1:13-14; 5:18-20; 6:10-18.

According to this text, a key role the Holy Spirit desires to play in the lives of Christ's followers is as an ethical empowerer. It's nothing short of profound, really. Given his way, the Holy Spirit will empower those he indwells to fully meet the "righteous requirement of the law."[48] In other words, this biblical text provides crucial support for the idea that one of the great desires of the Holy Spirit is to enable Christ's followers to actually live in such a way as to honor the heart of God. Though we can't say for sure that Paul had Jesus' two-commandment summary of the law in mind, it's fairly safe to say that he would be comfortable with the notion that the Holy Spirit can and will enable sincere Christian disciples to, like Jesus, love God supremely and their neighbors as themselves (cf. Rom 13:9-10; Gal 5:13-18).

However, and this is huge, the last lines of this first key passage indicate that there's some *contingency* involved: in order for the Holy Spirit to do this work of empowerment in our moral lives, his leadership must be surrendered to.[49] Indeed, a careful look at Romans 8:5-13—the context-providing verses that immediately follow this passage—only serves to reinforce this idea.[50] According to these verses, it's both possible and absolutely crucial for us as Christ's followers to:

- live in accordance with the Spirit (Rom 8:5a);

- set our minds on what the Spirit desires (Rom 8:5b);

- allow our minds to be governed by the Spirit (Rom 8:6); and

- with the Spirit's help, put to death the misdeeds of the body (Rom 8:12-13).

Galatians 5:22-25 (and the verses that precede). In the other pivotal text in which Paul indicates the importance of the Holy Spirit to a moral faithfulness, the apostle wrote:

> But the fruit of the Spirit is love, joy, peace, forbearance, kindness, goodness, faithfulness, gentleness and self-control. Against such things there is no law. Those who belong to Christ Jesus have crucified the flesh with its passions and desires. Since we live by the Spirit, *let us keep in step with the Spirit.* (Gal 5:22-25)

---

[48]John Murray, *The Epistle to the Romans*, New International Commentary on the New Testament (Grand Rapids: Eerdmans, 1987), p. 284.

[49]Ibid., pp. 293-94.

[50]See C. K. Barrett, *The Epistle to the Romans*, Harper's New Testament Commentaries (New York: Harper & Row, 1957), pp. 161-62.

I'm going to propose that the fruit of Spirit listed here, nine attributes that biblical scholar Ronald Fung describes as "ethical graces" and "graces of character," were manifestly present in the life of Jesus, himself.[51] Since the Holy Spirit is the Spirit of Christ (Acts 16:7; Rom 8:9; Phil 1:19; 1 Pet 1:11), it's possible to understand Paul inferring here that yet another role of the Holy Spirit in the life of the sincere Christian disciple is to produce within him or her the very virtues of Jesus himself![52]

And yet once again we find the apostle Paul indicating that the empowering work of the Spirit doesn't occur automatically; there's some contingency involved.[53] In this case, the disciple's responsibility is referred to in Galatians 5:24, where Paul speaks of the need for the follower of Christ to *crucify the flesh with its passion and desires* by *keeping in step with the Spirit*—that is, by saying "no" to the influence of the fleshly nature and "yes" to the guidance provided by Christ's Spirit.[54]

Moreover, a note of contingency is also sounded in the context-providing verses that immediately precede Galatians 5:22-25. To be specific, in Galatians 5:16 we find Paul exhorting his readers to "walk by the Spirit."[55] In Galatians 5:18 Paul refers to the tremendous importance of being "led by the Spirit." Both verses imply that keeping in step with the

---

[51]Ronald Y. K. Fung, *The Epistle to the Galatians*, New International Commentary on the New Testament (Grand Rapids: Eerdmans, 1988), pp. 271-72.

[52]According to F. F. Bruce, this list of "nine graces" is Paul's way of describing "the lifestyle of those who are indwelt and energized by the Spirit" (F. F. Bruce, *The Epistle to the Galatians*, New International Greek Testament Commentary [Grand Rapids: Eerdmans, 1982], p. 251). See also Fung, *Epistle to the Galatians*, p. 272; and Donald Guthrie, *Galatians*, New Century Bible Commentary (Grand Rapids: Eerdmans, 1973), p. 139.

[53]Fung makes this quite clear when he states: "While these virtues are presented as the product of the Spirit, it is worth emphasizing again . . . that the believer is not without responsibility, 'by attentive openness to God,' to allow the Spirit to produce these graces in him" (Fung, *Epistle to the Galatians*, pp. 272-73).

[54]For more on this, see Gary J. Tyra, "Proclaiming Christ's Victory over Sinful, Personal Desires," *Enrichment Journal*, Summer 2013, http://enrichmentjournal.ag.org/201303/201303_072_personal_victory.cfm. See also Fung, *Epistle to the Galatians*, p. 275.

[55]Douglas Moo observes, regarding the phrase "walk by the Spirit" found in Galatians 5:16, that "the present tense of the verb probably connotes continuous action: 'be always walking by the Spirit,' 'be a person characterized by walking in the Sprit,'" and that the dative form of the noun (Greek *pneumati*) suggests the idea that "the walk of the believer is determined by the Spirit, who both directs and empowers Christian living" (Douglas Moo, *Galatians*, Baker Exegetical Commentary on the New Testament [Grand Rapids: Baker Academic, 2013], p. 353). For more on the need for Christians to be "continually influenced by and directed by the Spirit," see ibid., pp. 356-57. See also Guthrie, *Galatians*, p. 136.

Spirit requires a choice. Commenting in particular on Galatians 5:18, Ronald Fung asserts:

> This conditional sentence clearly shows that Paul does not regard the believer as a helpless spectator or an unwilling pawn in the fierce battle between the flesh and the Spirit; the assumption is rather that the Christian can overcome the flesh by siding with the Spirit. Being "led by the Spirit" is in form passive; in its actual meaning, however, it is not entirely passive. The active leading of the Holy Spirit does not signify the believer's being, so to speak, led by the nose willy-nilly; on the contrary, he must let himself be led by the Spirit—that is actively choose to stand on the side of the Spirit over against the flesh. . . . The Holy Spirit is not a perpetual motion machine which operates automatically in the life of the believer, but a Person whose working the Christian can *respond* to, depend on, and cooperate with. Therefore, the Christian faces the decision whether to follow the Spirit in this way or to give in to the flesh.[56]

In sum, the New Testament seems to present us with passages that connect the moral life with the work of the Spirit. More than that, they seem to indicate that getting the moral life right as a Christian disciple mandates that we get serious about being led by the Spirit.

I'll conclude this discussion with the reminder that, according to passages such as Proverbs 2; Psalms 32:8-9; 143:10; Romans 8:1-4 and Galatians 5:22-25, some Spirit-enabled guidance and empowerment is available. However, this supernatural assistance in hearing and honoring the heart of God requires that we, recognizing the ambiguous nature of human existence and the relational nature of Christian discipleship, take seriously the apostle Paul's call to be led by the Spirit (Rom 8:4-6, 12-14; Gal 5:16-18, 25). Unfortunately, not every moral model sufficiently emphasizes the importance of a theologically and pneumatologically real approach to the Christian life. It's precisely because the ethic promoted in these pages does so that it should be embraced.

Having done my best in this work to indicate the possibility and importance of becoming a morally responsible Christian disciple, all that's left is a no-nonsense discussion of the process involved in our doing so. I'm convinced that the Holy Spirit wants to help the followers of Christ

---

[56]Fung, *Epistle to the Galatians*, pp. 251-52, emphasis added.

embody the moral faithfulness Jesus rendered to God on their behalf. But how is this done? What specific steps are involved? Can we (without giving in to a craving for certainty and control) be any more specific about those spiritual formation practices crucial to a morally faithful lifestyle? We can. Let's go on to discuss these very practical matters now.

Actually Becoming an
Ethically Responsible Christian Disciple

The Process Involved

In this book's introduction I referred to a young adult student's admission that prior to taking a college course on Christian ethics, he'd been guilty of making moral decisions in pretty much the same way his non-Christian friends did. In the previous chapter I alluded to a young woman—a new believer—who very nearly made one of the most important moral choices of her life in a manner that was almost completely void of any attempt to hear and honor the heart of God. I offer that both of these stories serve to illustrate a vitally important truth: we simply can't expect our culture at large to adequately encourage and enable us in the pursuit of a moral faithfulness before God. So how is a morally faithful lifestyle before God actualized in our lives? What spiritual/ecclesial experiences/activities do we need to engage in so as to cooperate with the Holy Spirit's ministry of helping us actually become ethically responsible Christian disciples? These are precisely the questions this final chapter will attempt to answer.

The book *Elements of a Christian Worldview* contains a chapter titled "The Ethics of Being: Character, Community, Praxis."[1] This chapter, written by Cheryl Bridges Johns and Vardaman White, endeavors to answer the questions posed above. To be even more specific, it provides a thoughtful response to a query every parent, church leader and college professor should be asking: What's the best way to help young Christians living in an

---

[1]Cheryl Bridges Johns and Vardaman W. White, "The Ethics of Being: Character, Community, Praxis," in *Elements of a Christian Worldview*, ed. Michael D. Palmer (Springfield, MO: Logion, 1998), pp. 283-312.

increasingly postmodern, morally relativistic world become truly Christlike?

In order to achieve their purpose, the authors tell their readers a story about a presumably fictional character named Jeff. Though no association is made between Jeff and the phenomenon of Moralistic Therapeutic Deism (the publication of this essay predated the NYSR), it would not be inappropriate to do so. Jeff's story can be viewed as a case study that, in a no-nonsense manner, portrays the process involved in someone sporting an "almost Christianity" eventually becoming, with the Holy Spirit's help, a fully devoted Christ follower both eager and able to render to God a moral faithfulness.

JEFF, POSTMODERNISM AND THE NEED FOR A NEW APPROACH TO ETHICS

The main character in this case study is a freshman attending a Christian college. A professing Christian, Jeff routinely attends a nearby church, helping out from time to time with the youth group. He has never used drugs and is not in the habit of drinking alcohol. However, he and his girlfriend are sexually active. Though Jeff is aware that his church does not endorse premarital sexual intimacy, he has convinced himself that sleeping with his girlfriend is not sinful because they love one another and plan to someday be married.[2]

So how is it that Jeff, a fairly regular attender at a Bible-believing church, can at the same time engage in a behavior he knows the Bible prohibits?[3]

According to Johns and White, it's crucial to understand just how significantly Jeff has been influenced by the cultural soup he's been swimming around in all his life. Referring to Jeff as a "product of his culture," they suggest that he is what may be called a "postmodern person." The authors explain that in an increasingly postmodern world people no longer share a "unified vision of right and wrong." In such a world, behavioral norms are not viewed as coming from God but are regarded as mere human inventions. Indeed, the concept of truth itself

---

[2]Ibid., p. 284.
[3]While it's true that there's no Bible verse that explicitly states "Thou shalt not have sex before marriage," it's clear that the teaching of Scripture as a whole proscribes such activity (e.g., see Gen 29:14-30; Ex 22:16-17; Deut 22:13-21; 1 Cor 7:1-2, 8-9; 2 Cor 11:2; Eph 5:1-3; Heb 13:4).

"has become relative and individualized." As a result, folks like Jeff are encouraged to "live by their *own* rules, define truth for themselves, and make their *own* world."[4]

The authors then proceed to spell out for their readers the challenge postmodernism presents for traditional Christian ethics. They explain that because Jeff has grown up in a cultural environment that is profoundly suspicious of absolute definitions of right and wrong, he needs something more than a list of rules to guide his ethical decision making, even if those rules come from the Bible. They point out that the mere fact that Jeff is "familiar with certain rules" does not mean he is adequately equipped to meet the challenges of a postmodern social context earmarked by a fairly strong embrace of moral relativism.

So what does a person living in such a world need in order to render to God the moral faithfulness a biblically informed version of Christianity calls for? According to the authors, "Jeff needs something that will center his life, unifying it, so that he will not only *have* Christian beliefs and actions but that he will *be* a Christian. Jeff needs to have the heart and the mind of a Christian, which will transform his view of reality."[5]

As its title infers, what we have in this essay is a case study that argues the need for a particular approach to the moral formation of Christians. After providing their readers with brief descriptions of the ways in which the question "What should I do?" is answered via the deontological (rules-oriented) and teleological (results-oriented) approaches to ethical decision making, Johns and White go on to suggest that perhaps the focus should actually be on character development.[6] It's at this point that the authors assert:

> In a postmodern world in which there is little given or assumed that would prescribe what one should do, it is imperative that Christian ethics begin with the transformation of being. Jeff must become someone distinctively Christian before he can express in action a clear Christian lifestyle. In other words, Jeff must develop the character of a Christian.[7]

---

[4]Johns and White, "Ethics of Being," p. 284, emphasis original.
[5]Ibid.
[6]Ibid., pp. 285-86.
[7]Ibid., p. 288.

But this raises the question: How does this character development occur?

There are a couple of reasons why I very much appreciate the content of this chapter so ably written by Johns and White. First, their fictional character, Jeff, could be one of the students who sits in front of me each day. Furthermore, like the young woman referred to earlier, Jeff is emblematic of so many churchgoing members of the emerging generations. Again, I don't believe it's going too far to suggest that Jeff might be viewed as representative of vast numbers of American youth whose lives have been dramatically impacted by the Moralistic Therapeutic Deism we discussed at length in chapter four of this book.

A second reason why I'm appreciative of the chapter penned by Johns and White flows from the fact that the manner in which they describe the process of Jeff's eventual character development resonates very strongly with my own personal and pastoral experience. The truth is that, except for the fact that I didn't grow up in the church, I could have been Jeff at his age. Moreover, the no-nonsense three-step process that Johns and White use to portray Jeff's transformation into a person who's eager and ready to become a responsible moral agent on the stage of human history rings true with my own spiritual journey. Furthermore, I've seen this same moral transformation process play out time and again in the lives of the people—students and parishioners—I've worked with over the years. It's for all of these reasons that I want to, with apologies to Johns and White, provide a necessarily condensed description of the three-pronged approach to Christian character development proffered by them.

JEFF AND THE CULTIVATION OF A MORALLY FAITHFUL LIFESTYLE

According to Johns and White, in order for any person to develop the virtues that Jesus himself possessed, it's necessary for them to experience three discipleship dynamics.

A transformative encounter with God enabled by his Spirit. The first thing that needs to happen if we fallen human beings are to end up possessing the very virtues of Christ is that our hearts need to be changed. We desperately need to experience a personal encounter with God through the Holy Spirit, whose regenerating and sanctifying work aims at producing a fundamental change at the core of our being.

Another former mentor of mine, the late Dallas Willard, famously suggested that such a transformation, taking place over a lifetime, is what a spiritual formation that is Christian in nature is all about. According to Willard, "the greatest need you and I have—the greatest need of collective humanity—is *renovation of our heart. That* spiritual place within us from which outlook, choices, and actions come has been formed by a world *away from God.* Now it must be transformed."[8] Willard goes on to assert that, for Christians, the intended direction of spiritual formation is nothing other than the very character of Christ. Says Willard: "Spiritual formation for the Christian basically refers to the Spirit-driven process of forming the inner world of the human self in such a way that it becomes like the inner being of Christ himself."[9]

Essentially echoing Willard's emphasis on the renovation of the heart, and speaking specifically of its implications for the moral life, Johns and White explain that a person's character matters greatly because, while circumstances may change, "the constant upon the shifting sands is the person facing the circumstances." A person's character—his or her dispositions, values, virtues, and vices—"move with that person across the landscape of his or her life." It's a person's character, say Johns and White, that "provides for consistency in action."[10] Citing Arthur Holmes, Johns and White remind us that it's character that "makes a person reliable, a responsible moral agent."[11]

To be more specific, at the heart of a person's character are his or her convictions and desires—deep-seated beliefs and longings that are constantly being shaped by family, experiences at school and church, and the larger society as reflected in the media.[12] The reason that human hearts need renovation stems from the fact that our convictions and desires can be out of sync with God's character and therefore antagonistic to our becoming responsible actors on the stage of human history.

---

[8]Dallas Willard, *Renovation of the Heart: Putting on the Character of Christ* (Colorado Springs: NavPress, 2002), p. 14.

[9]Ibid., p. 22.

[10]Johns and White, "Ethics of Being," p. 288.

[11]Arthur Holmes, *Ethics: Approaching Moral Decisions* (Downers Grove, IL: InterVarsity Press, 1984), p. 117, as cited in Johns and White, "Ethics of Being," p. 288.

[12]Johns and White, "Ethics of Being," p. 290.

When this is the case, our convictions and desires need to be transformed according to the will of God.

The good news, according to Willard, Johns and White, is that it's possible to experience God's presence and power in our lives in such a way as to be transformed at the core of our being. With the Holy Spirit's help we can gain the mind and heart of Christ, literally believing and desiring differently than we did before (see Ps 119:34-37; Ezek 36:26-27; Rom 2:29; 1 Cor 2:16; Col 2:11). Such a character transformation is crucial since, as Johns and White put it, "Only by this *becoming* can we avoid having a patchwork identity which pieces together moral choices based on what feels good or seems right in the moment."[13] The bottom line is that at the *heart* of a moral faithfulness is the need for our *hearts* to be renewed into the likeness of Christ through transformative encounters with God's Holy Spirit.

Johns and White picture Jeff having such an experience while attending a special revival meeting at his church. It's literally while kneeling in prayer at an altar service that Jeff encounters *at the same time* both the *holiness* and *forgiveness* of God. Such a profound spiritual experience is not only paradoxical but powerful also, producing within the sincere seeker "a powerful cleansing and healing."[14]

Of course, a transformative encounter with God through the Holy Spirit can occur at other locations as well (for example, at home, a dorm room, outdoors, etc.). Moreover, I would offer that there can and should be not just one but many experiences such as this in the course of a person's spiritual journey.

However, these caveats aside, I completely agree with the suggestion made by Johns and White that such existentially impactful encounters with God have the effect of either beginning or furthering the process of becoming a fundamentally different sort of person—someone more capable than before of hearing and honoring the heart of God, the press of an increasingly postmodern cultural environment notwithstanding (see Ezek 36:24-27).[15]

---

[13]Ibid., p. 292.
[14]Ibid., p. 293.
[15]Ibid.

A conscientious participation in genuine Christian community. Pressing further, as important as personal transformational experiences with God through the Spirit are to one's spiritual and moral formation, I'm convinced along with Johns and White that it's "nearly impossible to develop a Christian lifestyle without the fellowship of the church."[16] This is because character "formation occurs within the context of relationships."[17] It's only in community that a person learns who he or she is, begins to form character and learns to live according to that character in a consistent manner.[18] It's simply the case that character will not develop without an appropriate social environment.

However, this is not to say that, as far as a moral faithfulness before the God of the Bible is concerned, just any kind of community will do. Referring to the work of Stanley Hauerwas, Johns and White are correct to stipulate that *it's only a faithful Christian community that can form faithful Christians.*[19]

Ideally, what we're really talking about here is a small cadre of spiritual friends who will provide us with two dynamics crucial to spiritual transformation: a huge amount of acceptance (or support) and an equally significant measure of accountability. It's my sense that these two dynamics—interpersonal acceptance and accountability—are critical earmarks of a genuine rather than faux Christian community. Too many churches don't encourage a small group experience of any kind. Moreover, too many small group ministries fail to provide participants with both of these dynamics at the same time. All too often a small group will major on providing support/acceptance but lack the accountability factor, or they will emphasize accountability but fail to provide an ethos of unconditional acceptance/support. The truth be known, it's probably because of these two versions of imbalance, along with the fact that some small groups provide neither support nor accountability in sufficient measure,

---

[16]Ibid., p. 296. It should be noted that with regard to this assertion Johns and White reference Stanley Hauerwas and William H. Willimon, "Embarrassed by God's Presence," *Christian Century* 30 (January 1985): 99.

[17]See James W. Fowler, "Practical Theology and the Shaping of Christian Lives," in *Practical Theology*, ed. Don S. Browning (San Francisco: Harper & Row, 1983), p. 162, as cited in Johns and White, "Ethics of Being," p. 296.

[18]Johns and White, "Ethics of Being," p. 296.

[19]Ibid., pp. 295-96.

that most small group ministries initiated by churches end up dying, whether that demise is quick or slow in coming.[20]

For their part, Johns and White recommend an involvement in what they refer to as a "covenant group." Such a group "consists of people who commit themselves to pray, support, strengthen, and bless each other."[21] Obviously, for such a group to be truly Christian, the members must all share a common commitment to Jesus as Lord and to one another as brothers and sisters in Christ.[22]

In genuine community, people share their experiences with each other and come to feel as though they belong to one another. It has been the experience of many Christian disciples that as we relate to each other in such a group, we find ourselves relating to God himself.[23] Understood in terms of a theological realism, it's out of a spiritual communion with Christ realized by means of our communion with those who belong to his body (1 Cor 12:27) that the power for character transformation arises. For instance, being a part of a covenant group forces us to deal with the spirit of individualism (and consumerism) that saturates our society and that leads to an "almost Christianity" and the moral relativism and inconsistency associated with it. Thus Johns and White have Jeff making some dramatic changes in his relationship with his girlfriend, and then explaining to another friend that, as a result of the Christian community he was experiencing, "he no longer felt bound by the standards of the prevailing popular culture. He felt a new freedom to say no to what is evil and yes to what is righteous."[24] Wanting to make clear that Jeff wasn't attempting to white-knuckle his way to a more chaste lifestyle, these authors go on to say about Jeff that his

> participation in the body of Christ also gave him the courage to *be* what before he was unable to be. Jeff was free. He was free to be victorious over sin

---

[20]With this thought in mind I want to offer the observation that there's a crucial difference between a church that has some members meeting in small groups and a church that sees itself as being made up of small groups of Christians. In other words, for a small group ministry to both survive and thrive, it needs to be integral to both the nature and mission of the church.

[21]Johns and White, "Ethics of Being," p. 295.

[22]Ibid., p. 299.

[23]Ibid., p. 297.

[24]Ibid., p. 299.

and temptation, not just someone who was barely getting by. He continued to have struggles, but these struggles did not have power over him as they once did. Shame and guilt were no longer his constant companions.[25]

An ongoing engagement in Christian praxis. According to Johns and White, praxis is "reflective action . . . practice that is informed by theoretical reflection."[26] While there's more to praxis than our simply being careful to practice what we preach, there really is something to the idea that when we put into practice what we say we believe, we end up believing it even more intensely! We all know that the apostle James provides this important pastoral instruction: "Do not merely listen to the word, and so deceive yourselves. Do what it says" (Jas 1:22).

But James goes on to explain why actually putting the Word of God into practice is so important to one's spiritual and moral transformation. According to this apostle:

> Anyone who listens to the word but does not do what it says is like someone who looks at his face in a mirror and, after looking at himself, goes away and immediately forgets what he looks like. But whoever looks intently into the perfect law that gives freedom, and continues in it—not forgetting what they have heard, but doing it—they will be blessed in what they do. (Jas 1:23-25)

What James seems to be saying here is that *actually doing what we hear the Word of God saying to us is key to that word benefitting us in the way God intends.* The implication of this for our present discussion should be readily apparent. Praxis is following through on our faith, walking the walk instead of just talking the talk, actually living out what we say we believe, with the result that we end up believing it even more intensely (cf. Philem 6)!

Johns and White are, I believe, essentially saying the same thing when they indicate that a person's character is both revealed and shaped by his or her actions. In other words, there's a sense in which *we become what we do*! By our actions we not only reveal who we are; we also determine who we will be. This is why Stanley Hauerwas can refer to some actions as "acts of self-determination."[27] Say Johns and White: "By understanding who we

---

[25]Ibid.
[26]Ibid., p. 301.
[27]Stanley Hauerwas, *Vision and Virtue: Essays in Christian Ethical Reflection* (Notre Dame: University of Notre Dame Press, 1981), p. 49, as cited in Johns and White, "Ethics of Being," p. 302.

are and who we need to be, we self-consciously choose what we do (reflective action). By what we do we self-consciously choose who and what we will be (active reflection)."[28]

These authors go on to make the assertion that two kinds of praxis in particular are especially powerful in forming Christian character: (1) becoming involved in the sociopolitical dimensions of this world even though such involvement is costly and (2) becoming engaged in spiritual disciplines (e.g., solitude, prayer, study, worship, community, celebration, service, fasting, silence, etc.).[29] With regard to the latter form of engagement, Johns and White provide the important clarification that while the spiritual disciplines themselves do not transform us, they do put us in a place where God's Spirit can transform us into the image of Christ.[30] Put in terms I've made use of already, an encounter-seeking engagement in these tried-and-true spiritual practices produces within Christ's followers a desire and ability to discern and do the will of the Father.

With respect to praxis that requires an involvement in the sociopolitical dimensions of this world, the idea is that choosing to participate in a "contrast society" that seeks to bring the values of the come and coming kingdom of God to bear on the surrounding culture is hugely impactful, not only in terms of the condition of the world but ourselves as well. It's by belonging to such a contrast society (that is, the church or missional community), participating in its worship, nurture, community and mission in a theologically (and pneumatologically) real manner, that the character of Jesus himself is formed within us, enabling us and our brothers and sisters in Christ to more and more become responsible actors on the stage of human history.[31]

It's also important, say these authors, to keep in mind that there is such a thing as *sinful* praxis. This takes place when our actions are *not* guided by the authority of God's Word; instead, we (ironically) let the prevailing popular culture set our agenda and determine our methods for us. For example, Johns and White assert that the bombing of abortion clinics may

---

[28]Johns and White, "Ethics of Being," p. 302.

[29]Ibid., pp. 303, 309.

[30]Ibid.

[31]For more on what a theologically (and pneumatologically) real missional faithfulness involves, see Gary Tyra, *A Missional Orthodoxy: Theology and Ministry in a Post-Christian Context* (Downers Grove, IL: IVP Academic, 2013), pp. 345-61.

be reflective action but has "accomplished nothing righteous related to the problem of abortion," and the violence involved "only makes worse the alienation and anger found in our society."[32] This is a cogent reminder that there's a right and wrong way for Christians to engage in political or social action. Once again, I'll suggest the significance of Micah 6:8 to this discussion. It's never appropriate to engage in an act of so-called Christian praxis that ignores the need to act justly, love with mercy and walk humbly before God!

That said, the manner in which Johns and White portray Jeff's engagement in Christian practice is not only instructive but inspirational as well. Per the story told in the chapter, it was during the summer following his freshman year that Jeff participated in a short-term missions trip to South America. I appreciate the manner in which Johns and White indicate the various ways in which Jeff's worship and service among the desperately poor in Latin America affected him.

First, it altered his concept of Christianity. As the story goes, Jeff "began to understand that serving Christ involved more than merely attending church. It is a way of life that demands purposeful, informed, and circumspect action in the world. As Jeff discovered during his stay in Latin America, such action reveals one's real values and beliefs."[33]

Moreover, it was during this period of intense praxis that Jeff's social consciousness was raised. Heretofore he had been largely unaware of God's heart for justice. But, say Johns and White, "during his stay in Latin America Jeff heard stories of fellow Christians who had 'disappeared' because they had spoken against the violent treatment of the indigenous Indians." As a result,

> he began to see that a true Christian cannot help but relate to the political-social dimensions of this world, though he or she often pays a price for such involvement. Upon his return to the U.S. Jeff began to work as a construction volunteer in a local chapter of Habitat for Humanity. He also became more aware of the rise of pornography in his hometown and helped organize a campaign to close businesses that profited from it.[34]

---

[32]Johns and White, *Ethics of Being*, pp. 303-4.
[33]Ibid., p. 301.
[34]Ibid., p. 303.

Third, Jeff's engagement in Christian ministry had a dramatic effect on his understanding of God and Christian discipleship as well. As the authors put it: "No longer could he be 'part of the audience,' observing the Christian drama from a distance. Jeff became part of the drama and became part of its story. His knowledge of God became direct and personal and it nurtured him in a lifestyle of obedience."[35]

Finally, Jeff's relationship to the world as a whole was affected by his engagement in Christian praxis. It's with both skill and wisdom that Johns and White write:

> Jeff made a transition in his thinking about the relationship between the Christian and the world. He moved away from being part of a Christian sub-culture toward becoming part of a contrast-society. This move represented a major shift in his way of being in the world. For Jeff, there was now a marked difference between a Christian worldview and other worldviews prevalent in the culture. Whereas before he only saw Christianity as increasing the quality of his life, he now saw his faith as radically altering his life. His life was altered in such a way as to express a prophetic calling.[36]

JEFF, A MAN "AFTER" GOD'S OWN HEART

I trust that this adaptation of the excellent work of Cheryl Bridges Johns and Vardaman White has succeeded in helping my readers better understand the three main steps that must be taken if we want to help others (or ourselves) become more eager and able to hear and honor the heart of God. These authors conclude Jeff's story, indicating how, as a result of his having experienced a transformative encounter with God through the Holy Spirit, his becoming an active participant in genuine Christian community, and his serious engagement in some serious Christian praxis he has become "a very different person."[37] To be more specific, according to these authors, "Jeff's character now, more than before, reflects the *character* of God. . . . His actions as a Christian are more consistent with who he is as a believer in Christ."[38] This is the goal, isn't it: to

---

[35]Ibid., pp. 305-6.
[36]Ibid., p. 308.
[37]Ibid., p. 310.
[38]Ibid.

come to the place where our moral actions are consonant with the character of the one we claim to follow?

The goal of this final chapter of *Pursuing Moral Faithfulness* was to indicate the process by which the cultivation of a morally faithful lifestyle actually occurs. Toward this end, the chapter provided a response to the question: What's the best way to help young Christians living in a postmodern world to become truly Christlike? Once again, my personal experience as a Christian disciple, as well as my professional experience as a pastor and professor, convinces me that the three-step process put forward by Johns and White has what it takes to get the job done. Of course there's more involved in one's spiritual formation than three steps. That said, the fact remains that these three very basic steps were and are a part of my own spiritual journey, and I've seen the Holy Spirit work powerfully through them in the lives of others. So it's with some confidence that I assert that a thoughtful embrace of the ethic of responsible Christian discipleship, coupled with a serious engagement in the three-step spiritual formation process presented above, can and will help the sincere Christ follower see the moral faithfulness of Jesus actualized in his or her own life. We don't have to live our lives as almost Christians. If we let him, the Holy Spirit will help us render to God the missional and moral faithfulness he desires and deserves.

Conclusion

Ray Anderson, my theological mentor at Fuller Theological Seminary back in the early 1980s, would begin his courses by encouraging his students to, rather than get lost in the details, do their best to identify and wrestle with the really big ideas that would arise from his lectures. He referred to these big ideas as "$80 concepts." He had done the math, dividing the cost of the course by a rough (and humble) estimate of the number of big ideas likely to be conveyed. (A graduate education was much less expensive back then!) Every once in a while as he lectured, Ray would, with a satirical smirk, alert us students to the fact that he was about to articulate what he considered to be an $80 concept. I can't speak for my fellow students, but I for one took these playful warnings seriously. Never was I disappointed.

I'd like to think that scattered throughout *Pursuing Moral Faithfulness* are some big ideas that are worth my readers doing their best to identify and wrestle with. At the very least, it's my hope that the major premise of the work will prove to be provocative enough to warrant some ongoing reflection and perhaps application. I've spoken often in this book about the possibility of God's people "hearing" his heart. My argument has been that a moral faithfulness depends on this. God is a moral being with an opinion about how human beings made in his image relate to him, ourselves, one another and the planet. When faced with a moral choice of any kind, the faithful follower of Christ will want to do his or her best to, like Jesus, "hear" and then honor the heart of God. I want to bring the book to a close by endeavoring one last time to make a case for this crucial concept.

I was having lunch one day with some faculty colleagues when Rich Israel, an esteemed professor of biblical literature, made the observation that when

Solomon prayed for wisdom in 1 Kings 3:7-9 he was actually asking God to give him a *lēb šōmē'a*, a "listening heart," so that he might "distinguish between right and wrong." Since the Hebrew word *šōmē'a* is related to the word *šěma'*, "hear," I immediately began to wonder to myself whether we might also refer to *lēb šōmē'a* as a "hearing heart." *How interesting*, I thought to myself: *this possible connection between a hearing heart and a wisdom from God that imparts the ability to discern between right and wrong.*

We've seen how the book of Proverbs connects wisdom and moral guidance (e.g., Prov 2:1-22) while steering readers away from the practice of making life decisions based on their own instincts (e.g., Prov 14:12; 16:25). I'm suggesting this has the effect of prompting moral agents to open themselves to the experience of divine direction—their being guided by God in the moral moment rather than by their natural understanding of things. Here's a passage that can be understood as doing precisely that:

> Trust in the LORD with all your heart
>> and lean not on your own understanding;
> in all your ways *submit* to him,
>> and he will make your paths straight. (Prov 3:5-6)

Many of us are old enough to have originally committed this passage to memory as it appears in the King James Bible:

> Trust in the LORD with all thine heart; and lean not unto thine own understanding.
> In all thy ways *acknowledge* him, and he shall direct thy paths. (Prov 3:5-6 KJV)

Now the Hebrew word translated by the NIV as "submit" and by the KJV as "acknowledge" is *yāda'*, the most basic meaning of which is "to know" (in an intimate manner). Thus I want to humbly suggest that the best way to understand *yāda'* in Proverbs 3:6 would be with some word that combines the ideas of knowledge and submission. Perhaps this is why several modern translations (e.g., the NAS, ASV, ESV) also use the word *acknowledge* to translate the word *yāda'* in this particular context. My favorite translation of Proverbs 3:6, however, is the BBE (Bible in Basic English), which translates it thusly: "In all your ways *give ear* to him, and he will make straight your footsteps."

In other words, it's my contention that the best way to understand the use of *yāda'* in Proverbs 3:6 is as a call to *always have a spiritual ear tuned to the divine direction God can and will provide those who belong to him.* To the degree we do this, says the biblical author, we will find ourselves walking the right paths, doing the right things.

This is not to say, however, that doing the right thing is always easy. In a *Christianity Today* article, the focus of which is the kind of radical obedience we disciples of Jesus are sometimes required to render, Alec Hill, president of InterVarsity Christian Fellowship, reminds us:

> When Martin Luther King Jr. was 26, fellow clergy urged him to lead the Birmingham bus boycott. After agreeing to do so, he received regular death threats. Late one night, a caller threatened to bomb his house and kill him, his wife, and their infant daughter.
>
> As King prayed past midnight, he heard: "Martin Luther, stand up for righteousness. Stand up for justice. Stand up for truth. And lo, I will be with you, even until the end of the world." He said, "I heard the voice of Jesus saying still to fight on."
>
> King went to bed peacefully, no longer worried about death. That night changed his life. That night he accepted his duty. Whatever the cost might be to him or his family, he would be faithful to his calling.[39]

This poignant episode from King's life demonstrates the vital connection between a moral and missional faithfulness, and the importance of a hearing heart to both. It also serves to indicate that striving to hear and honor the heart of God can often be costly and inconvenient. Brueggemann was right: walking faithfully before the God of the Bible is no enterprise for wimps or sissies!

Perhaps this is why the apostle Paul prayed the way he did for the disciples he was responsible for. Paul knew firsthand that the kind of faithfulness God sometimes calls for simply cannot occur without a prior, personal word of command and promise uttered by the risen Christ himself. Keep this thought in mind as we ponder one last time the petition offered by Paul on behalf of the rank-and-file members of the church in Philippi:

> And this is my prayer: that your love may abound more and more in knowledge and depth of insight, so that you may be able to *discern what is best* and may

---

[39]Alec Hill, "The Most Troubling Parable," *Christianity Today* 58, no. 6 (July/August 2014): 79.

be pure and blameless for the day of Christ, filled with the fruit of righteousness that comes through Jesus Christ—to the glory and praise of God.
(Phil 1:9-11)

According to this passage (and parallels we find in Ephesians 1; 3), Paul's
most basic prayer for his fellow Christ followers focused on the need for
a "love" powerfully informed by a Spirit-imparted "knowledge" of who
God is, and a "depth of insight" as to what he's up to (see Eph 1:17-19; cf.
Eph 3:16-19). It's such a theologically informed love, says Paul, that allows
sincere Christian disciples to "discern what is best" so that they might be
"pure and blameless" on the day Jesus returns, "filled with the fruit of
righteousness" that comes through him. In other words, it's not just any
kind of love we Christians need in order to render to God the moral
faithfulness he's looking for. *It's a Christ-shaped capacity to care, accompanied by a Spirit-enabled revelation of what the Father is up to in the
world, that enables ethical decisions that do the very best job of honoring
the heart of our trinitarian God.*

So, convinced that the cultivation of a hearing heart is a big idea worth
wrestling with, I'm going to suggest that, the case of Martin Luther King
Jr. notwithstanding, all of us would do well to make the prayers of both
Solomon and Paul our own. May it ever be our prayer that God might
grant us a *lēb šōmēʿa*—a hearing heart that will enable us to *discern what
is best* in each moral choice we make. May we be careful to utter this
prayer in a theologically real manner over and over again for the rest of
our days. And may we pray thusly not only because we desire to be found
pure and blameless on the day of Christ, but because we are Christian
disciples genuinely eager to render to our faithful God the moral faithfulness he desires and deserves.

I hope your heart resonates with this holy ambition. If so, welcome to
the pursuit!

Author Index

Adams, Robert M., 19, 21, 170, 261
Alden, Robert L., 263, 265
Andersen, Francis I., 265-66
Anderson, Bernhard, 267
Anderson, Ray, 291
Arnett, Jeffrey Jensen, 129
Barclay, William, 222, 224-25
Barnette, Henlee H., 36, 187, 198, 204
Barrett, C. K., 273
Barth, Karl, 109
Bauman, Clarence, 216
Bellinger, W. H., Jr., 168-69
Bentham, Jeremy, 75-79
Birch, Bruce C., 24
Bird, Michael F., 20, 42, 72, 169-70, 174, 192, 270
Bishop, Stephen, 267
Bloesch, Donald, 22, 164-67, 178, 182-83, 188, 190
Blomberg, Craig L., 173, 211-12, 216
Bornhäuser, Karl, 216
Bowman, John Wick, 212, 216-17
Boyd, Gregory A., 170
Bruce, F. F., 173-74, 187, 198, 221-22, 224-25, 227, 274
Brueggemann, Walter, 167, 195, 262, 268, 293
Bruner, Frederick Dale, 220-23, 225-27
Brunner, Emil, 270
Buber, Martin, 202
Bush, Frederick William, 263-64, 268
Carson, D. A., 210-11, 221-22, 225, 227
Carson, H. M., 198
Childress, James, 82-85, 87, 103
Cholle, Francis P., 17
Christerson, Brad, 130
Christoffersen, Kari, 15, 57, 130, 147
Clark, Chap, 128, 156
Clark, David K., 19, 59, 72, 75, 81-82, 91, 98, 110
Clifford, Richard J., 201
Clines, David J. A., 260
Coleman, William, 212
Colson, Charles W., 128
Copan, Paul, 19, 21, 28, 35-36,

40-41, 44, 73, 75, 80, 90, 93, 95, 99, 103, 111, 114, 121, 166
Davidson, Hilary, 15, 57, 130, 147
Davidson, Robert, 258
Davies, W. D., 212
Dean, Kenda Creasy, 16, 128-31, 140-41, 155
Denton, Melinda Lundquist, 130-32
Dobrin, Arthur, 127
Dunn, James D. G., 23
Dunn, Richard R., 16, 141
Edwards, Korie, 130
Ferguson, Sinclair, 211, 219
Fletcher, Joseph, 81-87, 100, 102-3
Flory, Richard, 130
Fowler, James W., 283
France, R. T., 173, 177, 211, 213, 215
Franke, John R., 15, 138-39
Frankena, William, 14, 25, 35, 37, 39, 63, 64, 70-71, 75-79, 81-83, 115, 168, 176-77, 201
Fung, Ronald Y. K., 274-75
Geisler, Norman L., 24, 66, 75-79, 82-84, 91, 93, 96-97, 99-102, 104, 106, 108-12, 115-23
Gill, David W., 15-16, 36
Gosnell, Peter W., 72
Gray, G. Buchanan, 261, 263-64, 267-68
Green, Michael, 217
Grenz, Stanley J., 15, 22, 33-37, 44-45, 64, 70, 74-75, 78, 80-83, 86-87, 90, 98, 103, 109, 117, 138-39, 230, 270
Grovier, Trudy, 40
Guelich, Robert, 217
Gundry, Robert H., 213
Gushee, David P., 175
Gustafson, James M., 23-24, 26, 164, 178
Guthrie, Donald, 274
Hagner, Donald, 211, 213, 216
Harrington, Daniel, 23, 28, 176, 188
Hauerwas, Stanley, 18, 24-26, 193, 201, 283, 285
Henry, Carl F., 164
Herzog, Patricia Snell, 15, 57,

130-31, 147
Hiebert, Paul G., 15, 128, 135, 138
Hill, Alec, 293
Hollinger, Dennis, 14-15, 23, 35-37, 42, 53, 63-65, 75-78, 81-83, 90, 94-95, 103, 109, 169, 204
Holmes, Arthur, 68, 71, 145, 175-77, 281
House, Paul, 263-65
Hubbard, David Allan, 263-64, 268
Hughes, Philip E., 36
Johns, Cheryl Bridges, 277-89
Johnson-Mondragon, Ken, 130
Jonas, Hans, 163
Jones, Victoria Emily, 205
Jung, Patricia Beattie, 19
Jung, Shannon, 19
Kant, Immanuel, 14, 40, 91-98, 103
Keenan, James, 23, 28, 176, 188
Keener, Craig S., 194
Keller, Timothy, 170, 270-72
Kidner, Derek, 202
Kiel, Fred, 127
Kingsbury, Jack, 211
Kotva, Joseph, 15, 18, 24, 28, 168, 177, 178, 182, 187, 189, 193, 200-201, 214
Lamoureux, Patricia, 16, 177, 194, 198-200, 214
LaSor, William Sanford, 263-64, 268
Lehmann, Paul, 24
Lennick, Doug, 127
Lewis, C. S., 34-35, 37, 41-42, 270
Lewis, Paul, 25, 187, 192
Lovin, Robin, 21, 22, 24, 36-37, 44-46, 75-78, 80, 82-83, 87, 93, 96, 170, 175, 178, 200
Lutzer, Erwin, 108
Macchia, Frank, 23
MacIntyre, Alasdair, 68
Maston, T. B., 174
McQuilkin, Robertson, 19, 21, 28, 35-36, 40-41, 44, 73, 75, 80, 90, 93, 95, 99, 103, 111, 114, 121, 166
Michener, Ronald T., 14-15, 18, 22, 24-25, 35, 37, 40-41, 44-46,

51, 62, 64, 75, 78-79, 92-93,
95-96, 103, 129, 139, 143, 146,
163, 169, 172, 175, 182, 187, 191,
207, 212
Middleton, J. Richard, 104, 128
Mill, John Stuart, 77-79
Miller, Alexander, 19, 68-69
Moo, Douglas, 274
Morris, Leon, 222, 224-25, 227
Mueller, Walt, 15, 128, 146
Murphy, Roland E., 183, 194
Murray, John, 273
Newman, Judith, 267
Niebuhr, H. Richard, 163, 204,
232-33, 236
Nullens, Patrick, 14-15, 18, 22,
24-25, 35, 37, 40-41, 44-46, 51,
62, 64, 75, 78-79, 92-93, 95-96,
103, 129, 139, 143, 146, 163, 169,
172, 175, 182, 187, 191, 207, 212
Packer, J. I., 81
Parente, Pascal P., 264
Paterson, John, 183
Pearce, Lisa D., 129-30
Plato, 36, 107-8
Pojman, Louis P., 25, 201
Rae, Scott, 19, 24, 36-37, 39-40,
45-46, 51, 54, 59, 63-64, 68-69,
72-73, 75, 77-80, 82-83, 92-93,
99, 164, 168, 183, 187, 197, 200,
205-9

Rahn, Dave, 128
Rakestraw, Raymond V., 19, 59,
72, 75, 81-82, 91, 98, 110
Ramsey, Paul, 81-82, 168, 177-78
Rand, Ayn, 64-66
Rasmussen, Larry L., 24
Regnerus, Mark D., 130
Richter, Don C., 128
Ridderbos, Herman, 222, 224-25,
227
Ross, W. D., 120
Rush, Vincent E., 18
Sanders, E. P., 211
Sanders, Paul S., 258, 261
Schrage, Wolfgang, 28
Senior, Donald, 211
Sewall, Richard B., 258
Sheldon, Charles, 205
Simon, Marcel, 212
Singer, Peter, 40
Smedes, Lewis, 5, 15, 34, 36-37,
39, 41, 164, 168, 176, 178, 181,
204, 227, 230-41, 243-50, 252
Smith, Adam, 64
Smith, Christian, 15-16, 37, 42,
57, 129-57
Smith, R. Scott, 9, 19, 22, 42, 68,
99, 166
Spohn, William C., 164
Stassen, Glen H., 175
Stott, John R. W., 217, 272

Strecker, Georg, 211
Stump, Eleonore, 260, 265-66
Sundene, Jana L., 16, 141
Tapp, Roland W., 212, 216-17
Ten Boom, Corrie, 49
Thielicke, Helmut, 110-11, 116
Tholuck, August, 211
Thompson, James W., 261
Tolar, William B., 216
Tyra, Gary J., 16, 20, 90, 104, 109,
114, 167, 193, 197, 207, 210-11,
218, 250, 262, 274, 286
Vaughn, Lewis, 69
Vaught, Carl G., 211, 218-19
Wadell, Paul J., 16, 177, 194,
198-200, 214
Walsh, Brian J., 104, 128
Waltke, Bruce, 258-60, 266
Westermann, Claus, 264, 266
White, Vardaman W., 277-89
Whybray, R. N., 183, 194
Wilkens, Steve, 63-65, 74-78, 80,
82-83, 95, 103
Willard, Dallas, 191, 213, 281-82
Willimon, William H., 283
Wittmer, Michael, 128
Wolfers, David, 258, 261
Wright, N. T., 24, 193, 200,
221-22, 225, 227

Subject Index

absolutes, moral. *See* absolutism: moral

absolutism
  conflicting, 61, 92, 110-17, 124, 162
  graded, 61-62, 117-24, 162
  ideal (*see* absolutism: conflicting)
  moral, 59-62, 70, 74, 81-83, 87, 90-94, 96-124, 151, 162-66, 176, 179, 208, 232, 240, 246-48, 279
  nonconflicting, 61, 92, 98-102, 104-10, 113-14, 117, 124, 162
  unqualified (*see* absolutism: nonconflicting)
  See also legalism: ethical

accountability, moral, 115, 138, 152, 154-55, 233, 245, 283

action, reflective, 286-87

adults, emerging. *See* generation(s), emerging

agapism, 82-83, 177-78
  See also situationism, moral

alternative, third, 99-100, 105-7, 111

ambiguity
  moral, 97, 106, 117, 190, 193, 257
  purposeful, 257-59, 263-64, 268-69

anarchy, moral, 68, 87

antifoundationalism, 15

antinomianism, ethical, 66-67, 69, 71, 74, 82, 86-87, 91, 208

antirealism, 142-43

antitheses, ethical, 216-18

apathy
  ethical, 18
  moral, 154

areteology. *See* ethics: aretaic

Aristotle, 36, 78

autonomy, moral, 66, 69, 74, 92, 138-39, 152-55, 245
  See also individualism, moral; self, sovereignty of the; sovereignty, moral

biblicism, moral, 91, 192
  See also legalism: ethical

calculus, pleasure, 76-77
  See also utilitarianism,

ethical

calling, 138, 287, 293

capacity, prophetic, 166-67, 193-94

casuistry
  evangelical (*see* casuistry: prophetic)
  legalistic, 165
  prophetic, 163-65, 190
  see also contextualization: prophetic; guidance, moral

choice, existential, 233

Christ
  character of, 51-52, 54, 189, 274, 281-82, 286, 288-89
  image of, 286
  See also God

Christianity, almost, 16, 140-41, 155, 158, 278, 284, 289

Christianity Today, 293

Christology, high, 115-16, 211, 226

commitments, ethical
  significance of, 234-35, 242-44

community, Christian
  and acceptance, 283
  and accountability, 283
  faux, 283
  genuine, 284
  See also group

compromise, abject moral, 156-57

congruency, ethical, 234-35, 242-44
  See also hypocrisy; integrity, ethical

conscience, 17, 25, 40-42, 50, 143, 156-57, 191, 201

consciousness, 167
  historical, 15, 182
  social, 287

consumerism, 284
  See also individualism, moral

contextualization
  ethical, 22, 28, 52-53, 81, 83, 86-87, 162-63, 182, 189-90, 193-94, 197, 199, 218, 239
  prophetic, 162-63, 165, 190
  See also guidance, moral

conventionalism, moral, 61-62, 72-73, 143, 150, 162

Decalogue, 169, 185, 240

deism
  classical, 135-36
  moralistic therapeutic (*see* Moralistic Therapeutic Deism)

deontology. *See* ethics: deontological

development
  character, 279-80
  moral, 154
  sapiential, 259, 266-69
  spiritual, 258-59, 262, 268

differance, 145

dilemma
  Euthyphro, 166
  moral, 16-17, 43-46, 48-50, 52, 54, 63, 70-72, 76-77, 79, 81, 85, 98, 100-1, 105-7, 109, 111-12, 116, 121-24, 143, 148-50, 156-57, 164, 177, 182, 189-92, 206, 208, 222-26, 230, 233-35, 238-39, 242, 244, 246-47, 252

discernment, ethical, 13, 17, 22-25, 52-54, 70-71, 105, 110-12, 114, 116-17, 120, 122, 124, 163-65, 167, 179, 182, 186-90, 195, 198-200, 203-4, 225, 227, 234-35, 238-39, 242, 286, 292-94

discipleship
  pneumatologically real approach to, 272-75
  relational nature of, 271-72

disciplines
  academic, 26, 76
  empowerment, 25
  spiritual, 135, 286

drama, Christian, 288

egoism
  ethical, 60-69, 71, 146, 154
  psychological, 63

Eller, Cassia, 65-66, 68

emotivism, moral, 61-62, 68-69, 142-43, 145

empowerment, moral, 18, 25, 28, 43, 52-54, 58, 60, 74, 114, 124, 134, 166-67, 172, 179, 182, 204, 206, 208, 219, 226, 230, 236-37, 240, 247, 253, 273-75

Epicurus, 64

ethics
  absolutist approach to (see
    absolutism: moral; ethos,
    metaethical)
  altruistic approach to, 39,
    61-63, 65, 74, 80, 83
  analytical, 37
  antinomian approach to (see
    antinomianism, ethical)
  aretaic, 37, 45, 50, 59, 229
  autonomous principle, 92
  biblically informed, 18, 24, 28,
    42, 52, 58, 60, 114, 116,
    122-24, 134-35, 147, 168, 178,
    204, 208, 228-30, 236-37,
    241, 247, 249, 253, 279
  character, 18, 25, 34-35, 37,
    39, 46-47, 51-52, 54, 59,
    124, 175, 189-91, 225,
    229-30, 233, 248, 274, 277,
    279-86, 282-88
  Christ-centered, 18, 21-22,
    28, 52-53, 58, 60, 67, 74,
    114, 116-17, 165, 167, 172,
    204, 208, 230, 236-37, 247,
    269
  and consequences, 25, 37,
    44-45, 47, 49, 50, 62, 78, 80,
    83, 94, 96-97, 103, 105, 108,
    116, 144, 163, 183-84, 205,
    207, 224, 230-32, 234-35,
    237, 242, 245-46, 249, 268
  consequentialist, 62, 83, 144
  deontological, 44-45, 47-48,
    50, 59-61, 70-71, 91-92, 96,
    98, 162-64, 207-8, 229-30,
    240-41, 244, 278, 279
  descriptive, 36-37
  empirical, 37
  evangelical, 182 (see also
    casuistry: prophetic)
  and hedonism, 62, 64, 75-76,
    78, 93
  and justice, 36-37, 50, 52, 80,
    91, 123, 168-74, 176, 178,
    190-91, 209, 214, 225, 227,
    246-47, 271, 287, 293
  and logic, 40, 94-96 (see also
    rationalism, ethical)
  and mathematics, 77, 94
  and mercy, 89, 91, 101,
    168-79, 182, 190, 209, 214,
    225, 227, 246-47, 271, 287
  meta-, 19, 37, 68, 143, 145
    (see also ethos,
    metaethical)
  normative, 37, 59-60, 72, 81,
    189, 225

  philosophical, 19, 35-37,
    40-41, 44, 93, 115, 164 (see
    also philosophy, moral;
    rationalism, ethical)
  prescriptive, 36-37
  principled approach to,
    81-82 (see also absolutism:
    moral; legalism: ethical)
  relativistic approach to (see
    ethics: teleological; ethos,
    metaethical)
  situation (see situationism,
    moral)
  Spirit-empowered, 18, 28,
    52-53, 58, 60, 114, 124, 172,
    204, 208, 230, 236-37, 247,
    253
  teleological, 45, 47, 50, 58-63,
    68, 74, 83, 96, 162-64,
    229-30, 240, 242, 244, 279
  theocentric, 93, 103, 164
  theological, 19, 35, 37,
    40-41, 44, 83-85, 103-4,
    115, 164 (see also realism:
    theological
  Theonomous principle, 92
  trinitarian, 25, 166, 172, 294
  virtue, 18, 28, 37, 44-48,
    50-51, 59, 162, 168, 189,
    229-30
ethos, metaethical, 60-62, 81, 92,
  162
  See also ethics: meta-
eudaimonia, 78
evil, lesser, 61, 92, 110-17, 121-22,
  124
  See also hierarchy: of sin
faithfulness
  divine, 11, 171, 188
  ethical virtue of, 170-71, 173,
    178, 209, 273
  missional, 11, 27, 48, 54, 187,
    189, 197, 199, 206, 218, 226,
    228, 252, 256, 286, 289, 293
faithfulness quotient, moral, 28,
  125, 127, 129-30, 132, 134, 141,
  147-48, 158
fall
  humanity's, 15, 17, 24, 39, 43,
    72, 111, 113-15, 122, 150,
    178, 218, 280
  noetic effect of, 72
forgiveness, divine, 110, 112-14,
  117, 237, 282
fractal, complex, 266
generation(s), emerging, 14-16,
  29, 50, 57, 73, 109, 129-34,
  137-57, 280

God
  character of, 51, 99, 101-2,
    110, 113, 117, 122, 166,
    169-72, 175-76, 179, 281,
    288
  image of, 21, 33, 41-42, 55,
    67, 151-52, 179, 185, 218,
    270-71, 291
  kingdom of, 175, 210-16, 219,
    269-71, 286
  relational nature of, 270-71
  See also Christ
graces, ethical, 274
group
  covenant, 284
  small, 250-51, 283-84
  See also community,
    Christian
empowerment, moral, 18, 25, 28,
  43, 52-54, 58, 60, 74, 114, 124,
  134, 166-67, 172, 179, 182, 204,
  206, 208, 219, 226, 230, 236-37,
  240, 247, 253, 273-75
guidance, moral
  prophetic, 165-67, 190-91,
    193-98, 200, 202-3, 247-48,
    250
  Spirit-enabled, 22, 25, 165,
    167, 179, 183, 187-88,
    190-96, 198-200, 249, 275,
    294
  See also ethics: Spirit-
    empowered
heart
  hearing, 292-94
  listening, 292
hedonism, ethical. See ethics:
  and hedonism
hierarchialism. See absolutism:
  graded
hierarchy
  of divine commands, 118-19,
    122-23
  of sin, 111-12
  See also evil, lesser
Hobbes, Thomas, 64
Hugo, Victor, 89
humanity, new, 218
Hume, David, 14
humility
  as an ethical virtue, 46, 52,
    169-73, 178, 246-47
  relational, 153
  theological, 170
hypocrisy, 109, 173, 209, 213, 218,
  243
  See also congruency, ethical;
    integrity, ethical

imagination, ethical, 234-35, 239
imago Dei. See God, image of
imitatio Christi, 205
immorality, intentional, 156-57
imperative
  anthropological, 28
  categorical, 94-95
  conditional, 165
  divine, 122
  hypothetical, 94
  moral, 99, 108, 111, 120-21,
    123, 144, 156, 162, 165, 174,
    176, 182, 218, 240
  practical, 95
In His Steps, 205
individualism, moral, 65, 138-39,
  145, 152-54, 284
  See also autonomy, moral;
    self, sovereignty of the;
    sovereignty, moral
instinct(s)
  animal, 67
  ethical, 17, 24, 41, 43, 71, 292
  See also intuition, moral;
    intuitionism: moral
integrity, ethical, 48, 213-14,
  242-44, 258, 263
  See also congruency, ethical;
    hypocrisy
intelligence, moral, 127
  See also faithfulness
    quotient, moral; IQ, moral
intuition, moral, 17, 39, 61-62,
  69-71, 81, 143, 237, 244
  See also instinct(s): ethical;
    intuitionism: moral
intuitionism
  moral, 61-62, 69-72, 81, 120,
    143, 162, 164
  See also instinct(s): ethical;
    intuition, moral
IQ, moral, 127, 158
  See also faithfulness
    quotient, moral
Israel, Richard, 291
Jeremias, Joachim, 216
judgment, divine, 93, 97, 118,
  186, 217
  See also reckoning,
    eschatological
justice. *See* ethics: and justice
King, Martin Luther, Jr., 293
late-modernism, 14
  See also postmodernism
law, ceremonial, 101, 168, 183,
  185
legalism
  ethical, 70, 82, 86-87, 89-91,

97-98, 109, 162, 164, 241
  (*see also* biblicism, moral)
  religious, 90
Les Miserables, 89
McLuhan, Marshall, 128
mercy, 89, 91, 101, 168-79, 182,
  190, 209, 214, 225, 227, 246-47,
  262, 271, 287
midwives, Hebrew, 50
ministry, prophetic, 167
Moralistic Therapeutic Deism
  (MTD), 132-37, 139-42, 144,
  154, 156, 278, 280
multiculturalism, 145
myopia, moral, 173, 209
naiveté, ethical, 127-28, 144, 149
narcissism, ethical, 61-62, 64,
  72-73, 143, 154, 156
National Study of Youth and
  Religion (NSYR), 65, 129-33,
  136-38, 140-41, 143, 145-48,
  157-58
Nazis, 48-49, 111
Nietzsche, Friedrich, 14
norms, moral
  absolute, 82-83, 85-87, 144,
    165, 177, 181, 206, 211
  relative, 72-74, 78-79, 81-82,
    86, 165, 278
objectivism, 64-66
ought
  moral, 37, 39-44, 72, 128,
    178
  predictive, 39
  prudential, 39, 72
perfection, 219
perspectivalism, 142
Pharisaism, 16, 20, 90, 207,
  210-12, 215, 262-63
Pharisee(s), 97, 103, 109, 173,
  207-22, 224, 227, 229, 243, 245
phenomenon, prophetic, 166-67
  See also capacity, prophetic
philosophy, moral, 35, 58, 64
  See also ethics:
    philosophical
piety, Job's, 260-62
Plato, 36, 107-8
pornography, 43, 287
postmodernism, 14-16, 28, 50,
  58, 62, 69, 71-73, 87, 90, 125,
  128, 130, 135, 138, 139, 142,
  145, 182, 188, 224, 278-79, 282,
  289
praxis
  Christian, 23, 277, 285-88
  sinful, 286-87
prayer, 17, 20, 23, 25, 43, 46, 49,

52-53, 113, 124, 150, 187, 189,
  191, 197-98, 201-3, 211, 223,
  225-27, 230, 236-37, 242,
  247-49, 252, 257, 268, 282, 284,
  286, 292-94
prescience, 42-43
projection, psychological, 54, 192
Rahab, 50
rationalism, ethical, 35, 40-41,
  45, 92-97, 122, 199
  See also ethics: and logic;
    ethics: philosophical
realism
  metaphysical, 170
  moral, 21-22, 29, 41, 53, 121,
    137, 139, 142-43, 150-52,
    158, 161, 163, 175, 179, 181,
    188-89
  pneumatological, 20, 22-23,
    29, 52-53, 124, 150, 158,
    199, 206, 236, 272, 275,
    286
  theological, 19-23, 25, 28,
    136, 150, 158, 167, 179, 183,
    186, 188-89, 201-3, 206,
    218, 230, 236, 247-48, 262,
    271, 275, 284, 286, 294 (*see*
    also ethics: theological)
  See also antirealism
reason, practical, 95
reckoning, eschatological, 66
  See also judgment, divine
reflection, active, 286
relationship, real, 20, 257, 259,
  262, 268, 271
relationships, intratrinitarian,
  170
relativism
  cultural, 72-73
  epistemological, 139, 150
  moral, 14, 16-17, 21, 69, 72,
    82, 83, 90, 122, 150-51, 279,
    284
  various types of, 15
responsibility, ethical, 13, 18,
  27-29, 33, 36-37, 46, 48, 52, 59,
  82, 87, 100, 105, 107-10, 113-15,
  124, 127, 144-47, 149, 152,
  154-55, 158, 162-63, 167, 181,
  190, 192-93, 199, 201, 204, 224,
  228, 230-37, 239-40, 242-49,
  252, 255-57, 272, 275, 277,
  280-81, 286, 289
responsiveness, moral, 52, 224,
  228, 231, 236-37, 239-40, 242,
  244-45, 247-49, 252, 256-57
revelation
  biblical, 22, 43, 93, 164

divine, 20, 63, 81, 122, 165, 171-72, 179, 198, 202-3, 265, 294
  natural, 42, 122, 265
  special, 42, 94
ritualism, religious, 20, 268
roles, ethical significance of, 234-35, 242-44
Sabbath, 209, 220-21, 229
safety, psychological, 263, 265, 271
sanctification, 25, 54, 140, 220
Satan, 260, 263
self, sovereignty of the, 135-36, 145
  See also autonomy, moral; individualism, moral; sovereignty, moral
Sermon on the Mount, the, 118, 167, 176, 207, 210-19, 221
sin, seriousness of, 114, 118
situationism, moral, 61-62, 80-87, 116-17, 162, 164
  See also agapism
skepticism, epistemological, 142
Smith, Adam, 64
society, contrast, 286
Socrates, 44, 78, 107

Solomon, King, 292, 294
soup, religio-cultural, 28, 127-29, 131-32, 136, 140-41, 157-58, 278
sovereignty, moral, 152
  See also autonomy, moral; individualism, moral; self, sovereignty of the
subjectivism, moral, 61-62, 68-69, 72, 142-43, 150, 162
  See also subjectivity, ethical
subjectivity, ethical, 54, 66, 69, 70-71, 74, 94, 121, 142-43, 150, 152, 192, 238, 244
teleology. See ethics: teleological
Ten Commandments, 167, 169, 176, 240, 249
  See also Decalogue
theology
  biblical, 183
  and creation, 183
  and Jesus, 211
  moral, 35, 199
  natural, 42
  and Paul, 272
  trinitarian, 10, 20, 136, 166, 172, 269
Torah, 167, 196, 216, 262
transformation, moral, 39, 54, 89,

197, 279-86, 288-89
Trinity, the, 140, 170, 192
universalism, moral, 61, 92, 96, 98, 162
utilitarianism, ethical, 60-62, 74-80, 83, 85, 116-17, 162
utility, principle of, 74-75, 78-80, 85, 116, 144
virtue(s), 17-18, 24, 28, 37, 46-47, 50, 81, 100, 162, 168-75, 177-79, 182, 189, 191, 200, 208, 212-14, 216, 220, 224, 235, 237, 242-44, 246-47, 249, 260, 274, 280-81
  cardinal, 169-74, 177-79, 214
  ethics of (see ethics: virtue)
  generative, 170-71
  key, 18, 168, 171
  kingdom, 212-13
  theological, 47
  transcendent (see virtue(s): cardinal)
voice, still small, 23, 25, 189, 191, 201, 251
worldview, 66, 128-29, 131-32, 134-35, 138, 263, 277, 288
WWJD, 205-6

Scripture Index

OLD TESTAMENT

Genesis
3, *43*
9:7-14, *101*
12:10-17, *101*
16:1-12, *80*
17:1, *169*
22, *106, 120*
22:1-18, *119*
29:14-30, *278*
39:1-23, *80*

Exodus
1, *106, 119*
1:15-21, *50, 101, 120*
20:7, *217*
20:13, *217*
20:14, *217*
20:16, *49*
21:12, *217*
21:22-23, *121*
22:2, *115*
22:16-17, *278*
23:2, *73*
33:18, *171*
33:19-20, *171*
34, *171*
34:6-8, *172*

Leviticus
11, *101*
19:11, *49, 111*
19:16, *50, 111*
19:18, *217*
20:10, *217, 224*
21:18-20, *121, 123*
24:19-20, *217*

Numbers
30:2, *217*

Deuteronomy
6:13, *217*
22:13-21, *278*
22:22-24, *224*
24:1-4, *217*

Joshua
2, *50, 106*
2:1-13, *120*
2:1-21, *101*

6:1-7, *119*
6:17, *101*
6:23-24, *101*

Judges
2:11, *68*
3:7, *68*
3:12, *68*
4:1, *68*
6:1, *68*
10:6, *68*
13:1, *68*
16:29-30, *121*
17:6, *68*
21:25, *68*

1 Samuel
15:22, *261*

2 Samuel
11:1-26, *80*

1 Kings
2:4, *169*
3:7-9, *292*
8:25, *169*
9:4, *169*
9:4-5, *243*

1 Chronicles
29:17, *243*

2 Chronicles
7:17, *169*

Nehemiah
7:1-2, *243*

Job
1–20, *260*
1:1, *259*
1:1-5, *259*
1:4-5, *260*
1:6-12, *262, 263*
1:6–2:6, *263*
1:6–37:24, *263*
1:9, *260*
2:1-6, *262, 263*
3:1-26, *264*
3:25, *261*
4:7-9, *263*

4:17, *263*
7:17-21, *263*
8:3-7, *263*
9:16-18, *263*
9:22-24, *263*
10:1-3, *263*
10:2, *264*
10:18-19, *264*
11:1-6, *263*
13:3, *264*
13:7-8, *263*
13:15-24, *264*
15:11-16, *263*
16:7-17, *263*
18:5-21, *263*
19:1-7, *263*
19:7, *264*
20:4-29, *263*
22:1-5, *263*
22:21-30, *263*
23:3-9, *264*
23:11-17, *263*
23:15, *261*
24:1, *263*
24:12, *263*
25:1-6, *263*
27:2-6, *263*
28, *265*
29:1-17, *123*
30:20, *264*
30:20-26, *263*
31, *260, 261*
31:23, *261*
31:35-37, *264*
33:8-11, *263*
34:5-6, *263*
35:12-14, *264*
36:1-17, *263*
38–41, *264*
38:1–40:2, *265*
40:6–41:34, *265*
40:8, *263*
42:1-6, *266*
42:5, *267*
42:7-9, *268*
42:10, *268*

Psalms
5:5-6, *49*
16:7, *196*
22, *213*

23:3, *196*
24:3-6, *213*
25:4-5, *196*
25:12, *194, 196*
32:8-9, *80, 194, 275*
33:10-11, *104*
34:11-21, *213*
37:1-11, *213*
42:1-2, *213*
50:7-23, *261*
51:10-12, *53*
51:16-17, *261*
63:1-5, *213*
69, *213*
89:14, *171*
101:6, *169*
111:10, *66*
119, *213*
119:18, *191*
119:33-35, *195*
119:34-37, *282*
119:66, *195*
119:125, *195*
119:133, *195*
119:169, *202*
131:1-3, *265*
139:14-16, *121*
139:21-22, *217*
143:10, *195, 275*
145:1-21, *104*

Proverbs
1–9, *185, 188, 194*
1:8, *188*
1:20-33, *185, 188*
2, *183, 185, 186, 190,*
  202, 203, 230, 244,
  249, 269, 275
2:1, *201*
2:1-4, *188*
2:1-6, *185, 201, 202, 203*
2:1-9, *80*
2:1-22, *292*
2:2, *201*
2:3, *201*
2:4, *201*
2:6, *194, 201*
2:7-15, *183, 184*
2:16-22, *184, 185*
3:1, *188*
3:1-7, *185*

3:5-6, *72, 86, 192, 292*
3:6, *292*
3:7, *66*
4:1, *188*
4:5, *188*
4:5-6, *188*
4:10-19, *185*
4:13, *188*
4:24-27, *243*
4:27, *18*
5:1-2, *188*
5:1-23, *185*
5:7, *188*
6:20, *188*
6:20-21, *188*
6:20-35, *185*
7:1-4, *188*
7:1-27, *185*
8–9, *194*
8:1-6, *188, 194*
8:10, *188*
8:12-16, *185*
8:17, *188*
8:32-34, *188, 194*
8:33, *188*
8:36, *188*
9:1-6, *185, 194*
10:9, *242*
11:3, *243*
12:15, *249*
12:22, *49*
13:16, *238*
14:12, *17, 24, 43, 67, 72,*
    80, 86, 292
16:6, *66*
16:9, *104*
16:25, *17, 24, 43, 67, 72,*
    80, 86, 292
17:3, *233*
19:21, *104*
20:24, *104*
21:1-8, *105*
21:3, *261*
21:5, *105*
24:11-12, *107*
25:26, *73*
28:26, *17, 24, 43, 86*
29:25, *73*
31:8-9, *123*

Ecclesiastes
7:18, *18*
12:13-14, *66*

Isaiah
1:11-17, *261*
30:21, *192*
32:16-18, *271*

57:15, *212*
61:1-3, *212*
66:1-2, *212*

Jeremiah
31:33-34, *271*

Ezekiel
36:24-27, *196, 282*
36:26-27, *282*

Daniel
3, *106, 119*
3:1-30, *80*
6, *119*
6:1-28, *80*

Hosea
2:19-20, *172*
6:1-6, *261*
8:11-14, *261*
12:6, *191*

Amos
5:21-24, *261*

Micah
6:6-8, *168, 261*
6:8, *52, 167-78, 182, 185,*
    189, 190, 191, 193, 194,
    212, 213, 214, 224,
    227, 239, 246, 247,
    260, 271, 287

Zechariah
7:9-10, *213*

Malachi
3:6, *99*

NEW TESTAMENT
Matthew
1–13, *211, 213, 216*
4:17, *210*
4:23, *210*
5, *213, 215*
5–7, *210*
5:3-12, *210, 214, 218*
5:17, *215*
5:17-19, *48*
5:17-20, *21, 52, 67, 103,*
    124, 215
5:17-48, *210, 214, 221*
5:18-19, *215*
5:19, *118*
5:20, *214, 215, 216*
5:21, *216, 217*
5:21-47, *216, 218*

5:21-48, *80, 109, 216*
5:22, *217*
5:27, *216, 217*
5:27-32, *185*
5:28, *217*
5:31, *216, 217*
5:32, *217*
5:33, *216, 217*
5:34-37, *217*
5:38, *216, 217*
5:39-42, *217*
5:43, *216, 217*
5:48, *110, 215, 218, 219*
6:1, *73*
6:2, *243*
6:5, *243*
6:15, *243*
6:19-24, *212*
6:24, *120*
6:31, *144*
7:5, *243*
7:7-11, *249*
7:12, *144*
7:21, *225*
9:10-13, *47, 213*
10:37, *120*
11:16-19, *47*
12:1-14, *209*
12:32, *112*
12:36, *66*
13:41, *48*
15:1-9, *243*
15:10-20, *185*
15:18-19, *46*
16:24-27, *270*
18:6-9, *48*
18:19-20, *249, 252*
19:16-19, *185*
22:15-18, *243*
22:34-40, *86, 99, 118,*
    177, 272
22:37-38, *119*
23, *213*
23:1-12, *213*
23:13, *243*
23:13-15, *212*
23:15, *243*
23:23, *118, 173, 209, 214,*
    221, 243
23:23-24, *213*
23:25, *243*
23:25-28, *213*
23:27, *243*
23:29, *243*
23:29-32, *213*
23:33-39, *213*
24:45-51, *243*

Mark
1:14-15, *269*
1:35, *249*
2:4, *120*
2:23-28, *109, 229*
3:1-6, *229*
3:2, *229*
3:29, *118*
7:1-20, *209*
7:9-13, *20*
7:14-19, *101*
8:38, *270*
12:18-27, *20*
12:28-34, *177*

Luke
2:41-51, *241*
2:52, *211, 241*
3:21-22, *226*
4:1-2, *226*
4:14, *226*
5:16, *226, 249*
5:32, *48*
6:20-26, *213*
6:36, *219*
6:46-49, *225*
9:23, *205*
9:59-60, *120*
10:25-28, *177*
11:42, *173*
14:25-33, *119*
14:26, *120*
15, *270*
16:13-15, *212*
18:1-8, *249*
18:9-14, *212*
18:10-14, *211*

John
1:1-2, *20*
1:14, *20*
1:18, *20, 172*
3:3-8, *272*
3:16, *80, 236*
5, *221*
5:1-18, *221*
5:16-18, *221*
5:17, *240*
5:19, *16, 21, 240, 249*
5:30, *16, 21, 53, 224,*
    228, 240, 249
7:1, *245*
7:1-52, *245*
7:14-24, *220, 221*
7:17, *270*
7:21-24, *109, 220*
7:24, *220, 221, 239*
8, *226, 245*

8:1-6, *222*
8:1-11, *53, 222, 225, 238, 242, 245, 246, 252*
8:6, *223*
8:6-11, *227*
8:7, *227*
8:11, *48, 227*
8:28, *224*
8:28-29, *21, 249*
9:13-16, *221*
9:16, *221*
10:3, *270*
10:33-35, *207*
10:37, *21, 249*
12:42-43, *73*
12:49, *224*
12:49-50, *21, 249*
13–17, *54, 197*
13:15, *205*
14:10, *21, 224, 240, 249*
14:15-26, *186*
14:23, *270*
14:23-24, *21, 249*
14:24, *224*
14:26, *20, 186, 191*
14:30-31, *21, 249*
14:31, *224*
15:15, *224*
16:5-13, *53*
16:7-14, *186*
16:7-15, *272*
16:13-15, *20*
16:14, *186*
19:10-11, *112*
19:11, *118*

Acts
1:8, *272*
4, *107*
4:1-31, *119*
5:17-41, *119*
5:29, *120*
6:3, *186*
10:19, *191*
10:39-43, *66*
13:1-3, *249*
13:2, *191*
15:22-29, *197, 249*
16:6-10, *272*
16:7, *274*
17:29-31, *66*
20:34, *53*
24:16, *156*
26:18, *28*

Romans
2:5-16, *66*
2:14-15, *41*

2:29, *282*
8, *54*
8:1-4, *203, 272, 275*
8:1-14, *198*
8:4, *53*
8:4-6, *275*
8:5, *273*
8:5-13, *273*
8:6, *273*
8:9, *53, 274*
8:12-13, *273*
8:12-14, *275*
8:15-16, *272*
8:26-27, *272*
8:28, *104, 108, 113*
8:29, *205*
9:3, *121*
10:4, *101*
10:11, *270*
12:2, *187*
12:11-12, *249*
13:1-2, *119*
13:5, *156*
13:8, *82*
13:9-10, *273*
14:10, *66*
14:17, *271*
15:7, *174*
15:13, *272*
15:14-16, *28*

1 Corinthians
1:2, *28*
1:20, *198*
2:5, *198*
2:6, *198*
2:6-16, *20, 198*
2:13, *198*
2:14, *54*
2:16, *282*
3:17, *270*
3:19, *198*
4:2, *169*
4:4-5, *66*
6:9-11, *28*
7:1-2, *278*
7:8-9, *278*
8:7-13, *156*
10:13, *101, 106*
11:29, *270*
12:4-8, *272*
12:8, *186*
12:27, *284*
13:4-7, *177*
13:12, *170*
13:13, *176*
16:22, *270*

2 Corinthians
1:12, *186, 197, 243*
3:18, *54*
5:9-11, *66*
5:17, *270*
5:21, *116*
6:14-18, *73*
7:8-13, *114*
11:2, *278*
12:1-10, *268*
12:21, *46, 114*
13:5, *128*

Galatians
1:10, *73*
1:15-16, *270*
2:19-21, *270*
5:6, *101*
5:13-18, *273*
5:16, *54, 274*
5:16-18, *275*
5:16-25, *198*
5:16-26, *53*
5:18, *274, 275*
5:19, *46*
5:22-23, *54*
5:22-25, *272, 273, 274, 275*
5:24, *274*
5:25, *275*

Ephesians
1, *294*
1:3-4, *28*
1:13-14, *272*
1:15-19, *187*
1:17, *186*
1:17-19, *294*
2:8-9, *91, 98, 134*
3, *294*
3:14-19, *187*
3:16-19, *294*
4:1, *28*
4:15, *108*
4:17-19, *198*
4:25-32, *198*
4:30, *198*
4:32, *174*
5, *199*
5:1, *205*
5:1-2, *51, 174*
5:1-3, *278*
5:3, *46*
5:8-10, *21, 199*
5:15-17, *21*
5:17-18, *199*
5:18-20, *272*
6:1-4, *102*

6:10-18, *272*
6:18, *249*

Philippians
1:9-11, *21, 187, 198, 239, 294*
1:19, *274*
2:3-8, *53*
2:5, *205*
4:6, *249*
4:13, *270*

Colossians
1:5, *169*
1:9, *198*
1:9-10, *21, 187, 198*
2:11, *282*
2:16-17, *101*
2:20-23, *101*
3:5, *46*
3:9-10, *49*
3:12-14, *173*
3:14, *176*
3:16, *46*
4:1, *174*
4:2, *249*

1 Thessalonians
2:10, *174*
2:10-12, *197*
4:1-8, *28*
5:17, *249*
5:19-22, *54*

1 Timothy
1:5, *156*
1:18-20, *156*
4:1-2, *156, 243*
5:5, *249*
5:8, *46*

2 Timothy
1:3, *156*
2:22, *169*
3:14-17, *20*
4:1, *66*
4:8, *66*

Titus
1:5-8, *197*
1:8, *174*
1:15, *156*
2:6-8, *243*
2:7-8, *197*
3:1, *119*

Philemon
6, *285*

Hebrews
1:1-3, *172*
1:3, *20*
2:10-18, *226*
3:12, *270*
3:12-13, *114*
4:1, *270*
4:10, *270*
4:15, *116*
8:1-13, *101*
9, *261*
9:1-28, *101*
9:6-14, *156*
10:19-22, *156*
10:23-25, *252*
11:17-19, *119*
11:31, *50*
13:4, *278*
13:18, *156*

James
1:5, *186*

1:22, *225,*
    285
1:23-25,
    285
1:23-26, *270*
1:27, *174*
2:10, *118*
2:12-13, *66*
2:14, *270*
3:1, *66*
3:13-17, *186*
4:17, *107*
5:16, *114*

1 Peter
1:11, *53, 274*
1:17, *67*
2:13-15, *119*
2:13-23, *53*
2:21, *51, 205*
3:13-16, *156*
4:5, *67*

2 Peter
1:8-9, *270*
2:12, *67*
3:7, *67*
3:9, *270*
3:17, *67*

1 John
1:8-10, *114*
2:1, *51*
2:1-2, *114*
2:4-6, *270*
2:6, *205*
3:17, *174*
4:8, *270*
4:15-16,
    270
4:15-17, *67*

Jude
3, *140*
4, *67*

14-15, *67*
17-19, *67*

Revelation
2–3, *199*
2:7, *199*
2:11, *199*
2:17, *199*
2:29, *199*
3:1-3, *114*
3:6, *199*
3:13, *199*
3:20-22, *270*
3:22, *199*
6:10, *67*
14:6-7, *66*
20:12-13, *67*
21:1-4, *271*
21:8, *49*
22:3-5, *271*
22:12, *270*
22:17, *270*

www.ingramcontent.com/pod-product-compliance
Lightning Source LLC
La Vergne TN
LVHW040327070125
800701LV00006BA/174